# Black Women and Popular Culture

# Black Women and Popular Culture

*The Conversation Continues*

Edited by Adria Y. Goldman, VaNatta S. Ford, Alexa A. Harris, and Natasha R. Howard

LEXINGTON BOOKS
Lanham • Boulder • New York • London

Published by Lexington Books
An imprint of The Rowman & Littlefield Publishing Group, Inc.
4501 Forbes Boulevard, Suite 200, Lanham, Maryland 20706
www.rowman.com

16 Carlisle Street, London W1D 3BT, United Kingdom

Copyright © 2014 by Lexington Books

*All rights reserved.* No part of this book may be reproduced in any form or by any electronic or mechanical means, including information storage and retrieval systems, without written permission from the publisher, except by a reviewer who may quote passages in a review.

British Library Cataloguing in Publication Information Available

**Library of Congress Cataloging-in-Publication Data**

Black women and popular culture : the conversation continues / edited by Adria Y. Goldman, VaNatta S. Ford, Alexa A. Harris, and Natasha R. Howard.
pages cm
Includes bibliographical references and index.
ISBN 978-0-7391-9228-3 (cloth : alk. paper) -- ISBN 978-0-7391-9229-0 (electronic)
1. African American women--Social conditions--21st century. 2. African American women in popular culture--History--21st century. 3. United States--Race relations--History--21st century. 4. Popular culture--United States--History--21st century. I. Goldman, Adria Y.
E185.86.B5416 2014
305.48'8960730905--dc23
2014020835

∞ ™ The paper used in this publication meets the minimum requirements of American National Standard for Information Sciences Permanence of Paper for Printed Library Materials, ANSI/NISO Z39.48-1992.

Printed in the United States of America

# Contents

Black Women in Popular Culture: An Introduction to the Reader's Journey     1
*Alexa A. Harris and Adria Y. Goldman*

**I: Television and Film**     13

1. Scandalous: Olivia Pope and Black Women in Primetime History     15
*Joshua K. Wright*

2. Meet the Braxtons and the Marys: A Closer Look at Representations of Black Female Celebrities in WE TV's *Braxton Family Values* and *Mary Mary*     33
*Adria Y. Goldman*

3. Visible but Devalued through the Black Male Gaze: Degrading Images of the Black Woman in Tyler Perry's *Temptation*     55
*Christopher K. Jackson*

4. "Don't Make Me Hop After You . . .": Black Womanhood and the Dangerous Body in Popular Film     71
*LeRhonda S. Manigault-Bryant*

5. Learning to Conquer Metaphysical Dilemmas: Womanist and Masculinist Perspectives on Tyler Perry's *For Colored Girls*     89
*Robin M. Boylorn and Mark C. Hopson*

**II: The Music Industry**     109

6. Mother Appreciation Rap (MAR) as a Genre and Representation of Black Motherhood     111
*VaNatta S. Ford and Natasha R. Howard*

| | |
|---|---|
| 7 I Am Not My Sister's Keeper: Shifting Themes in Female Rap Videos (2005–2011)<br>*Natasha R. Howard* | 125 |
| 8 "Bey Feminism" vs. Black Feminism: A Critical Conversation on Word-of-Mouth Advertisement of *Beyoncé's Visual Album*<br>*Elizabeth Y. Whittington and Mackenzie Jordan* | 155 |
| 9 Black Women and Gender Violence: Lil' Wayne's "How to Love" as Progressive Hip Hop<br>*Joshua Daniel Phillips and Rachel Alicia Griffin* | 175 |
| **III: Advertising, Print, and Digital Media** | **197** |
| 10 Apparitions of the Past and Obscure Visions for the Future: Stereotypes of Black Women and Advertising during a Paradigm Shift<br>*Joanna L. Jenkins* | 199 |
| 11 Writing (about) the Black Female Body: An Exploration of Skin Color Politics in Advertising within *Ebony* and *Essence*<br>*Simone Puff* | 225 |
| 12 Black Millennial Women as Digital Entrepreneurs: A New Lane on the Information Superhighway<br>*Alexa A. Harris* | 247 |
| 13 The Classification of Black Celebrity Women in Cyberspace<br>*Andre Nicholson* | 273 |
| 14 Identity as a Rite of Passage: The Case of Chirlane McCray<br>*Sheena C. Howard* | 293 |
| Index | 307 |
| About the Contributors | 321 |
| About the Editors | 325 |

# Black Women in Popular Culture

*An Introduction to the Reader's Journey*

Alexa A. Harris and Adria Y. Goldman

A 2012 issue of *Vibe* magazine featured four women of color on the cover with the tagline, "Meet Your New Role Models: Kandi, Tamar, Evelyn, and Chrissy."[1] The cover featured Evelyn Lozada, Chrissy Lampkin, Kandi Burrus, and Tamar Braxton—four ladies with a common thread—they all have been featured on reality television programming. Many went to blogs and online forums to express their frustrations with the magazine's choice of "role models," arguing that the women selected were not worthy of such a title.[2] Yet, the fact remains that each female has garnered a large amount of fans because of their presence in popular culture.

Regardless of the public's take on *Vibe*'s choice of role models for their cover, the choice to include four reality stars helps illustrate the role and prevalence of popular culture in American society. In addition, *Vibe* magazine was originally created by Quincy Jones to give voice to urban youth and the hip hop community.[3] Thus, the inclusion of four reality television stars speaks to their perceived relevance for the magazine's target market. Yes, it can be argued that these women are mothers, daughters, aunts, and businesswomen, like many other women outside of the public's eye. However, these women are in the spotlight—and somewhat celebrated—because of their presence and behavior (whether good or bad) in media and popular culture. *Vibe*'s decision to include the women on the cover shows that these women are considered to be a relevant part of America's popular culture and is only evidence of how the conversation on Black women in popular culture is far from over.

Popular culture has long been a part of America's history. What started as a rebellious form of culture giving voices to those outside of the mainstream continues to exist as a means for expression, socialization, and entertainment.[4] One reason why this form of culture continues to thrive is because of the constant emergence of new artifacts. As mentioned earlier, reality television remains popular for producers and audiences. Blogging and social media carry on as popular activities for many individuals logging on to the Internet. New films, music, and television shows continue to emerge. The fact remains—popular culture is here to stay.

Countless scholars attest to the fact that media is influential. Its images and messages teach individuals how to think, act, believe, and perceive the world around them. In fact, scholars have argued that mass media is one of the strongest agents in the socialization process, along with family, friends, and school.[5] Oftentimes, it is the messages within media that help active audience members construct their reality—even if subconsciously.[6] Because of this relationship between media and its audiences, individuals exist in a mediated society that only intensifies as mass media continue to grow.[7] Since popular culture is often communicated through mass media, the two can go hand-in-hand when considering the influence on audiences.

With media and popular culture educating society about how individuals should view themselves and others, the way in which groups are featured in these cultural artifacts has garnered much research attention. More specifically, Black women's battle with inclusion in popular culture artifacts is a common research topic. Because of their sex and race, Black women have dealt with a long battle of limited quality media representation.[8] In addition, Brenda Allen explains how Black women are in a unique position that is oftentimes not recognized: ". . . [Researchers] may classify Black women with Black men, with White women, or with women of color. This bias neglects to consider the unique position of being both Black and woman. Thus, it renders Black women invisible rather than as distinct persons who experience and resist multiple jeopardy or interlocking oppressions based on their race, their gender, and intersections of these and other aspects of their identity."[9] For these reasons, Black women's place in popular culture deserves additional attention, as the genre continues to grow.

The objectification of Black women for the sake of entertainment dates back to the eighteenth century. This can even be seen in the experience of Saartjie (Sarah) Baartmann, also known as the Hottentot Venus, who was a member of the Khoikhoi tribe in South Africa. Against her will, she was taken from her birthplace, caged and treated as a freak show on exhibit across the world by White European men. Featured unclothed, her large breasts and buttocks were fully exposed to masses that paid money to view her body because of her uncommon physical traits.[10] Although in a different form, Black women were continuously objectified throughout history—which includes their media representations.

A review of the history of media representations of women, in general, shows how the group was included less often than men.[11] However, this media exclusion was more intense for Black women. Originally, when represented in media, Black women were objectified and limited to stereotypical roles such as the domestic Mammy, hypersexual Jezebel, or the overly aggressive Sapphire.[12] As times changed and Black women were included more, images began to change. However, many researchers argued that a closer look revealed how even more recent images were reminiscent of past stereotypical characters. These recycled versions of stereotypes were found to be subtler than its original form. Many scholars have also argued that an increase in media representation did not translate to an automatic improvement, since demeaning images continued to exist in large numbers.[13] This helps explain the importance of continuing to examine Black women and their relationship to popular culture. As different media forms continue to emerge and grow, there are possibilities for increased inclusion, improvement of images, the use of recycled stereotypes, and/or the creation of new ideologies.

Once upon a time, the *greatest* debates were about Black women casted in stereotypical roles due to the actions of non-Black Americans in powerful positions. However, we are currently living in a society where White men are no longer the only individuals responsible for the presentation of Black women in popular culture. The amount of Black writers, creators, and directors has increased. In some instances, audiences have still been dissatisfied by the representations even when from the creative minds of Black people. For example, Mona Scott Young, creator of *Love & Hip Hop* and Shaunie O'Neal, creator of *Basketball Wives*—both reality television shows on *VH1*—have received mixed reviews for their presentations of Black women. In 2012, online petitions were created to have both shows cancelled, garnering 3,239 supporters in response to *Love & Hip Hop Atlanta*[14] and 29,665 supporters in response to *Basketball Wives*.[15]

Black women have fought long and hard for their own space in the public eye and on their own terms. Many of these women have had great success, such as Debbie Allen, Neema Barnette, Ayoka Chenzira, Julie Dash, and Euzhan Palcy. These women brought their experiences to the screen and paved a way for others, like Ava DuVaernay. In 2012, DuVaernay became the first Black woman to win the "Best Director" award at the Sundance Film festival with her film, *Middle of Nowhere*.[16] DuVaernay worked in Hollywood as a publicist for many years until she began creating her own film projects. One of the documentaries she produced, *My Mic Sounds Nice*, became BET's first original film about Black female hip hop artists. It was a major milestone in the history of BET, hip hop, film, and for the presentations of Black women. DuVaernay was able to take the stories of other Black women and bring them to life on a cable network. Her work and success help illustrate multi-dimensional representations of Black women in popular culture are possible and do exist. *Black Women and Popular Culture: The Conversation Continues* provides a survey of Black women in popular culture by not only focusing on the lack of inclusion, but also examining the positive strides Black women have made, as well as the trails they have blazed in popular culture.

With such a troubling history of media inclusion, Black women have often had to find these personal means of expression. From quilting during slavery and stitching coded symbols to serve as guides through the Underground Railroad, to writing narratives, Black women have historically found innovative ways to share their voices and perspectives. Black women continue to value the need to share their own stories. These creative outlets of expression are often seen in various forms of popular culture. When considering popular Black celebrity gossip blogs such as Natasha Eubanks's *theYBF.com*, Nicki Minaj's continuous popularity in the music industry, Nene Leakes' rise to fame from *The Real Housewives of Atlanta* and *The New Normal* (now cancelled), Issa Rae's critically acclaimed webseries *Awkward Black Girl* resulting in a television deal with HBO, and even Mabel "Madea" Simmons' [Tyler Perry] representation of Black womanhood from the eyes of a man—it is evident Black women are featured in today's popular culture in some way.

Furthermore the relevance and popularity of such presentations is clear. Reality television stars are continuing to become household names, with accompanying slogans. For example, consider the growing popularity of Nene Leakes and her famous decree to her castmate saying she is *very rich* as a result of participating in NBC's *Celebrity Apprentice* with Donald Trump. Fan followings for Black American popular culture icons are becoming a way of life as the number of Tamartians (fans of singer Tamar Braxton), Barbz (fans of rapper Nicki Minaj), and members of the Beyhive (fans of singer Beyoncé) continue to grow. Tamar Braxton's single *Love and War* had great success and earned a number one spot on iTunes within twenty-four hours of its release.[17] Tamar took to Twitter to express her gratitude to the Tamartians who made her success possible.[18] Her fans from reality television and music, the identification of the group, as well as her communication with them via Twitter each illustrates the significance of Black women and popular culture. In fact, Tamar's music success and role on reality television are topics discussed in one of our chapters titled, "Meet the Braxtons and the Marys: A Closer Look at Representations of Black Female Celebrities in WE TV's *Braxton Family Values* and *Mary Mary*."

What is especially interesting is how these fans do not fit the bill of traditional celebrity fan club members of yesterday. Perhaps it is due to access through social media that fans feel more connected than ever with their celebrity idols. As a result, they are quite protective of their beloved celebrity leaders; this also expresses the importance of these Black women. For example, on March 18, 2013, R&B singer Keyshia Cole shared her perspective about the divisive nature of Beyonce's song "Bow Down/I Been On." Members of Beyonce's fan club, the Beyhive, quickly logged onto Twitter to defend Beyoncé by *stinging* Cole with an array of put downs and insults.[19] Because of the high amount of attention the exchange brought to Twitter, it became a trending topic on the social media site. The relevancy and significance of both Black women and popular culture is seen in this incidence.

But, one cannot get overly excited about the increased presence of Black women in popular culture and the popularity it has earned from audiences. The group's history of media inclusion illustrates how an increase in representations does not always translate to an improvement in images, messages, and accompanying perceptions. Some may argue the rise of new stars on television, such as Wendy Williams, and the continued presence of more seasoned stars, such as Oprah Winfrey, illustrate that Black women have finally arrived! However, the editors and contributing authors of *Black Women and Popular Culture: The Conversation Continues* recognize this presence of Black women as a reason to continue researching in order to see how Black women are presented and included in popular culture.

*Black Women and Popular Culture: The Conversation Continues* was initially an idea for a research panel incorporating the scholarly works of four communication scholars with a common interest in Black women and popular culture. While conducting their individual research on contemporary issues relating to images, representations, relationships, *voice* and portrayals, all of the women found voids in current academic research. The groundbreaking work of many scholars such as Jacqueline Bobo, Johnetta B. Cole, Patricia Hill Collins, bell hooks and Beverly Guy-Sheftall, served as foundation for the research presented in this text. With new forms of television shows, movies, social networking sites, music, and other popular culture artifacts, the conversation on Black women's representations those scholars started only continues.

In all actuality, discourses have already begun on Black women in popular culture in the digital realm. Audience members have taken to blogs, social networking sites, magazines and other outlets to express their views of different forms of popular culture. As mentioned earlier, several petitions were circulated through the Internet as viewers voiced their concern with the presentation of Black women in reality television. This was not only the case for VH1, as another petition led to the cancellation of the Oxygen's original series *All My Babies' Mommas*—a show featuring rap artist, Shawty Lo, who fathered eleven children with ten women.[20] Millions take to Twitter, Facebook, or even face-to-face conversations in order to discuss what's hot and what's not in popular culture today. These conversations often include discussions of Black women and their representations, or lack thereof. As another example, one could consider Shonda Rhimes' hit show *Scandal*, which brings in an average of 9 million viewers a week and features a Black woman as the protagonist.[21] The show, which was also created by a Black woman (Rhimes), has beat *American Idol* in the category of the number of tweets surrounding one episode alone by receiving 119,000 on Twitter.[22] More details about the show are further explored in an upcoming chapter, "Scandalous: Olivia Pope and Black Women in Primetime History." This anthology helps add to the conversation on Black women and popular culture by deconstructing different forms of popular culture, similar to those mentioned thus far, in order to see if and how this group is featured. In addition, chapters within this text explore the ways Black women are producing, participating in, and curating popular culture.

*Black Women and Popular Culture: The Conversation Continues* is edited by a group of women with educational backgrounds in mass communication, media studies, rhetoric, and intercultural communication. Each has dedicated a large amount of her research agenda to examining the representations of groups, such as Black women in popular culture. The anthology also features the work of multiple researchers who have used a variety of methods and theoretical frameworks to add their perspectives to the discussion. Each scholar uses a critical lens to look at one of three categories—television and film, music, or advertising—to examine how Black women are presented, whether through images, messages, or self-presentation.

Part I features articles that examine messages about Black women communicated via traditional forms of media. Although both television and film are not new platforms to share stories through audiovisual media, each continues to produce new projects that warrant further research. Scholars discuss the participation and presentations of Black women in drama and reality television genres, and implications of those images. Additionally, film, another traditional media platform, continues to thrive as new movies featuring Black women continue to emerge. Despite the strides Black women filmmakers have made in this arena, writers who contributed to this section provide critiques of popular films featuring Black women. "Visible but Devalued through the Black Male Gaze: Degrading Images of a Black Woman in Tyler Perry's *Temptation*," "Learning to Conquer Metaphysical Dilemmas: Womanist and Masculinist Perspectives on Tyler Perry's *For Colored Girls*," and "'Don't Make Me Hop After You . . .': Black Womanhood and the Dangerous Body in Popular Film," are three upcoming chapters that examine representations of Black women constructed by men.

Part II focuses on another long standing media form that continues to find new ways to attract audiences—the music industry. Writers in this section provide in-depth analyses of lyrical content about Black women in popular music and images presented by female artists. "I Am Not My Sister's Keeper: Shifting Themes in Female Rap Videos (2005–2011)" explores Black women emcees, while others focus on Black male perspectives of women in hip-hop. More specifically, in the chapters, "Black Women and Gender Violence: Lil'Wayne's 'How to Love' as Progressive Hip Hop" and "Mother Appreciation Rap (MAR) as a Genre and Representation of Black Motherhood," scholars delve into the presentations of Black family dynamics, female sexuality, and domestic relations in rap music.

Part III includes research about Black women in advertising, print, and digital media. Advertising is a form of media with historical roots that span into an array of sectors in this day and age. What once included a ten- to thirty-second spot on radio or television now ranges to pop-ups on websites and commercials on YouTube videos. Innovative methods continue to emerge in order to persuade consumers to purchase products—from hair, makeup, and fashion *must haves* to music albums. In an era where popular culture often teaches its audiences to glorify materialism and high end spending, it is especially important to research how Black women are targeted and presented within advertisements. Author of the chapter, "Apparitions of the Past and Obscure Visions for the Future: Stereotypes of Black Women and Advertising during a Paradigm Shift," not only explores these notions, but also offers a deeper investigation of topics that surfaced in promoting products to Black women.

Print is another traditional media form, with newspapers being a historical source of information. However, as time has passed, lifestyle publications have become a popular medium to promote trends, daily activities, inspirational stories, and feature advertisements. This third section also focuses on magazines and their potential implications for Black women. One of the chapters, "Writing (about) the Black Female Body: An Exploration of Skin Color Politics in Advertising within *Ebony* and *Essence*," calls attention to ways colorism continues to exist in popular culture. In addition, the chapter "Identity as a Rite of Passage: The Case of Chirlane McCray," touches on the way in which a powerful 1979 *Essence* article plays a role in a larger narrative about sexual identity.

While many publications continue to thrive in print form, others have ventured to the digital space. Because of the massive opportunities the Internet provides for content producers and businesses, a discussion of popular culture would not be complete without also examining this medium. Although not as old as other media forms, the Internet has proven to be just as powerful and long lasting. The digital space has allowed Black women the opportunity to create online communities and engage in conversations that were once limited to their time around the "kitchen table."[23] Scholars with research experience in this area discuss Black women's presentations on the Internet, as well as their use of the medium. Because this is a relatively new focus of study, historical representations of Black women in television, film, and society help serve as reference points for these types of analyses. The chapter, "The Classification of Black Celebrity Women in Cyberspace," highlights ways social networking sites can provide a new way for Black female celebrities to define themselves, while engaging with their fans. Another author contributes, "Black Millennial Women as Digital Entrepreneurs: A New Lane on the Information Superhighway," which sheds light on those who have used the Internet to capitalize on entertainment business ventures.

In addition to analyzing the activity of Black women in the digital space, it is interesting to note the use of media convergence also examined within the cutting edge research of *Black Women and Popular Culture: The Conversation Continues*. The anthology explores the presentation of Black women in an array of media platforms that often merge. For example, the chapter, "'Bey Feminism' vs. Black Feminism: A Critical Conversation on Word-of-Mouth Advertisement of *Beyoncé's Visual Album,*" touches on the intersection of the music industry and advertising. In addition, the relationship between music and social networking is discussed in, "The Classification of Black Celebrity Women in Cyberspace," where the author considers the interactive nature of the Internet and its impact on media representations. The editors and writers of *Black Women and Popular Culture: The Conversation Continues* recognize the need to discuss such media convergence in the overall conversation of media representations of Black women.

It is important to explain the editors' classification of *Black* women as we explore this topic. Some of the researchers rely on demographic information while also considering Dubrofsky's argument of racial ambiguity.[24] Dubrofsky argues that if a woman "is not marked physically as a woman of color, [a television] series can represent her ethnicity in a mutable fashion."[25] This same argument is applied to many of our discussions of Black women in different vehicles of popular culture. The researchers also examine women who *appear* Black while not explicitly self-identifying as otherwise and thus serve as a representation of this group in viewers' eyes.

Each of the articles included in *Black Women and Popular Culture: The Conversation Continues* provides fresh insight into how Black women are presented in contemporary media. Reading the articles will increase your knowledge of the topic while also helping you form a critical lens to use for future popular culture consumption. The history of this art form helps illustrate its staying power and influence. Thus, learning more about popular culture and ways to comprehend its messages is valuable for both researchers and active audience members. As we take you on a journey of Black women in popular culture, you are encouraged to take the information from here and add to the conversation, whether it is through additional research or a conversation with your friends.

So, now that you have a little background, let the voyage begin!

## NOTES

1. Bossip Staff, "VIBE Magazine Cover Girls Evelyn Lozada, Tamar Braxton, Kandi Burruss And Chrissy Lampkin Talk Being Bad (And Good) Girls On TV." *Bossip.* May 22, 2012. Accessed May 2, 2013 http://bossip.com/588595/vibe-magazine-cover-girl-evelyn-lozada-blasts-isht-startin-star-jones-nobody-gives-a-fawk-about-her-says-show-has-helped-her-check-herself/.
2. Brittni Danielle, "If These Are Our New Role Models, We're In Serious Trouble." *Clutch Magazine.* May 22, 2012. Accessed May 3, 2013 http://www.clutchmagonline.com/2012/05/if-these-are-our-new-role-models-were-in-serious-trouble/; Demetria L. Lucas, "Vibe Magazine's Cover: No Real Role Models." *The Root.* May 25, 2012. Accessed May 5, 2013 http://www.theroot.com/buzz/vibe-magazine-role-models.
3. Alan Mirabella, "Where is Johnathan Van Meter Now," *Crain's New York Business.* October 12, 2012. Accessed April 30, 2013 http://mycrains.crainsnewyork.com/40under40/profiles/1993/jonathan-van-meter.
4. Marcel Danesi, *Popular Culture: Introductory Perspectives* (Lanham, MD: Rowman & Littlefield, 2008).
5. Patricia Hill Collins, *Black Sexual Politics* (New York: Routledge, 2005); David Croteau and William D. Hoynes, *Media/Society: Industries, Images, and Audiences* (3rd ed.). (Thousand Oaks, CA: Pine Forge Press, 2003); Susan J. Douglas, *Where the Girls Are: Growing Up Female With the Mass Media* (New York: Times Books, 1994); Linda Holtzman, *Media Messages: What Film, Television, and Popular Music Teach Us About Race, Class, Gender, and Sexual Orientation* (Armonk, NY: M. E. Sharpe, 2000); K. Sue Jewell, *From Mammy To Miss America and Beyond: Cultural Images & the Shaping of US Social Policy* (New York, NY: Routledge, 1993); Rebecca Ann Lind, "Laying a Foundation For Studying Race, Gender, and the Media," in *Race, Gender, Media: Considering Diversity Across Audiences, Content, and Producers.* Edited by Rebecca Ann Lind (Boston, MA: Pearson Education, 2004), 1–10; Myra Macdonald, *Representing Women: Myths of Femininity in Popular Media* (New York, NY: Edward Arnold, 1995); Sharon R. Mazzarella, and Norma Odom Pecora, "Introduction," in *Growing Up Girls: Popular Culture and the Construction of Identity.* Edited by Sharon R. Mazzarella & Norma Odom Pecora (New York, NY: Peter Lang Publishing, 1999), 1–8.
6. Danesi, *Popular Culture: Introductory Perspectives*, 2010; Jennifer L. Pozner, *Reality Bites Back: The Troubling Truth About Guilty Pleasure TV* (Berkeley, CA: Seal Press, 2010).
7. Croteau and Hoynes, *Media/Society: Industries, Images, and Audiences*; Deni Elliott, "Moral Responsibilities and the Power of Pictures," in *Images That Injure: Pictorial Stereotypes in the Media.* Edited by Paul Martin Lester & Susan Dente Ross (Westport, CT: Praeger Publishers, 2003), 7–14.
8. Beretta E. Smith-Shomade, *Shaded Lives: African-American Women and Television* (Piscataway, NJ: Rutgers University Press, 2002).
9. Brenda J. Allen, "Goals for Emancipatory Communication Research on Black American Women," in *Centering Ourselves: African American Feminist and Womanist Studies of Discourse.* Edited by Marsha Houston and Olga Davis (Cresskill, NJ: Hampton, 2002), 23.
10. Clifton Craise and Pamela Scully, *Sara Baartman and the Hottentot Venus: A Ghost Story and a Biography* (Princeton, NJ: Princeton University Press, 2010).
11. Croteau and Hoynes, *Media/Society: Industries, Images, and Audiences*; Myra Macdonald, *Representing Women: Myths of Femininity in Popular Media.*
12. Patricia Hill Collins, *Black Sexual Politics* (New York: Routledge, 2005); Shawna V. Hudson, "Re-Creational Television: The Paradox of Change and Continuity Within Stereotypical Iconography." *Sociological Inquiry* 68, no. 2 (1998): 242–57; Anita Jones Thomas, Karen McCurtis Witherspoon, and Suzette L. Speight, "Toward the Development of the Stereotypic Roles of Black Women Scale." *Journal of Black Psychology* 30 (2004): 426–41; Carolyn M. West, "Mammy, Sapphire, and Jezebel: Historical Images of Black Women and Their Implications For Psychotherapy." *Psychotherapy* 32, no. 3 (1995): 458–66.
13. Linus Abraham, "Media Stereotypes of African Americans," in *Images That Injure: Pictorial Stereotypes in the Media.* Edited by Paul Martin Lester & Susan Dente Ross (Westport, CT: Praeger Publishers, 2003), 87–92; Collins, *Black Sexual Politics*; Croteau and

Hoynes, *Media/Society: Industries, Images, and Audiences*; Robert Entman and Andrew Rojecki, *The Black Image in the White Mind*. Chicago, IL: University of Chicago Press, 2000; Stuart Hall, "The Whites of Their Eyes: Racist Ideologies and the Media," in *Gender, Race, and Class in Media: A Text-Reader* (2nd ed.) Edited by Gail Dines and Jean M. Humez (Thousand Oaks, CA: Sage Publications, 2003), 89–93; Holtzman, *Media Messages: What Film, Television, and Popular Music Teach Us About Race, Class, Gender, and Sexual Orientation*; Shawna V. Hudson, "Re-Creational Television: The Paradox of Change and Continuity Within Stereotypical Iconography." *Sociological Inquiry* 68, no. 2 (1998): 242–57; K. Sue. Jewell, *From Mammy to Miss America and Beyond: Cultural Images & the Shaping of US Social Policy* (New York, NY: Routledge, 1993); Clint C. Wilson II, Felix Guiterrez, and Lena M. Chao, *Racism, Sexism, and the Media: The Rise of Class Communication in Multicultural America* (3rd ed.) (Thousand Oaks, CA: Sage Publications, 2003).

14. Erin Harper, "Boycott VH1 (Love & Hip Hop: Atlanta, Specifically): Stop Dealing Digital Crack and Tell Balanced Stories." Petition, 2012, *Change.org*. http://www.change.org/petitions/boycott-vh1-love-hip-hop-atlantaspecifically-stop-dealing-digital-crack-and-tell-balanced-stories.

15. Alexis M., "Boycott "Basketball Wives" & "Evelyn Lozada": Don't support Evelyn Lozada's spinoff show "EV and OCHO" on VH1." Petition, 2012, *Change.org*. http://www.change.org/petitions/boycott-basketball-wives-evelyn-lozada-don-t-support-evelyn-lozada-s-spinoff-show-ev-and-ocho-on-vh1.

16. Kirsten West Savalli, "Straight Outta Compton: Ava Makes Black History at Sundance!" *NewsOne*. June 19, 2012. Accessed March 1, 2014 http://newsone.com/1833555/ava-duvernay-sundance-festival/

17. Bene Viera, "Tamar Braxton's 'Love and War' Is Like A Sexy Photoshoot On the Beach." *VH1*. January 18, 2013. Accessed February 22, 2014 http://www.vh1.com/music/tuner/2013-0118/tamar-braxtons-loveand-war-is-like-a-sexy-photoshoot-on-the-beach/.

18. TamarBraxtonHer. Twitter post, December 6, 2012, 9:43 pm. https://twitter.com/TamarBraxtonHer/status/276924984889323520.

19. Rachel Maresca, "Keyshia Cole Slams Beyonce's New Single, 'Bow Down/I Been On' Via Twitter." *New York Daily News*. March 19, 2013. Accessed May 6, 2013. http://www.nydailynews.com/entertainment/gossip/keyshia-cole-slams-new-beyonce-song-twitter-article-1.1293023.

20. Gene Demby, "All My Babies' Mamas" Won't Be Happening, But What If It Had?: *NPR*. January 17, 2013. Accessed May 5, 2013 http://www.npr.org/blogs/monkeysee/2013/01/16/169535025/all-my-babies-mamas-wont-be-happening-but-what-if-it-had.

21. Mary McNamara, "Scandal Has Become Must-Tweet TV.'" *LA Times*. May 11, 2013. Accessed March 5, 2014. http://articles.latimes.com/2013/may/11/entertainment/la-et-st-scandal-abc-social-media-20130511.

22. Ibid.

23. Johnnetta Cole and Bevery Guy-Sheftall, *Gender Talk: The Struggle for Women's Equality in African American Communities* (New York: Ballantine Books, 2003).

24. Rachel E. Dubrofsky, *The Surveillance of Women on Reality Television: Watching The Bachelor and The Bachelorette* (Lanham, MD: Lexington Books, 2011).

25. Ibid., 31.

# BIBLIOGRAPHY

Abraham, Linus. "Media Stereotypes of African Americans." In *Images That Injure: Pictorial Stereotypes in the Media*. Edited by Paul Martin Lester & Susan Dente Ross. Westport: Praeger Publishers, 2003: 87–92.

Allen, Brenda J. "Goals for Emancipatory Communication Research on Black American Women." In *Centering Ourselves: African American Feminist and Womanist Studies of Discourse*. Edited by Marsha Houston & Olga Davis. Cresskill: Hampton, 2002: 21–34.

Bossip Staff. "VIBE Magazine Cover Girls Evelyn Lozada, Tamar Braxton, Kandi Burruss and Chrissy Lampkin Talk Being Bad (And Good) Girls On TV." *Bossip*. May 22, 2012. Accessed May 2, 2013 http://bossip.com/588595/vibe-magazine-cover-girl-evelyn-lozada-blasts-isht-startin-star-jones-nobody-gives-a-fawk-about-her-says-show-has-helped-her-check-herself/.

Carlson, Erin. "Keyshia Cole Calls Out Beyonce for 'Bow Down.'" *Billboard.* March 19, 2013. Accessed May 4, 2013 http://www.billboard.com/articles/columns/the-juice/1552529/keyshia-cole-calls-out-beyonce-for-bow-down.

Cole, Johnnetta, and Beverly Guy-Sheftall. *Gender Talk: The Struggle for Women's Equality in African American Communities.* New York: Ballantine Books, 2003.

Collins, Patricia Hill. *Black Sexual Politics: African Americans, Gender, and the New Racism.* New York: Routledge, 2005.

Craise, Clifton and Pamela Scully. *Sara Baartman and the Hottentot Venus: A Ghost Story and a Biography.* Princeton: Princeton University Press, 2010.

Croteau, David and William D. Hoynes. *Media/Society: Industries, Images, and Audiences.* 3rd ed. Thousand Oaks: Pine Forge Press, 2003.

Danesi, Marcel. *Popular Culture: Introductory Perspectives.* Lanham: Rowman and Littlefield Publishers, 2008.

Danielle, Brittni. "If These Are Our New Role Models, We're In Serious Trouble." *Clutch Magazine.* May 22, 2012. Accessed May 3, 2013 http://www.clutchmagonline.com/2012/05/if-these-are-our-new-role-models-were-in-serious-trouble/.

Demby, Gene. "All My Babies' Mamas" Won't Be Happening, But What if it Had?: *NPR.* January 17, 2013. Accessed May 5, 2013 http://www.npr.org/blogs/monkeysee/. 2013/01/16/169535025/all-my-babies-mamas-wont-be-happening-but-what-if-it-had

Douglas, Susan J. *Where the Girls Are: Growing Up Female with the Mass Media.* New York: Times Books, 1994.

Dubrofsky, Rachel E. *The Surveillance of Women on Reality Television: Watching The Bachelor and The Bachelorette.* Lanham: Lexington Books, 2011.

Elliott, Deni. "Moral Responsibilities and the Power of Pictures." In *Images That Injure: Pictorial Stereotypes in the Media.* Edited by Paul Martin Lester & Susan Dente Ross. Westport: Praeger Publishers, 2003: 7–14.

Entman, Robert and Andrew Rojecki. *The Black Image in the White Mind.* Chicago: University of Chicago Press, 2000.

Hall, Stuart. "The Whites of Their Eyes: Racist Ideologies and the Media." In *Gender, Race, and Class in Media: A Text-Reader.* 2nd ed. Edited by Gail Dines & Jean M. Humez. Thousand Oaks: Sage Publications, 2003: 89–93.

Harper, Erin. "Boycott VH1 (Love & Hip Hop: Atlanta, Specifically): Stop Dealing Digital Crack and Tell Balanced Stories." Petition, 2012, *Change.org.* http://www.change.org/petitions/boycott-vh1-love-hip-hop-atlanta-specifically-stop-dealing-digital-crack-and-tell-balanced-stories.

Holtzman, Linda. *Media Messages: What Film, Television, and Popular Music Teach Us About Race, Class, Gender, and Sexual Orientation.* Armonk: M. E. Sharpe, 2000.

Hudson, Shawna V. "Re-Creational Television: The Paradox of Change and Continuity Within Stereotypical Iconography." *Sociological Inquiry* 68, no. 2 (1998): 242–57.

Jewell, K. Sue. *From Mammy To Miss America and Beyond: Cultural Images & the Shaping of US Social Policy.* New York: Routledge, 1993.

Lind, Rebecca Ann. "Laying a Foundation for Studying Race, Gender, and the Media." In *Race, Gender, Media: Considering Diversity Across Audiences, Content, and Producers.* Edited by Rebecca Ann Lind. Boston: Pearson Education, 2004: 1–10.

Lucas, Demetria L. "Vibe Magazine's Cover: No Real Role Models." *The Root.* May 25, 2012. Accessed May 5, 2013 http://www.theroot.com/buzz/vibe-magazine-role-models.

M, Alexis. "Boycott "Basketball Wives" & "Evelyn Lozada": Don't Support Evelyn Lozada's Spinoff Show 'EV and OCHO' on VH1." Petition, 2012, *Change.org.* http://www.change.org/petitions/boycott-basketball-wives-evelyn-lozada-don-t-support-evelyn-lozada-s-spinoff-show-ev-and-ocho-on-vh1.

Macdonald, Myra. *Representing Women: Myths of Femininity in Popular Media.* New York: Edward Arnold, 1995.

Maresca, Rachel. "Keyshia Cole Slams Beyoncé's New Single, 'Bow Down/I Been On' Via Twitter." *New York Daily News*. March 19, 2013. Accessed May 6, 2013 http://www.nydailynews.com/entertainment/gossip/keyshia-cole-slams-new-beyonce-song-twitter-article-1.1293023.

Mazzarella, Sharon R., and Norma Odom Pecora. "Introduction." In *Growing Up Girls: Popular Culture and the Construction of Identity*. Edited by Sharon R. Mazzarella & Norma Odom Pecora. New York: Peter Lang Publishing, 1999:1–8.

McNamara, Mary. "Scandal Has Become Must-Tweet TV." *LA Times*. May 11, 2013. Accessed March 5, 2014 http://articles.latimes.com/2013/may/11/entertainment/la-et-st-scandal-abc-social-media-20130511.

Mirabella, Alan. "Where is Johnathan Van Meter Now." *Crain's New York Business*. October 12, 2012. Accessed April 30, 2013. http://mycrains.crainsnewyork.com/40under40/profiles/1993/jonathan-van-meter

Pozner, Jennifer L. *Reality Bites Back: The Troubling Truth About Guilty Pleasure TV*. Berkley: Seal Press, 2010.

Savalli, Kirsten West. "Straight Outta Compton: Ava Makes Black History at Sundance!" *NewsOne*. June 19, 2012. Accessed March 1, 2014 http://newsone.com/1833555/ava-duvernay-sundance-festival/.

Smith-Shomade, Beretta E. *Shaded Lives: African-American Women and Television*. Piscataway: Rutgers University Press, 2002.

TamarBraxtonHer. Twitter post, December 6, 2012, 9:43 pm. https://twitter.com/TamarBraxtonHer/status/276924984889323520.

Thomas, Anita Jones, Karen McCurtis Witherspoon, and Speight, Suzette L. Witherspoon. "Toward the Development of the Stereotypic Roles of Black Women Scale." *Journal of Black Psychology* 30, (2004): 426–41.

Viera, Bene. "Tamar Braxton's 'Love and War' Is Like A Sexy Photoshoot On the Beach." *VH1*. January 18, 2013. Accessed February 22, 2014 http://www.vh1.com/music/tuner/2013-01-18/tamar-braxtons-love-and-war-is-like-a-sexy-photoshoot-on-the-beach/.

West, Carolyn M. "Mammy, Sapphire, and Jezebel: Historical Images of Black Women and Their Implications for Psychotherapy." *Psychotherapy* 32, no. 3 (1995): 458–66.

Wilson II, Clint C., Felix Guiterrez, and Lena M. Chao. *Racism, Sexism, and the Media: The Rise of Class Communication in Multicultural America*. 3rd ed. Thousand Oaks: Sage Publications, 2003.

*I*

# Television and Film

*Chapter One*

# Scandalous

*Olivia Pope and Black Women in Primetime History*

## Joshua K. Wright

The president has been shot. The nation has gone into a panic after watching their commander-in-chief nearly assassinated at his birthday gala. As the president breathes through a tube in a hospital bed while his disloyal vice president not so subtly tries to steal his job, there is only one person who can restore order. When a deranged mother takes the White House hostage threatening to detonate explosives, to avenge the death of her son at the hands of the government, only one person can save the day. Olivia Pope. Whoever thought the nation's survival would rest in the hands of a Black woman? In just two years ABC's *Scandal* has become a primetime television phenomenon and solidified its heroine, Olivia Pope, as one of the most influential and infamous Black women in American history. The image of Black women in television has been debated for decades as a result of racism, sexism, and struggles for equality. The following chapter uses the fictional Pope and the television series *Scandal* to do the following: (1) Examine the evolution of Black women's images in primetime television since 1939; and (2) Assess *Scandal*'s overall historical significance in the depiction of Black women in television and popular culture.

### PRIMETIME TELEVISION BEFORE *SCANDAL*

The image of Black women on television has evolved considerably since *The Ethel Waters Show* (1939) starring the legendary blues singer Ethel Waters. The show was a one night special, aired on NBC to test the new medium of television as a vehicle for entertainment. One could argue 1950 was a watershed year for Black women in television. The DuMont Network, in competition with the three major television networks, launched a new variety program called *The Hazel Scott Show*.[1] Scott, a beautiful native of Trinidad, was a classically-trained pianist and jazz singer briefly married to Harlem congressman Rev. Adam Clayton Powell Jr. She was the first Black woman to have her own television series. Scott would perform various show tunes on each episode. Unfortunately, this fifteen-minute variety show was cancelled within a year, a casualty of Senator Joseph McCarthy's Red Scare.[2] Scott's series lost its sponsorship after she was accused of being sympathetic toward the Communist Party.

The same year that Hazel Scott's show premiered, ABC also premiered *The Beulah Show*, originally a CBS radio series (1945–1954), starring Hattie McDaniel (and later Louis Beavers) as the faithful maid of the Hendersons, a White middle class family. "Don't let nobody tell you I'm in the market for a husband. Of course I would be but they don't sell husbands at the market," said Beulah at the start of an episode. On a weekly basis viewers watched Beulah solve the family's problems such as teaching their ten year old son Donnie to dance. The following year CBS adapted *The Amos 'n' Andy Show* from radio. The series followed the adventures of the bumbling Andy Brown, the responsible entrepreneur Amos Jones, and their lazy, shiftless, and always unemployed friend George "Kingfish" Stevens. The National Association for the Advancement of Colored People (NAACP) found *Amos 'n' Andy* to be full of negative stereotypes defiling the image of African Americans. In August 1951, the NAACP published "Why the *Amos 'n' Andy* TV Show Should be Taken Off the Air." Among its grievance list the civil rights organization accused the series of depicting Black women as "cackling screaming shrews."[3] Earnestine Wade and Amanda Randolph played the Kingfish's wife and mother-in-law. Randolph played Beulah on the radio version of the series from 1953 to 1954. *Amos 'n' Andy* portrayed Randolph and Wade as loud, angry, unattractive, and overbearing. The national protest forced the series chief sponsor, Blatz Beer, to end its partnership and CBS pulled the show from its airwaves.

During the turbulent 1960s Black women continued to be visible on television. The most notable primetime examples were *Star Trek* and *Julia*. Gene Roddenberry's science fiction series *Star Trek* (1966–1969) was a groundbreaking show that combined the Cold War era's fascination with outer space and Martin Luther King Jr.'s dream for an equal society. The series dealt with issues of feminism, the anti-war movement, race, and civil rights. Nichelle Nichols played communications officer Lieutenant Uhura aboard the USS Enterprise. Nichols's role was a breath of fresh air for the African-American community. King applauded her work, which inspired Mae Jemison to become an astronaut for NASA. Nichols and her co-star William Shatner made history in the November 22, 1968, episode "Plato's Stepchildren" by engaging in television's first interracial kiss.[4] The five second kiss was one of the most groundbreaking moments in television history. Nearly two months earlier NBC debuted *Julia*, the first sitcom about a Black middle class woman (not set in outer space). Diahann Carroll played the mother of a young son, the widow of a Vietnam veteran, and a nurse in a White doctor's office. The series ran for three seasons.

In the wake of the civil rights and Black power era, Hollywood became enamored with African Americans. Blaxploitation cinema introduced the mainstream public to tales of working class Blacks and to hustlers, pimps, and prostitutes in the "ghetto." Pam Grier emerged as the brightest star of the blaxploitation era with films like *Coffy* (1973) and *Foxy Brown* (1974). Grier's characters were praised by some for being empowering symbols of strong Black womanhood and lambasted by others for promoting negative stereotypes about Black women being hyper-violent and hyper-sexual.[5] Another significant figure in the Blaxploitation era was Tamara Dobson. Dobson, a six foot two inch model for *Vogue,* viewed herself as the anti-Grier because she refused to appear nude in her films. In 1973 she starred in the action heroine film, *Cleopatra Jones.* The success of Grier and Dobson as action heroines inspired ABC's 1974 series *Get Christie Love!* The series began as a made for television film starring Teresa Graves as an undercover police detective fighting drug dealers. "You're under arrest, sugah!" was Graves's famous catchphrase on the show.

*Get Christie Love!* is often cited as the last dramatic series on network television to feature a Black woman prior to *Scandal.* During the nearly forty years between the two shows, various images of Black women have been presented in television ranging from Louise Jefferson, the wife of a rich businessman, to her maid Florence Johnston (*The Jeffersons,* 1975–1985). The 1980s and 1990s introduced diverse characters such as Lydia Grant, a dance teacher (*Fame,* 1982–1987), Claire Huxtable, a successful attorney and married mother of five (*The Cosby Show,* 1984–1992); Whitley Gilbert, the sassy southern bell (*A Different World,* 1987–1993); and Dr. Jennie Boulet, a HIV positive medical doctor (*ER,* 1994–2009). Hip hop stars Queen Latifah (*Living Single,* 1993–1998) and Brandy (*Moesha,* 1996–2001) also assumed lead roles in sitcoms.

From 2000 to 2008 Mara Brock Akil's series, *Girlfriends* kept younger Black women tuned into UPN and the CW. The show's success led to Akil's spin-off series *The Game* (2006–the present) depicting the mothers, wives, girlfriends, and "Baby Mamas" of professional Black football players. In 2009 TNT's *Hawthorne* made Jada Pinkett Smith the first Black woman to have the lead role in a television drama (though not on network television) since *Get Christie Love!* Smith played Christina, a widow and single mother, who works as a nurse in a "(stereotypically) chaotic urban hospital."[6] Nine months after *Scandal*'s pilot episode NBC premiered *Deception,* the second network television drama with a Black female lead. Meagan Goode, another Hollywood star, played Detective Joanna Locasto who goes undercover to investigate the mysterious death of her best friend Vivian Bowers, a wealthy White socialite. Locasto's mother was the Bower family maid for years. Unfortunately, *Deception* was cancelled after its first season. In January 2014 BET launched a new dramatic series from Mara Brock Akil titled, *being mary jane,* about a television talk show host (Gabrielle Union) juggling her career, family, and complicated love life.

## WELCOME TO SHONDALAND

On April 5, 2012, ABC debuted *Scandal*, a trailblazing new series that is part political-crime drama, soap opera, and action adventure. *Scandal* is the brainchild of Shonda Rhimes, arguably Hollywood's hottest African-American screenwriter, director, and producer. Rhimes first rose to prominence with her hit ABC medical drama *Grey's Anatomy* (2005–present). *Scandal* is loosely based on the life of Judy Smith, an African-American CEO of Smith & Company, a crisis management firm. Smith, who formerly worked as the Deputy Press Secretary and a Special Assistant to President George H. W. Bush, handled some of the nation's most titillating scandals including the Iran Contra Affair, Clarence Thomas-Anita Hill senate hearing, Monica Lewinsky's assignations with President Bill Clinton, and Michael Vick's post-prison image makeover.

Smith inspired Rhimes's creation of *Scandal*'s lead character Olivia Pope, portrayed by Kerry Washington. Washington is on a growing list of movie stars who have recently turned to primetime television having starred in such films as *Ray* (2004), *Mr. and Mrs. Smith* (2005), *The Last King of Scotland* (2006), and *Django Unchained* (2013). In spite of her past success on the big screen, Washington's defining role is Olivia Pope.

Kerry Washington is the first Black actress to receive an Emmy nomination for lead actress in a television series since Cicely Tyson in 1995. In 2013 she received a Golden Globe nomination for best actress in a dramatic series. Washington's recent success has led to many prestigious opportunities. She serves on President Barack Obama's Committee on Arts and Humanities. She was the 2013 commencement speaker at George Washington University, her alma mater. She also made history in 2013 by becoming the eighth Black woman to ever host NBC's *Saturday Night Live*.[7]

Washington's character Olivia Pope is the CEO of Washington, DC's most successful crisis management firm, Pope & Associates. Olivia and her band of merry misfits, referred to as "gladiators in suits," fix the problems of the nation's most powerful figures, occasionally solving murders and averting catastrophes that threaten national security. They even run a brief campaign for a female presidential candidate. Olivia began working in Washington after serving on the presidential campaign for California's Republican Governor Fitzgerald (Fitz) Thomas Grant III. In return for helping Fitz to win the election she is made the White House Director of Communications. She leaves the White House after a brief stay and opens her firm.

Olivia may be great at fixing other people's problems, but her own personal life is not drama-free. She is an only child whose mother died in a plane crash when she was twelve. Her father is a curator for the antiquities collection at the Smithsonian. Following her mother's death Olivia's father sends her overseas to a prestigious boarding school, a decision that marks the beginning of their estrangement. Olivia goes on to graduate from Princeton University and Georgetown University Law School. Years later she learns that her father is really the commander of a classified CIA program called B613 that kills and tortures enemies of the state. She also learns that her mother is still alive and could possibly be a terrorist.

Olivia does not have any children and has never been married. She was twice engaged to a Black senator named Edison Davis and briefly dates Jake Ballard, a high-ranking White military officer who served with the president in the Navy and is a member of B613. The series revolves around Olivia's on again off again affair with the president. She and Fitz began dating during his presidential campaign. She quit her job at the White House because she grew sick of the affair only to reconcile with him months later. Fitz is unhappily married to Melody "Mellie" Grant and they have an infant son. Fitz is a spoiled senator's son who joined the Navy to escape his father's shadow. After signing up for Black Ops missions he is ordered to shoot down a commercial plane killing 329 passengers on board but preventing a bomb on board the plane from detonating and killing millions. Olivia's mother was originally thought to have been killed on the plane. After his father pulls some strings to clear him of all criminal charges he earns a law degree from Harvard and enters politics.

Olivia, Mellie, and the other members of Fitz's campaign team rig the ballots in Defiance, Ohio, to ensure his presidency. Fitz is unaware of the Defiance scandal until the liberal Supreme Court Justice Verna Thornton reveals the news to him, and tells him she was responsible for his near assassination, as she lies in a hospital bed dying from cancer. Upon learning the news an enraged Fitz shuts off her oxygen causing her sudden death. He delivers her eulogy days later. Nevertheless, in spite of his flaws Olivia loves this man and believes that he will divorce Mellie, leave his family, and move her into the White House.

## OLIVIA POPE AS THE POST-RACIAL HEROINE

*Scandal* is currently one of the most successful television shows on television with more than 12 million viewers per episode. It ranks number one in the ratings among viewers ages eighteen to thirty-four.[8] In this age of social media *Scandal* is what everyone seems to be talking about on Thursday evenings, as the series averages over 500,000 tweets an episode.[9] *Vanity Fair*, *Vogue*, *Harpers Bazaar*, and other publications geared toward women have dedicated websites and blogs to Olivia Pope's wardrobe.

One of the reasons the series is so popular is because it successfully crosses racial lines. Luchina Fisher published an article for an ABC News blog titled, "Kerry Washington: 'White Women Want to Be Olivia Pope'" discussing Olivia's popularity beyond African-American viewers.[10] Fisher's article highlighted Washington's popularity among women of all races. A group of White female graduate students in their thirties were interviewed for this article. Each of the women claimed not to see race while watching the series *Scandal*, which could indicate that America has come a long way in how interracial relationships are perceived since Uhura's *Star Trek* kiss and Helen and Tom Willis, on *The Jeffersons*.[11]

Olivia Pope is primetime television's first post-racial Black heroine. Unlike previous Black heroines like Christie Love and Christina Hawthorne, race is seldom a roadblock for her. The election of President Barack Obama and the widespread embrace of his wife, Michelle, in 2008 led some Americans to claim that the nation had finally moved beyond its preoccupation with race. With the exception of a weekly soundtrack that includes music from renowned Black singers, Rhimes chooses to avoid making race an issue, directly addressing it briefly and only rarely in the first twenty-nine episodes of the series. "You have to be twice as good as them (White people) to get what they have," Olivia's father tells her in the premiere episode of season three.[12] In another episode Fitz tells his Chief-of-Staff that he plans to divorce his wife for Olivia and use the moment to begin a national dialogue on race. In another episode Olivia's father chastises Fitz, repeatedly referring to him as a "boy," for not having to work for anything in life and using his daughter as an escape from his father's shadow. As a result of his uppity behavior Fitz fires him and gives his job to Jake Ballard. In another episode a new White client is surprised to learn that Olivia is Black. Perhaps the most infamous episode pertaining to race revolved around the Sally Hemings incident. In season two Olivia, tired of feeling like Fitz's glorified booty call, tells him, "I am feeling a little Sally Hemings, Thomas Jefferson about all of this."[13] Olivia continues, "I take my clothes off for you. . . . My whole life is you . . . you own me. You control me. I belong to you."[14] Fitz responds, "I am in love with you. . . . There's no Sally and Thomas here. You're nobody's victim. I belong to you."[15]

The exchange between the two lovers is daring because it forces the audience to consider the secret relationship between President Thomas Jefferson and his mixed-race slave girl Sally Hemings. Just fourteen when she accompanied Jefferson and his youngest daughter to Paris in 1787, Sally Hemings was coaxed into a sexual relationship with the president which spanned four decades and produced six children.[16] Professor Kaila Story, the Audre Lorde Chair of Race, Class, Gender and Sexuality Studies at the University of Louisville, said of the exchange, "Rhimes is so smart. The whole institution of enslavement in and of itself does not engender romantic relationship."[17] Unfortunately, Rhimes avoids exploring this subject further in the episode or providing any historical context for her viewers unfamiliar with the Hemings-Jefferson reference.

Many Black feminists applaud Rhimes for refusing to dwell on race. "There's an audience of African-Americans who just want to see themselves in a good story, not necessarily a race-specific show," says hip hop feminist Joan Morgan.[18] "I think the success of the show speaks to how we have become more inclusive as a society," says Professor Brittney Cooper, Rutgers University professor and co-founder of the Crunk Feminist Collective.[19]

But not everyone agrees with Rhimes's post-racial optimism. In her critique of the series *The New Yorker*'s Emily Nussbaum faults Rhimes for making Pope's ethnicity and other issues of race seemingly non-existent. She compares *Scandal* to CBS's hit series *The Good Wife*, starring Julianna Marguilies as a lawyer and wife of a disgraced state's attorney. Nussbaum praises *The Good Wife* for having the courage to frequently tackle uncomfortable issues of institutional racism and White guilt.[20]

University of Michigan professor Tiya Miles disputes the show's premise that interracial relationships, especially between Black women and White men, are so common and acceptable. Miles points out an interesting statistic found in data released by the popular online dating site OkCupid. While Black women respond to more initial overtures than other women, their initial contacts are the most ignored.[21] The majority of Americans still marry within their race and Black women are more likely to remain single than women of other races. In a *New York Times* article, Kevin Noble Maillard, co-editor of *Loving v. Virginia in a Post-Racial World*,[22] contends, "Interracial relationships are scandalous because people still believe them to be rare." In her book, *According to Our Hearts: Rhinelander v. Rhinelander and the Law of Multiracial Family*, Professor Angela Onwuachi-Willig argues that interracial relationships are of interest because they are often framed as deviant.[23] Would the Rhimes series be such a hit if Olivia and Fitz were of the same race?

In the weeks leading up to the fiftieth anniversary of the March on Washington, Rev. Martin Luther King Jr.'s protégé Congressman John Lewis told a reporter that the idea of a post-racial America is more fantasy than reality.

Oprah Winfrey, arguably the most beloved Black woman in America, told a BBC reporter in 2013 that much of the criticism of President Barack Obama is racially motivated. The 98th Annual Meeting for the Association for the Study of African American Life & History in 2013 included a panel called "Crashing the Ol' Boys' Club: Interrogating Power and Representation in ABC's *Scandal.*" Ironically the panel, featuring three Black female doctoral candidates from Florida State University, occurred the night after the season three premiere. Some of the panelists, as well as Black women in the audience, commented that Rhimes should deal more with race considering the state of the country. Season three debuted just months after the controversial verdict in the George Zimmerman trial and in the year of historically based films about race by Black writers and directors, such as: *The Butler, Fruitvale Station,* and *12 Years a Slave.*

*Scandal* is not the first series with a Black female lead to be criticized for downplaying race. NBC's *Julia* (1968–1970) starred Diahann Carroll as Julia Baker, a nurse and single mother of a six-year-old son. Julia lived in a middle class mixed-race apartment building, she was the only Black person in her office, and her son's best friend was White. The fact that Julia represented a strong independent woman at the dawn of the second wave of feminism was largely ignored. The series and Carroll were subjected to rampant criticism. *Ebony* said the show presented a fictional middle class Black life that working class Blacks could not relate to. Robert Lewis Shayon of *The Saturday Review* accused the series of diluting the nation's race problem and masquerading one fortunate Black woman's life as the common African-American experience in the late sixties.[24] Gil Scott Heron compared *Julia*'s relevance to that of the animated *The Bullwinkle Show* in his classic poem and song, "The Revolution Will Not Be Televised." The scrutiny was too much for Diahann Carroll to bear; she was hospitalized twice due to stress and declined to renew her contract for a fourth season.[25]

*The Cosby Show* was also accused of selling out on racial issues. From 1985 to 1989 it was the most watched television series in America. The sitcom followed the funny experiences of the Huxtables, an upper middle class Black family in Brooklyn, New York. Cliff (Bill Cosby) was an obstetrician, and his wife Claire (Phylicia Rashad) was a partner at a law firm. Both graduated from the same historically Black college and had five children. Although Cliff was the star Claire often stole the show with her beauty, smarts, charm, and wit. "If you don't get it together and drop these macho attitudes you are never gonna have anybody bringing you anything, anywhere, anyplace ev-errr," she famously told her sexist son-in-law Elvin.[26]

Just like *Scandal, The Cosby Show* dealt with race in subtle ways like featuring cameos from Black musicians like Lena Horne and B. B. King or displaying Black art work prominently featured on the walls. In one episode the family watches King's "I Have a Dream" speech. Nevertheless, Black scholars such as Michael Eric Dyson and Henry Louis Gates Jr. have criticized the series for not shining light on crucial issues of the day such as crack addiction, gang violence, the rising rates of Black male incarceration, poverty, and failing schools.[27] Others accused the show of being unrealistic, downplaying social issues to appease White viewers and the mainstream masses unconcerned with race.

During a 2013 episode of *Oprah's Next Chapter* Phylicia Rashad defended the series and its role in promoting positive groundbreaking images of a middle class Black family and displaying that the Black experience was not monolithic.[28] Hopefully, Rhimes will devote at least one episode to the issue of race. She has the platform and a highly educated audience in social media to create one of the most insightful discussions on race in years.

## SHAMING, STEREOTYPES, AND *SCANDAL*: DEBATING RESPECTABILITY

When Brandon Maxwell published his online article "Olivia Pope and the Scandal of Representation," calling Pope a glamorous updated version of the Mammy and Jezebel stereotypes historically associated with Black women, the comment section exploded with responses from Black women rushing to Olivia's defense. David Dennis responded to the attacks on Maxwell by publishing "It's not a Scandal to think Olivia Pope's a rogue not a hero." Far too often criticism of *Scandal* becomes an argument between Black men and women over patriarchy and feminism. Black men who attack Olivia are often accused of engaging in the practice of shaming and respectability politics. The final section of this chapter will explore this issue by providing historical context about Black women's images in the media.

During the early twentieth century, middle class Blacks used respectability politics to improve the image of African Americans circulated by late nineteenth century southern media. Southern propaganda excluded Black women from the Cult of True Womanhood, which associated womanhood with virtues of piety, purity, submissiveness, and domesticity.[29] In her book *Sister Citizen* Melissa Harris-Perry says Black women have been shamed by these negative stereotypes and forced to view the world from the vantage point of a crooked room in which they appear as only Mammies, bitches, and Jezebels.[30]

In his article Brandon Maxwell refers to Olivia as a hybrid of all three stereotypes. He says that her role as the fixer for everyone else's problems makes her a twenty-first century sophisticated Mammy. Olivia's "gladiators" are so loyal to her because she has saved each of them in the past. Her right-hand man Harrison was a disgraced lawyer facing prison for insider trading. Huck is a tortured soul and B613 outcast who had been living in a Washington, DC, subway station. Abby is a survivor of domestic violence. Olivia helps her divorce her abusive husband and put her life back together. And then there is Quinn who Olivia helps beat a charge of murdering seven people.

According to many historians the Mammy image first appeared with the advent of Aunt Jemima pancake mix and syrup in 1889. The company's founders were inspired by a minstrel performance featuring a White man in Blackface playing a southern Black maid. The company hired Nancy Green, a former slave to serve as their Mammy mascot from 1890 until 1923. Educator Anna Julia Cooper said this represented White men's exploitation of Black female bodies in the Jim Crow era.[31]

Southern White women looking to redeem the defeated Confederacy's broken image, invented the Lost Cause myth, a philosophy that portrayed the confederates as noble heroes who fought and sacrificed for the cause of state rights, *not* slavery. The Lost Cause myth said Abraham Lincoln and the Union were bad. Slavery was not immoral, but alternatively slaves were happy with their existence.[32] The Mammy, the faithful, deeply religious domestic servant was the manifestation of this myth about slavery. Historian Catherine Clinton says the Mammy, who tended to be a dark skinned, overweight, asexual woman, was used to counter the fair skinned bi-racial Black woman that White men lusted. The fair skinned woman became the Jezebel or the whore who tempted God fearing White men to cheat on their saintly wives. The Mammy became the all-knowing, problem solving, mother figure.[33]

Hattie McDaniel became the first African American to win an Oscar for her portrayal as Mammy in the 1939 film *Gone with the Wind*. She reprised that role on television in *The Beulah Show* (1950–1952). The Mammy has remained a dominant image of Black womanhood in popular culture. Nell Carter played the Mammy in the 1980s sitcom *Gimme a Break!* For six seasons Carter played the housekeeper of a widowed White police chief and his three daughters. Later in the series she also assumes responsibility of two little orphaned White boys. In recent years the Mammy has appeared in the AMC series *Mad Men*, Tyler Perry's Madea films, and the popular 2011 film *The Help* about Black Mississippi maids during the 1960s. Nanchez, Mississippi still has a restaurant called Mammy Cupboard Café. The restaurant's front door is in Mammy's apron (right near her vaginal area).

In 1923 two thousand Black women from the Phyllis Wheatley Y.W.C.A. protested U.S. Senate approved plans to erect a monument honoring Black Mammies in the nation's capital.[34] Olivia's role as the fixer can be identified with the Mammy's problem solving skills, but the comparison ends there. The Mammy was generally less educated. Olivia is a cosmopolitan woman who graduated from Princeton and Georgetown. Her father is an alumnus of Princeton too. She is not rearing anyone's "chillum" or frying chicken in a

White person's kitchen. Her thin figure and lighter brown complexion is what has historically been appealing to White men. No one will ever accuse her of being asexual or overly religious.

Maxwell says Olivia also fits the stereotype of the strong Black woman (or Bitch) who empowers herself by emasculating Black men. He accuses her of belittling her assistant Harrison Wright (Columbus Short). "It's getting crazy in here. What do you need . . . I am your gladiator. Give me some marching orders," Harrison tells Olivia.[35] Angry female readers responded to Maxwell's comment by calling him a Black man that is uncomfortable with the idea of a woman with agency. In the 1920s, Black women were told that the best way they could uplift the race was through motherhood. Black women who failed to fulfill their duties as good mothers and obedient wives were blamed for the race's failure.

Historian Peniel Joseph says that sexism was a problem within the Black Power Movement in the 1960s.[36] Stokely Carmichael, arguably the most influential Black power leader, once quipped that a woman's best position in the movement was "prone."[37] Maulana Karenga, founder of US Organization, stated the following: "What makes a woman appealing is her femininity and she can't be feminine without being submissive. A man has to be the leader. There is no virtue in independence. Black women should remember this."[38]

As a result of such rhetoric, strong Black women who refused to be subordinate were perceived as Sapphires. Sapphire was the wife of George (Kingfish) Stevens in the 1950s television series *Amos 'n' Andy*. She was portrayed as being angry, loud, overbearing, and asexual. A similar image reappeared during the 1970s in the form of *Sanford and Son*'s Aunt Esther, and in the 1990s with *Martin*'s Pam. Olivia Pope does not fit this description of the strong Black woman, but she does fit another description of this stereotype.

Historical research by scholars like Herbert Gutman confirms that Black families were not completely destroyed by slavery. Nevertheless, many Black women were forced to serve in roles typically held by men as the breadwinners, due to slavery and later Jim and Jane Crow. As a result the average Black woman was viewed as being exceptionally strong and able to endure more than her privileged White female counterpart. Black women could not show too much emotion because it was a sign of weakness. On a 1974 episode of *Good Times* the matriarch Florida Evans is hosting guests after her husband's funeral. She remains strong as a rock throughout the entire episode. Her children question her lack of emotion. She finally breaks down at the end the episode; overcome with grief she shouts the famous phrase: "Damn, daamn daaaamn."

Similar to Florida, Olivia is unable to publicly show emotion. She cries in front of Fitz, Jake, and her father, but she typically remains cool in all other situations. After Olivia shows little emotion over the return of her mother, after twenty-two years of thinking she was dead, her assistant Abby says to Harrison: "a normal person would have had a nervous breakdown by now." Later on Abby forces Olivia to hug her mother before she boards a plane to Hong Kong [at the time Olivia was unsure if she would ever see her mother again]. Olivia's mother lauds her power, but expresses displeasure with her lack of happiness and a social life. Olivia can be cold, but would a man be criticized for appearing "too strong" in difficult situations? Would he be expected to cry? No.

Maxwell received the most criticism for labeling Olivia a Jezebel. Is Olivia Pope a slut? During the premier of season three Cyrus and his team of crisis managers consider playing the "ambitious slut" card when Olivia is publicly named as the president's mistress. A background check into Olivia's past shows that she was a party girl in college who dated and slept with wealthy, powerful men during and after law school. The Black slut or Jezebel has been a common figure in television. At times she is just an accessory for the male stud. Other times she is a "Gold Digger" expecting a man to be her lottery ticket. In the 2007 episode of *The Game*, "Turkey Basting Bitches," a young woman attempts to use a turkey baster to impregnate herself with the semen of a famous professional football player.

In addition to using the Jezebel label, Maxwell indirectly suggested that Olivia was little more than an object of sexual pleasure for her powerful White boss, Fitz. Rhimes introduced the issue of slavery and sexual relationships with the Sally Hemings reference. "You control me," says Olivia. The 2013 Oscar winning film adaptation of Solomon Northrup's chilling tale of enslavement *12 Years a Slave* depicts the sexual abuse that a female slave named Patsey (Lupita Nyong'o) receives at the hands of her master, Mr. Edwin Epps.[39] Such horrific images are also found in Harriet Jacobs's 1861 autobiography *Incidents in the Life of a Slave Girl*. From the age of fifteen until she ran away, Harriet feared being raped by her master Dr. James Norcom. In the case of Patsey and Harriet their masters controlled their bodies and every aspect of their lives. Fitz does not control Olivia.

Slave women and girls were often despised by their plantation mistresses who viewed them as whores and blamed them for their husbands' philandering. Harriet Jacobs describes her plantation mistress's cruel treatment. In the film *12 Years a Slave* Mrs. Epps gleefully watches her husband and Solomon nearly whip Patsey to death and takes part in physically and emotionally abusing her. Catherine Clinton's *The Plantation Mistress* and Elizabeth Fox-Genovese's *Within the Plantation Household* reveal countless examples of these rivalries that existed between Black and White women on the plantation. If the White House is a metaphor for the plantation, as Maxwell's article indirectly suggests, those rivalries are still present. Fitz's wife Mellie despises Olivia and frequently calls her a whore. Nevertheless, she needs Olivia and is forced to put up with her. When Fitz is depressed and having trouble sleeping Mellie secretly invites Olivia to a state dinner. When he asks Mellie why she did that her reply is, "because you needed to see her . . . I trust now you will sleep like a baby."[40]

Olivia Pope fans will hate this next comment, but Mellie has every right to hate her. Mellie sacrificed a promising career as a partner at a law firm to be a governor's wife. She left her family in North Carolina and followed Fitz to California and Washington, DC. She wants to play a role in the White House, but Fitz refuses to give her any role of significance. She has remained faithful to Fitz in spite of his transgressions. Mellie is a contemporary version of the White suburban housewife found in Betty Freidan's 1963 book *The Feminine Mystique*.[41] She is a more cunning version of *Mad Men*'s Betty Draper. Finally, she is secretly living with the shame of being raped by Fitz's drunken father. The rape led to a pregnancy, which ended in miscarriage. The plantation mistress was a victim of patriarchy and infidelity, yet her suffering hardly compared to that of the slave women and girls. But in this case Olivia has just as much education and more power than Mellie, sleeps with her husband by choice, and thus deserves whatever resentment Mellie directs toward her.

Although Mellie is the only woman to be raped in the series, Janeen Price argues in her 2013 conference paper "Interrogating Power in ABC's Scandal" that Fitz's sexual advances toward Olivia are dominating, overly aggressive, and subtle forms of rape. Price uses several examples from the series to make her point such as when Fitz invites Olivia to a hunting trip, during which he pushes her up against a tree in the woods, aggressively kisses her, and tries to rip open her blouse in the presence of his two secret service agents. In another instance Olivia goes storming out of a White House reception following the christening of Fitz's newborn son. A drunken Fitz follows her, pulls her into an empty room, and attempts to kiss her. She slaps him and pushes him away, but then proceeds to have sex with him. During one of Fitz's inaugural balls he takes Olivia into the Oval Office, removes her panties, and has sex with her on his desk.

Do these examples in *Scandal* qualify as rape? Rape is a serious matter in the African-American community. Danielle McGuire's *At the Dark End of the Street* explores the connection between rape and Black women's activism in the Civil Rights Movement. According to McGuire only ten White men in Mississippi were convicted for raping Black females between 1940 and 1965.[42] The *Black Women's Blueprint* reports that 60 percent of Black females have been sexually abused by their eighteenth birthday.[43] The Department of Justice reports that for every Black woman that reports rape, at least fifteen others do not.[44]

Is Olivia Pope a victim of rape? Rape is defined as the unlawful act of forcing another person into sexual intercourse. It is doubtful that Price's rape theory will find universal support. Olivia clearly enjoys having sex with Fitz and is always a willing participant even if she plays hard to get. She may even enjoy Fitz's rough behavior. Katie Roiphe's 2012 *Newsweek* article "Spanking Goes Mainstream" discusses the popularity of sexual domination among women in their twenties and thirties. Roiphe points to the success of the domination filled sex novel *Fifty Shades of Grey* and discussions of domination on the HBO series *Girls* as proof of her theory. In a *Girls* episode the protagonist Maya (Lena Dunham) tells her friend, "I am seeing this guy and sometimes I let him hit me."[45]

Janet Jackson's 1997 song "Rope Burn" and Rihanna's 2010 hit "S&M" celebrate this desire to be dominated in the bedroom. In Beyonce's 2014 hit single "Drunk In Love," her husband Jay-Z hints at rough behavior in their bedroom where he raps about "beating it up" and "biting" like a famous boxer.[46] Jay-Z's lyrics reference Mike Tyson's 1992 conviction for rape and his biting Evander Holyfield's ear during a 1997 heavyweight boxing prize fight. Jay-Z also references Tina Turner's (Anna Mae Bullock) abusive relationship with her ex-husband Ike Turner. In spite of the controversial lyrics many women support the song.

Roiphie also points to a 2010 *Psychology Today* article by Michael Castleman, which estimates that between 31 and 57 percent of women have rape fantasies once a month, in which they are coerced into having sex.[47] A 2009 report in the *Journal of Sex Research* includes the findings of a survey of 355 college women conducted by psychologists at North Texas University. It reveals that 62 percent of the women have such fantasies. But it should be noted that the North Texas University survey does point out that while 52 percent of women typically fantasized about being sexually dominated by men, only 32 percent fantasized about being raped.[48]

Is Olivia Pope a rape victim? This question is difficult to answer for several reasons. Some fans who do not have a problem with S&M may simply excuse Fitz's behavior and say that Olivia just likes it rough. Other fans may argue that defining what type of sexual behavior is appropriate is just another form of oppressing women. But there are many women who find Fitz's actions, especially the scene in the woods, to be repulsive. Olivia clearly was not in control in this particular instance. Unlike their other aggressive sexual encounters, which were in private, this was done in the clear sight of other men. Fitz demonstrated no respect for Olivia, her body, or her role as a well-respected high profile professional. Olivia was clearly bothered and felt violated by Fitz's behavior and proceeds to tell him, "I am not yours. This is over."[49] If Fitz was Black and Olivia was White would more people view that scene as rape? Unfortunately, we will never have an answer. Although Janeen Price's rape argument may not gain universal acceptance it certainly adds an interesting point of discussion.

Olivia Pope is a flawed person, but she is no more flawed than the White women on *Sex and the City* or the White men on *Mad Men*. She is a real human being not an idealized figure. Olivia should be criticized when it is necessary, but beginning conversations with labels like Mammy, bitch, slut, and Jezebel is not conducive for a productive discourse.

## CONCLUSION

Does television need more Olivia Popes? Professor Arnetra Pleas from Holmes Community College in Mississippi admits that she knows many professional women who refuse to watch *Scandal* because they strongly object to Oliva's relationship with Fitz and believe that it encourages female viewers to engage in affairs with married men. They further assert that she is a bad role model for young Black girls because she is engaged in a relationship that does not nurture who she really is and sends the message that, "some man is better than no man at all."[50] At the same time many of these same women dislike the idea of not supporting Shonda Rhimes and Kerry Washington due to the lack of opportunities for Black women in Hollywood.[51] Professor LaKeisha Harris from the University of Maryland Eastern Shore responds to such criticism of the series: "While her romantic life does not appeal to all, one of the main reasons *Scandal* has a large following is because many can empathize with the duality of maintaining a superwoman persona during the day while simultaneously hosting a multitude of personal problems at night."[52]

*Scandal* is a fresh breath for millions of Black women sick of unflattering depictions in reality shows like *Basketball Wives* and *Love & Hip Hop* and being equated to twenty-first century Hottentot Venuses in hip hop videos. Olivia Pope is a welcomed sight for Black women sick of seeing their bodies used as props in twerking videos for White performers like Miley Cyrus.[53] Olivia Pope is not Beulah or Sapphire. She encompasses the beauty, intelligence, grace, and sophistication of Claire Huxtable, Julia, and Hazel Scott.

Olivia Pope also gives non-Black women a powerful, well educated, beautiful figure to admire. Although Olivia's decision making does not sit well with everyone, Shonda Rhimes sees her as an antihero rather than the perfect person.[54] The antihero has become a common fixture in television in recent years thanks to the success of *Breaking Bad, The Sopranos*, and *The Wire*. Olivia Pope is television's first beloved Black female antihero. The fact that such a character exists demonstrates considerable progress. In the 1960s it was believed that all Black characters had to be as squeaky clean as those portrayed by Sidney Poitier. The NAACP was quick to boycott anything that failed to meet their standards of respectability. Today the NAACP honors Kerry Washington, Shonda Rhimes, and *Scandal* at their annual Image Awards.

Professor Takiyah Nur Amin from the University of North Carolina Charlotte says the following about Olivia Pope's significance: "She does not have to be perfect or a pillar of moral rectitude to be desired, respected, admired, or trusted. Olivia is deeply satisfying for many—especially Black women— who are often marginalized on television and in real life."[55]

Hate it or love it *Scandal* has a huge impact on the Black woman's image and will go down in history as a series that is still being discussed and debated fifty years from now.

## NOTES

1. Donald Bogle, *Toms, Coons, Mulattoes, Mammies & Bucks: An Interpretive History of Blacks in American Films* (New York: Continuum, 2001), 9–15.
2. http://www.aaregistry.org/historic_events/view/exceptional-talent-and-appeal-hazel-scott.
3. Bogle, 33.
4. J. William Snyder Jr., "*Star Trek*: A Phenomenon and Social Statement on the 1960s," http://www.uni-kiel.de/medien/stj/essays/trek.html, accessed on September 2, 2013.
5. Stehane Dunn, "*Baad Bitches" and Sassy Supermamas*: *Black Power Action Films*. (Champaign: University of Illinois Press, 2008).
6. Allison Samuels, "Alternative Medicine," *Newsweek,* Vol. 153, Issue 25, June 22, 2009, 64.
7. Greg Braxton, "'Scandal's' Kerry Washington: Is She a Sellout for Hosting 'SNL'?" *Los Angeles Times,* November 1, 2013, http://articles.latimes.com/2013/nov/01/entertainment/la-et-st-scandals-kerry-washington-is-she-a-sell-out-for-hosting-snl-20131101, accessed on October 16, 2013.
8. Andrew Meola, "ABC Reduces Scandal Season 3 order from 22 to 18 episodes," December 6, 2013, http://www.mstarz.com/articles/22916/20131206/abc-reduces-scandal-season-3-order-22-18-episodes.htm, accessed on February 26, 2014.
9. "Ebony Power 100," *Ebony,* December 2013/January 2014, 130.
10. Luchina Fisher, "Kerry Washington: 'White Women Want to Be Olivia Pope,'" http://abcnews.go.com/blogs/entertainment/2013/07/kerry-washington-white-women-want-to-be-olivia-pope/, accessed on July 2, 2013.
11. Helen and Tom Willis were a fictional interracial couple on *The Jeffersons* television series.
12. *Scandal*, Episode no. 30, first broadcast October 3, 2013, by ABC. Directed by Tom Verica and written by Shonda Rhimes.
13. *Scandal*, Episode no. 16, first broadcast 13 December 2012 by ABC. Directed by Jessica Yu and written by Mark Wilding.
14. Ibid.
15. Ibid.
16. Annette Gordon-Reed, *Thomas Jefferson and Sally Hemings: An American Controversy* (Charlottesville: University of Virginia Press, 1997), 217.
17. "'Scandal' on ABC is Breaking Barriers." http://scandalmoments.tumblr.com/post/40750602188/scandal-on-abc-is-breaking-barriers.
18. Tanzina Vega, "'Scandal' on ABC Is Breaking Barriers," *The New York Times,* January 16, 2013, http://www.nytimes.com/2013/01/17/arts/television/scandal-on-abc-is-breaking-barriers.html?_r=0, accessed on August 9, 2013.
19. Ibid.

20. Emily Nussbaum, "Primary Colors: Shonda Rhimes's 'Scandal' and the Diversity Debate," *The New Yorker*, http://www.newyorker.com/arts/critics/television/2012/05/21/120521 crte_television_nussbaum, accessed on May 21, 2012.

21. Tiya Miles, "Black Women, Interracial Dating, and Marriage: What's Love Got to Do With It?" *The Huffington Post,* November 5, 2013, http://www.huffingtonpost.com/tiya-miles/ interracial-dating-and-marriage_b_4213066.html, accessed on December 1, 2013.

22. Kevin Noble Maillard, "Interracial Couples are Still Seen as Rare," *New York Times*, June 27, 2013. Retrieved from http://www.nytimes.com/roomfordebate/2013/06/13/is-interracial-marriage-still-scandalous/interracial-couples-are-still-seen-as-rare.

23. Angela Onwuachi-Willig, "Is Interracial Romance Still Scandalous," http://www.huffingtonpost.com/angela-onwuachiwillig/is-interracial-romance-st_b_3331640.html, accessed on May 24, 2013.

24. Bogle, 142–45.

25. Actress and singer Diahann Carroll describes her role in the 1960s TV show *Julia* in this eighth of ten excerpts from the NVLP Oral History Archive.

26. *The Cosby Show*, episode 28, (first broadcast on October 17, 1985) by NBC. Directed by Jay Sandrich and written by Ed Weinber.

27. Darnell M. Hunt (ed.), *Channeling Blackness: Studies on Television and Race in America.* (New York: Oxford University Press, 2005), 163.

28. "How The Cosby Show Represented Race in America—Oprah's Next Chapter—OWN," http://www.youtube.com/watch?v=mio8JacwoYQ, accessed on December 12, 2013.

29. Barbara Welter, "The Cult of True Womanhood: 1820–1860," 1966.

30. Melissa V. Harris-Perry, *Sister Citizen*: *Shame, Stereotypes, and Black Women in America.* (New Haven: Yale University Press, 2011), 76.

31. Kimberly Wallace Sanders, *Mammy*: *A Century of Race, Gender, and Southern Memory* (Anne Arbor: University of Michigan Press, 1962), 65.

32. Sarah E. Gardner, *Blood and Irony*: *Southern White Women's Narratives of the Civil War, 1861* (Chapel Hill: University of North Carolina Press, 2004).

33. Catherine Clinton, *The Plantation Mistress*: *Woman's World in the Old South* (New York: Pantheon, 1984).

34. Tony Horwitz, "The Mammy Washington Almost Had." *The Atlantic.* May 31, 2013. http://www.theatlantic.com/national/archive/2013/05/the-mammy-washington-almost-had/276431/. Accessed on December 28, 2013.

35. *Scandal*, Episode no. 13 (first broadcast November 15, 2012) by ABC. Directed by Bethany Rooney and written by Chris Van Dusen.

36. Peniel Joseph, *Waiting 'Til The Midnight Hour: A Narrative History of Black Power in America* (New York: Henry Holt and Company, 2006), 212–13.

37. Johnnetta B. Cole and Beverly Guy-Sheftall, *Gender Talk: The Struggle for Women's Equality in African American Communities* (New York: One World/Ballantine, 2003), 80.

38. Susan Brownmiller, *In Our Time: Memoir of a Revolution.* (New York: Dial Books, 2000). http://www.nytimes.com/books/first/b/brownmiller-time.html. Accessed July 28, 2013.

39. *12 Years a Slave* was awarded Best Picture at the 2014 Academy Awards. Lupita Nyong'o received an Academy Award for Best Supporting Actress for her portrayal of Patsey.

40. *Scandal*, Episode no. 3 (first broadcast April 19, 2012) by ABC. Directed by Allison Liddi-Brown and written by Matt Byrne.

41. Betty Friedan, *The Feminine Mystique.* (New York: W.W. Norton & Company, 2001).

42. Danielle L. McGuire, *At the Dark End of the Street*: *Black Women, Rape, and Resistance—A New History of the Civil Rights Movement from Rosa Parks to the Rise of Black Power.* (New York: Vintage, 2011).

43. Brooke Axtell, "Black Women, Sexual Assault and the Art of Resistance," *Forbes*, April 25, 2012 http://www.forbes.com/sites/shenegotiates/2012/04/25/black-women-sexual-assault-and-the-art-of-resistance/. Accessed on September 1, 2013.

44. Ibid.

45. Katie Roiphie, "Spanking Goes Mainstream," *Newsweek*, April 16, 2010.

46. Beyoncé Knowles, Noel Fisher, Shawn Carter, Andre Eric Proctor, Rasool Diaz, Brian Soko, Timothy Mosley, and Jerome Harmon, "Drunk in Love," performed by Beyoncé featuring Jay-Z, *Beyoncé,* 2013, Columbia Records, compact disc.
47. Ibid.
48. Michael Castleman, "Women's Rape Fantasies: How Common? What Do They Mean?" *Psychology Today*, January 14, 2010. http://www.psychologytoday.com/blog/all-about-sex/201001/womens-rape-fantasies-how-common-what-do-they-mean. Accessed on December 29, 2013.
49. *Scandal*, Episode no. 10 (first broadcast October 18, 2012) by ABC. Directed by Allison Liddi-Brown and written by Matt Byrne.
50. Dr. Arnetra Pleas was interviewed for this study on December 29, 2013.
51. Ibid.
52. Dr. LaKeisha Harris was interviewed for this study on December 30, 2013.
53. "When Your (Brown) Body is a (White) Wonderland." August 27, 2013 http://tressiemc.com/2013/08/27/when-your-brown-body-is-a-white-wonderland/. Accessed on December 14, 2013.
54. Rick Porter, "'Scandal' creator Shonda Rhimes: Olivia Pope is an antihero," January 17, 2013 http://blog.zap2it.com/frominsidethebox/2013/01/scandal-creator-shonda-rhimes-olivia-pope-is-an-antihero.html. Accessed on October 31, 2013.
55. Dr. Takiyah Amin was interviewed for this study on December 16, 2013.

# BIBLIOGRAPHY

Bogle, Donald. *Toms, Coons, Mulattoes, Mammies & Bucks: An Interpretive History of Blacks in American Films.* New York: Continuum, 2001.
Clinton, Catherine. *The Plantation Mistress: Woman's World in the Old South.* New York: Pantheon, 1984.
Cole, Johnnetta B., and Beverly Guy-Sheftall. *Gender Talk: The Struggle for Women's Equality in African American Communities.* New York: One World/Ballantine, 2003.
Dunn, Stephane. *"Baad Bitches" and Sassy Supermamas: Black Power Action Films.* Champaign: University of Illinois Press, 2008.
Friedan, Betty. *The Feminine Mystique.* New York: W.W. Norton & Company, 2001.
Gardner, Sarah E. *Blood and Irony: Southern White Women's Narratives of the Civil War, 1861.* Chapel Hill: University of North Carolina Press, 2004.
Gordon-Reed, Annette. *Thomas Jefferson and Sally Hemings: An American Controversy.* Charlottesville: University of Virginia Press, 1997.
Harris-Perry, Melissa V. *Sister Citizen: Shame, Stereotypes, and Black Women in America.* New Haven: Yale University Press, 2011.
Hunt, Darnell M. *Channeling Blackness: Studies on Television and Race in America.* New York: Oxford University Press, 2005.
Joseph, Peniel. *Waiting 'Til The Midnight Hour: A Narrative History of Black Power in America.* New York: Henry Holt and Company, 2006.
McGuire, Danielle L. *At the Dark End of the Street: Black Women, Rape, and Resistance—A New History of the Civil Rights Movement from Rosa Parks to the Rise of Black Power.* New York: Vintage, 2011.
Sanders, Kimberly Wallace. *Mammy: A Century of Race, Gender, and Southern Memory.* Anne Arbor: University of Michigan Press, 1962.

*Chapter Two*

# Meet the Braxtons and the Marys

*A Closer Look at Representations of Black Female Celebrities in WE TV's* Braxton Family Values *and* Mary Mary

Adria Y. Goldman

Over the years, reality television has made its staying power clear. Ratings and message boards evidence how some audience members are fans of this type of programming. Because of its low cost and high profitability, reality television also has a mass appeal for producers. Thus, it is no surprise reality television has earned itself a slot on many television station line-ups. As its name describes, this programming promises to deliver continuously to its audiences. Reality television programming has allowed viewers behind the scenes of everything from repossession shops and restaurant kitchens, to the luxurious lifestyles of those in the sports or hip hop industry. This is one of the appeals of reality television—it gives viewers a "fly-on-the-wall perspective" into the lives of people they may not know.[1]

Yet despite this claim, one could argue that reality television is actually a *constructed reality*. Although participants are not always given a script and storyline, the use of editing and strategic casting takes away from the shows' authenticity. In fact, audience members often recognize this lack of reality, but identify the shows as entertainment and continue to tune into the programs.[2] But, research has shown that even fictional programming is influential. All television programming has the potential to shape views and reinforce ideologies about different groups.[3] The way in which a group is represented on the screen could impact the way they are perceived in real life. This is especially problematic for individuals who are underrepresented or treated unfairly in media, such as Black women.

Members of the press have voiced concerns about the presentations of Black women in reality television and the genre's tendency to present stereotypical portrayals.[4] For them, reality television has failed to present the diversity that was once expected of this programming. Some blame these one-dimensional representations on the lack of true reality in reality television. Consequently, production teams are often credited for the final product presented to audiences.

Several Black reality television stars have blamed producers and editing for their negative portrayals. Following an explosive episode of Bravo's *The Real Housewives of Atlanta,* which aired on January 27, 2014, Nene Leakes used her blog to reach viewers and explain her side of the story. After a couples' pajama party goes wrong and results in physical fights involving multiple cast members, several viewers used social media to discuss their outrage. In her blog, Nene points the blame at one specific cast member while also alluding to editing procedures that led to a false presentation. She writes,

> We really had fun with it contrary to what you thought you saw and I stress "what you thought you saw" . . . why do you think they let Kenya narrate the whole fight scene? Why do you think they took the part out when Kenya was charging across the room? All the housewives would say we were having a good time! Why do you think they showed it as if we were not?[5]

Readers can assume Nene's mention of *they* refers to Bravo's production team. But despite issues with editing and portrayals, there never seems to be a shortage of reality show participants. Even celebrities have joined in on the action.

Celebrity docusoaps are one of the many genres of reality television that earns high ratings. Viewers get a chance to see famous stars behind the scenes and in their everyday lives. The celebrities that were once only featured in magazines, gossip blogs, or as famed characters are now presented as themselves, in their own settings. As expected with docusoaps, the shows present celebrities in a style very similar to documentaries. In each episode, viewers follow along with the characters' lives. Monica Brown allowed viewers into her life with the BET original *Still Standing* (2009–2010). VH1 continues to give viewers a front row seat in the home and family life of music couple Clifford *T.I.* Harris and Tomeka *Tiny* Cottle-Harris in their reality show, *The Family Hustle* (2011–present). Audiences get to learn about their favorite *R&B Divas-Atlanta* such as Angie Stone, Monifah Carter, and Sylenna Johnson Moore thanks to TV One's series (2012–present).

When Black female celebrities perform as fictional characters, they serve as a representation of Black women. This is still the case with their presentations in reality television. Black female celebrities provide presentations that impact the way Black women are viewed by society—whether fiction or nonfiction. Thus, when studying images in reality television, celebrities cannot be excluded. This chapter takes a closer look at how Black female celebrities are represented in reality television docusoaps. This introduces an interesting dynamic as celebrities on reality television (or their management team) oftentimes have production credits on their shows. Will this result in a more positive, realistic portrayal?

In order to help narrow the focus and add another dimension, I selected shows based on a common theme—family. More specifically, the shows analyzed all centered on the relationship among sisters who share their personal and business worlds. Black culture has always celebrated family and sisterhood. Even the way in which these values are presented communicates something about Black women. A closer examination of these images can reveal what reality television communicates about Black women in general, as well as their roles in the family and workplace. In addition, it helps to show how Black women are presented in relationship to other Black women.

While researching to identify shows that fit the focus of this study, the mission statement for one cable network, in particular, stood out. Women's Entertainment Television, or WE tv, expressed to the public their desire to present more family centered entertainment. The mission of the cable station is to provide entertainment that presents and caters to strong women.[6] The channel currently features two celebrity reality shows that focus on Black sisters—*Braxton Family Values* and *Mary Mary*. Considering the mission of the station as well as the leading cast of the shows and focus on family, the two shows were good candidates for analysis. Focusing in on shows only from WE tv will also help assess if a network that promises positive images of family and women, delivers with its presentations of Black women. This chapter starts with background information on Black women's struggle with media portrayals, leading up to their current place in reality television. Further details are provided about each show, followed by an analysis and discussion on ways the women are presented and the societal implications.

## BLACK WOMEN IN TELEVISION

Researchers have continuously studied television representations of Black women, for good reason. Television plays a big role in the socialization process for its viewers. People use messages communicated through this medium to construct their identity and reality about the social world.[7] Thus, media representations are a source of power. When a group is excluded, or presented in a derogatory fashion, a negative impact can be left beyond the screen.

Unfortunately, Black women suffered from media exclusion as a double minority because of their race and their sex. As women, they were often featured in stereotypical ways that highlighted qualities such as femininity, domesticity, submissiveness, dependency on men, romance-driven, and physical appearance (according to Eurocentric Beauty Standards).[8] But as *Black* women, they were also often presented in racially stereotypical ways.

Mammy, Sapphire, and Jezebel were three popular characterizations used to describe and portray Black women. Historically, the Mammy and Sapphire were depicted as dark skin characters. Mammy was also an obese character, further deeming her as unattractive according to Eurocentric beauty standards.[9] Another similarity the two characters shared was their use of sassiness and aggression, though in different ways. As a nurturing and content domestic servant, Mammy had to be careful with how she used her assertiveness. She was able to use her sass toward other African-American women. However, she was not allowed to use it toward her White employers in a way that would make them feel uncomfortable or disrespected. Because of this understanding, and her physical appearance, she did not pose a threat to White people.[10] On the other hand, Sapphire's loud, aggressive, and sometimes obnoxious personality was used as a source of humor. The character, which originally aired on *The Amos 'n' Andy Show,* used her anger and dramatic behaviors (e.g., neck-rolling) to tear others down, especially Black men.[11] Her anger was framed more as unexplainable, unnecessary, and unattractive.

In contrast to Mammy and Sapphire, the Jezebel was historically a lighter skin Black woman who aligned more with Eurocentric beauty standards. The key component of this character was her hypersexuality. She enjoyed using her sexuality to attract and seduce men. Unlike Mammy, her provocativeness and sex appeal made her a threat to White people. The image was a way to justify White slave owners who often engaged in sexual activities with their Black female slaves. The Jezebel characterization allowed them to put blame on the women and their sexual desires. Instead of raping Jezebel, she wanted "it" and she asked for "it" through her actions and appearance.[12]

Through the years, more positive images of Black women emerged. This was due in part to changing times, including the Civil Rights Movement.[13] Production teams also began to acknowledge Black audiences as a profitable, niche market.[14] Viewers saw a change in the quality of images, as well. For example, Claire Huxtable of *The Cosby Show* (NBC, 1984–1992) presented an educated Black woman who was able to have a happy marriage, maintain a successful career as an attorney, and manage a household. Although some may have considered Claire's portrayal to be idealistic, it can also be argued that she presented a different and more flattering image from past stereotypical images. However, all representations were not quite *Claire-esque*. Stereotypes managed to travel and reappear in television, but in a new form.

Newer images of Black women appeared, yet they featured certain characteristics from past stereotypes. For example, Patricia Hill Collins discusses the evolution and modernization of the Mammy character. While the historical image of the Mammy was reserved for lower class, a different image—the Black Lady—was able to gain entry into middle class and the professional world. Her career is very important to her and is necessary if she wants to maintain her social status. According to Collins, the Black Lady can be linked to the modernized version of Mammy. While the older image was asexual, the newer portrayal had sexual desires but had to learn how to deal with them appropriately and in relation to other aspects of her life.[15]

Yet, this newer image can still use aggression in a way that was more acceptable than Sapphire. Assertiveness is appropriate for her when used to succeed or in service to others. But the modernized Mammy had to be careful to maintain, "a balance between being appropriately subordinate to White and/or male authority yet [maintain] a level of ambition and aggressiveness needed for achievement in middle-class occupations."[16] Thus despite her economic improvement, her place below White people and men remained the same. Claire Huxtable (as mentioned earlier), is identified by Collins as an example of the *new* Black Lady—she is educated and professional, a wife who knew to keep her sexuality restricted to her home, and viewers even saw her as a mother.

Yet all modernized images were not as big of an improvement as the Black Lady (e.g., from working class to middle-class/professional). Some of the newer, subtler stereotypical images were still just as troubling as past images, if not more. The recycled form made their staying power stronger and helped the images go unnoticed by some. For example, unexplainable anger is inherent with stereotypes such as the Bitch or the Angry Black Woman.[17] The Sapphire character shared that same quality. With newer images, the physical appearances have evolved, as Black women of all complexions and body styles can now exhibit that unexplainable anger.

Over the years, we have also witnessed how media can present Black women in the same role—but frame them either positively or negatively. Take for example the portrayal of Black women as mothers. Images that represent bad motherhood, such as the Welfare Mom or Baby Mama, present Black women as unfit mothers who had children due to their hypersexuality, irresponsibility, or other selfish reasons.[18] On the other end of the spectrum, and as times changed, television began to present images of Black women as good mothers. For example, Reid-Brinkely discusses the strong mothering skills possessed by the Black Queen.[19] The newer image of the Black Lady (discussed earlier) also has the potential to be a good mother,[20] *only if* she is able to successfully juggle her tasks as a mother and business woman—as exhibited by Claire Huxtable.

As time progressed and new types of media became popular, we were also introduced to images of Black women that were not featured in the past. For example, Dionne Stephens and Layli Phillips identify several new characterizations of Black women. Some of the characters still featured common demeaning characteristics from the past—such as the theme of hypersexuality inherent in the newer image, Golddigger. She uses her sexuality for financial gain. But, we were also introduced to newer characters, such as the Diva who has more of a contained sexuality and is not dependent on men. She is conceited, enjoys luxuries, and basks in her high social status.[21] Now that reality television has become so popular, those inside and outside of academe have begun to raise questions about how Black women are presented. Looking at reality television images, while also considering the history of Black women in television, helps to determine whether portrayals have evolved or remained the same.

## Reality Television

The amount of reality television programming has continued to increase substantially throughout the years, in both amount and variety. Now, various networks such as MTV, BET, ABC, and BRAVO are known for featuring reality shows. These shows are expected to be unscripted and feature *real* people in their everyday lives, routines, and/or specific situations. Footage is then formatted and presented to audiences in a narrative form.[22] Since the programming does not require big name actors, screenwriters, and as many resources as other programming types, it is fairly cheap to produce.[23] Editing and strategic casting contributes to the reason why reality television lacks the realism promised by its name.

The reality shows still garner large audiences and profits. Viewers appreciate the way shows offer entertainment. Reality television can provide an escape from their own reality. So, despite the lack of a true *reality,* the shows give them an opportunity to look into the lives of new people and subjects, while also giving them the chance to participate in the television process. Reality television is the chance for an *ordinary person* to be featured in television and/or join in on conversations and decisions.[24]

Several different types of television shows fall under the umbrella of reality television, including dating shows, competition shows, and talent shows. One popular type of reality programming is the docusoap. Anisa Biressi and Heather Nunn define docusoaps as, "multi-part series, each episode featuring strong recurrent 'characters' engaged in everyday activities, whose stories are interleaved in soap opera style."[25] Viewers tune in weekly to see how the storyline continues for each character, causing them to become more invested in the show.

Although reality television can be traced back to the 1940s with *Candid Camera*,[26] the first docusoap was *An American Family*, which debuted in 1973.[27] MTV's docusoap *The Real World* helped revive the genre in the 1990s.[28] In fact, the show is still on the air. Today, viewers have several other examples of docusoaps such as Bravo's *The Real Housewives* franchise, MTV's *Teen Mom* franchise, and VH1's *Love & Hip Hop* franchise. Celebrity docusoaps feature celebrities as they deal with their personal and professional lives.

Reality television was very promising. Researchers believed that this new programming would open up the doors for groups who were traditionally excluded from the media.[29] Reality television shows had the potential to increase diversity and educate society about its importance. Yet, some argue that it has failed to do so. Critics have voiced concerns with how images of Black women in reality television have remained one-dimensional and stereotypical. In a Twitter chat facilitated by TheGrio.com, audience members expressed their concerns: "Many participants shared that they felt shows like Real Housewives of Atlanta, Love and Hip Hop, and Basketball Wives reinforce harmful racial stereotypes and teach viewers to disrespect black women."[30] Other bloggers and critics have expressed similar concerns over the way the genre communicates messages about Black women.

Additionally, research has found that problematic images of Black women have reappeared in reality television. For example, Jennifer Pozner argues reality television relies on several derogatory images of Black women such as "the Black Bitch, Hootchie Mama, Ghetto Girl, and Entitled Diva."[31] Tia Tyree also found the Hoochie (spelled differently by each scholar) as a common image when examining Black women in reality television, specifically game docs,[32] talent contests, and docusoaps.[33] She also found multiple instances of the Angry Black Woman and the Chicken Head,[34] the latter of which featured an overly sexualized nature, which is a trait also possessed by the Jezebel. Other researchers found images of Black women as angry within shows including *The Real Housewives of Atlanta* (Bravo, 2008–present), *Bad Girls Club—New Orleans* (Oxygen, 2011). *The Real World—Cancun* (MTV, 2009), *Basketball Wives—Miami* (VH1, 2010–present), *Love & Hip Hop—New York* (VH1, 2011–present),[35] *Road Rules* (MTV, 1995–2007),[36] and *I Love New York* (VH1, 2007–2008).[37]

This is not to say that all presentations found in reality television were demeaning. For example, in a previous examination of reality television, I found that, amidst the drama, *The Real Housewives of Atlanta*, *Love & Hip Hop—New York*, and *Basketball Wives—Miami* presented Black women as good mothers, through show presentations and/or their cast biographies. This was an improvement from past images of bad Black mothers, as discussed earlier. The analysis of docusoaps also revealed instances where Black women were presented in the shows and/or cast biographies as professional, career-driven women. However, the image of the Angry Black Woman was highlighted more than the positive images.[38]

Members of the popular press have also acknowledged that some people do not find reality television images of Black women to always be bad. Discussing the relationship between Black viewers and cable networks, journalist Evette Dionne writes,

> We drive ratings, and in exchange, the networks give us a rare chance to see black women humanized in the media.... The average black woman can live vicariously through the housewives of Atlanta, basketball wives of Miami and hip-hop lovers of New York. Reality television [lets] us see the humanity of other women of color, even if their fancy lives will never be ours.[39]

While completely idealistic, do-no-wrong characters are not expected (nor are they realistic) the key is to examine if a balance exists among images. It is no denying that television drama is a guilty pleasure for many viewers—and this is the same for reality programming. What is important to examine is who and what is always the source of such drama. We must also consider what other images and messages are presented along with such drama.

In order to add to the current discussion on Black women in reality television, I offer an analysis of Black female celebrities. This is beneficial to our understanding of Black women in reality television for multiple reasons. Black female celebrities have continuously served as representations of this group. Although they are now featured in a new genre and no longer in character, it is still important to consider how they represent Black women. Furthermore, celebrities carry the task of serving as role models. It is common for their fans to want to mimic their behaviors. This could especially be the case when audiences are able to see their favorite celebrities in their *real* lives.

## SISTERS, CELEBRITIES, AND REALITY STARS

WE tv, a branch of *AMC Networks*, "showcases and celebrates modern women who are bold, independent and taking control of their lives."[40] In 2011, the cable channel premiered *Braxton Family Values* as part of their rebranding strategy. Their new goal was to present more shows centered around family and other topics that viewers could relate.[41] Kim Martin, then president and general manager of WE tv, explained the channel's new tagline "Life as WE Know It": "At the heart of every WE tv original show is a story that allows a woman to see herself, someone she knows or someone she'd love to know. Whether the shows feature celebrities or real people, viewers can relate to the situations and share in the experience."[42]

*Braxton Family Values* continued to be a large success, causing WE tv to label it as one of their signature shows. The show has already been renewed for a fourth season, which comes as no surprise since the third season averaged 1.4 million viewers.[43] The show documents the lives of Grammy award winning singer, Toni Braxton and her four sisters, Towanda, Traci, Trina, and Tamar. Due to the show's success, WE tv decided to release another reality docusoap focusing on Black celebrity sisters, their family lives, and careers. In a press release announcing the new series, Martin is quoted saying,

> WE tv has experienced incredible success with *Braxton Family Values*, especially among African-American women. By developing more shows for this underserved audience, we are super serving a valuable fan base that consumes more television than any other audience and is highly engaged with their favorite shows on social media platforms. Through research and ongoing conversations with our viewers we know that this audience is hungry for content that reflects their lives and we are thrilled to be the network to bring it to them.[44]

The show *Mary Mary,* named after the gospel-singing duo, follows the lives and careers of sisters Erica and Tina Campbell. Their younger sister and stylist, Goo Goo, also makes frequent appearances. The series grows in popularity from season to season. Prior to the season two finale the series already experienced more than a 16 percent growth in viewership. WE tv continued to include the show in its line up with the third season premiering on February 27, 2014.[45] That particular season had not ended at the time of this research.

Both series have proven successful for WE tv. Each also aligns with the cable network's goal to provide quality programming focusing on a family dynamic to which viewers can relate. Season three of *Braxton Family Values* and season two of *Mary Mary* were examined. The third season of *Braxton Family Values* was broken into two halves, with a five-month break in between. Each half was treated as its own mini season, with a premiere and finale. In order to keep the amount of episodes equitable between the shows, the second half of season three was used. This sampling strategy also helped to create an ongoing timeline of the two series—*Braxton Family Values* season three, part two aired one month after *Mary Mary* season two ended. More specifically, I sought to identify themes shared across the episodes of both shows. This helps add to the discussion on Black women in popular culture by providing additional examples of how the group is portrayed in a branch of reality programming. To assist the reader throughout the analysis, the shows are abbreviated as follows: *BFV* for *Braxton Family Values* and *Mary* for *Mary Mary*. Mentions of Mary Mary (without italics) references the gospel duo, and not the show as a whole.

## BLACK FEMALE CELEBRITIES IN REALITY TELEVISION

### She's About Her Business

As celebrities, it is no surprise that each of the series focuses heavily on the women's occupations. Success is highlighted as the women continue with their career or begin the journey. For example, both Erica and Tina of Mary Mary have earned major accolades for their work as musical artists. But now, viewers are able to see why they are successful. The women are shown rehearsing, traveling, and performing. The show communicates how their success is earned. We also see how their lives as professionals are not always easy. Viewers witness Mary Mary work long hours, run into issues while practicing, and stressing over how to juggle multiple tasks. In episode 6, Erica and Tina have two big obligations in one day. They have an early morning performance on *The Tom Joyner Morning Show*. Later that night they have to perform at a tribute concert for Bishop T. D. Jakes. The women are stressed about fitting both performances into the day, in addition to sound checks, resting their voices, and other errands. In the end, however, the women have two good performances, as illustrated by the crowd's response.[46] The Black female celebrities are shown as being professional, hardworking career women.

The show also allows viewers to see Black females who are working toward meeting their career goals. For example, in episode sixteen of *BFV*, Traci debuts her radio show on Bliss.fm, Tamar is rehearsing for her tour, and Trina learns about a new opportunity to perform her original music at Toni's upcoming concert.[47] Because of a docusoap's format, those invested in the series are able to follow along and see how the women's success unfolds.

As professionals, the women are also shown perfecting their skills. Mary Mary is excited about their upcoming performance at the *Essence* Festival in New Orleans, LA. It has always been a dream of the group's and they explain to their fans how it is the biggest stage on which they have ever performed. The women go through countless rehearsals and planning to make sure they are prepared. Episode seven, for example, shows the women at one of their many rehearsals with choreographer Laurieann Gibson. Even Tina, who is well over seven-months pregnant, is there to prepare for the show.[48] We see this same work ethic on *BFV* as Toni and Tamar prepare for their own tours. Their dedication to the craft is clear as Tamar rehearses while sick and Toni stays on top of her sisters to make sure all of the singing and dance moves are correct.[49]

As part of the women's professionalism, they believe in delivering a strong product—no matter the cost. In fact, during one performance Tina makes the band stop and re-start the music during the concert. She explains to the fans that it has to be right, because that is what they paid for. The work on their careers, as well as dedication to their craft, helps present the Black women in a light similar to the new image of the Black Lady, as discussed earlier. The women are ambitious, motivated, and successful which are qualities shared with the Black Lady. But did this impact their mothering skills?

## Wonder Mom

Not only are the celebrities career women, they are working moms. We see multiple examples of the women while at work, but we also have images of the women interacting with their children. Both Tamar, from *BFV*, and Erica, from *Mary*, recently had a baby. Following their concerts and other business, we see the mothers spending time with their infants.[50] On the stage, Tina may be one half of the group Mary Mary, but at home we see her cooking dinner for her family and throwing a birthday party for her daughter.[51] Of course, this is in addition to Tina's constant traveling and performing on stage up to her ninth month of pregnancy. Towanda helps her sister Toni with background vocals, but we also see her shopping with her family to purchase football gear for her son.[52]

The women manage to juggle their career and family, although it is not always an easy task. Tamar, from *BFV*, shares that she feels guilty about her performance as a mother. She is new to handling her career and family life at once, and fears she is preventing her son from having a real childhood. Her friends and sister remind her that she is, in fact, a successful career woman who still makes time for her son.[53] Many of the women seem to make their children a priority, even if their career has to take a back seat. For example, Towanda does not join her sisters Traci and Trina for an appearance at the *Essence* Festival because she needed to be with her children.[54]

During a tribute performance to Mary Mary, Tina steps off of the stage to comfort her son who has called from home. Although her manager and sister/group member are not happy about the decision, Tina insists she must take the time to soothe her son by talking and singing to him. We also see Tina turn down gigs in order to spend more time with her children.[55] Although she is ambitious and dedicated to her job, it is clear that family comes first. In one scene she explains, "I'm not willing to lose what I have at home to pursue everything that I want career wise."[56]

You can also see passion for motherhood through their actions. While out of town, Tina is visibly upset she is not able to be with her husband and children while they are at the zoo.[57] She also has a tough time leaving her newborn son when it is time to return to work.[58] On *BFV*, Trina and Traci show passion for their children through their protective natures. Although her son is eighteen years old, Trina is sad when he decides to leave college and join the army. She still wants to protect him from what she considers to be a dangerous situation.[59] When the second part of *BFV* season three returns, Traci is dealing with rumors that her husband had an illegitimate child outside of their marriage. Yet her main concern is not her own feeling, but the way in which the situation is impacting her son. She explains, "It doesn't matter what his father or his mother does. Do not take it out on my child!"[60] Traci's statement and nonverbal behaviors communicate her anger. But here, we see anger is used for a purpose. Unlike the unexplainable anger of the Sapphire or Bitch, as a mother, Traci uses her anger strategically to protect her child.

Being a good mother appears to be something the women learned by example. Their own mothers are present in several episodes, still providing support to their daughters, even as adults. On *BFV*, their mother, Ms. Evelyn, travels with her daughter Tamar, helping to take care of the baby.[61] Ms. Honey, the mother of Erica and Tina, also travels with the music group so she can watch after Erica's infant daughter.[62] Both Ms. Evelyn and Ms. Honey serve as an advisor and mediator for their children. When an issue she is having with her sisters saddens Tamar, she confides in her mother while they are at lunch. Her mom comforts her daughter while also giving her advice.[63] Ms. Honey advises her pregnant daughter, Tina, to slow down with all she was trying to accomplish, for her own health and wellbeing.[64]

Both moms also serve as peacemakers when their daughters are disagreeing. While a feud between Towanda and Tamar continues, Ms. Evelyn takes it upon herself to sit down with Towanda to urge her to work things out with her sister.[65] On *Mary*, Erica reaches out to her mother following a heated argument with her sister Tina over business and personal issues. Mom is there to comfort Erica while also explaining the need for them to work out their issues.[66] So while we do see the ladies as professional and ambitious, the women on both shows are able to succeed as good mothers, despite their careers.

## I Am My Sister's Keeper

Since each of the series centers on sisters, it is no surprise that one of the messages communicated about Black women is about their relationship with their siblings. In this regard, the women are presented in a flattering light. As sisters, the women are protective and supportive. Despite their individual careers and personal lives, several of the women made time for bonding with their sisters. From helping their sister clean out her closet on *BFV*,[67] to attending their baby sister's bachelorette party on *Mary*,[68] viewers witness a range of activities that illustrate the closeness of their sisterhood on both shows.

As the women's relationships with each other are displayed, other characteristics of their personality shine through. The same protective nature displayed as a mother is also displayed as a sister. During their trip to the *Essence* Festival, the Braxton sisters Trina and Traci are nervous about questions they might be asked during the interview. The last time fans saw the women, Trina was dealing with an impending divorce and Traci had learned about her husband's alleged infidelity. The sisters admitted they are not looking forward to answering questions related to their situation. Instantly, as the host turns her attention to Traci she begins to ask about the infidelity. Trina quickly interjects and asks the host (and audience) to first pay attention to how Traci's hard work dieting and exercising resulted in weight loss and a new look.[69] Although Traci eventually has to discuss the topic, Trina's attempt to deflect for even a moment shows her desire to protect her sister. As a woman going through marital issues herself, it appears Trina understands Traci's situation and does not want her sister to endure an interview focused on her relationship.

Erica and Tina show their protective nature as sisters when attending their younger sister Alana's wedding. During the reception they pull aside the new boyfriend of their other sister (and stylist) Goo Goo. They want to know more about his intentions and make it clear they will not allow anyone to hurt their sister.[70] Their approach and tone at times could be considered aggressive. Yet, this aggression comes with reason. This serves as another example of how the women are not aggressive by nature, but instead they are able to turn it on when they feel it is necessary.

As sisters, they continuously provide support for one another. Despite a full schedule, Erica decides to accompany her sister Tina to the doctor. Their manager suggests their assistant go instead so that Erica can handle business for the group. Yet, despite his disapproval, Erica insists on taking her sister to the doctor. She even hangs up the phone on the manager when he uses sarcasm to further express his disapproval.[71] Providing support to her sister Tina was more important.

While Toni is shown working on her autobiography, viewers learn about a huge way she supports her sisters. The Grammy winner reveals she did not want to participate in the reality show. Yet, she did so for her sisters. Her goal was to allow the world to see how talented they are and to provide a platform for them to launch their careers.[72] Her selflessness portrays her as a supportive and caring person. The sisters also help each other out in a number of instances, such as planning events or being there to hear about each other's frustrations.[73]

Support from one another seems to be an expectation. When it is not received, the women are visibly upset. Tamar is mad because she feels all of her sisters are not supporting her during her blossoming career. At a dinner with three of her sisters, Tamar addresses Towanda about what she perceives as a lack of adequate support: "[I] was there for you on your 40th birthday. You [weren't] there for me during [my] success story."[74] Before beginning her tour, Tamar invites her sisters to come with her. Trina obliges and Tamar is clearly appreciative of the support. During a dinner together, Trina is able to console Tamar when she is discussing her concerns about being a good mother. But we also see how Tamar is disappointed that her sisters Traci and Towanda did not come to support her.[75] In the end, all of the sisters are shown supporting Tamar as she wins her first Soul Train Award, celebrates her Grammy nominations,[76] and then deals with the upset of not winning.[77] Although there are rocky moments, overall the women in both series are portrayed as Black women who are willing and able to support their sisters.

## Let's Talk About Sex

Although not a daily topic, the women do not appear ashamed of their sexuality. The women are not portrayed as hypersexual beings that were obsessed with sex. They were also not portrayed as being irresponsible with their sexual activities. This illustrates a nice improvement from images such as (or similar to) the Jezebel. On *Mary,* older sisters Erica and Tina give advice about sex to their younger sister, Alana. Viewers learn that, for this family, sex is reserved for those who are married. The morning of Alana's wedding when she is stressed, Tina responds: "You gonna be having sex tonight. You should be thinking about that." Following her statement is a flashback to a previous episode where Tina tells Alana she will be "sore and oversexed" in the beginning of the marriage, since this is new for the couple.[78]

Prior to the wedding, while arranging the bachelorette party, sexuality emerges as a theme. While sister Goo Goo wants to hire strippers (which she is shown interviewing in a later episode), Tina is opposed to the idea. In the end the male entertainers are invited to the party and are shown shirtless while serving the women food. Viewers are left to imagine if the men ever strip for the women. When she feels as if the party is getting a bit sexually explicit, Tina quickly looks at the camera crew and says, "Cut! Thank you for coming. You guys may be dismissed."[79] The show presents Black females who are interested in sex, with certain conditions. It is not a careless act, but instead something that is reserved for marriage—and especially for Tina, something that is not on display for strangers.

The Braxtons' discussions related to sexuality also hint to the importance of appropriateness. Trina and Toni are both shown expressing concerns with their attire being too revealing.[80] As Trina explained, they want to make sure the clothing was not "giving too much."[81] To celebrate her fortieth birthday, Towanda participates in a photo shoot. After being convinced by her team and photographer, she agrees to take a picture wearing only a thong.[82] When she shows her pictures to her mom and sisters, some raise concerns with that particular picture. They are relieved when they find that the pictures are for her personal collection. Her reason behind the photos was to celebrate her beauty and not to share with others. Everyone then agrees that the pictures are fine.[83] They felt celebrating their own sexuality, even if this includes partially nude photos is acceptable, as long as they are not used to arouse others. One could even see this as an example of a woman (Towanda) owning her sexuality. Again, the Black woman's sexuality is presented in a more responsible way than stereotypes of the past. Viewers also witness Trina and Towanda visit a sex toy store,[84] further illustrating how the women are sexual beings.

**Fight Hard, Love Harder**

In a voiceover during the opening of the season three, part two premiere one of the Braxton sisters explains, "There's always drama with the Braxtons."[85] The season delivers just that with one of the reoccurring storylines being a feud between Tamar and Trina. The two are shown arguing with each other on more than one occasion, which sometimes includes yelling, sarcasm, and insults.[86] The same is the case for Erica and Tina who are shown arguing over business and issues about disrespect. Their biggest argument happens at the end of the season and results in the women deciding to take a break from the group, Mary Mary.[87] However, disagreements between the sisters never turn physical in either series.

Several attempts were made to mediate and solve conflicts among the sisters. Mother to the Braxtons, Ms. Evelyn, and the remaining sisters encourage Towanda and Tamar to work through their issues.[88] The sisters also feel that the issues should not be discussed with those outside the public. For example, when on the red carpet for the Soul Train Music Awards, Towanda discusses the upcoming season of *BFV*: "A lot of drama ahead . . . but we love each other. We just don't like each other right now."[89] Trina is shown in a commentary scene explaining that Towanda should not have shared that information: "There are some things that you shouldn't do or say in front of the company."[90] Toni shares that same sentiment in a later commentary scene before urging Towanda to sit down one-on-one with Tamar.[91] Of course, this is quite interesting considering all information discussed in front of the cameras has the potential to air on their show for the viewing public. Perhaps it is more acceptable when viewers are able to see the conflict in a context that involves attempts to mediate and other positive interactions. Of course, viewers can only assume this point, as the women do not explain it during the show. Mary Mary also made similar attempts to mediate their conflicts, sometimes with the help of a third party such as their mother or manager.[92]

Regardless of the drama, bonds and relationships remain intact. Towanda explains, "You know, it's interesting. Even when we have big or heated arguments . . . I don't have any ill feelings whenever I am with my sisters.

It's always refreshing to see each other. Even though we had a big argument."[93] On the season finale of *Mary*, Tina discusses the importance of fixing her issues with Erica. As she explains, the business side can come and go, but their relationship as sisters is more important.[94] So, while the ladies do engage in conflict it serves as an example of healthy conflict. The women disagree, attempt to mediate, and maintain relationships while dealing with disputes—an unavoidable element of interpersonal relationships.

**She's Just Like Me**

The women featured on both shows have earned fame, whether from their careers pre-reality television, their popularity after the shows aired, or both. The shows allow viewers to see their celebrities as ordinary people. As discussed earlier, WE tv strives to present images of women to whom viewers could relate. The viewers see that Black female celebrities are not perfect. Instead—they are human. The women have successful careers and luxurious lifestyles. But the series also acknowledges their flaws.

Trina and Traci from *BFV* discuss their marital issues.[95] Their sister Tamar shows her vulnerability when she shares her concerns with being a first time mother.[96] Different episodes of *Mary* show the women make a mistake during their performances and/or admit that they did not deliver a good show.[97] Viewers also learn that, even as professionals and celebrities, the Braxtons and the Campbells experience nervousness. For example, Erica admits she is nervous when performing alone as one of the celebrity performances at the *How Sweet the Sound* gospel competition.[98] Traci also explains the anxiety she experiences on her first day at her new radio show.[99]

Each series addresses issues with health and physical appearance. On *Mary*, Erica deals with severe headaches and high blood pressure[100] while Tina has a scare associated with her pregnancy during rehearsals.[101] With the Braxtons, several of the sisters mention issues with body size and their desire to lose weight.[102] The celebrities deal with issues that the average viewer may experience, as well. The Black female celebrities are not presented as perfect or idealistic. Instead, they are shown experiencing both good and bad times.

## REVISITING THE POTENTIAL OF REALITY TELEVISION

WE tv delivered on their promise to offer reality television programming centered on family. *Braxton Family Values* and *Mary Mary* present Black female celebrities as they balance their family and careers. These family centered storylines also communicate ideas about Black women. The reality show presents Black women as ambitious businesswomen who are able to care for and protect their children. Anger and sexuality are not absent from the images, but instead, are used with purpose and appropriateness. Despite an abundance of drama, their love and support for one another manages to shine through, due in part to their attempts to resolve conflict. Their success may have been obvious before viewing the show, but afterwards, audiences can learn that family comes first for these women.

Presentations of the Braxton and Campbell sisters communicated a positive image. The shows present Black women who are ambitious and successful. They possess strong mothering skills and know the difference between hypersexuality and acceptable sexuality. In addition, their use of aggression is purposeful and to protect others. The women are not solely presented as one specific stereotype. Instead, they are featured as multifaceted women who experience several highs as well as lows. Thus, more positive images of Black women in reality television can and do exist.

Peter Berger and Thomas Luckmann's Social Construction of Reality discusses how we use different information as we continuously make sense of our surroundings. Different social institutions—including media messages—provide us with some of this information.[103] Fictional and nonfictional information is used as viewers shape ideas about their own identity as well as their perceptions of others. Although media are not the only part of this process, it does serve as a powerful influence for many. As discussed earlier, television is a big part of the socialization process—which includes a social construction of reality. In applying this theory to the current topic, these show presentations could be beneficial. When trying to shape perceptions of Black women, many will turn to media to help construct ideas. If using the women within *BFV* and *Mary* as examples, this could help people realize the multidimensionality of Black women. Furthermore, Black women may use this information in constructing their own identity. Seeing professional, family oriented Black women may motivate others to strive for the same.

Reality television *does* still have the potential to increase diversity. The success of *BFV* and *Mary* are evidence that reality television programming with more flattering images of Black women can succeed. The shows also illustrate how drama and sexuality—selling points for television—can still exist, without being at the expense of Black women's identities. However, we cannot ignore the fact that celebrity reality television participants may have more input on the way they are portrayed. This could certainly play a role in the type of representations that make it to our television airways. For reality television to truly meet its potential, more positive images of Black women, as well as other underrepresented groups, need to appear in noncelebrity reality television programming, as well. It is important to reiterate the goal is not for idealistic Black female characters that only exhibit perfection. Instead, presentations within reality television should present more of a *reality*—multidimensional Black women, flaws and all. For examples, see Toni, Trina, Towanda, Traci, Tamar, Tina, and Erica.

## NOTES

1. Susan Murray, "I Think We Need a New Name for It: The Meeting of Documentary and Reality TV," in *Reality TV: Remaking Television Culture*, edited by Susan Murray and Laurie Ouellete (New York: New York University Press, 2009), 65.
2. Mark Andrejevic, *Reality TV: The Work of Being Watched* (Lanham: Rowman & Littlefiled, 2004), 3–4.
3. David Croteau and Williams Hoynes, *Media/Society: Industries, Images, and Audiences*, 3rd ed. (Thousand Oaks: Pine Forge Press, 2003), 176–79.
4. Jessica Johnson, "Johnson: Reality TV Offers Scraps to Black Women," *Athens Banner Herald*, October 28, 2013, accessed March 3, 2014, http://onlineathens.com/opinion/2013-10-28/johnson-reality-tv-offers-scraps-black-women; Allison Samuels, "Reality TV Trashes Black Women," *Newsweek*, May 1, 2011, accessed January 7, 2012, http://www.newsweek.com/reality-tv-trashes-black-women-67641; Terry Shropshire, "Is This the Black Reality," *Rolling Out*, July 12, 2012, accessed March 3, 2014, http://rollingout.com/covers/is-this-the-black-reality/#_.
5. Nene Leakes, "Pillow Talk," *Nene Leakes Official* (blog), January 27, 2014, accessed April 1, 2014, www.neneleakesofficial.com/page/8/.
6. "WE tv," AMC Networks, accessed April 4, 2014, http://www.amcnetworks.com/we-tv.
7. Croteau and Hoynes, *Media/Society*, 13–18.
8. Croteau and Hoynes, *Media/Society*, 213–16; Susan Douglas, *Where The Girls Are: Growing Up Female with the Mass Media* (New York: Times Books, 1994). Linda Holtzman, *Media Messages: What Film, Television, and Popular Music Teach Us About Race, Class, Gender, and Sexual Orientation* (Armonk: M. E. Sharpe, 2000), 72–81; Myra Macdonald, *Representing Women: Myths of Femininity in the Popular Media* (New York: Edward Arnold, 1995); Marian Meyers, "Fracturing Women," in *Mediated Women: Representations in Popular Culture*, ed. Marian Meyers (Cresskill: Hampton Press, 1999), 10–12.
9. Beretta E. Smith-Shomade, *Shaded Lives: African-American Women and Television* (Piscataway: Rutgers University Press, 2002), 60–61; K. Sue Jewell, *From Mammy to Miss America and Beyond: Cultural Images and the Shaping of US Social Policy* (New York: Routledge, 1993), 37–49.
10. Shawna V. Hudson, "Re-creational Television: The Paradox of Change and Continuity within Stereotypical Iconography," *Sociological Inquiry* 68, no. 2 (1998): 244; Jewell, *Mammy to Miss America*, 37–44.
11. Hudson, "Re-creational Television," 246–47; Jewell, *Mammy to Miss America*, 45.
12. Hudson, "Re-creational Television," 244–45; Jewell, *Mammy to Miss America*, 46–47.
13. Croteau and Hines, *Media/Society*, 27–29.
14. Herman Gray, *Watching Race: Television and the Struggle for Blackness* (Minneapolis: University of Minnesota Press, 2004), xix–xxi.
15. Patricia Hill Collins, *Black Sexual Politics: African Americans, Gender, and the New Racism* (New York: Routledge, 2005), 138–48.
16. Ibid, 140.
17. Ibid, 123.
18. Collins, *Black Sexual Politics,* 130; Dionne P. Stephens and Layli D. Phillips, "Freaks, Gold Diggers, Divas and Dykes: The Sociohistorical Development of Adolescent African American Women's Sexual Scripts," *Sexuality and Culture* (2003): 32–34.
19. Shanara R. Reid-Brinkely, "The Essence of Res(ex)pectability Black Women's Negotiation of Black Femininity in Rap Music and Music Video," *Meridians: Feminism, Race, Transnationalism* 8, no. 1 (2008): 236–60; Tia Tyree, "Lovin Momma and Hatin on Baby Mama: A Comparison of Misogynistic and Stereotypical Representations in Songs about Rappers' Mothers and Baby Mamas," *Women and Language* 32, no. 2: 50–58.
20. Collins, *Black Sexual Politics,* 139–40.
21. Stephens and Phillips, "Freaks and Gold Diggers," 15–20.
22. Robin L. Nabi et al., "Reality-Based Television Programming and the Psychology of Its Appeal," *Media Psychology* 5 (2003): 304.

23. Jennifer L. Pozner, *Reality Bites Back: The Troubling Truth About Guilty Pleasure TV.* (Berkeley: Seal Press, 2010), 14–15.

24. Andrejevic, *Reality TV,* 2–6; An example of the participatory nature of reality television, outside of cast members, is the voting process that is a part of competition shows such as Fox's *American Idol.*

25. Anita Biressi and Heather Nunn, *Reality TV: Realism and Revelation,* (New York: Wallflower Press, 2005), 64.

26. Bradley D. Clissold, "Candid Camera and the Origins of Reality TV: Origins of Reality TV," in *Understanding Reality Television,* eds. Su Holmes and Deborah Jermyn, (New York: Routledge, 2004), 33.

27. Andrejevic, *Reality TV,* 66.

28. Ibid, 71.

29. Laurie Ouellette and Susan Murray, introduction to *Reality TV: Remaking Television Culture,* by Susan Murray and Laurie Ouellete (New York: New York University Press, 2009), 11.

30. Sil Lai Abrams, "From 'Julia' to 'Nene': The Impact of Reality TV on Black Women," *theGrio,* June 5, 2013, accessed March 3, 2014, http://thegrio.com/2013/06/05/from-julia-to-nene-thoughts-on-the-impact-of-reality-tv-on-black-women/.

31. Ted Madger, "Television 2.0: The Business of American Television in Transition," in *Understanding Reality Television Reality TV: Remaking Television Culture,* eds. Susan Murray and Laurie Ouellete (New York: New York University Press, 2009), 141–42; Pozner, *Reality Bites Back,* 166.

32. A game doc is a show that follows cast members during their daily routines, while they are competing for a prize. An example of such is CBS' *Survivor.*

33. Tia Tyree, "African American Stereotypes in Reality Television," *The Howard Journal of Communications* 22, no. 2 (2011): 406.

34. Ibid, 404–405.

35. Adria Goldman, "Constructing a Woman's Reality: Examining Images of African-American Women in Six Selected Reality Television Docusoaps" (PhD diss., Howard University, 2012); It is rumored that *Basketball Wives—Miami* was canceled, however at the time of this analysis, that was not confirmed by VH1.

36. Mark Andrejevic and Dean Colby, "Racism and Reality TV: The Case of MTV's Road Rules," in *How Real is Reality TV?: Essays on Representation and Truth,* ed. David S. Escoffery (Jefferson: McFarland & Company, 2006).

37. Shannon B. Campbell et al., "I Love New York: Does New York Love Me?" *Journal of International Women's Studies* 10, no. 2 (2008), 20–28.

38. Goldman, "Constructing Woman's Reality."

39. Evette Dionne, "Wealthy Reality Stars Humanize Black Women," *The New York Times,* January 16, 2014, accessed March 3, 2014, http://www.nytimes.com/roomfordebate/2014/01/16/why-we-like-to-watch-rich-people/wealthy-reality-stars-humanize-black-women.

40. "WE tv," AMC Networks, accessed March 3, 2014, http://www.amcnetworks.com/we-tv.

41. AMC Networks, "WE tv Announces Pair of Original Series for 2011," under "Press Releases," http://www.amcnetworks.com/pressreleases/wetvannouncespairoforiginalseriesfor2012 (accessed March 3, 2014); David Bauder, "Toni Braxton, Family Get New WE Reality Series," *Huff Post Entertainment,* January 3, 2011, accessed March 3, 2014, http://www.huffingtonpost.com/2011/01/03/toni-braxton-family-get-new-we-reality-series_n_803903.html?view=print&comm_ref=false.

42. AMC Networks, "WE tv Announces"; Kim Martin is the former president and general manager of WE tv. According to AMC Networks website, Marc Juris was named as her successor.

43. AMC Networks, "WE tv Orders New Seasons of Hit Shows Braxton Family Values and SWV Reunited," under "Press Releases," http://www.amcnetworks.com/press-releases/we-tv-orders-new-seasons-of-hit-shows-braxton-family-values-and-swv-reunited (accessed March 3, 2014).

44. AMC Networks, "WE tv Greenlights Mary Mary for 2012," under "Press Releases," http://www.amcnetworks.com/pressreleases/wetvgreenlightsmarymaryfor2012 (accessed March 3, 2014).

45. Amanda Kondolojy, "WE tv Renews Mary Mary for Third Season," *TV by the Numbers*, February 27, 2013, accessed March 3, 2014, http://tvbythenumbers.zap2it.com/2013/02/27/we-tv-renews-mary-mary-for-third-season/171108/.

46. *Mary Mary*, "The Showdown," episode 6, March 14, 2014 (originally aired January 10, 2013).

47. *Braxton Family Values*, "Back to Braxton Business," episode 16, March 7, 2014 (originally aired November 28, 2013).

48. *Mary Mary*, "Pregnant Pause," episode 7, March 14, 2014 (originally aired January 17, 2013).

49. *Braxton Family Values*, "Back to Braxton Business," November 28, 2013.

50. *Braxton Family Values*, "Chix in a Row," episode 22, March 14, 2014 (originally aired January 23, 2014); *Mary Mary*, "Road Test," episode 1, March 7, 2014 (originally aired December 6, 2012).

51. *Mary Mary*, "Bachelorette Party," episode 2, March 7, 2014 (originally aired December 13, 2012); *Mary Mary*, "The Showdown," January 10, 2013.

52. *Braxton Family Values*, "I Don't Have No Baby," episode 15, March 14, 2014 (originally aired November 21, 2013).

53. *Braxton Family Values*, "Chix in a Row," January 23, 2014.

54. *Braxton Family Values*, "A Very Public Affair," episode 14, March 14, 2014 (originally aired November 14, 2013).

55. *Mary Mary*, "Essence of the Conflict," episode 10, March 7, 2014 (originally aired February 7, 2013).

56. *Mary Mary*, "Boyfriend Drama," episode 3, March 7, 2014 (originally aired December 20, 2012).

57. *Mary Mary*, "Road Test," December 6, 2012.

58. *Mary Mary*, "Beginning of the End," episode 12, March 7, 2014 (originally aired February 21, 2013).

59. *Braxton Family Values*, "I Don't Have No Baby," November 21, 2013.

60. *Braxton Family Values*, "A Very Public Affair," November 14, 2013.

61. *Braxton Family Values*, "Chix in a Row," January 23, 2014.

62. *Mary Mary*, "Road Test," December 6, 2012.

63. *Braxton Family Values*, "Award Show Shade," episode 25, March 14, 2012 (originally aired February 13, 2014).

64. *Mary Mary*, "All Night Wrong," episode 4, March 7, 2014 (originally aired December 27, 2012).

65. *Braxton Family Values*, "It's All Good," episode 26, March 14, 2014 (originally aired February 20, 2014).

66. *Mary Mary*, "Crossroads," episode 13, March 7, 2014 (originally aired February 28, 2013).

67. *Braxton Family Values*, "Award Show Shade," February 13, 2014.

68. *Mary Mary*, "Bachelorette Party," December 13, 2012.

69. *Braxton Family Values*, "A Very Public Affair," November 14, 2013.

70. *Mary Mary*, "Wedding Crasher," episode 5, March 7, 2014 (originally aired January 3, 2013).

71. *Mary Mary*, "Beginning of the End," episode 12, March 7, 2014 (originally aired February 21, 2013).

72. *Braxton Family Values*, "Who Wants to be a Braxton," episode 24, March 14, 2014 (originally aired February 6, 2014).

73. *Mary Mary*, "The Showdown," January 10, 2013; *Braxton Family Values*, "Chix in a Row," January 23, 2014.

74. *Braxton Family Values*, "Birthday Bare-All," episode 19, March 14, 2014 (originally aired December 19, 2013).

75. *Braxton Family Values*, "Chix in a Row," January 23, 2014.

76. *Braxton Family Values*, "Award Show Shade," February 13, 2014.
77. *Braxton Family Values*, "It's All Good," February 20, 2014.
78. *Mary Mary*, "Wedding Crasher," January 3, 2013.
79. *Mary Mary*, "Bachelorette Party," December 13, 2012.
80. *Braxton Family Values*, "A Very Public Affair," November 14, 2013.
81. *Braxton Family Values*, "A Very Public Affair," November 14, 2013; *Braxton Family Values*, "I Don't Have No Baby," November 21, 2013.
82. *Braxton Family Values*, "Birthday Bare-All," December 19, 2013.
83. *Braxton Family Values*, "Who Wants to be a Braxton," February 6, 2014.
84. *Braxton Family Values*, "They Threw a Shoe at You?!?" episode 21, March 14, 2014 (originally aired January 16, 2014).
85. *Braxton Family Values*, "A Very Public Affair," November 14, 2013; No one is shown while this statement was made, although the voice sounds like Trina Braxton.
86. *Braxton Family Values*, "Birthday Bare-All," December 19, 2013; *Braxton Family Values*, #Wack # Family," episode 20, March 14, 2014 (originally aired January 9, 2014); *Braxton Family Values*, "Award Show Shade," February 13, 2014.
87. *Mary Mary*, "Beginning of the End," February 21, 2013; *Mary Mary*, "Crossroads," February 28, 2013.
88. *Braxton Family Values*, "Award Show Shade," February 13, 2014; *Braxton Family Values*, "It's All Good," February 20, 2014.
89. *Braxton Family Values*, "It's All Good," February 20, 2014.
90. Ibid.
91. Ibid.
92. *Mary Mary*, "Crossroads," February 28, 2013.
93. *Braxton Family Values*, "They Threw a Shoe at You?!?" January 16, 2014.
94. *Mary Mary*, "Crossroads," February 28, 2013.
95. *Braxton Family Values*, "A Very Public Affair," November 14, 2013.
96. *Braxton Family Values*, "Chix in a Row," January 23, 2014.
97. *Mary Mary*, "All Night Wrong," December 27, 2012; *Mary Mary*, "Beginning of the End," February 21, 2013.
98. *Mary Mary*, "Beginning of the End," February 21, 2013.
99. *Braxton Family Values*, "Back to Braxton Business," November 28, 2013.
100. *Mary Mary*, "All Night Wrong," December 27, 2012
101. *Mary Mary*, "Pregnant Pause," January 17, 2013.
102. *Braxton Family Values*, #Wack # Family," January 9, 2014; *Braxton Family Values*, "They Threw a Shoe at You?!?" January 16, 2014; *Braxton Family Values*, "Award Show Shade," February 13, 2014.
103. Peter L. Berger and Thomas Luckmann, *The Social Construction of Reality: A Treatise in the Sociology of Knowledge* (Garden City: First Anchor Books, 1966); Stanley J. Baran and Dennis K. Davis, *Mass Communication Theory: Foundations, Ferment, and Future*, 5th ed. (Boston: Wadsworth Cengage Learning, 2009), 309; William A., Gamson et al., "Media Images and the Social Construction of Reality," *Annual Review of Sociology* 18, (1992): 374.

## BIBLIOGRAPHY

Andrejevic, Mark. *Reality TV: The Work of Being Watched*. Lanham, MD: Rowman & Littlefield, 2004.

Andrejevic, Mark, and Dean Colby. "Racism and Reality TV: The Case of MTV's Road Rules." In *How Real is Reality TV? Essays on Representation and Truth*, edited by David S. Escoffery, 195–211. Jefferson: McFarland and Company, 2006.

Baran, Stanley J., and Dennis K. Davis. *Mass Communication Theory: Foundations, Ferment, and Future*, 5th ed. Boston: Wadsworth Cengage Learning, 2009.

Berger, Peter L., and Thomas Luckmann. *The Social Construction of Reality: A Treatise in the Sociology of Knowledge*. Garden City: First Anchor Books, 1966.

Biressi, Anita, and Heather Nunn. *Reality TV: Realism and Revelation.* New York: Routledge, 2005.

Campbell, Shannon B., Steven S. Giannino, Chrystal R. China, and Christopher S. Harris. "I Love New York: Does New York Love Me?" *Journal of International Women's Studies* 10, no. 2 (2008), 20–28.

Clissold, Bradley D. "Candid Camera and the Origins of Reality TV: Remaking Television Culture." In *Understanding Reality Television*, edited by Su Holmes and Deborah Jermyn, 33–53. New York: Routledge, 2004.

Collins, Patricia H. *Black Sexual Politics: African Americans, Gender, and the New Racism.* New York: Routledge, 2005.

Croteau, David, and William Hoynes. *Media/Society: Industries, Images, and Audiences.* 3rd ed. Thousand Oaks: Pine Forge Press, 2003.

Douglas, Susan. *Where the Girls Are: Growing up Female with the Mass Media.* New York: Times Books, 1994.

Gamson, William A., David C. Croteau, William Hoynes, and Theodore Sasson. "Media Images and the Social Construction of Reality." *Annual Review of Sociology* 18 (1992), 373–93.

Goldman, Adria. "Constructing a Woman's Reality: Examining Images of African-American Women in Six Selected Reality Television Docusoaps." PhD dissertation, Howard University, 2012.

Gray, Herman. *Watching Race: Television and the Struggle for Blackness.* Minneapolis: University of Minnesota Press, 2004.

Holtzman, Linda. *Media Messages: What Film, Television, and Popular Music Teach Us About Race, Class, Gender, and Sexual Orientation.* Armonk: M. E. Sharpe, 2000.

Hudson, Shawna. "Re-creational Television: The Paradox of Change and Continuity within Stereotypical Iconography." *Sociological Inquiry* 68, no. 2 (1998), 242–57.

Jewell, K. Sue. *From Mammy to Miss America and Beyond: Cultural Images and the Shaping of US Social Policy.* New York: Routledge, 1993.

Macdonald, Myra. *Representing Women: Myths of Femininity in the Popular Media.* New York: Edward Arnold, 1995.

Madger, Ted. "Television 2.0: The Business of American Television in Transition." In *Understanding Reality Television: Remaking Television Culture*, edited by Susan Murray and Laurie Ouellete, 141–64. New York: New York University Press, 2009.

Meyers, Marian. "Fracturing Women." In *Mediated Women: Representations in Popular Culture*, edited by Marian Meyers, 3–24. Cresskill: Hampton Press, 1999.

Murray, Susan. "I Think We Need a New Name for it: The Meeting of Documentary and Reality TV." In *Reality TV: Remaking Television Culture*, by Susan Murray and Laurie Ouellete, 65–81. New York: New York University Press, 2009.

Nabi, Robin L., Erica Biely, Sarah J. Morgan, and Carmen R. Stitt. "Reality-Based Television Programming and the Psychology and Its Appeal." *Media Psychology* 5 (2003), 303-30.

Ouellettte, Laurie, and Susan Murray. "Introduction." In *Reality TV: Remaking Television Culture*, edited by Susan Murray and Laurie Ouellette, 1–19. New York: New York University Press, 2009.

Pozner, Jennifer L. *Reality TV Bites Back: The Troubling Truth About Guilty Pleasure TV.* Berkeley: Seal Press, 2009.

Smith-Shomade, Beretta E. *Shaded Lives: African-American Women and Television.* Piscataway: Rutgers University Press, 2002.

Stephens, Dionne P., and Layli D. Phillips. "Freaks, Gold Diggers, Divas and Dykes: The Sociohistorical Development of Adolescent African American Women's Sexual Scripts." *Sexuality and Culture* (2003), 3–49.

Tyree, Tia. "African American Stereotypes in Reality Television." *The Howard Journal of Communications* 22, no. 2 (2011), 394–413.

*Chapter Three*

# Visible but Devalued through the Black Male Gaze

*Degrading Images of the Black Woman in Tyler Perry's* Temptation

Christopher K. Jackson

Popular culture produces images that shape identities.[1] These images represent a political struggle over how people are represented as well as the embedded meanings that are attached to these representations. Historically, there was a "war of images" of African Americans in the media. White producers of African-American images reflected their omission and distortion, which resulted in these images to be contested by Black image-makers.[2] Today, we are inundated with images from successful Black filmmakers who are giving African-American actors and actresses more visibility in films. Yet, it is important to caution against the rise of this visibility of African-American images in film and popular culture because they do not necessarily represent progress.[3] For women in particular, their image in popular culture is a fractured one. One that is inherently contradictory, presenting misogynistic images on one hand and ideals of inequality on the other.[4] Many images of Black women have relied on recycled stereotypes in which there is a constant assault on their womanhood. Stuart Hall argues that "invisibility" has been replaced by a "carefully regulated, segregated visibility."[5]

Viola Davis, an African-American actress, recently spoke out about the segregated visibility that Black women receive in terms of their movie roles. During a taping of *Oprah's Next Chapter* (OWN, June 23, 2013), Davis contends that Black actresses are in crisis mode: "Not only in the sheer number of roles that are offered and that are out there. But in the quality of the roles. We are in deprivation mode because we are in the same category.

But if you take a Caucasian actress there are roles for them. But when you just have 2–3 different types of roles for Black actresses . . ." In this quote, Davis addresses the problem that Black women face in film. Due to the limited type of roles afforded to African-American actresses, a simplistic type of image is created for them that fails to address their many layers and complexity. Although this segregated visibility has historically been prevalent in White productions, it has also become a mainstay in many Black productions as well. Tyler Perry, currently one of the most successful Black image-makers and producers, has committed himself to telling the emotional stories of African-American women.[6] However, in the midst of telling these stories, Perry has relied on recycled stereotypes in his films.

Donald Bogle, one of the premier historians of African Americans in film and television contends that it is a tremendous burden for an African-American filmmaker to "liberate audiences from illusions" in which they have faced historically in the media, justly or unjustly.[7] Previous research has examined how Perry's films rely on historical stereotypes of African Americans in films.[8] There is no empirical evidence to support the argument that Perry's success resulted from his reliance on recycled stereotypes; however, the inclusion of stereotypical imagery of African Americans in his films has led to much financial success for him. According to a *60 Minutes* report (CBS, October 22, 2009), from 2005–2009, Perry had five movies to open number one at the box office, a major feat that no other filmmaker was able to accomplish during that span. Perry's movies, sitcoms, and stage plays have grossed nearly 1 billion dollars in revenue.[9]

Perry's success has placed him in a position to effect change in terms of how African-American men and women are portrayed in film. However, his image portrayals "represent refashioned stereotypes" while simultaneously creating new ones.[10] For women specifically, in which Perry holds a special affinity in his films, their visibility reflects more of their domination than their progress. Perry's films operate from a system of patriarchy in which Black female characters are oppressed.[11] Although Perry's movies provide Black women more visibility in media, his image portrayals also attack their true womanhood. Instead of challenging the historical stereotypes and structures of domination that have plagued Black women in films, Perry's image of the Black woman reverts back to their subjugation.

Representation has a major effect on how social identity is constructed and the image offers the visual for that construction. The image not only represents how people are perceived and viewed; it also represents an ideology on how people understand and "make sense" of their social existence.[12] The image cannot go unchecked. If so, it can easily be accepted as real, true and natural. Ian Angus and Sut Jhally described the importance of examining the image in our society in their seminal work, *Cultural Politics in Contemporary America*:

> In contemporary culture the media have become central to the constitution of social identity. It is not just that media messages have become important forms of influence on individuals. We also identify and construct ourselves as social beings through the mediation of images. This is not simply a case of people being dominated by images, but of people seeking and obtaining pleasure through the experience of the consumption of these images. An understanding of contemporary culture involves a focus on both the phenomenology of watching and the cultural form of images.[13]

Images represent something that was already there and "through the media, has been represented."[14] Images of African-American women in media, whether accurate or not, play a major role in how they are defined.[15] Black women have rarely been discussed in popular culture on their own terms. Instead they are "bombarded with warped images of their humanity."[16]

This chapter takes a critical look at the leading female character in Perry's 2013 movie, *Temptation: Confessions of a Marriage Counselor*. Throughout the movie, Judith (played by Jurnee Smollett-Bell) is only viewed as an object. According to bell hooks, as an object "one's reality is defined by others, one's identity created by others, one's history names only in ways that define one's relationship to those who are subject."[17] There is no sense of agency in Judith's character. Instead, she is presented as an object to fulfill the roles and expectations placed on her by her mother, husband, and lover. Judith's character fails to show any complexity. Instead, her character goes from one extreme to another. She is introduced as the doting wife but quickly transitions to the hypersexual being whose eagerness for money and attention leads to life changing consequences. Her character endures interlocking forms of oppression, such as neglect, abuse, and domination. The social and cultural implications of Judith's character present a troublesome image for African-American women. More specifically, Judith's happiness is dependent upon submission to the will of her mother, husband, and lover, in which she fulfills the role of an object.

A textual analysis of the film allowed for a more critical look at Judith's character. Using leading feminist scholar bell hooks' theory in regards to the devaluation of Black womanhood, this essay demonstrates how Perry's work operates within a system of patriarchy in which the woman's value is taken away.[18] The subsequent sections will first highlight the troublesome image of Black women in film, then an account of the theoretical framework, and an analysis of the image that Judith presents in the film.

## TROUBLESOME IMAGES OF BLACK WOMEN IN FILM

Black women face a dual challenge in regards to their portrayal in the media, "sexism and racism."[19] Black feminist scholar Patricia Hill Collins argues, "portraying [African-American] women as stereotypical mammies, matriarchs, welfare recipients, and hot mommas help justify U.S. Black women's oppression."[20] These stereotypical images of African-American women hold a certain belief system of this marginalized group in popular culture. One popular stereotype for African-American women is that they are hypersexual beings, which predates the media but has been a mainstay since its inception.[21]

Previous studies have demonstrated the troublesome images of Black women in film. During the 1970s, Blaxploitation films emerged offering Black audiences' representations of themselves in leading roles. Although the films primarily cast Black men as drug dealers, pimps, and vigilantes, this genre did produce Black female stars such as Pam Grier.[22] These women were able to seek agency in their roles by demonstrating strength, while also fulfilling the stereotypes of hypersexuality, the angry Black woman, and being considered dangerous. Grier's image, and other Black actresses in these films, "privileged a male perspective that objectified and sexualized [African-American] women."[23]

During the 1990s, the stereotypical iconography reemerged. The popular Mammy image reappeared and was repackaged. The refined Mammy image does not fit the physical qualities of the traditional Mammy, who is large and unattractive. However, she still fits the qualities of the nurturing and caretaking attributes that support racial and gender-based hierarchies. The 1995 movie *Showgirls* offered a repackaged version of this popular imagery with the character of Molly Abrams (played by Gina Ravera). Molly's character fulfills the asexual role of the Mammy. In a film where sex and sexuality are central, Molly fulfills the role of the seamstress. Her normal attire includes baggy clothing. She acts as caretaker and nurturer for Nomi Malone (played by Elizabeth Berkely).[24]

Tina Harris examined two popular films, *Waiting to Exhale* and *Set It Off*, which had a leading all female African-American cast. There was a dialectical tension that existed in both films when the entertainment of the films was overshadowed by the perpetuation of stereotypes.[25] It has been argued that *Waiting to Exhale* also presented a simplistic image of Black women who were willing to do anything to become involved in a relationship with a Black man. The film also shows how Blackness, with a leading Black female, can act as a commodity and be exploited for Hollywood.[26]

Then, at the turn of the twenty-first century Black men in drag reappeared with their assault on Black womanhood. Leading Black male actors such as Eddie Murphy (*Norbit*, the *Nutty Professor* films 1996, 2000), Martin Lawrence (*Big Momma* films 2000, 2006, 2011), and of course Tyler Perry (*Madea* films) presented images of debasement and scandal for viewers, which must be challenged before they become dominant.[27] These images serve as a new form of minstrelsy. The Black woman embodies less feminist traits, which highlights a new form of racism and sexism.[28] Madea is one of Perry's most popular characters in his films. The Madea character, Perry dressed in drag at more than six feet tall, presents a number of stereotypical images of Black women. Of course her physical appearance and authoritative posture presents her as a contemporary Mammy. Yet, her vengeful attitude, gun toting ways, and eye-for-an-eye persona remind us of the angry Black woman and the Jezebel, which is not "reflective of the contemporary black woman on film or in society."[29]

Aside from the Madea character, the portrayal of women in some of Perry's films has been a complicated one. Robert Patterson argues that Perry's films operate from a system of Black patriarchy that produces problematic stereotypes based on the intersectionality of race, class, and gender ideologies. Instead of presenting a transformative image of the Black woman, his film forces them to submit to roles assumed due to their gender.[30] Perry's images flourish and are prominent due to lack of other quality images of Blacks on films.[31] His films offer a conflicting message for African Americans. In one vein he challenges the dominant ideologies of patriarchy, but these same women end up needing men in order to find true happiness.[32] His portrayal of African-American women fails to offer a progressive message. They have the potential to educate the audiences instead of just offering entertainment; yet, his films primarily reinforce old stereotypes and myths.[33] This study adds to the previous discussions on Perry's work by taking a critical look at the leading female character in his 2013 movie *Temptation: Confessions of a Marriage Counselor* (referenced hereafter as *Temptation*).

## DEVALUATION OF BLACK WOMEN: UNDERSTANDING CINEMATIC IMAGES

The attack on Black womanhood has been a long and complicated one. Being mindful of the history of slavery, Jim Crow laws, urban segregation, racism, and patriarchy, the role and image of Black women has been one of expected conformity. The devaluation of Black womanhood, posited by bell hooks, was used as the conceptual framework for the analysis of *Temptation* in order to highlight the impact that these images have on the status of African-American women in popular culture and society in general. The devaluation of Black womanhood has its roots in the historical system of patriarchy from White and Black men. Both of the aforementioned groups had a "shared sexism" to promote male dominance and view women as inherently inferior.[34]

Black men were able to view "black women as objects with no human value or worth. This anti-woman attitude is endemic to patriarchy."[35] In a patriarchal system, a woman's happiness is inherently linked to her submission to a man. As such, women are also the recipients of male aggression in the form of physical abuse in these relationships. Black women designations as sexually loose, depraved, and immoral arise from slavery. This designation came from Black women being raped and sexually exploited by the patriarchal system they were a part of during and after their enslavement. However, instead of being seen as victims, they were seen as people who lost their value and worth. The devaluation of Black womanhood is a form of social control.

## MOVIES AS TEXT: STORYLINE OF TYLER PERRY'S TEMPTATION: CONFESSIONS OF A MARRIAGE COUNSELOR

An account of the movie will provide the proper context in order to comprehend the true nature of the images and their impact. In order to fully understand Judith's expected role and how she is portrayed in the movie, a description of the storyline must be provided. *Temptation* is a story about a young woman named Judith who is a marriage counselor reflecting on a tragic mistake that she made when she was younger. She has an inner ambition to own her own marriage counseling practice but this ambition never materializes outwardly in order for her to achieve her goal. She grew up in a small town in the South, where she met her first love, Brice (played by Lance Gross). They eventually married and moved to Washington, DC. He obtained a job at a local pharmacy and she obtained a job at a matchmaking service. Ironically enough, despite having a goal of owning her own marriage counseling practice, Judith is unable to address and fix her own marriage problems. The following analysis will examine the image of Judith in relation to the three people who directly impacted and influenced her actions throughout the film.

### Judith's Relationship with Her Mother

Judith's mother, Sarah, is the first person to prescribe a life for Judith. She was a single parent who raised Judith with a strict church upbringing. In the opening scenes of the film, we learn that they attended church at least six times a week. Later in the film, viewers learn that her mother left her father once she joined the church in their hometown; however, Sarah told Judith that her father was dead. Sarah's character is perplexing. Now a Reverend, she represents a change from tradition in terms of women's role in the church. Traditionally, the role of women in the church was relegated to a support role and not ordination to the ministry.[36] Although Sarah has broken the traditional boundaries of patriarchy in the church, she still expects her daughter to submit to the system of patriarchy in her own marriage. Sarah imparts on her daughter about the importance of going to church on Sundays, having dinner ready for her husband, and keeping the house clean.

During her first visit to Judith and Brice, Sarah chastises her daughter at the dinner table for not fulfilling the expected duties of a wife. This interaction presents the image of Judith as a child that is scolded by her mother for not doing what is expected of her as a wife. Eventually, Judith develops a level of resentment toward her mother for placing all of these demands on her. Religion has been a constant in Perry's movies. A strong reliance on God as a source of divine intervention and retribution has been a consistent theme.[37] Sarah offers an extreme case of this in the film. At every instance where she appears or is mentioned in the film, religion and prayer followed. When Sarah discovers that Judith is having an extramarital affair, she declares that her relationship with the other man will send her to hell. This acts as a form of foreshadowing for Judith who endures life-changing consequences for her mistakes.

## Judith's Relationship with Her Husband

Judith and Brice were supposed to have the traditional marriage. Her initial appearance also reflects that tradition. Her normal attire, aside from when she is out for her morning run, includes long dresses and a blouse or a pants suit. Hence, she is covered head to toe. As we see Judith and Brice's relationship develop, audiences notice the problem in their marriage by trying to fit within that mold. In a patriarchal system, the woman is expected to submit to the will of her husband and he is supposed to be sole provider. Traditionally, the sexist roles had the man as "the breadwinner and the subject, the woman the helpmate and the object."[38]

However, Black men have failed to fulfill this sexist role of the protector and provider in the patriarchal system. As a result, women must work in order to provide for their family.[39] Although both of them worked, Judith was still responsible for the roles historically reserved for women such as cleaning and tending to the home. Her role to fulfill her *wifely duties is* reinforced in one of the opening scenes of their adult relationship. Judith comes home after a frustrating day at work to vent. She also talks about the pressures placed on her by her mother who wants to make sure that Judith is cooking, cleaning, and having sex with her husband regularly. It is apparent that Judith is unhappy fulfilling these expected duties as prescribed by her mother and the Bible. She has a graduate degree, finished undergrad in three years, and is really frustrated in her life. She felt that she should aspire to do more to achieve her goal of becoming a marriage counselor. However, Brice immediately dismisses this notion and tells her that she needs to wait ten to fifteen years until they are more established. Judith puts her goals aside and does what is expected of her as a loving wife.

Nonetheless, in an effort to console his wife, Brice relieves his wife of her cooking duties for the night and decides to take her out for dinner. After dinner, they encountered three guys where one of them objectified Judith with verbal obscenities in regards to her body. Judith immediately responded and felt violated by this incident. Black women have been known to be outspoken and assertive as an act of resistance.[40] Brice instantly tries to quell her resistance and urges Judith to ignore them while immediately rushing her into the car. Upon returning home, Judith mentioned to Brice that she did not feel safe. Although many would not expect for Brice to get into a physical altercation with the guys, he defended his behavior and explained that the guys could have had guns. However, this scene demonstrates a crack in the patriarchal premise of the film. Brice was unable to protect the honor of his wife. Judith's outspokenness in this scene represents a sign of resistance and Brice's urging her to be quiet can be viewed as a form of passivity.

Brice is unable to fulfill other needs of his wife. After a meeting with Harley, which included a tantalizing sexual conversation, Judith rushes home in an attempt to have wild sex with her husband. She enters the home demanding that Brice manhandle her. She grabs him, slaps him, and demands that he treat her like an animal. Brice rebuffs Judith's sexual desire. He tells her to calm down and then they can have sex the "right way" in the bedroom. We also see Brice's lack of attention to his wife when he forgets her birthday for the past two years. On the morning of her birthday Brice fails to even acknowledge the day. The scene ends with him leaving out of the bathroom and Judith reciting to him that his breakfast is on the table as she finished getting ready for work. Judith was visibly disappointed that he forgot her birthday. Then, when she arrived to work she had a bouquet of roses waiting for her that she thought was from her husband. However, she later realizes they are from Harley, as she physically shows her disappointment. Later, Brice blames his absentmindedness on work responsibilities. To make up for this oversight, Brice attempts to cheer his wife up by stripping down to his underwear and playing his guitar.

Brice's lack of attention to his wife eventually leads her to seek out the attention of another man. He is completely unaware that she is sneaking out of the house to spend time with Harley until it is too late. During one scene, while her mother was visiting, Judith left the house to see Harley. Although Brice was home, he was watching football and did not acknowledge that Judith was leaving. This lack of attention eventually leads Judith to leave Brice for Harley, whom she thinks can give her a better life. Ultimately Judith's relationship with Harley did not last, as he became abusive and she needed rescuing by Brice. Brice learns of Harley's abusive past and HIV status and immediately goes over to rescue Judith. He finally defends her honor by brutally assaulting Harley, who is high off of cocaine. Brice then carries Judith out in his arms to safety.

## Judith's Relationship with Her Lover

There is an inherent contradiction in the narrative Perry creates for Judith. She can accept that her husband just cannot fulfill his expected duties in this patriarchal narrative or she can rebel. Her form of rebellion led her to receive fulfillment from another man. While at work, Judith meets Harley, a successful young businessman who is considering investing in the matchmaking service company where she is working. There is an immediate attraction between them. Harley acts as a predator and Judith is the object of his desire. In a patriarchal system women are seen as possessions. For Harley, Judith is the object and he actively pursues her. His interest is deepened when she reveals that she is married.

They spent many late nights working together. As previously mentioned, during one meeting the topic of sex was discussed in detail. This really piqued the interest of Harley, who is shocked when Judith informs him that she does not believe in sex before marriage because she is a Christian. In response, Harley begins to speak in a sexy tone and alludes to the many places that people could have sex, such as the kitchen, at work, etc. The language that Harley uses accentuates the meaning of every word and clearly gets Judith aroused. It is apparent that Judith's sexual appetite is not being fulfilled at home because she is moved by Harley's words. There is an apparent sexual desire and longing that she has that she has not received from her husband.

The temptation begins when Judith leaves her house the next morning for her morning jog so that she can intentionally run into Harley. After encountering Harley on the route, she bumps into a biker. Harley, physically upset, is about to assault the guy until Judith pleads with him to stop. Judith is moved by the gesture that Harley is willing to defend her. Harley picks up Judith and takes her back to his apartment to provide first aid. While at Harley's apartment, he comes on to Judith questioning her marriage to Brice. He asks her if Brice notices the small intricate details about her hair and breathing. She responds by acknowledging that she is *not* naïve. Judith notices women's artifacts such as high heel shoes by the bed, earrings on the table, and the smell of perfume as a sign that another woman was recently there.

Judith continues to resist the sexual advances made by Harley until she is even more disappointed in her marriage. This disappointment led her to make a change in her appearance before she takes a business trip with Harley. Her attire changes from the long dresses and blouse to a more twenty-first-century look, a business suit that includes a skirt. On the plane back from the trip Harley makes another sexual advance toward Judith. He gets up from his seat to approach her, uncrosses her legs, and begins to manhandle her. At each instance, she is begging him to stop and tries to fight him off. However, he does not stop. Then Harley tells Judith to stop trying to fight it and proclaims that she can say she resisted. This pronouncement by Harley is used to pacify Judith from feeling guilty about cheating on her husband. At that point, she lets her guard down, succumbs to the temptation, and has sex with him on the plane. This presents a damaging image for Judith. Apparently she was so lustful with sexual desire that she allowed her libido to take control.

After that encounter, Judith tries to fight her feelings for Harley but gives in to temptation. She slowly begins to invest more time and emotion into her extramarital affair. Her growing feelings for Harley are shown when she leaves at night to go be with him. Judith makes dramatic changes in her life; she quits her job, begins to do drugs, and hangs out in clubs. Her relationship with Harley becomes abusive after he manhandles her mother in a physical altercation at Judith's old apartment that she shared with Brice. When they arrive back to his house, Harley physically assaults Judith. This physical abuse is endemic of patriarchy and acts as a form of control. Judith was not submitting to her role in her relationship; as such, she was on the receiving end of male aggression.

## DISCUSSION

The movie ends with Judith as the victim and leaves the audience no indication that transformation has occurred. The film ends with Judith, about twenty years older, visiting Brice (at the pharmacy that he now owns) to get her prescription filled for the sexually transmitted disease, HIV, she contracted from Harley. While there, Judith witnesses Brice embrace his new wife and daughter. This presents an image of what Judith could have had if she would have not made the mistake of having an affair. This humiliation from her relationship with her mom, husband, and lover overshadows the entire movie. After receiving her prescription, Judith leaves the pharmacy. She is apparently crippled from the abuse she suffered from Harley. She walks out into the cold alone. This final image of Judith acts as a residual message for viewers to see what can happen when one makes a mistake; one can receive a severe judgment. In this vein, Perry acts as a moral leader to punish Judith for her sins. This punishment acts as an object of scorn and humiliation in an effort for Judith to learn from her sins.

In many of Perry's films the Black woman is always portrayed as the victim. If the Black woman is not the victim of physical, sexual, or emotional abuse she is viewed as powerless in a patriarchal society.[41] Judith was unable to seek agency in her victimization. There is no sense of self-sufficiency in her life. Instead of confronting and learning to cope with the mistake she made she had to be rescued by Brice. In the end, Brice also acts as her caretaker by providing her with prescriptions. She is alone, unhappy, and still needs to rely on the resources of a *man* for safety. Men are seen as the catalyst for women in Perry's films. He repackages the same Hollywood patriarchal formula into a Black context in which the Black women have to sacrifice, suffer, and overcome.[42] Judith was aware that Harley was sleeping with other women. She even noticed his violent temper when he attempted to assault the guy on the bicycle. Yet, the storyline shows that she was driven by her own sexual appetite to be tempted to have unprotected sex with Harley, leave her husband, and quit her job. This sexual longing is reminiscent of the Jezebel stereotype, the image of the seductive and hypersexual woman. However, Judith's sexual urges could be seen as a break from the repressive sexist roles of patriarchy. Her sex with Harley can be interpreted as a liberating act to insert fun and excitement, which could be a form of sexual agency for Judith.[43]

The first sexual encounter between Judith and Harley on his private jet could actually be considered rape. She resisted and tried to fight him off; then Judith eventually gave in after he told her she could say she resisted. The historical and political implications of this act are troubling. Judith became a desiring subject and willing participant. This reflects a "sexist mindset" where the responsibility is placed on the female.[44] This scene alludes to the historical oppression and exploitation that Black women have endured at the hands of White and Black men in America. America has played a major role in trying to control the Black woman by questioning their morality, chastity, and respectability. During slavery, Black women were raped and any attempts by Black women to avert the sexual advances were interpreted as feigning.[45] According to the Rape Crisis Center, one out of every six American women has been the victim of an attempted or completed rape. Out of that group, African-American women have more incidents of rape than White women.

Judith pays the ultimate price for her mistakes. Her infidelity is compounded because she contracts HIV from her sexual encounter with Harley. The implications of this punishment are troubling. According to the Centers for Disease Control and Prevention in 2010, African Americans accounted for 44 percent of all new HIV infections amongst adults and adolescents thirteen and older. Out of that number, African-American women accounted for 29 percent of all new cases. Now, the audience does not know if Perry is trying to spread awareness here or just using this disease as a form of punishment. Either way, Judith is seen as a naïve woman who is completely ignorant to the consequences of having unprotected sex.

## CONCLUSION

Tyler Perry's movies started from his plays that gained a huge following on the "chitlin circuit." Today, these movies are representative products of a capitalistic patriarchal society reverting back to dominant ideologies in regards to Black women. The image of Judith represents a dialectical tension. Her visibility could be seen as a form of progress for a Black actress. However, the lack of development in her character reifies the one-dimensional aspect of roles traditionally given to Black actresses in popular culture. The aim of popular culture is to focus on everyday people and their experiences. As a form of entertainment and even an educational tool, films provide audiences a glimpse into the American landscape embedded with various ideologies.[46] These ideologies and images that are presented in film must be challenged consistently because they "determine how blackness and black people are seen."[47] One would assume that the presence of more African-American women in feature roles would change how they are represented on screen especially from a Black filmmaker. However, Judith's character is representative of the problem that Black women face in popular culture, no multidimensionality and no control over their own narrative. The politics of these representations of Black women oftentimes reflect a distorted image.

Echoing the sentiments offered by bell hooks, we must move beyond the dualistic notion of positive and negative portrayals and focus more on questioning the quality of the image portrayals. The image of Black women should represent a form of progress and agency that subvert the historical, stereotypical portrayals. Until then, we must continue to hold Perry and other Black image-makers accountable for their portrayal of Black women in film. If the Black woman is only going to be seen as the victim in her own exploitation, one has to wonder what progress has really been made. What value is the Black woman image if it only represents the traditional iconography? A Black woman's true value is not contingent upon her desire to get a man or endure the physical and emotional abuse that may ensue. Instead, a Black woman's value demonstrates her autonomy, independence, and self-determination to achieve her own goals.

## NOTES

1. Henry A. Giroux, *Breaking into the Movies: Film and the Culture of Politics* (Malden: Blackwell Publishers, 2002), 6; Herman Gray, *Watching Race: Television and the Struggle for Blackness* (Minneapolis: University of Minnesota Press, 2004), 4–6.

2. Jannette L. Dates and William Barlow, "Introduction: A War of Images," in *Split Image: African Americans in the Mass Media* (Washington: Howard University Press, 1990), 3.

3. bell hooks, *Reel to Real: Race, Sex, and Class at the Movies* (New York: Routledge, 1996), 6.

4. Marian Meyers, "Fracturing Women," *Mediated Women: Representation in Popular Culture*, ed. Marian Meyers (Creskill: Hampton Press, 1999), 12.

5. Stuart Hall, "What is This 'Black' in Black Popular Culture," in *Black Popular Culture: A Project by Michele Wallace,* ed. Gail Dent (Seattle: Bay Press, 1992), 24.

6. Wesley Morris, "The Year of Tyler Perry. Seriously: America's Most Important Black Filmmaker," *Film Comment,* Jan/Feb 2011, 47.

7. Donald Bogle, *Toms, Coons, Mulattos, Mammies, & Bucks,* 4th ed. (New York: Continuum, 2009), 433.

8. Cheris A. Harris and Keisha Edwards Tassie, "The Cinematic Incarnation of Frazier's Black Bourgeoisie: Tyler Perry's Black Middle Class," *Journal of African American Studies* 16, (July 2011): 321–44; Jamel S. C. Bell and Ronald L. Jackson II. eds. *Interpreting Tyler Perry: Perspectives on Race, Class, Gender, and Sexuality* (New York: Routledge, 2013), 5.

9. Drew Jubera, "Tyler Perry Runs the Table," *Men's Health* November 2012, 27(9).

10. Harris and Tassie, "The Cinematic Incarnation of Frazier's . . ."

11. Robert J. Patterson, "'Woman Thou Art Bound': Critical Spectatorship, Black Masculine Gazes, and Gender Problems in Tyler Perry Movies," *Black Camera* 3(1) (Winter 2011), 9–30.

12. Stuart Hall, "The Whites of Their Eyes," in *Gender, Race, and Class in Media,* 3rd ed., ed. Gail Dines and Jean M. Humez (Los Angeles: Sage, 2011), 67–70.

13. Ian Angus and Sut Jhally, "Introduction," in Ian Angus and Sut Jhally, *Cultural Politics in Contemporary America* (New York: Routledge, 1988), 2.

14. Stuart Hall, "Representation & the Media" (lecture, Media Education Foundation, Northampton, MA, 1997), 6.

15. K. Sue Jewell, *From Mammy to Miss America and Beyond* (London: Routledge, 1993).

16. Janet Sims-Wood. "The Black Female: Mammy, Jemima, Sapphire, and Other Images," in *Images of Blacks in American Culture: A Reference Guide to Information Sources,* ed. Jessie C. Smith (Westport: Greenwood); Melissa V. Harris-Perry, *Sister Citizen: Shame, Stereotypes, and Black Women in America* (New Haven: Yale, 2011), 29.

17. bell hooks, *Talking Back: Thinking Feminist, Thinking Black* (Boston: South End Press, 1989), 42.

18. bell hooks, *Ain't I A Woman: Black Women and Feminism* (Boston: South End Press, 1981).

19. Clint C. Wilson II., Felix Guiterrez, Lena M. Chao eds., *Racism, Sexism and the Media: The Rise of Class Communication in Multicultural America* (Thousand Oaks: Sage, 2003), 191.

20. Patricia Hill Collins, *Black Feminist Thought: Knowledge, Consciousness, and the Politics of Empowerment* (New York: Routledge, 2000), 69.

21. Robert M. Entman and Andrew Rojecki, *The Black Image in the White Mind: Media and Race in America* (Chicago: University of Chicago Press, 2000); Carolyn Byerly, "Situating 'The Other': Women, Racial, and Sexual Minorities in the Media," in *Women in Mass Communication,* 3rd ed., ed. Pamela J. Creedon and Judith Cramer (Thousand Oaks: Sage, 2007), 226.

22. Angelique Harris and Omar Mushtaq, "Creating Racial Identity Through Film: A Queer and Gendered Analysis of Blaxploitation Films," *Western Journal of Black Studies,* 37 (1) (Spring 2013), 28–38.

23. Lakesia D. Johnson, *Iconic: Decoding Images of the Revolutionary Black Woman* (Waco: Baylor University Press, 2012), 45–65.

24. Carmen R. Gillespie, "Mammy Goes to Las Vegas: *Showgirls* and the Constancy of African American Female Stereotypes," in *Mediated Women: Representations in Popular Culture,* ed. Marian Myers (Cresskill: Hampton), 90.

25. Tina M. Harris, "Interrogating the Representation of African American Female Identity in the Films *Waiting to Exhale* and *Set It Off,*" in *African American Communication & Identities: Essential Readings,* ed. Ronald L. Jackson II (Thousand Oaks: Sage, 2004), 189–96.

26. bell hooks, *Reel to Real: Race, Sex and Class at the Movies,* (New York: Routledge, 1996), 52–59.

27. Robin Means Coleman, "'Roll Up Your Sleeves!,' Black Women, Black Feminism in Feminist Media Studies," *Feminist Media Studies, 11*(1) (Spring, 2011), 38.

28. Ilian De Larkin, "If the Fat Suit Fits: Fat-Suit Minstrelsy in Black Comedy Films," in *Interpreting Tyler Perry: Perspectives on Race, Class, Gender, and Sexuality,* eds. Jamel S. C. Bell and Ronald L. Jackson II (New York: Routledge, 2013), 47–56.

29. Sheri Parks, *Fierce Angels: The Strong Black Woman in American Life and Culture* (New York: One World, 2010), 131–132; Bishetta D. Merritt and Melbourne S. Cummings, "The African American Woman on Film: The Tyler Perry Image," in *Interpreting Tyler Perry: Perspectives on Race, Class, Gender, and Sexuality,* ed. Jamel S. C. Bell and Ronald L. Jackson II (New York: Routledge, 2013), 187–95.

30. Patterson, "Woman Thou Art Bound . . . ," 10; Harris and Tassie, "The Cinematic Incarnation of Frazier's . . . ," 321.

31. Ibid.

32. Marcia A. Dawkins and Ulli K. Ryder, "Passing as a Woman(ist)?: A Look at Black Women's Narratives in Tyler Perry's Films," in *Interpreting Tyler Perry: Perspectives on Race, Class, Gender, and Sexuality,* ed. Jamel S. C. Bell and Ronald L. Jackson II (New York: Routledge, 2013), 267.

33. Rockell Brown and Kimberly D. Campbell, "Representing the Ladies: A Negotiated Response to Tyler Perry's Portrayal of African American Female Characters," in *Interpreting Tyler Perry: Perspectives on Race, Class, Gender, and Sexuality,* ed. Jamel S. C. Bell and Ronald L. Jackson II (New York: Routledge, 2013), 270.

34. bell hooks, *Ain't I A Woman . . . ,* 99; bell hooks, *Killing Rage: Ending Racism* (New York: Holt Paperbacks, 1995), 78–79.

35. hooks, *Ain't I A Woman,* 101.

36. Jacquelyn Grant. "Black Women and the Church" in *But Some of us Are Brave: All the Women Are White, All the Blacks Are Men: Black Women's Studies,* ed. Gloria T. Hall, Patricia B. Scott, and Barbara Smith (New York: Feminist Press of The City University of New York, 1993), 145.

37. Leah Aldridge, "Mythology and Affect: The Brands of Cinematic Blackness of Will Smith and Tyler Perry," *Spectrums 31,* no.1 (Spring 2011).

38. Toni Cade Bambara, "On the Issue of Roles," in *The Black Woman: An Anthology* (New York: Washington Square Press, 2005), 103.

39. bell hooks, *Ain't I A Woman.*

40. Patricia Hill Collins, *Black Feminist Thought.*

41. Harris & Porter, 2013; Brown & Campbell, 2013.

42. Patterson, "Woman Thou Art Bound," 20.

43. bell hooks, *Outlaw Culture: Resisting Representations* (New York: Routledge, 1994), 85–93.

44. bell hooks, *Reel to Real . . . ,* 232.

45. Deborah Gray White, *Ar'n't I a Woman: Females Slaves in the Plantation South* (New York: W. W. Norton & Company, 1999).

46. bell hooks, *Black Looks: Race and Representations* (Cambridge: South End Press, 1992), 5.

47. Giroux, *Breaking Into the Movies,* 3.

## BIBLIOGRAPHY

Aldridge, Leah. "Mythology and Affect: The Brands of Cinematic Blackness of Will Smith and Tyler Perry." *Spectrums 31,* no.1 (Spring 2011), 41–47.

Angus, Ian, and Sut Jhally. "Introduction." In *Cultural Politics in Contemporary America,* edited by Ian Angus and Sut Jhally, 1–16. New York: Routledge, 1988.

Bambara, Toni Cade. "On the Issue of Roles." In *The Black Woman: An Anthology*, edited by Toni C. Bambara, 101–10. New York: Washington Square Press, 2005.

Bell, Jamel S. C., and Ronald L. Jackson, II., eds. *Interpreting Tyler Perry: Perspectives on Race, Class, Gender, and Sexuality.* New York: Routledge, 2013.

Bogle, Donald. *Toms, Coons, Mulattos, Mammies, & Bucks.* 4th ed. New York: Continuum, 2009.

Brown, Rockell, and Kimberly D. Campbell. "Representing the Ladies: A Negotiated Response to Tyler Perry's Portrayal of African American Female Characters." In *Interpreting Tyler*

Perry: Perspectives on Race, Class, Gender, and Sexuality,* edited by Jamel Santa Cruz Bell and Ronald L. Jackson, II., 270–87. New York: Routledge, 2013.
Byerly, Carolyn M. "Situating 'The Other': Women, Racial, and Sexual Minorities in the Media. In *Women in Mass Communication,* 3rd ed., edited by Pamela J. Creedon & Judith Cramer, 221–32. Thousand Oaks: Sage, 2007.
Coleman, Robin Means. "'Roll Up Your Sleeves!,' Black women, Black Feminism in Feminist Media Studies." *Feminist Media Studies 11,* no. 1 (March 2011): 35–41.
Collins, Patricia Hill. *Black Feminist Thought: Knowledge, Consciousness and the Politics of Empowerment.* New York: Routledge, 2000.
Dates, Jannette L., and Barlow, William. "Introduction: A War of Images." In *Split Image: African Americans in the Mass Media,* edited by Janette L. Dates & William Barlow, 1–21. Washington: Howard University Press, 1990.
Dawkins, Marcia A., and Ulli K. Ryder. "Passing as a Woman(ist)? A Look at Black Women's Narratives in Tyler Perry's Films." In *Interpreting Tyler Perry: Perspectives on Race, Class, Gender, and Sexuality,* edited by Jamel Santa Cruz Bell and Ronald L. Jackson, II., 257–69. New York: Routledge, 2013.
De Larkin, Ilian. "If the Fat Suit Fits: Fat-Suit Minstrelsy in Black Comedy Films." In *Interpreting Tyler Perry: Perspectives on Race, Class, Gender, and Sexuality,* edited by Jamel Santa Cruz Bell and Ronald L. Jackson, II., 47–56. New York: Routledge, 2013.
Entman, Robert M., and Andrew Rojecki. *The Black Image in the White Mind: Media and Race in America.* Chicago: University of Chicago Press, 2000.
Gillespie, Carmen R. "Mammy Goes to Las Vegas: *Showgirls* and the Constancy of African American Female Stereotypes." In *Mediated Women: Representations in Popular Culture,* edited by Marian Meyers, 81–90. Cresskill: Hampton.
Giroux, Henry A. *Breaking into the Movies: Film and the Culture of Politics.* Malden: Blackwell Publishers, 2002.
Grant, Jacqueline. "Black Women in the Church." In *But Some of us Are Brave: All the Women Are White, All the Blacks Are Men: Black Women's Studies,* edited by Gloria T. Hull, Patricia Bell Scott, and Barbara Smith, 141–56. New York: The Feminist Press at the City University of New York, 1993.
Gray, Herman. *Watching Race: Television and the Struggle for Blackness.* Minneapolis: University of Minnesota Press, 2004.
Hall, Stuart. "The Whites of Their Eyes." In *Gender, Race, and Class in Media,* 3rd ed., edited by Gail Dines and Jean M Humez, 67–70. Los Angeles: Sage, 2011.
———. "Representation & The Media." Lecture, Media Education Foundation. Northampton, MA, 1997, 6.
———. "What is This 'Black' in Black Popular Culture." In *Black Popular Culture: A Project by Michelle Wallace,* edited by Gina Dent, 21-33. Seattle: Bay Press, 1992.
Harris, Angelique, and Omar Mushtaq. "Creating Racial Identity Through Film: A Queer and Gendered Analysis of Blaxploitation Films." *Western Journal of Black Studies 37,* no. 1 (Spring 2013): 28–38.
Harris, Cheris A., and Keisha Edwards Tassie. "The Cinematic Incarnation of Frazier's Black Bourgeoisie: Tyler Perry's Black Middle Class." *Journal of African American Studies, 16,* (July 2011): 321–44.
Harris-Perry, Melissa V. *Sister Citizen: Shame, Stereotypes, and Black Women in America.* New Haven: Yale, 2011.
Harris, Tina M. "Interrogating the Representation of African American Female Identity in the Films *Waiting to Exhale* and *Set it Off.*" In *African American Communication & Identities: Essential Readings,* edited by Ronald L. Jackson, II., 189–96. Thousand Oaks: Sage, 2004.
hooks, bell. *Reel to Real: Race, Sex, and Class at the Movies.* New York: Routledge, 1996.
———. *Killing Rage: Ending Racism.* New York: Holt Paperbacks, 1995.
———. *Outlaw Culture: Resisting Representations.* New York: Routledge, 1994.
———. *Black Looks: Race and Representation.* Boston: South End Press, 1992.
———. *Talking Back: Thinking Feminist, Thinking Black.* Boston: South End Press, 1989.
———. *Ain't I A Woman: Black Women and Feminism.* Boston: South End Press, 1981.
Jewell, K. Sue. *From Mammy to Miss America and Beyond.* London: Routledge, 1993.

Johnson, Lakesia D. *Iconic: Decoding Images of the Revolutionary Black Woman.* Waco: Baylor University Press, 2012.
Jubera, Drew. "Tyler Perry Runs the Table." *Men's Health,* November 2012.
Merritt, Bishetta D., and Melbourne S. Cummings. "The African American Woman on Film: The Tyler Perry Image." In *Interpreting Tyler Perry: Perspectives on Race, Class, Gender, and Sexuality,* edited by Jamel Santa Cruz Bell and Ronald L. Jackson, II., 187–95. New York: Routledge, 2013.
Meyers, Marian, "Fracturing Women." In *Mediated Women: Representation in Popular Culture,* edited by Marian Meyers, 3–22. Cresskill: Hampton Press, 1999.
Morris, Wesley. "The Year of Tyler Perry. Seriously: Americas Most Important Black Filmmaker," *Film Comment,* Jan/Feb 2011, 59–61.
Parks, Sheri. *Fierce Angels: The Strong Black Woman in American Life and Culture.* New York; One World, 2010.
Patterson, Robert J. "'Woman Thou Art Bound': Critical Spectatorship, Black Masculine Gazes, and Gender Problems in Tyler Perry Movies." *Black Camera 3*, no. 1 (Winter 2011): 9–30.
Sims-Wood, Janet. "The Black Female: Mammy, Jemima, Sapphire, and Other Images." In *Images of Black in American Culture: A Reference Guide to Information Sources*, edited by Jessie C. Smith, 235–56. Westport: Greenwood, 1988.
White, Deborah Gray. *Ar'n't I a Woman: Female Slaves in the Plantation South,* Rev. ed. New York: W.W. Norton & Company, 1999.
Wilson, Clint C. II., Felix Gutierrez, and Lena M. Chao. *Racism, Sexism and the Media: The Rise of Class Communication in Multicultural America,* 3rd ed. Thousand Oaks: Sage, 2003.

*Chapter Four*

# "Don't Make Me Hop After You..."

*Black Womanhood and the Dangerous Body in Popular Film*

## LeRhonda S. Manigault-Bryant

The cult classic *I'm Gonna Get You Sucka* (1988) is Keenan Ivory Wayans's riotous parody of 1970s Blaxploitation films.[1] The film follows Jack Spade (Keenan Ivory Wayans), a war veteran who returns to his hometown ("Any Ghetto U.S.A") following his brother's death. Soon after his arrival, Jack discovers that crime lord Mr. Big (John Vernon) his taken over his neighborhood, and that Mr. Big's bullying has left the locals living in terror. And, to make matters worse, Mr. Big's drug industry has become so successful that it has fueled how Black males in the community have become addicted to *overgolding*, the excessive wearing of gold chains. With his community in crisis, Jack takes it upon himself to avenge his brother's murder and to reclaim the community from Mr. Big's stronghold. He soon realizes, however, that he lacks the skill and muscle to defeat Mr. Big on his own, so he builds an army of local heroes who were crime fighters in their own right during the 1970s. Comprised of his childhood idol John Slade (Bernie Casey), Flyguy (Antonio Fargas), Kung Fu Joe (Steve James), and the deadly duo Hammer (Isaac Hayes), and Slammer (Jim Brown), Jack's army is a cast of characters who do their best to take down Mr. Big. *I'm Gonna Git You Sucka* (hereafter *Sucka*) is exemplary of what William Covey calls an "African American Neo-Noir film," where a filmmaker cognizant of a particular filmic heritage places his or her own interpretation upon a remake or new narrative.[2] It is also notable for its homage to the Blaxploitation era, and especially for its illustration of Black male cultural stereotypes prevalent in the American film industry.

*Sucka* is situated within a collection of popular Black films released in the 1980s.[3] These films featured Black actors and actresses, were marketed primarily to Black audiences, were directed and/or produced by Black Americans, and demonstrated the positive economic potential of films geared toward Black audiences. The film's star-studded cast of well-known Blaxploitation actors (Bernie Casey, Antonia Fargas, and Steve James), a popular Black R&B musician (Isaac Hayes), and a superstar Black athlete (Jim Brown) assured its acceptance and popularity within Black communities. The film's overall gross of thirteen million, while low according to modern blockbuster expectations, was quite successful at the time. This is especially the case in light of the movie's three million dollar budget. Considering the film's popularity at the time it was released, it is remarkable that it has seemed to fade into relative obscurity in the annals of Black film. Fans of Keenan Ivory Wayans, his popular sketch show *In Living Color*,[4] and the generations of the Wayans family (especially Damon, Kim, Shawn, and Marlon), know the film well, however, and are likely to recall many of its memorable lines (such as "they shootin,' they shootin'!") with fondness and amusement.

The pace of current production rarely allows scholars who work in popular culture to consider a film as a historical document. In that vein, this essay is a retrospective reading of *Sucka* that coincides with the twenty-fifth anniversary of the film's release (December 16, 1988). This essay also suggests that filmic representations of Black women from the past have great bearing on our cinematic present. A contemporary review of *Sucka* reveals, rather unsurprisingly, that many of the negative stereotypes associated with Black people as outlined by film critic Donald Bogle in the 1970s[5] continued to be a part of the American film industry in the 1980s—even those produced by Black filmmakers. More substantive evaluation of the film, however, exposes something deeper about the popular comedy. In *Sucka*, negative constructs of Black masculinity are centered, and, in keeping with the form of comedic film, openly made fun of with the purpose of identifying and disrupting the negative constructs outright. What is less obvious about the film are the ways that Black femininity is also parodied. But rather than being contested, off-putting tropes associated with Black women are reified. I contend that the negative perceptions of Black women exemplified in *Sucka* have directly influenced how we interpret the Black female body as dangerous in contemporary popular film. This is especially the case in the legacy of Black popular comedies, which often use sarcasm, satire, and parody to identify and potentially contest stereotypes. The goals of this essay are fourfold: (1) to examine the ways *Sucka* centers the Black male character, often at the expense of the Black female figure; (2) to demonstrate how *Sucka* dangerously reinscribes negative tropes associated with Black women; (3) to consider how Black female characters in *Sucka* are treated as a danger to

Black masculinity; and (4) to consider the implications of *Sucka* upon modern imaginations of the Black female body in popular comedies.

## A MAN'S MAN'S WORLD

*Sucka* explicitly suggests that the world of Black America is that of Black men. Yet viewers would be negligent if they ignored the ways that constructions of Black masculinity in the film directly influence its treatment of Black femininity, and the film's depictions of Black female characters. Black male heroism is certainly *Sucka*'s primary trope, which is signaled by the film's tag line "it's tough to be a hero." Arguably, the Black male heroism Wayans centers in the film is a direct response to what has been articulated as a "crisis of Black masculinity" in the 1980s and 1990s. This crisis was the direct result of centuries of criminalization, stereotyping, public policy, negative publicity, and popular perceptions, all of which culminated into the (mis)reading of Black male figures and bodies as dangerous, problematic, and in need of control.[6] During this time, interrogation of Black American male citizenry, questions regarding Black male stability, and concern about the role of Black male figures in the "traditional" American family structure became the focus of the popular imagination. The subsequent highly publicized moments including the controversy surrounding Clarence Thomas's appointment to the Supreme Court (1991), the brutal beating of Rodney King (1991), the uprising surrounding the acquittal of King's abusers (1992), and the Million Man March (1995) exemplify the broad arch of the public concern about the place of the Black male figure in American life during that time.

Film critic Ed Guerrero suggests that this purported crisis of Black masculinity had a particular impact on popular film.[7] While noting America's treatment of Black men as "prized media fetishes" Guerrero explains, "The construction of the Black male image in commercial cinema follows a paradoxical mix of stereotype and adoration that has taken a convoluted course over cinema history. . . ."[8] This "convoluted course" vacillates between relentless stereotyping and a type of idolatry where Black male exceptionalism is heralded as another form of typical representation. The stakes of this wavering are high, as they lead to extremely narrow mappings of Black masculinity, trap viewers into perpetuating limited (and often negative) tropes about Black men, and consequently fail to fill in the much-needed filmic gaps with the complex, layered figures that are more representative of Black experiences broadly. The stakes are also especially high for the ways that the popular (mis)conceptions about Black masculinity that make their way onto the screen directly influence filmic representations of Black femininity.

*Sucka* struggles with a particular kind of indecisiveness, where Black male figures are simultaneously heralded and mocked for their performance of certain aspects of Black masculinity. In a rhetorical strategy recognized as what Harriet Margolis calls "self-directed stereotypes," *Sucka* satirically depicts stereotypes to undermine and expose the ridiculous underpinnings of said stereotypes.[9] As such, the film takes its analysis of myths about Black supermen, Black male sexuality, and Black criminality seriously, even as it presents its analysis in sardonic form. In the film, Wayans's response to the purported crisis of Black masculinity is demonstrated by the presentation of four tropes: the aggressive Black male, the macho (read hypermasculine) Black male hero, the emasculated Black male, and the well-endowed, virile Black male.

*Sucka* directly responds to popular perceptions about Black male aggression. Viewers' initial encounter with John Slade occurs during the First Annual Youth Gang Competition where local gang members battle for prizes and street credibility in events such as a foot race with stolen items (while being chased by police dogs, naturally), and stripping cars. While being interviewed about the event, Slade tells a reporter that the purpose of the competition is "To provide for these young people an opportunity to let steam off in a very positive way by competing in events that are, familiar, if you will, to their environment." Another example occurs in the film when viewers are introduced to the duo Hammer and Slammer, who are the owners of a soul food restaurant. Viewers witness how it takes everything in Hammer not to beat the brakes off a customer (Chris Rock) who is hoping Hammer can "hook a brotha up" to cover the cost of "one rib" and a "sip of soda," even though the wad of cash in his pockets indicates he can afford to pay any price. Hammer does everything he can to not become enraged, which is exemplified by his exaggerated deep breathing and the quelling of his angered responses into a more calm expression. In addition, the phrases "stay cool" or "be cool" are frequently used throughout the film to prevent Black male characters from acting out in an aggressive manner. In all of these instances, it is made clear to viewers that Black men have a problem with anger, and that problem must be dealt with by the systematic repression or channeling of that anger through more constructive means. Keenan Ivory Wayans's directorial choices informs the viewer that he is well aware of public perceptions of Black men as angry. Wayans's mocking and the extremes to which his characters go to diminish their rage are indicative of the public perceptions about the need to control Black male aggression.

Just as *Sucka* explicitly engages the idea of controlling Black male aggression, it also plays up notions of the Black male as hypermasculine, which are transmuted into the film's scenes between men and women. The film's presentation of Black machismo is over the top. Jack Spade constantly has to prove he is "tough enough" to be a Black hero and part of Slade's crew, and he frequently references the numerous badges he earned while in the Army (including, hilariously, one he earned for typing). The use of music in the film is also suggestive of machismo's significance. In addition to being accompanied by theme music that follows Jack, John, and company wherever they go, staccato horns and a jumping bass line in the background are nondiegetic insertions into the filmic narrative. This incorporation of "hero theme music" certainly pays homage to the use of funk and soul accompaniment popular in Blaxploitation films and centers the importance of the Black male hero. It also, as Christopher Hight notes, allows "the subliminal effects of cinematic sound to surface, suggesting that sound is equally as implicated as visual representation in constructions of racial identity."[10]

The best representation of hypermasculinity in the film, however, is demonstrated in the character Flyguy, the imprisoned pimp[11] who served time for refusing to "sell out" his comrades. Flyguy, who recalls with nostalgia how he was "the biggest and baddest guy out there," is cast as the player who, in his prime, won the Pimp of the Year award. Notably, Flyguy's participation in the competition is best remembered for the rendering of his poem "Bitch Betta Have My Money." Flyguy's release from prison and re-entry into the world is resplendent. He emerges from jail in a bright yellow, fur-lined zoot suit with a matching wide-brimmed hat, and platform shoes complete with fish. Even as locals mock him for his over-the-top style dress we are made aware of how fashion choices and Black male identity become intertwined.[12] Most significantly, Flyguy's resurgence signals the sustained imagery of the Black male as pimp and player in the American popular imagination.

To be sure, Wayans's directorial efforts explicitly critique the negative tropes associated with Black male identity, including especially hypermasculinity and aggression. As Guerrero aptly notes, ". . . the black cinema experience ha[d] grown so sophisticated and commodified that it ha[d] reached the dialectical moment of self-parody with the release of *Sucka*."[13] By addressing these themes through the form of parody, Wayans effectively combats stereotypes with extreme stereotypes, even as he does so in a rather nostalgic way.[14] *Sucka* thus becomes a particularly important film for the ways it uses parody. Ironically, even as *Sucka* pays homage to the litany of successful Blaxploitation films such as *Sweet Sweetback's Baadasssss Song* (1970), *Shaft* (1971), and *Super Fly* (1972), it notably ignores *Cleopatra Jones* (1973), *Foxy Brown* (1974), and the other *sheroes* of the Blaxploitation era in its character choices and its storyline. This omission, which was initially acknowledged by Jennifer DeVere Brody,[15] signals the male dominance of Black popular film. Focusing on how the film centers Black male experiences renders only a surface-level reading of the ways that *Sucka* constructs Black male and female relationships. Rather, examining how the third and fourth tropes surrounding Black masculinity—emasculation and virility—are presented in the film, and how Black women are used to affirm these tropes, arguably leads to a more substantive analysis of Black male and female relationships, and how the Black female body becomes read as dangerous.

## PIECE BY PIECE (OR, "*THAT* IS FOR GETTING LAID")

Even as *Sucka* focuses predominantly on Black men, there are three female characters who play an important part in how the film's presentation of Black male experiences are interpreted: Cheryl (Dawnn Lewis), Jack's sister-in-law; Ma Bell (Ja'net Dubois), Jack's mother; and Cherry (Anne-Marie Johnson), Jack's brief love interest. As a collective, what is most striking about these female characters is that, unlike their male counterparts, they are not presented as important to the narrative in their own right or because they add something distinct to the storyline. Rather, they are incorporated into the filmic narrative in relationship to the Black male characters (especially Jack) and for the ways that they bring to light the very stereotypes that Keenan Ivory Wayans uses the film to critique. On the one hand, this relational construction makes sense given that the film follows Jack's efforts to defeat Mr. Big. On the other hand, that the women are not treated as characters that add something substantive to the storyline in ways akin to male characters reinforces their position as secondary and affirms the ways that Black women are presented as being a threat to Black masculinity.

More significantly, the female characters are literally *used* to play up the tropes of emasculation and virility in the film, a feature that perpetuates dangerous stereotypes about Black women. Ma Bell is presented as the well intentioned, yet emasculating Black woman. Her enthusiasm for Jack's return home is overshadowed by her efforts to protect Jack at any cost. In a scene nearly thirty minutes into the film, Jack arrives at Cheryl's workplace to take her home. Cheryl, who was waiting for Ma Bell to pick her up, is more than happy to have Jack as an escort. She affectionately calls him "Soldier Boy" in recognition of his status as a military man and to express her delight at his offer. Before they can leave however, two of Mr. Big's unnamed henchmen enter the diner and threaten Jack, who willingly faces the confrontation even as he is outsized and outnumbered. Jack tells a very nervous Cheryl, "don't you worry about a thing, I can handle this." Embodying the damsel in distress persona, Cheryl virtually swoons in awe and a scuffle nearly ensues. Just as Jack removes his jacket in preparation for the fight, Ma Bell bursts into the diner shouting, "Hold it right there! Ain't nobody layin' a finger on my baby." As the quintessential strong Black woman she then reaches Mr. Big's men by way of a back flip and somersault, and proceeds to beat them up handily. All the while, Jack stands aside helplessly, and looks sheepish and embarrassed. Even as the intentionally poor editing demonstrates that Wayans is well aware of the scene's absurdity (it was quite obvious that Ja'net Dubois as Ma Bell was not the person flipping and subsequently beating up the two men), the fact remains that Ma Bell's intervention emasculated Jack by taking away his ability to defend himself and protect Cheryl. At the end of the sequence, Jack confronts Ma Bell exclaiming, "You didn't have to do that, that was *my* fight." Even with that, Ma Bell infantilizes Jack by telling him "That's alright sugar, mama don't want her baby fightin' that street trash," and admonishing him to put his coat on because it was cold outside.

Ma Bell's chastisement, while amusing, harkens to a traditional role of motherhood—that of the self-sacrificial, overly devoted mother. Ma Bell's intervention is also suggestive of the perceived place of Black motherhood in the lives of Black men—that Black men cannot survive without their mothers. Even though Jack had left home, lived on his own, and served in the military, he continued to need a seemingly unsuitable kind of maternal support. Rather than allowing her son to "become a man" and handle situations on his own, the Black mother as construed in *Sucka* is overprotective, interventionist, and, like society at large, prevents Black men from becoming adults. The film therefore implies that Ma Bell is a threat to Jack's progression from boyhood into manhood, or put another way, that Black mothers are a deterrent to young Black men's growth and development. Also suggestive is the idea that in addition to having to deal with the crisis of Black masculinity as interpreted by popular culture broadly, Black men also have to deal with infantilization in the home—and Black women are central to that infantilization. This idea that Black men are emasculated, and that Black women play a particular role in their emasculation is quite dangerous as is perpetuates the negative trope of Sapphire—the emasculating, attitudinal Black woman.[16] The film fails to provide a context for why Ma Bell may be overprotective of Jack beyond the fact that he was bullied as a kid, which is strange considering the fact that her son Junebug had recently been murdered. Rather, viewers are left with a limited explanation for Ma Bell's overprotective nature and are led to believe that her desire to protect Jack is inappropriate. In this way, Keenan Ivory Wayans's directorial efforts diverge from Blaxploitation forms by attributing the negative tropes surrounding Black masculinity to Black women as well as to "the Man."

The character Cheryl is uniquely positioned in the film for the ways she highlights two tropes: Black male emasculation by way of the "Black bitch"[17] and Black male virility. Cheryl is a stark contrast to Ma Bell's character as an overbearing matriarch, and she waffles between being the docile, demure woman and the angry Black bitch. In her most prim moments, Cheryl sighs, coos, and plays coy with Jack. The uses of canted angle and medium close-ups frame her exchanges with Jack as filled with longing and desire. Yet, her mutual desire for Jack is inappropriate. She is, after all, a widow who should be mourning the recent loss of her husband who was also

Jack's brother. Cheryl's character certainly reflects a *softer* side of Black femininity. Yet the underlying message is that Black women have an overwhelming desire and need to be rescued by Black men. This message is contradictory to the film's response to Ma Bell, who does the rescuing herself, yet is reprimanded for her efforts.

The "bitch" aspect of her character is invoked when Cheryl is experiencing a natural, physiological aspect of womanhood: her menstrual cycle. In one of the most memorable scenes in the film, we see Cheryl seamlessly transition from demure woman to emasculating bitch. Due to the onset of her menstrual cycle, Cheryl is not feeling one hundred percent, and she leaves work early. While en route home, Mr. Big's goon Leonard (Damon Wayans) follows her, and attempts to pick her up in order to settle her deceased husband's debt. Leonard initially seeks Cheryl's compliance through sexual suggestion, saying "Alright sweet thing, it's time to come home to daddy." Cheryl, who is in distress because of the severity of her menstrual cramps, responds, "Please, please just leave me alone" with exceptional politeness considering she is being followed and is alone on a dark street. Leonard responds to her suggestion with "Bitch, I said you're coming with *me*." Cheryl turns around, and at that moment is dramatically transformed into a terrifying, wild hair, yellow-eyed monster (an obvious homage to Michael Jackson's "Thriller" video). Leonard fearfully responds, "Oh shit, you must got the devil in you!" Cheryl then gurgles the retort "Nooooo, craaaamps!" She subsequently accosts Leonard, throws him against a wall, and threatens to "cut his balls off" while he screams in a high-pitched manner suggestive of a woman's voice.

It seems like Leonard is doomed, but he is rescued when his partner Willie (Kadeem Hardison) bludgeons Cheryl, and they carry her away. Their capture of Cheryl does not occur, however, before Willie lets Leonard know that he could hear him screaming from a block away, to which Leonard adamantly responds, "I wasn't screaming, I was *whistling*!" It is striking how swiftly Leonard's character transitions from being kind to objectifying Cheryl as a bitch when, prior to that moment, Cheryl had been no less than a polite woman. More notably, however, this scene is significant because it suggests that the range of hormones literally invokes a rage in Black women, even among the most demure. That the physiological processes of womanhood result in the explicit emasculation of Black men by Black women further positions the Black female body as dangerous to Black men. Yet again, *Sucka* is guilty of using its Black female characters to reinscribe dangerous, negative stereotypes of Black women suggested in Cheryl's "emotional instability," bitchy attitude, and explicit threat toward Black manhood.

Despite these more subtle references to sexual suggestion in Cheryl and Jack's relationship and the overarching trope of Black male emasculation, it is through the character Cherry that *Sucka* most obviously highlights the trope of Black male virility. We are introduced to Cherry when Jack and Slade go to a bar to see One Eyed Sam and gather materials to settle their score with Mr. Big. Other than the waitress and the exaggerating lounge singer (who is referred to and is literally "The Director's Sister," [Kim Wayans]), Cherry is the only woman in the bar. Slade begins lecturing Jack about the importance of "being laid," and, on cue, Cherry struts over to their table in a skin-tight, form fitting, fire-engine red and black leather dress with a matching red jacket. Accented by red-stained lips and shoulder-length, wavy curls Cherry swiftly makes her desire for Jack known. In addition to over-annunciating words to bring attention to her mouth and tongue, she speaks in breathy tones, frequently licks her lips, and maneuvers her tongue in ways suggestive of sexual prowess. Channeling the trope of the Jezebel—the highly sexual Black woman—Cherry propositions Jack, and tells him that in him she has found Mr. Right who can give her exactly what she needs: a twelve inch penis. Jack concedes she is correct in her quest for finding Mr. Right, and departs with Cherry to her place around the corner.

Things quickly get hot and heavy between them, but shortly after they arrive at Cherry's place, Jack feels compelled to admit that he does not have the twelve inches Cherry desires. Jack's admission stalls the moment and also leads to a rather unexpected turn of events. Cherry is obviously disappointed, but surprisingly has her own series of confessions: her eyes are not green, she is wearing a wig and is almost totally bald, her breasts and ass are not real, and, to top it off, she has a prosthetic leg. Cherry's revelations coincide with her throwing her faux parts across the room, and are too much for Jack, so he scrambles out of the apartment. This is not, however, before Cherry begs him to stay and threatens in a most memorable line, "Don't make me, don't make me hop after you!" which she exclaims while jumping after Jack with her single leg. The entire sequence unfolds in just under five minutes, but the implications of Cherry's character belie the length of her screen time. Even as Cherry's actions and Jack's own admissions call his manhood into question, of greater importance is what the scene with Cherry signifies. Explicit in Cherry's performance is the message that Black women are so immensely sexual, utterly insatiable, and outright desperate to find Mr. Right that they would literally become the embodiment of a lie to give the illusion of desirability. This striking scene suggests that female characters in *Sucka* are focused upon only insofar as they reinforce troubling, negative stereotypes about Black women.

More specifically, *Sucka* highlights, and even celebrates the objectification of Black women. As if the explicit portrayal of Cherry's heightened sexual prowess is not suggestive enough, Cheryl's "damsel in distress" persona represents another aspect of Black womanhood. Cheryl and Cherry represent extremes of Black femininity, but what brings their characters together is that they are the objects of Jack's desire. Cheryl is the focus of Jack's sexual desire and also serves as the catalyst for his takedown of Mr. Big when he kidnaps her and threatens her life. Jack's original focus on Mr. Big's empire (drugs, gold chains, illicit businesses, etc.) falls to the wayside as his love (and lust) for Cheryl takes over. Cheryl and Jack's mutual desire becomes so significant to the story that we forget that they should be in mourning. Some may read this as Wayans's critique of the appropriation of Black respectability politics where the Black female becomes, like many White matriarchs, in need of salvation. Many read this form of parody, like Harriet Margolis suggests, as Wayans's "attack on stereotyping as a process that is presented by the media as a means of conceptualizing the world."[18] I contest this idea however, because *Sucka* is a satiric homage to Blaxploitation era films, and there were few, if any, where salvation of the Black female is the central plot. In the popular film *Shaft* (1971), for example, the daughter of the main character, Bumpy [Richard Roundtree] was kidnapped. Yet, that positioning of a Black female character in the plot functioned as a secondary means for the White Mafia to blackmail Bumpy rather than a consuming focus for which Bumpy chooses to take on "the Man."

The viewer's introduction to Cherry is mediated by John Slade's explanation of the exact purpose for a woman's body and his efforts to give Jack a lesson about being a hero. When Slade sees Cherry, he immediately objectifies her, even as he offers an explanation to Jack that differentiates between "being loved" and "being laid." Instead of calling Cherry "her" or "she," or even by her name, he instead identifies her as "that." The objectification is made obvious by Slade's pronoun designation inasmuch for his description of "that's" purpose, which is "for getting laid," and he encourages Jack to "help himself" to Cherry, as if she were a plate of food.

Certainly, Cherry's character reflects a kind of ridiculousness and, in that way, keeps in line with the overall form of parody demonstrated throughout the movie. Yet, Cherry's function does something different than the male absurdities played up in the film. Rather than mocking the ways that women may be perceived as the hypersexualized Jezebel—the obvious negative filmic trope for which Cherry is a stand-in—the character Cherry appears to be mentally unwell. She is in fact, a kind of drag parody whose unmasking performance[19] of herself as the voluptuous and desirable woman gives way to the *real* woman underneath the prosthetics—a Black woman who is fake, empty, and desperate.

When compared to how the male parodies occur in the film, the women are continuously mocked without redemption. For example, Jack's military experience is outright made fun of. His numerous badges and role as an "Inter-military Administrator" or a "Secretary" are humorously engaged, and their role in Jack's efforts to reclaim his old neighborhood from Mr. Big (aka the Man) on his own is a large part of the film's critique. Yet, his limited military experience, naiveté, and innocence do not preclude him from being the hero. Rather, these features makes a case for seeing him in a more appealing light, as he, after all, can be read as the *everyday hero*. In contrast, there are no redemptive qualities for Ma Bell, the overbearing Black mother or Cherry, the one-legged, lying Jezebel who is filled with such great longing for a man's attention and to fulfill her need for "twelve inches" that she literally hops in desperation after him. This suggests, as bell hooks poignantly notes, that "representations of black female bodies in contemporary popular culture rarely subvert or critique images of black female sexuality which were part of the cultural apparatus of nineteenth century racism and which still shape perceptions today."[20]

## "DON'T MAKE ME HOP AFTER YOU..."

bell hooks's argument about how popular culture fails to disrupt negative imagery of Black female bodies gives us much to consider in light of *Sucka*'s representations of Black women. *Sucka* highlights negative tropes associated with Black masculinity (virility, emasculation, hypermasculinity, and aggression) and mocks the absurdities of popular expectations related to Black male identities. When Black female characters are introduced, they too are hyperbolized stereotypes, but they do not get equal footing in terms of debunking. Whereas *Sucka* plays up and actively disrupts notions of the Black male as hypersexualized and violent through its characters Jack Spade, John Slade, Hammer, Slammer, and others, it never actually critiques the representations it highlights for Black women. Rather, the film presents them as normative and features for which Black men must escape, as in "Momma, I don't need you to fight for me" and "don't make me hop after you!" *Sucka*'s bottom line—made most explicitly through Cherry's hop—is that Black women's bodies are inherently dangerous, and must literally be cast aside for Black men to embrace their masculinity and become "the hero." In the end, Wayans's directorial efforts are, as Margolis suggests, vulnerable to charges of furthering the very stereotypes he chooses to confront.[21]

To be clear, I do not suggest that *Sucka* had to be about Black women or to center Black women's experiences. Rather, that Wayans chose to center Black male experiences at the expense of developing Black female characters is what I find curious. Whereas the film's critique about hypermasculinity and Black male aggression directly responds to larger, societal claims and concerns about Black men that are arguably directed toward "the Man" (aka "Whitey"), its commentary about Black male virility and emasculation is directed toward Black women. This too is a break from the Blaxploitation film, where Black solidarity often takes precedent over and against intra-race politics. In this case, the use of Black female characters to prove points about

Black male virility and emasculation is problematic because it takes attention from the film's Blaxploitation roots of "sticking it to the Man." Consequently, the positioning of Black female bodies in the films renders the female characters as lacking any depth and as unable to transcend the very stereotypes they bring to the forefront.

In her provocative essay "Inauguration Day 2001" Hortense Spillers describes her outrage with the controversial outcome of the 2000 presidential election, where George W. Bush ascended into the presidency without having amassed a majority of the popular vote and without having to count a significant number of votes in the state of Florida.[22] Citing Slavonian intellectual Slavoj Žižek, Spillers notes the importance of irony and sarcasm as a means of rejecting dominant beliefs. More than just the mere critique of popular ideals, cynicism becomes a mode of confronting and exposing official ruling ideologies so as to make them the objects of ridicule. Certainly, the stakes of parody in a 1980s film may not be perceived to be as significant as the mockery surrounding the outright theft of an American presidential election. That withstanding, the use of parody in *Sucka* is meant to ridicule "official ruling ideologies" that would suggest that there is, in fact, a "crisis of Black masculinity" and that Black men can be relegated to relentless negative stereotyping. Yet, the question remains: where does parody intervene and ridicule popular ideologies surrounding Black women's embodiment in the film?

One could argue that Keenan Ivory Wayans was unaware of the implications of his character choices or worse, that he was totally aware but did not care how Black female bodies would be read in *Sucka*. Given that "no character in *Sucka* goes without ridicule, and no point of view remains secure for viewer identification" as Margolis suggests,[23] both of these alternatives are plausible. A third alternative to consider, is that intention aside, there is something inherent in the filmic *form* of parody that leaves much to be desired in its characterizations of Black women. In the case of *Sucka* self-directed parody means that the Black filmmaker (Wayans) satirizes stereotypes that are about Black people—people who would arguably see the film and immediately be equipped to identify the stereotypes being parodied whether they agree with them or not. As effective a strategy as parody may be, given that, as Tommy Lott suggests, the relationship between the concepts of Black identity and of cinema itself is one that is fraught with numerous tensions,[24] the use of parody in film to disrupt Black stereotypes may in and of itself be a largely ineffective strategy. Factors such as varied interpretations, demographics, and experiences among viewers can result in the exaggerated form doing more harm than good. In addition, that the film does little to develop its female characters so as to forthrightly identify—let alone critique—popular stereotypes about Black women further detracts from the effectiveness of the use of satire.

I believe there is something about the *form* of the Black comedic film that lends itself to a less than substantive critique of negative representations of Black female bodies. This is certainly evident in *Sucka*, where representations of Black women are riddled with stereotypes that are left unchecked. Even if we are willing to excuse *Sucka* as exemplary of its time, we must consider its lasting implications upon subsequent films, and especially those written, directed, and/or produced by Black artists. Whether pitched as the bitch, strong Black woman, damsel in distress, emasculating maternal figure, or hypersexual Jezebel, the female characters (or caricatures) of *Sucka* continue to be present in today's popular films. Of special note are the contemporary films that emerged from the roots of *Sucka* including a series of comedies that mock Black women by way of drag performance. With parody at its core, these films—which are best exemplified by the comedies featuring Black men with stand-up and stage experience in fat suits—pay explicit homage to Wayans's sketch comedy routines that are incorporated into *Sucka*. Films such as the three installations of the *Big Momma's House* franchise that feature Martin Lawrence, *Norbit* (2007) which includes Eddie Murphy, and the numerous films that center Tyler Perry as the character Madea (e.g., *Madea's Family Reunion* [2006], *Madea's Big Happy Family* [2011], *Madea's Witness Protection* [2012], and *A Madea Christmas* [2013]) can all be read as part of *Sucka*'s legacy. Like *Sucka*, all of these films are comedies or comedy-dramas (versus romantic comedies or dramas), they feature Black actors and actresses, are financially lucrative, have accompanying R&B soundtracks, and are, for marketing purposes, targeted toward Black audiences in addition to their crossover appeal.[25]

These comedy dramas utilize a different kind of costuming from *Sucka* because of their use of fat suits. That withstanding, these popular films, like *Sucka*, share the use of extreme parody to bring stereotypes to the forefront. Most significantly, they have the frequent reinscription of negative tropes geared toward Black women's bodies in common, and with a particular emphasis on the three caricatures brought to the forefront in *Sucka*: the angry Black woman or bitch, the emasculating Black mother, and the hypersexualized Jezebel. At first glance, Eddie Murphy's character Rasputia *(Norbit)* is indicative of the attitudinal, angry Black bitch, while Tyler Perry's Madea and Martin Lawrence's Big Momma embody the overly doting yet emasculating Black mother figure. Murphy's Rasputia also represents the quintessential, hypersexualized Jezebel.

Yet, the modern iteration of these tropes is not the three distinct characters as they were in *Sucka*. Rather, they have merged into a hybrid Black female figure I call Sapphmammibel—a combination of Sapphire, Mammy, and Jezebel that is so stylized and hidden in her fat suit that she is increasingly difficult to decipher. In this contemporary cinematic era, a transition has occurred to a point where Black women are not actually portrayed by Black women, but are parodied and caricatured by Black men who dress in drag. In all of these cases from *Sucka* until now, what has remained constant is comedy's poor ability to disrupt negative stereotypes as they make fun of them. In short, when it comes to Black filmic comedies and the treatment of women, parody loses its critical edge.

It is ironic that on the twenty-fifth anniversary of *I'm Gonna Git You Sucka*, a review of the tropes, caricatures, and satirical elements of the film reveals that little has changed in regards to representations of Black women in popular film. From *Sucka* until now, negative tropes have been used to present Black women as explicit threats to Black masculinity. To put it frankly, Black women have historically been—and continue to be—the butt (no pun intended) of the joke of negative representations in popular comedic films. Taking the Black, fat drag, comedy drama as a modern iteration of the Blaxploitation parody helps us see the lasting implications of the dangerous, negative readings of Black women that popular film seems to uncritically perpetuate and that the masses incredulously consume. Because there is such limited engagement and critique in popular culture about the rendering of Black women's bodies as dangerous in popular film, we are left to conclude that parody does little to disrupt, and in fact, actively perpetuates a long history of negative stereotyping of Black women.

## NOTES

1. Blaxploitation films, which began in the 1971 with Melvin Van Peeble's *Sweet Sweetback's Baadasssss Song* and coincided with the end of the Black power era, were best known for their predominantly Black actors and actresses, their treatment of Black men and women as anti-heroes and heroines, their critique of white supremacy and the white establishment (also known as The Man), their positive valuation of Black pimps and drug dealers as protectors of urban ghettos, and the accompanying soundtrack of funk and soul music (and especially the wah-wah guitar). The functions and features of Blaxploitation era films, as well as their complex and controversial impact on American cinema, are examined in an extensive body of literature. Refer especially to *Women of Blaxploitation: How the Black Action Film Heroine Changes American Popular Culture* by Yvonne D. Sims (McFarland and Company, 2006); *Blaxploitation Cinema: The Essential Reference Guide* by Josiah Howard (FAB Press, 2008); *"Baad Bitches" and Sassy Supermamas: Black Power Action Films* by Stephanie Dunn (University of Illinois Press, 2008; *Blaxploitation Films* by Mikel J. Koven (Oldcastle Books, 2010); *What It Is...What is Was! The Black Film Explosion of the '70s in Words and Pictures* by Gerald Martinez, Denise Chavez and Andres Chavez (Miramax Books, 1998); and the iconic text, *Tom, Coons, Mulattoes, Mammies and Bucks: An Interpretive History of Blacks in American Films*, 4th edition by Donald Bogle (Bloomsbury Academic, 2001).

2. Wiliam Covey, "The Genre Don't Know Where it Came From: African American Neo-Noir Since the 1960s" in *Journal of Film and Video*, 55, no. 2/3 (Summer/Fall 2003): 59–72.

3. Other films in this category included *Purple Rain* (1984), *Brother from Another Planet* (1985), *Hollywood Shuffle* (1987), *School Daze* (1988), and *Harlem Nights* (1990). See Jacqueline Bobo, "'The Subject is Money': Reconsidering the Black Film Audience as a Theoretical Paradigm," in *Black American Literature Forum*, 25, no. 2 (Summer 1991): 421–32.

4. *In Living Color* was an American sketch comedy series created by Keenan Ivory Wayans and Damon Wayans. The show aired weekly on Fox Network from April 1990 to May 1994.

5. Bogle, *Toms, Coons, Mulattoes, Mammies and Bucks* (originally published in 1973).

6. There are extensive sources that engage (and at times contest) the notion of a "crisis of black masculinity." Refer especially to Mark Anthony Neal, *New Black Man* (Routledge, 2006); Maurice O. Wallace, *Constructing the Black Masculine: Identity and Ideality in African American Men's Literature and Culture, 1775–1995* (Duke University Press, 2002); Anthony J. Lemelle Jr., "Africana Studies and the Crisis of Black Masculinity" in *Afrocentric Traditions*, edited by James L. Conyers Jr., 63–82 (Transaction Publishers, 2011); *Cool Pose: The Dilemmas of Black Manhood in America* by Richard Majors and Janet M. Billson (Touchstone, 1992); Hortense J. Spillers, "Mama's Baby Papa's Maybe: An American Grammar Book" in *Black, White and in Color: Essays on American Literature and Culture*, 203–230 (University of Chicago Press, 2003); and Natalie Hopkinson and Natalie Moore, *Deconstructing Tyrone: A New Look at Black Masculinity in the Hip-Hop Generation* (Cleis Press, 2006). See also the entirety of *AmeriQuests*, volume 6, which was devoted to the topic "On Manliness: Black American Masculinities" and especially the introduction "On Manliness: Black Masculinity Revisited" by Gilman W. Whiting and Thabiti Lewis (*AmeriQuests* 6, no. 1 [2008]: 1–8). As the notion of "crisis" is highly contested in the literature for the ways it potentially pathologizes black male experiences, I bracket the term throughout this essay.

7. See "Black Men and the Movies: How Does it Feel to Be a Problem (and an Answer)" in *Traps: African American Men on Gender and Sexuality*, edited by Rudolph P. Byrd and Beverly Guy-Sheftall, 270–77 (Indiana University Press, 2001). See also Guerrero's text *Framing Blackness: The African American Image in Film* (Temple University Press, 1993).

8. Guerrero, "Black Men and the Movies," 271.

9. Margolis, "Stereotypical Strategies: Black Film Aesthetics, Spectator Positioning, and Self-Directed Stereotypes in 'Hollywood Shuffle' and 'I'm Gonna Git You Sucka,'" *Cinema Journal*, 38, no. 3 (Spring 1999): 50–66.

10. See his essay "Stereo Types: The Operation of Sound in the Production of Racial Identity," *Leonardo*, 36, no. 1 (2003): 13–17.

11. Arguably, that Flyguy is imprisoned is yet another not-so-subtle reference to the criminalization and policing of Black men.

12. Covey, "The Genre Don't Know Where it Came From," 65.

13. Ed Guerrero, "Black Film: Mo' Better on the '90s," *Black Camera* 6, no. 1 (Spring/Summer 1991): 2–3.

14. Henry Louis Gates, Jr. "Harlem on Our Minds" in *Critical Inquiry* 24, no. 1 (Autumn 1997): 1–12.

15. "The Returns of Cleopatra Jones." *Signs: Journal of Women in Culture and Society* 25, no. 1 (Autumn 1999): 91–121.

16. See especially Hortense Spiller's incomparable essay, "Mama's Baby, Papa's Maybe."

17. There is extensive literature about reading of Black women through the trope of the "bitch." See bell hooks, *Reel to Real: Race, Sex, and Class at the Movies* (Routledge, 1996); Ed Guerrero, *Framing Blackness*; Patricia Hill Collins, "Mammies, Matriarchs and Other Controlling Images" in *Feminist Philosophies: Problems, Theories and Applications*, edited by Janet A. Kournay, James P. Sterba, and Rosemarie Tong, 142–52 (Prentice Hall, 1999); Kimberly Springer, "Divas, Evil Black Bitches and Bitter Black Women: African-American Women in Postfeminist and Post-Civil Rights Popular Culture" in *Interrogating Postfeminism: Gender and the Politics of Popular Culture*, edited by Yvonne Tasker and Diane Negra, 249–76 (Duke University Press, 2007); Melissa Harris-Perry, *Sister Citizen: Shame, Stereotypes, and Black Women in America* (Yale University Press, 2011); and Tamura A. Lomax, "Mad Black Bitches and Lady-Like Saints: Representations of African American Women in Tyler Perry Films" in *Womanist and Black Feminist Reponses to Tyler Perry's Productions*, edited by LeRhonda S. Manigault-Bryant, Tamura A. Lomax, and Carol B. Duncan (Palgrave Macmillan 2014).

18. Margolis, "Stereotypical Strategies," 50.

19. For sources that engage the use of drag performance as a means of simultaneous unmasking and exaggeration, see Judith Lorber, *Paradoxes of Gender* (Yale University Press, 1995) and *Gender Inequality: Feminist Theories and Politics* (Oxford University Press, 2009); Marjorie Garber, *Vested Interests: Cross-Dressing and Cultural Anxiety* (Harper Perennial, 1992); and Steven P. Schact and Lisa Underwood, *The Drag Queen Anthology: The Absolutely*

*Fabulous but Flawlessly Customary World of Female Impersonators* (Harrington Park Press, 2004).

20. hooks, "Selling Hot Pussy: Representations of Black Female Sexuality in the Cultural Marketplace," in *Black Looks: Race and Representation* (South End Press, 1992), 62.

21. Margolis, "Stereotypical Strategies," 53.

22. Spillers, "Inauguration Day 2001." *boundary 2*, 29, no. 1 (Spring 2002): 1–10. I extend my sincere thanks to James Manigault-Bryant for reminding me of the importance of this essay.

23. Margolis, "Stereotypical Strategies," 55.

24. Lott, "A No-Theory Theory of Contemporary Black Cinema" in *Black American Literature Forum*, 25, no. 2 (Summer 1991): 221–36.

25. I outline six features of the fat drag comedy-drama in the essay "Fat Spirit: Obesity, Religion, and Sapphmammibel in Contemporary Black Film," in *Fat Studies: An Interdisciplinary Journal of Body Weight and Society* 2, no. 1 (Spring 2013): 56–69. Quite notably, *I'm Gonna Git You Sucka* shares four of the six features. The two features that are not shared are a focus or emphasis on Black religiosity and the use of fat suits. That said, however, Cherry's role in *Sucka* can certainly be read as a form of drag performance.

# BIBLIOGRAPHY

Bobo, Jacqueline. "'The Subject is Money': Reconsidering the Black Film Audience as a Theoretical Paradigm." *Black American Literature Forum* 25, no. 2 (Summer 1991): 421–32.

Bogle, Donald. *Toms, Coons, Mulattos, Mammies, & Bucks.* 4th ed. New York: Bloomsbury Academic, 2001.

Brody, Jennifer DeVere. "The Returns of Cleopatra Jones." *Signs: Journal of Women in Culture and Society 25*, no. 1 (Autumn 1999): 91–121.

Byrd, Rudolph P., and Beverly Guy-Sheftall. "Black Men and the Movies: How Does it Feel to Be a Problem (and an Answer)." In *Traps: African American Men on Gender and Sexuality*, edited by Rudolph P. Byrd and Beverly Guy-Sheftall, 270–77. Bloomington: Indiana University Press, 2001.

Collins, Patricia Hill. "Mammies, Matriarchs and Other Controlling Images." In *Feminist Philosophies: Problems, Theories and Applications*, edited by Janet A. Kournay, James P. Sterba, and Rosemarie Tong, 142–52. Upper Saddle River: Prentice Hall, 1999.

Covey, Wiliam. "The Genre Don't Know Where it Came From: African American Neo-Noir Since the 1960s." In *Journal of Film and Video* 55, no. 2/3 (Summer/Fall 2003): 59–72.

Dunn, Stephanie. *"Baad Bitches" and Sassy Supermamas: Black Power Action Films.* Chicago: University of Illinois Press, 2008.

Garber, Marjorie. *Vested Interests: Cross-Dressing and Cultural Anxiety.* New York: Harper Perennial, 1992.

Gates, Henry Louis, Jr. "Harlem on Our Minds." *Critical Inquiry* 24, no. 1 (Autumn 1997): 1–12.

Guerrero, Ed. *Framing Blackness: The African American Image in Film.* Philadelphia: Temple University Press, 1993.

———. "Black Film: Mo' Better on the '90s." *Black Camera* 6, no. 1 (Spring/Summer 1991): 2–3.

Harris-Perry, Melissa V. *Sister Citizen: Shame, Stereotypes, and Black Women in America.* New Haven: Yale, 2011.

Hight, Christopher. "Stereo Types: The Operation of Sound in the Production of Racial Identity." *Leonardo 36*, no. 1 (Winter 2003): 13–17.

hooks, bell. *Reel to Real: Race, Sex, and Class at the Movies.* New York: Routledge, 1996.

———. "Selling Hot Pussy: Representations of Black Female Sexuality in the Cultural Marketplace." In *Black Looks: Race and Representation.* Boston: South End Press, 1992.

Hopkinson, Natalie, and Natalie Moore. *Deconstructing Tyrone: A New Look at Black Masculinity in the Hip-Hop Generation.* San Francisco: Cleis Press, 2006.

Howard, Josiah. *Blaxploitation Cinema: The Essential Reference Guide.* Goldaming: FAB Press, 2008.

Koven, Mikel J. *Blaxploitation Films.* United Kingdom: Oldcastle Books, 2010.

Lemelle Jr., Anthony J. "Africana Studies and the Crisis of Black Masculinity." In *Afrocentric Traditions,* edited by James L. Conyers Jr., 63–82. Piscataway: Transaction Publishers, 2011.

Lomax, Tamura A. "Mad Black Bitches and Lady-Like Saints: Representations of African American Women in Tyler Perry Films." In *Womanist and Black Feminist Reponses to Tyler Perry's Productions,* edited by LeRhonda S. Manigault-Bryant, Tamura A. Lomax, and Carol B. Duncan. United Kingdom: Palgrave Macmillan, 2014.

Lorber, Judith. *Paradoxes of Gender.* New Haven: Yale University Press, 1995.

———. *Gender Inequality: Feminist Theories and Politics.* New York: Oxford University Press, 2009.

Lott, Tommy L. "A No-Theory Theory of Contemporary Black Cinema." *Black American Literature Forum* 25, no. 2 (Summer 1991): 221–36.

Majors, Richard, and Janet M. Billson. *Cool Pose: The Dilemmas of Black Manhood in America.* New York: Touchstone, 1992.

Manigault-Bryant, LeRhonda S. "Fat Spirit: Obesity, Religion, and Sapphmammibel in Contemporary Black Film." *Fat Studies: An Interdisciplinary Journal of Body Weight and Society 1* (Spring 2013): 56–69.

Margolis, Harriet. "Stereotypical Strategies: Black Film Aesthetics, Spectator Positioning, and Self-Directed Stereotypes in 'Hollywood Shuffle' and 'I'm Gonna Git You Sucka.'" *Cinema Journal 38,* no. 3 (Spring 1999): 50–66.

Martinez, Gerald, Denise Chavez, and Adres Chavez. *What It Is...What is Was! The Black Film Explosion of the '70s in Words and Pictures.* New York: Miramax Books, 1998.

Neal, Mark Anthony. *New Black Man.* New York: Routledge, 2006.

Schact, Steven P. and Lisa Underwood. *The Drag Queen Anthology: The Absolutely Fabulous but Flawlessly Customary World of Female Impersonators.* New York: Harrington Park Press, 2004.

Sims, Yvonne D. *Women of Blaxploitation: How the Black Action Film Heroine Changes American Popular Culture.* Jefferson: McFarland and Company, 2006.

Spillers, Hortense J. "Mama's Baby Papa's Maybe: An American Grammar Book." In *Black, White and in Color: Essays on American Literature and Culture,* 203–30, Chicago: University of Chicago Press, 2003.

———. "Inauguration Day 2001." *Boundary 2 29,* no. 1 (Spring 2002): 1–10.

Springer, Kimberly. "Divas, Evil Black Bitches and Bitter Black Women: African-American Women in Postfeminist and Post-Civil Rights Popular Culture." *Interrogating Postfeminism: Gender and the Politics of Popular Culture,* edited by Yvonne Tasker and Diane Negra, 249–76. Durham: Duke University Press, 2007.

Wallace, Maurice O. *Constructing the Black Masculine: Identity and Ideality in African American Men's Literature and Culture, 1775–1995.* Durham: Duke University Press, 2002.

*Chapter Five*

# Learning to Conquer Metaphysical Dilemmas

## *Womanist and Masculinist Perspectives on* Tyler Perry's For Colored Girls

## Robin M. Boylorn and Mark C. Hopson

Being alive and being a woman is all I got, but being colored is a metaphysical dilemma I haven't conquered yet. —Tangie/Lady in Yellow

Ever since I realized there was someone callt/
a colored girl an evil woman a bitch or a nag/
i been tryin not to be that & leave bitterness/
in somebody else's cup . . . —Juanita/Lady in Orange

Political consciousness is locating the self in the mundane scheme where realities such as race, gender and economics are profoundly considered and injustices of power and privilege are resisted. —Akasha Hull, 2001

By definition, black popular culture is a contradictory space. It is a site of strategic contestation. —Stuart Hall, 2004

### BLACK WOMANIST AND MASCULINIST PERSPECTIVES

The nature of critique is complex. To make an argument for one thing is seen as making an argument against something else. Our objective here is not to demean the artistic works of Tyler Perry. We recognize the value and importance of bringing Black experiences to the big screen, and we commend Perry for his commitment to doing so. However, we also believe that a critical[1] and oppositional gaze[2] concentrated through a womanist and Black masculinist lens offers an intervention of Black popular culture and can be applied to the Tyler Perry genre. We realize not all viewers will interpret Perry's work in the same way, nor will all readers agree with every sentiment of our critique. By responding to Tyler Perry's *For Colored Girls* through the particularities of our own lives, we open our ideas for review. Exploration is necessary on all fronts. We are likely to tread on sensitive ground in that our discussion requires airing some dirty laundry—Perry's and our own.

Daryl Cumber Dance[3] argues that Black/African-American sensibilities have long been viewed as an in-house affair where critical examination is concealed from the White public. Perhaps Tyler Perry's infamy is increased by his open invitation to examine and evaluate the lives of Black people. As such we expand Dance's assertion with our critique of Perry's critique. The gaze works in both directions. Consider Robert Penn Warren's *Pondy Woods* where the author writes "Nigger your breed ain't metaphysical," to which Sterling Brown retorted nearly fifty years later, "Cracker your breed ain't exegetical."[4] Certainly the dilemma between what is real and surreal, and logical and illogical continues to be relevant to discussions concerning race and gender identity.

Black feminist and womanist scholarship[5] works to foreground unique perspectives, increase intellectual and active resistance to subjugation, and energize critical discourse necessary to rise out of domination. The value of feminist work includes its potential for transformation in all aspects of social life. In *Soul Talk*, Akasha Hull examines a transformative paradigm for the political, economic, and spiritual health of Black womanhood to address an essential question of life: Having worked on political fronts to honor concrete identities and improve material realities, having developed a spiritual consciousness with its attendant creative results, how then do African-American women pull it all together?[6] Pulling it together requires multiple contributions. Transformative energy moves to encompass spirituality in a deeper, explicit way for grappling with social issues on a more profound level. Thus Hull might argue that Tyler Perry's film *For Colored Girls* has great potential for transformation and healing, while his treatment of race and gender may contribute to constrictive identity politics.

A progressive Black masculinist approach to Tyler Perry's work seeks to critique and deconstruct hegemonic descriptions of masculinity that limit the dimensionality of Black manhood. A Black masculinist approach is also concerned with creat[ing] new tropes of Black masculinity that challenge the most negative stereotypes and counter stringently sanitized images.[7] In many ways a Black masculinist perspective works together with a Black feminist/womanist perspective to emphasize and challenge problematic depictions and characterizations of Black men and women. Here, we examine the recurring fragmented identities—rather, parts of a metaphysical dilemma—that provide the impetus for Perry's film.

The popularity of entertainment created by Black people for Black people has resulted in an increased interest in the competing images therein. As such we engage perspectives of the Black feminist/womanist and the Black masculinist to examine Tyler Perry's rhetorical treatment of race and gender in *For Colored Girls*.

Indirectly associated with Ntozake Shange's choreopoem *For Colored Girls Who Have Considered Suicide When The Rainbow Is Enuf*, Perry's film has been credited with reprising Black womanhood by bringing her story to the big screen. However, the representation(s) of Blackness in the film are problematic because Perry's adaptation stigmatizes Black women and men into stereotypical social roles.[8] Perry's characters lack nuance and instead of adding new relevance to the original text, fall short of the concerns set forth by Shange. The film's reinterpretation largely masks the poem's objective of female empowerment and exaggerates Black men as irredeemably violent or ineffectually masculine, both tropes failing at respectable masculinity. Perry does not pull together the brokenness and pain that results from such difficult realities as abortion, rape, unreciprocated love, depression, domestic violence, and child murder. Instead of contributing to the political consciousness of a largely Black and working-class, Christian, female audience, the original feminist text is "Tyler-Perry'd" by de-centering Black women and (de)masculinizing Black men. Thus we are forced to ask: Is the limited interrogation of the Black voice a way of framing familiar and marketable conundrums? What does Perry teach the rest of the world about Black culture?[9] Otherwise is Perry adding to the viability of Black stories?

## IMAGES OF WOMEN IN *FOR COLORED GIRLS*

Tyler Perry is undeniably one of the most powerful, influential, and controversial filmmakers of the twenty-first century. He has written and directed numerous stage plays, films, and network television shows, and written a best-selling book (under the moniker of Madea, the main character of many of his plays and films, which he himself portrays in drag).[10] His rise from humble beginnings and childhood abuse to unrefuted household name has generated a fan base in the millions, mostly Black women and Christians.

Perry's plays and films can be very seductive to audiences looking for Black representations in film,[11] but we must consider the larger implications of these images.[12] It is important to consider whether the representations do more harm than good, particularly for Black women.[13] In obtaining the rights to *For Colored Girls Who Have Considered Suicide When the Rainbow Is Enuf*, Perry took on "a Black girl's song" about girlhood, the transition to womanhood, and the various embedded pains therein (including yearning for but never quite achieving traditional, Christian, heterosexual, reciprocated love; and learning to love oneself in the absence of those things). Perry's overwhelming message in his repertoire of films, however, is grounded in women's fallibility and the need to be rescued and/or saved (either by the love of a man or through a redeeming relationship with God). While Perry is staying true to his bread and butter market of Black women's pain, some consumers may feel like he has already told the story several times over. Why did he need *For Colored Girls*?

Perry has been criticized for stereotypical generalizations. His overemphasis of Black women as inherently flawed leaves little space for redemption. His body of work is both praiseworthy and problematic. It has been called "coonery buffoonery" by filmmaker Spike Lee, and "the KFC of Black cinema" by Touré. Means Coleman writes that Perry is well-meaning but his version of womanhood defines women as victims who cannot extract themselves from this status, because they are not men.[14] At the same time Perry's plays and films have been considered groundbreaking.[15] *For Colored Girls*, a film that is adapted from a Black woman playwright, is considered Perry's first *serious* work.

A critical reading of Perry's films exposes a tendency toward blame and antifeminism.[16] Perry's version of Ntozake Shange's work strips the all-Black woman characters of their human and redeemable qualities.[17] Further, he creates characters that are non-existent in the original choreopoem to fit his genre and to "Tyler-Perry" what is otherwise an empowering commentary on Black womanhood. The film becomes a proscriptive account about the lives of women.

Rather than inspiring survival and sisterhood, *For Colored Girls* presents a series of unfortunate circumstances that do not integrate larger societal forces (racism, sexism, classism) in the lives of Black people. The film lacks the necessary moments of sass, laughter, innocence, bravery, recovery, self-love, self-actualization, and strength found in Shange's original work. There are few moments for breath; little air or space for connection with characters. Where the choreopoem is based on pride, mystery, sexual empowerment, resilience, and recovery—the film simply offers moment after moment of trauma. The audience is not allowed the same naïveté Perry often gives the characters.

Shange[18] is open to the various metamorphoses of her work, but says her intended message with *For Colored Girls* was an affirmation of Black women's possibilities. She has remained committed, through the various incarnations of her work, to adapting to/for the audience, while maintaining it as a feminist text.[19] Likewise, in *Soul Talk* Hull draws from Morrison's *The Bluest Eye*, Angelou's *I Know Why The Caged Bird Sings*, and Walker's *The Color Purple* to reveal themes of transcendence in literature which is not restricted to monolithic images or narratives where one-pain-fits-all, and asserts "African American women are quite definitely a marvelous mix of hardship and grace, whim and caring."[20]

Yet, in *For Colored Girls*, possibility is replaced by a constraining force. That force is replete with power and control which inform an overwhelming atmosphere of violence. Responding to the film, Hollywood reporter Kirk Honeycutt calls attention to the redundancy of self-sabotage and victimhood:

> In Perry's peculiar view . . . the women often collaborate in their victimhood. They invite the stranger into the home or let men stay when they clearly should go. They all fall from grace . . . he [Perry] can't resist turning *For Colored Girls* into a Tyler Perry Movie, which means imposing diva worship where nuance is called for and a pleasure-punishing Christian worldview where a certain moral ambiguity might have been more appropriate.[21]

Conversely, Jimi Izrael argues that the film's only shortcoming is the lack of context and over-ambition of translating a choreopoem to a film.[22] Perry attempts to modernize a timeless narrative. While there are likely issues with any attempt to translate a performance piece into a film, *For Colored Girls* speaks to the limitations of the medium and the implications of Perry's larger body of work. The pathologies of the Black community are told and sold at their expense. Stories of angry Black women, emasculated Black men, and tragedy are consistent throughout the tapestry of his film work.

A pseudo-feminist film, *For Colored Girls* misrepresents Black women by reinforcing a so-called singularity of experience between Perry's characters and Shange's characters. The choreopoem has survived various metamorphoses and transformations, including criticisms of tone and politics (too anti-male, too pro-Black), and yet it remains a performance which opens up the mind and heart. In contrast Perry's film opens old wounds and transforms a woman-centered text into something patriarchal and parochial. The text humanized Black women in a way that the film only accomplishes, although hardly convincingly, at the end.

## HISTORICAL REPRESENTATIONS AND CHARACTERIZATIONS

Black women have long endured negative representations.[23] Consequently there is an ongoing need to respond. Trudier Harris spoke to the necessary act in this way:

> Called Matriarch, Emasculator and Hot Momma. Sometimes Sister, Pretty Baby, Auntie, Mammy and Girl. Called Unwed Mother, Welfare Recipient and Inner City Consumer. The Black American Woman has had to admit that while nobody knew the troubles she saw, everybody, his brother and his dog, felt qualified to explain her, even to herself.[24]

Speaking to/with/for his mostly Black female audience, Perry and others use a language of troubled stock characters which depict Black women according to any one or combination of specific stereotypes, including but not limited to the Mammy, Matriarch, Jezebel, Sapphire, and Black Lady.[25] Today these stereotypes include *educated* Bitches or *bad* Black mothers.

The Mammy stereotype conjures images of slavery and the Black woman. Historically her allegiance was to the White family. She often cared for White children at the expense of her own. This character is rhetorically constructed as big bodied, intimidating, matronly, asexual, and nurturing. She does not have to be married or a biological mother to perform her function as self-sacrificing support for others. The Mammy stereotype is celebrated for knowing her place and tending to the needs of other people.

In contrast, the Matriarch character is situated as a failed Mammy because of her rejection of willing subjugation. The Matriarch as featured in the Moynihan Report[26] was often blamed for the plights of the Black family and community. Matriarchs are seen as "overly aggressive, unfeminine women" who "allegedly emasculate their lovers and husbands"[27] because of her place as head of the household. Usually masculinized, Matriarchs share some physical characteristics with their Mammy counterparts, but are characteristically independent.

The historical Jezebel image is related to Black women's presumed hypersexuality and lack of sexual agency during slavery. Jezebel was seen as a temptress and seductress whose indiscriminate sexual appetite condoned slave master rape.[28] Modern representations of the Jezebel are the Hoochie and Welfare Queen. These representations express a deviant female sexuality wherein Black women have insatiable sexual appetites. Promiscuity and fertility are dominant traits of the Jezebel.

The Sapphire image combines stereotypes of the sassy Mammy and the angry Black woman. Sapphire is considered "rude, loud, malicious, stubborn and overbearing."[29] She is an antagonizing verbal emasculator who continuously berates and nags Black men. She is both offensive and easily offended, and aggressively defends herself or speaks her mind. Sapphire is often represented as uneducated, undereducated, and unsophisticated.

The Black Lady is a class-specific image of the "middle-class professional Black woman" who is independently successful and educated.[30] This stereotype is a unique mix of the modern Mammy and the Matriarch due to her work ethic and dedication to work above family. The Black Lady's obsession with her own success is usually at the expense of her domestic pursuits. Generally she is unmarried and childless.

One commonality of controlling images—including the Mammy, Matriarch, Jezebel, Sapphire, and Black Lady—is their assumed inept ability to mother properly. The bad Black mother label can be attached to any of the preceding stereotypes for various reasons. For example, a Mammy might be a bad mother because of her focus on White people's children, oftentimes to the detriment of her own. The Matriarch might be considered a bad mother because of the circumstantial absence of a father-figure, which leads to the emasculation of sons and the indoctrination that a daughter's independence is paramount to happiness. The Black Lady might be framed as bad because of her refusal or inability to be a mother, while the Jezebel (which is directly linked to the Welfare Queen stereotype) is a bad mother because she is selfish and uninterested in her children, using them as a means to an end to either manipulate men or get over on the system.

## LESSONS ON BLACK WOMEN

Not all women in *For Colored Girls* are the same. Their universal albeit different experiences of oppression do not necessarily remove the texture of their individual lives. Yet where Shange offers multiple possibilities for the Black woman, Perry's film reverts to a limited scope which sets the blame at her door. Not unlike the Moynihan Report[31] Perry found a way to blame the ills and demise of the Black community on its women. And while Shange acknowledges that Black women are oftentimes complicit in their own circumstances, it is not to the exclusion of other factors and conditions beyond their control.

In addition, Perry created controlling images where none existed. Tangie's character is the Jezebel, oversexed and unapologetic she is a disgrace to her religious fanatic mother. Instead of representing sexual freedom and expression, Tangie represents an unfeeling nymphomaniac with little respect for herself or others. Crystal is framed as a victim. Weak and complicit in her own demise, Crystal is the antithesis of all Black woman stereotypes. She is voiceless and without agency (which is entirely different from her description in the choreopoem). She is the quintessential bad Black mother stereotype, unable and unwilling to protect her children by remaining in an unhealthy and unstable intimate relationship. Like the others, Crystal is held fully responsible for what happens to her (and her children). Both Tangie and Crystal's voices are represented by the Lady in Red in the choreopoem, but are significantly differentiated in the film.

Furthermore, Perry created actual characters which do not exist in the original choreopoem. Writing new characters into existence is allowed through creative agency and not inherently troublesome. However, certain issues arise with the new characters. Shange indiscriminately created colors of representation (the rainbow) without distinguishing the voices or the experiences because the collective voice and experience is that of a Black girl. Shange's ambiguity leaves room for interpretation. Perry's design however is more about staying true to a limited sense of possibility. The new characters are extreme and in some cases peculiarly pitiful. Perry's characters fit a preexisting mold: the educated Black bitch (Jo), the Mammy-like religious fanatic (Alice) who is also a bad Black mother, and the childless Matriarch shrew (Gilda). Perry also situates the stories around women's issues with each other, including jealousy (which exists between Tangie and her sister Nyla) and colorism (demonstrated in the scene between Alice and Tangie).

The women who are mothers, or able to be mothers, are presented in a derogatory light. Whether through abortion, ignorance, infertility, or death, none of the women are capable of being good mothers. The one exception potentially is Loretta Devine's character, a nurse, community service worker, and mentor. However, because she is not a biological mother and is incapable of emulating a traditional, heterosexual, Christian relationship, her good deeds are canceled out by her loneliness (and her man's infidelity). The character Kelly is also a bad Black mother because she is unable to conceive due to a previously untreated sexually transmitted infection, and she is unable to save/help/protect Crystal's children though she had time and opportunity.

Perry's film also mires Black women's sexuality. Sex is seen as violent, regrettable, forgettable and full of consequences. Sex represents unwanted pregnancy, scandal, violent rape, unhealthy promiscuity, infertility from disease, and the contraction of a life-threatening illness. Conversely, the choreopoem builds on a narrative of healthy sexuality that, while not always framed in positive circumstances or without consequences, is empowering and liberating in its own right. For example, the "graduation nite" poem is about losing one's virginity intentionally. The poem "One" chronicles Lady in Red, who is like Tangie in that her sexual exploits reveal desperation to be held, wanted, and loved. Her nightly tears signal the pain and need for something more, but the fear is that it may never be possible. Tangie's character is not humanized enough to allow viewers to sympathize or empathize with her. The film skews her sexuality by insinuating that a Black woman who embraces her sexuality, enjoys non-monogamous sex, or adopts a masculinized view of sex must have endured some kind of sexual abuse and must be inherently bad. Perry creates issues that were not there. Issues with men manifest themselves in failed attempts at intimacy (Tangie), a loveless marriage giving way to a husband on the down-low (Jo), and rape that is blamed at least partially on the victim's unbelievable naiveté (Yasmine).

In *Black Looks: Race and Representation*, bell hooks talks about the absence of Black women's criticism of movies. Some Black women admit "they never went to movies expecting to see compelling representations of Black femaleness."[32] While hooks's critique predates the decade of the Tyler Perry franchise, there has been ample opportunity for a shift in representation and response by audiences. Currently Perry might argue that he is catering to his audience. However, controlling images of Black womanhood take on special meaning because the authority to define these symbols is a major instrument of power. Perry's power and influence to shape social and cultural imaginations about the everydayness of Black life is undeniable—the question is what does he do with that power?

## LESSONS ON BLACK MEN

What does *For Colored Girls* teach us about Black men? Black masculinity and manhood perspectives call attention to fluctuating and conflicting identities resulting largely from Western definitions of manhood.[33] By questioning popular misperceptions of race and gender, Black masculinity and manhood research emphasizes how the daily practices of Black men are impacted within dominant structures. Black masculinity research in its truest form speaks to Black men's societal health and wellness.

Positioning Black men as people rather than objects of human history is a viable means of exploring and explaining the Black/African-American experience. What roles do Black men play in Perry's film? With regard to popular culture, Perry's depiction of Black women's strength is shaped at the expense of the Black man. *For Colored Girls* centralizes the demonization of Black men by presenting Black women as perpetual victims of Black masculinity. Too often the Black man is framed negatively (e.g., a rapist or psychopath), and women are warned of his potential for violence.

Perry's characterizations are more disturbing when aligned with historic stereotypes of Black men. Throughout the film an implied circumstantial absence of a positive father-figure leads to the emasculation of men and the indoctrination of women who assume their independence is paramount to happiness. The absence of good Black men is a primary theme. Fathers and husbands are "missing in action" to the extent their absence and their presence serve to construct trauma in the lives of women. Does Perry mean to bring to screen the private discussions of the Black community?

In *The Impact of Fatherlessness on Black Women*, the author examines the manifestations of pain attributed to the missing Black man. Barras outlines the consequence of "father deprivation" as a series of traits experienced by some Black women. 1) The "un"factor: The fatherless daughter/woman believes she is unworthy and unlovable. 2) The triple fears factor/abandonment syndrome: The fatherless daughter/woman fears rejection, abandonment, and commitment. 3) The sexual healing factor: The fatherless daughter/woman's sexual behavior may range from promiscuity to an aversion to intimacy. 4) The over factor: The fatherless daughter/woman is determined not to allow anyone, man or woman, to discover her wound. 5) The rage factor: The fatherless daughter/woman holds unexplained anger and rage, sometimes on the surface and sometimes out of sight.[34]

Perry's lens constructs the Jezebel, the angry Black woman, the middle class professional obsessed with achievement, and the religionist who trusts no masculine figure but God. Throughout the film there are overt and subtle references to the "crazy bitch." This rhetorical framing reflects ongoing allegations of Black men dehumanizing Black women, which is often associated with the African Diaspora and now popular culture. Indeed, the power of language is evident throughout a film. Meaning starts with the title: *For Colored Girls*. The film is for and about this specific audience. Meaning occurs with the first scene: After sex Tangie is called a bitch. Poetry is performance where seeing and hearing become assumptions about "truth."

We do not assert that *For Colored Girls* intends to recreate or reinforce a narrative about men. Instead we seek to understand how images occur here. The task is to interrogate depictions of manhood. Men are created via imaginative memory and interaction with the main female characters. On film we see what is absent from the choreopoem: literal interactions between men and women. On film men are detrimental to women and present only long enough to cause emotional and physical damage (e.g., giving women HIV, leaving women pregnant, causing infertility through the transmission of an sexually transmitted infection, and rape).[35]

Although the original choreopoem did not feature Black male actors, it may have contained more substance. Shange was criticized for her rhetorical depictions[36] but the play managed to reflect the pain of women without completely disparaging men. There was no emphasis on the male voice. By extension, the play did not present a holistic and homogenous representation of Black men. We do not necessarily see the woman beater, child abuser, rapist, and pedophile. Yet we understand that consequences of a White, patriarchal culture include the limited views of Blackness which make filmic representations all the more influential.

Arguably, Perry had the opportunity to expand on the play and create more than one positive Black male character. Perry's treatment could have been reimagined with more contextualization on the external factors that impact the Black male psyche and demeanor.[37] For example, the inclusion of a character on the down-low[38] could have been an opportunity to speak out about homophobia in the Black community, and the ways in which fear contributes to silencing non-heterosexuality (often at the expense of unsuspecting Black women). Likewise, there was also an opportunity to address miseducation around undiagnosed mental illness, as a way to better understand Beau Willie Brown's struggles with what we are led to believe is post-traumatic stress disorder as a war veteran.

In his article "Does Tyler Perry Have a Problem With Black Men," Mychel Denzel Smith argues that Black women are the most damaged by Perry's limited and limiting representations, but Black men also do not fare well:

> In his [Perry's] black-and-white world of morality, Black men are narrowly confined to two camps: the righteous and the evil, with many more falling into the evil category. They are all too often portrayed as drug dealers with a taste for blood, womanizers with no heart, abusive with no chance for redemption (save for through joining the church and accepting Jesus Christ as their personal savior), or thugs without respectable jobs or hope for a brighter day.[39]

Perry's work can be best understood in the context of Black representations in American films. Donald Bogle explains that Black re/presentations in films are most often not intended to do harm, yet they do reinforce problematic stereotypes.[40] Perry's characterizations of Black men are an amalgamation of historical assumptions, existing realities, and unredeemable possibilities. In his collection, Perry routinely creates Black male characters in diametrically opposed extremes (idiotic or brilliant; responsible or comical; and good or bad). He fails to create representations of Black men as human and vulnerable.

Bogle also identifies basic characterizations of Black male stereotypes that have been reproduced on film, including the Uncle Tom, the Coon, and the brutal Black Buck.[41] These characters are largely gender-specific. The Tom character is based on Harriet Beecher Stowe's novel *Uncle Tom's Cabin*, which glamorizes the submissive Black man. Considered a *Good Negro* character, the Tom is a Black male version of Mammy. Toms are generally emasculated by their feminized demeanor and their unfailing submission to Whiteness. Next, the Coon characterization presents Black men as buffoons whose sole purpose in film is comedic relief. This character exists less in *For Colored Girls*, but is very apparent in Perry's larger body of work. The Coon will dance, sing, clown, and inspire laughter based on ignorant antics. Bogle identifies two types of Coon: a) the Pickaninny is childlike, and b) the Uncle Remus is elderly, harmless, and congenial. Uncle Remus is a first-cousin to the Tom, yet he distinguishes himself by his quaint, naïve, and comic philosophizing.[42] Another popularized version of the Coon is the Sambo whose character is lazy, irresponsible, and humorous.

The Black Buck character was popularized in D. W. Griffith's *The Birth of a Nation*. The Black Buck type could be broken into two categories, the Black Brute and the Black Buck. "The Black brute was a barbaric black out to raise havoc. Audiences could assume that his physical violence served as an outlet for a man who was sexually repressed."[43] By comparison, the pure Black Bucks are "always big, baadddd niggers, oversexed and savage, violent and frenzied as they lust for white flesh."[44] The Black Buck is similar to the Mandingo character, which links Black men to animalistic, violent, and predatory sexual behaviors.

Perry's critics often cite his work as grossly reliant on centuries-old stereotypes. Spike Lee's claim that Perry's work is *coonery* speaks to the commonalities between contemporary work and minstrel shows that depicted Black characters in similar ways (superstitious, ignorant, naïve, and happy-go-lucky). Until *For Colored Girls*, Perry had not engaged the Black man as dangerous. Most of his other films, plays, and television shows present Black men as clownish, feminized characters, usually abusing women through their absence or emotional neglect.

Beau Willie Brown's character exemplifies stereotypes of Black men as inherently angry, violent, and sexually aggressive.[45] Two additional male characters that do not exist in the original choreopoem are Donald (the police officer) and Carl (Jo's down-low husband). They are framed as the good and bad Black man respectively. Both are professionals and married to Black women (marriage is also not present in the choreopoem). The men fail to be good husbands for different reasons. Donald is unable to heal his wife from past trauma, and Carl is deceptive and untruthful regarding his same-sex attraction to men. The men also fail as lovers due to Donald's inability to impregnate his infertile wife and Carl's bisexuality which leads to his unsuspecting wife contracting HIV. Last, manhood is also represented by the nameless men involved in sexual encounters with Tangie, and Frank who is Juanita's on-again, off-again lover.

Counter to the bad Black mother stereotype is the bad Black father. Beau Willie Brown fails as a father because of his inability to provide for his children. Further, he is a bad Black Buck because he is abusive and mentally ill. He eventually murders his own children as a way of punishing their mother. Other examples of the bad Black father include the incestuous pedophile alluded to in a conversation between Alice and Tangie, and the man who impregnates Nyla but is absent throughout her consideration of parenthood and eventual decision of abortion. Donald is also framed as a bad Black father because of his inability/failure to be a father.

Donald's character offers an alternative to the other bad Black men in the film. He represents a particular type of Black man for women who are lucky enough to find him. He is the patriarchal poster child; a provider and a protector for his wife and other women in the film. He is faithful, supportive, and present. Donald's existence however does not challenge the egregiousness he attempts to rectify.

Interestingly, the choreopoem's positive Black male character is not manifested in the film. Toussaint L'Ouverture, a figment of Lady in Brown's imagination, manifests in a boy with the same name (Toussaint Jones). She recounts her love for this Black man. Toussaint is not present in Perry's film but discussed while Gilda tries to distract Crystal's children from their father's rage. Toussaint may have been Shange's way of redeeming Black men. His absence from *For Colored Girls* may have limited possibilities to show positive images of Black men on screen.

## HE SAID, SHE SAID: TYLER PERRY'S WORDS (IN BLACK WOMEN'S MOUTHS)

Perry's words are blended between Shange's beautifully subtle poetry, and his literal language, which is often abrupt and distracting. From the beginning it is difficult for an unfamiliar viewer (one who has not read Shange's choreopoem) to distinguish between the original and remake. The implications in the words, however, make it remarkably clear when he is speaking and what he is saying (about/to Black women). If *For Colored Girls Who Have Considered Suicide When The Rainbow Is Enuf* is about Black women's empowerment and self-actualization, Perry's version is about pushing Black women to the periphery and centering the pathologies that surround them, making them interchangeable.

As a writer of Black women's stories, Perry puts words in the mouths of Black women. For example, when playing Madea he is creating a script for the Black woman to speak: Seasoned Black women speak to younger Black women (on the screen and in the audience) about what they need to do and/or what they should want in life. This includes the unintentional wisdom sometimes blanketed between Madea's rants and two Matriarch characters in *For Colored Girls*. Phylicia Rashad and Whoopi Goldberg both play the roles of judgmental Matriarchs. Perry's words in their mouths become pronouncements, judgments, and proclamations that are contrary to the purpose of the original work. Consistent with Perry's other films, his words berate Black women while disguising it as celebration.

In one scene Tangie and Alice exchange lines of the poem One, which in its original context chronicles the complicated and nuanced sex/love life of Lady in Red, whose promiscuity is a result of having been abandoned many times by lovers. She sees her own exploits as devastating and delightful. Perry's reinterpretation traces the words of the monologue, and repeats them in judgment rather than the vulnerable honesty in which the work is intended. At the end of one poem, he inserts words that are not there, speaking to Tangie and seemingly any Black woman who dares to embrace non-traditional, non-monogamous sex(uality):

Tangie: "You don't know me."

Alice: "I know you. You're the devil."

The conversation makes a claim that does not exist in the original text. Tangie's promiscuity is characterized somewhere between religion and a response to childhood sexual abuse. Additionally, Perry shows that abuse has arrested both mother and daughter, causing one woman to become chaste and the other promiscuous.

Another example of Perry's words pushing judgment on Black women is the exchange between Gilda and Crystal after her children are murdered by their father.

> Gilda: "What is your plan? What are you doing baby? You just gonna lay in here and die? . . . It wasn't just him honey."
>
> Crystal: "But I tried to stop him."
>
> Gilda: "You had to stop him long before he got to that window."
>
> Crystal: "Are you saying this is my fault?"
>
> Gilda: "What I'm saying Crystal is you gonna have to take responsibility in some of this. How much of it you take is up to you. But you gotta take some of it. Until you do, you're just gonna be living to die. Mark my words. But you gotta get up from here."

In these and other exchanges, Perry manages to put words of judgment against Black women in the mouths of Black women.

## WE WANT OUR STUFF BACK: CONCLUDING THOUGHTS ON RECLAIMING OURSELVES THROUGH OUR WOMANIST AND MASCULINIST PERSPECTIVES

> Like a kleptomaniac workin hard & forgettin while stealin this is mine/this ain't yr stuff/now why don't you put me back & let me hang out in my own self . . . hey man/where are you goin wid alla my stuff/this is a woman's trip & I need my stuff . . . i want my stuff back/my rhythms & my voice/open my mouth/& let me talk ya outta/throwin my shit in the sewer/this is some delicate leg & whimsical kiss . . . I want my own things/ how I lived them/ & give me my memories/ how I waz when I waz there/ you can't have them or do nothing wit them/ stealin my shit from me/ don't make it yrs/ makes it stolen.[46]

The aforementioned poem "somebody almost walked off wid alla my stuff"[47] illustrates the ways in which Perry re-centered the narrative of Black womanhood in the filmic version of *For Colored Girls*. Perry's agency as a producer and director is not above reproach. We seek to reimagine ways of reclaiming our imagined possibilities and call for more distinction in how Black women and men are represented. Perry's bread and butter audience has increased beyond his church-play days—but the message has not matured. The moral integrity of Perry's storylines overlaps into what seems like the same stock characters reintroduced over and over again. We want Black characters made visible without being vilified.

We want our stuff. Agency for Black women and men is linked to our struggle to claim and retain our self-respect, dignity, self-love and self-power. For some men, agency attempts to challenge myths that are often perpetuated (myths of inferiority, violence, sexual aggression, and irresponsibility). For some women, agency may include the robust characters on Shange's page (imaginative, resilient, and interesting).

As was stated in this chapter's introduction, we acknowledge that Perry's work resonates with a large audience and not everyone will find our critique compelling. Perry has an audience because he responds to the public's fascination with stories about the lives of Black women. We believe *For Colored Girls*, in its original context, was a call for transformation. Any interpretation of the original text should deemphasize former scripts, and reemphasize vulnerabilities and contradictions of race and gender in everyday life. Shange gave what Perry takes away—voice. Shange puts it this way:

> I was very concerned about and very passionately committed to the idea of creating new rituals and new mythologies for people of color . . . [because] the mythologies that were available to us were negative images . . . their images of [B]lack people were not necessarily false images, but they were certainly images that were concerned with our relationship with the Other as opposed to our relationship with ourselves.[48]

Perry's rendition does little to challenge negative images. Returning to the notion of the gaze, his version met the demands of marketing race and gender. Shange directly refutes this view and since the 1970s has worked to keep the play accessible for the Black female audience it was originally intended to reach.

As a well-intentioned visionary, Perry offered a new reading. As a storyteller, he was redundant in his interpretations. Yes his characters exist, but there are more versions of Black womanhood and manhood that include versatility, emotional viability, confidence, and self-awareness. *For Colored Girls* was a unique opportunity to explore the myriad possibilities. Black folks do not have the luxury of multiple representations in the media, so every representation counts. Being Black on screen (or anywhere for that matter) is a metaphysical dilemma we have not yet conquered.

## NOTES

1. Stuart Hall, "Encoding, Decoding" in *The Black Studies Reader*, ed. Jacqueline Bobo, Cynthia Hudley, and Claudine Michel (New York: Routledge, 2004), 255–63.

2. bell hooks, *Reel to Real: Race, Sex, and Class at the Movies* (New York: Routledge, 1996).

3. Daryl Cumber Dance, ed., *Honey Hush: An Anthology of African American Women's Humor* (New York: W.W. Norton and Company, 1998).

4. John F. Callahan, "A Brown Study: Sterling Brown's Legacy of Compassionate Connections" *Callaloo* 21, no. 4 (1998): 896–910.

5. Patricia Hill Collins, *Black Feminist Thought: Knowledge, Consciousness, and the Politics of Empowerment*, 1990. Reprint (New York: Routledge, 2008); Layli Phillips, ed., *The Womanist Reader* (New York: Routledge, 2006).

6. Akasha Gloria Hull, *Soul Talk: The New Spirituality of African American Women* (Rochester, VT: Inner Traditions International, 2001), 217.

7. Mark Anthony Neal, *New Black Man* (New York: Routledge, 2006), xx–xxi.

8. Rockell Brown and Kimberly D. Campbell, "Representin' the Ladies: A Negotiated Response to Tyler Perry's Portrayal of African American Female Characters" in *Interpreting Tyler Perry: Perspectives on Race, Class, Gender and Sexuality*, eds. Jamel Santa Cruze Bell and Ronald L. Jackson II (New York: Routledge, 2014), 270–87.

9. Jamel Santa Cruze Bell and Ronald L. Jackson II., eds., *Interpreting Tyler Perry: Perspectives on Race, Class, Gender and Sexuality* (New York: Routledge, 2014).

10. Kia M. Natisse, "Tyler Perry Thumbs Nose at Critics with New 'Madea' Movie" *The Grio*, April 22, 2011, http://www.thegrio.com/entertainment/tyler-perry-thumbs-his-nose-at-critics-with-madeas-big-happy-family.php.

11. bell hooks, *Black Looks: Race and Representation* (Boston, MA: South End Press, 1992).

12. Robin M. Boylorn, "As Seen on TV: An Autoethnographic Reflection on Race and Reality Television" *Critical Studies in Media Communication* 25, no. 4 (2008): 413–33.

13. Donald Bogle, *Toms, Coons, Mulattoes, Mammies, and Bucks: An Interpretive History of Blacks in American Films*, 4th ed. (New York: Continuum, 2001); Brown and Campbell, "Representin' the Ladies"; hooks, *Black Looks*; Means Coleman, "The (Self-Appointed) Savior."

14. Ibid.

15. Jimi Izrael, "In Defense of For Colored Girls" *NPR: Tell Me More*, November 12, 2010, http://www.npr.org/blogs/tellmemore/2010/11/12/131275640/in-defense-of-colored-girls.

16. Robin Means Coleman, "Tyler Perry: The (Self-Appointed) Savior of Black Womanhood" in *Our Voices: Essays in Culture, Ethnicity and Communication*, eds. Alberto Gonzalez, Marsha Houston, and Victoria Chen (New York: Oxford, 2011), 53–59; Armond White, "For Oprah Winfrey Fans Who've Considered Victimhood When Too Many Coincidences are Enough" *New York Press*, http://nypress.com/for-oprah-winfrey-fans-whove-considered-victimhood-when-too-many-coincidences-are-enough/.

17. Ashoncrawley, "On Audience" *Crunk Feminist Collective* (blog), http://crunkfeministcollective.wordpress.com/2010/07/08/on-audience/; Moyazb, "On #ForColoredGirls" *Crunk Feminist Collective* (blog), http://crunkfeministcollective.wordpress.com/2010/11/08/on-forcoloredgirls-spoiler-alert/; Sheridf, "Tyler Perry Almost Walked Off Wid Alla my Stuff" *Crunk Feminist Collective* (blog), http://crunkfeministcollective.wordpress.com/2010/11/22/tyler-perry-almost-walked-off-wid-alla-my-stuff/.

18. Amber West, "Metamorphic Rainbows: The Journey of Shange's For Colored Girls From Poetry to Television and Beyond" *Journal of Research on Women and Gender* 1 (2010): 191–208.

19. Ibid.

20. Hull, *Soul Talk*, 163.

21. "Critics Rip Tyler Perry's 'For Colored Girls' to Pieces" *Eurweb.com*, Last modified October 22, 2010, http://www.eurweb.com/2010/10/critics-rip-tyler-perrys-for-colored-girls-to-pieces/.

22. Izrael, "In Defense of For Colored Girls."

23. Boylorn, "As Seen on TV"; Collins, *Black Feminist Thought*; hooks, *Black Looks*.

24. Trudier Harris, *From Mammies to Militants: Domestics in Black American Literature* (Philadelphia: Temple University Press, 1982), 4.

25. Brown and Campbell, "Representin' the Ladies"; Collins, *Black Feminist Thought*.

26. Daniel Patrick Moynihan, *The Negro Family: The Case for National Action* (Washington, DC: Government Printing Office, 1965).

27. Ibid.

28. Marilyn Yarbrough and Crystal Bennett, "Cassandra and the 'Sistahs': The Peculiar Treatment of African American Women in the Myth of Women as Liars" *Journal of Gender, Race, and Justice* 3, no. 2 (2000): 625–48.
29. Ibid.
30. Collins, *Black Feminist Thought*.
31. Moynihan, "The Negro Family."
32. hooks, *Black Looks*, 119.
33. Ronald Jackson II and Mark C. Hopson, eds., *Masculinity in the Black imagination: Politics of Communicating Race and Manhood* (New York: Peter Lang, 2011).
34. Jonetta R. Barras, *Whatever Happened to Daddy's Little Girl?: The Impact of Fatherlessness on Black Women* (New York: Ballantine, 2002).
35. Courtland Milloy, "For Black Men Who Have Considered Homicide After Watching Another Tyler Perry Movie" *The Washington Post*, November 8, 2010, http://www.washingtonpost.com/wpdyn/content/article/2010/11/07/AR2010110704428.html?nav=email page.
36. Neal A. Lester, *Ntozake Shange: A Critical Study of the Plays* (New York: Garland, 1995).
37. Merc80, "Tyler Perry Versus . . ."
38. This character does not exist in the original choreopoem, but does appear in the revised edition released alongside the film in a new poem Shange penned to address the dangers of Black men being on the down low called, "Positive."
39. Mychal Denzel Smith, "Does Tyler Perry Have a Problem With Black Men?" *The Grio*, November 4, 2010, http://www.thegrio.com/entertainment/does-tyler-perry-have-a-problem-with-black-men.php.
40. Bogle, *Toms, Coons, Mulattoes, Mammies*.
41. Ibid.
42. Ibid, 8.
43. Ibid, 13.
44. Ibid, 13–14.
45. Mark P. Orbe and Mark C. Hopson, "Looking at the Front Door: Exploring Images of the Black Male on MTV's 'The Real World'" in *Readings in Intercultural Contexts: Experiences and Contexts*, eds. Judith N. Martin, Thomas K. Nakayama, and Lisa A. Flores (Boston, MA: McGraw Hill, 2002), 219–26.
46. Ntozake Shange, *For Colored Girls Who Have Considered Suicide When the Rainbow is Enuf*, 1975. Reprint (New York: Scribner, 2010), 49–50.
47. Ibid.
48. Lester, *Ntozake Shange*, 13.

# BIBLIOGRAPHY

Ashoncrawley. "On Audience." *Crunk Feminist Collective* (blog), http://crunkfeministcollective.wordpress.com/2010/07/08/on-audience/.
Barras, Jonetta R. *Whatever Happened to Daddy's Little Girl?: The Impact of Fatherlessness on Black Women*. New York: Ballantine, 2002.
Bell, Jamel Santa Cruze, and Ronald L. Jackson II., eds. *Interpreting Tyler Perry: Perspectives on Race, Class, Gender and Sexuality*. New York: Routledge, 2014.
Bogle, Donald. *Toms, Coons, Mulattoes, Mammies, and Bucks: An Interpretive History of Blacks in American Films*. 4th ed. New York: Continuum, 2001.
Boylorn, Robin M. "As Seen on TV: An Autoethnographic Reflection on Race and Reality Television." *Critical Studies in Media Communication* 25, no. 4 (2008): 413–33.
Brown, Rockell, and Kimberly D. Campbell. "Representin' the Ladies: A Negotiated Response to Tyler Perry's Portrayal of African American Female Characters." In *Interpreting Tyler Perry: Perspectives on Race, Class, Gender and Sexuality*, edited by Jamel Santa Cruze Bell and Ronald L. Jackson II, 270–87. New York: Routledge, 2014.

Callahan, John F. "A Brown Study: Sterling Brown's Legacy of Compassionate Connections." *Callaloo* 21, no. 4 (1998): 896–910.

Collins, Patricia Hill. *Black Feminist Thought: Knowledge, Consciousness, and the Politics of Empowerment.* 1990. Reprint, New York: Routledge, 2008.

"Critics Rip Tyler Perry's 'For Colored Girls' to Pieces." *Eurweb.com.* Last modified October 22, 2010. http://www.eurweb.com/2010/10/critics-rip-tyler-perrys-for-colored-girls-to-pieces/.

Dance, Daryl Cumber, ed. *Honey Hush: An Anthology of African American Women's Humor.* New York, W.W. Norton and Company, 1998.

*For Colored Girls.* Directed by Tyler Perry. 2010. Santa Monica, CA: Lions Gate Entertainment, 2011. DVD.

Hall, Stuart. "What is this 'Black' in Black Popular Culture?" In *The Black Studies Reader*, edited by Jacqueline Bobo, Cynthia Hudley, and Claudine Michel, 255–63. New York: Routledge, 2004.

Hall, Stuart. "Encoding, Decoding." In *The Cultural Studies Reader*, edited by Simon During, 1977. Reprint, 90–103. New York: Routledge, 1993.

Harris, Trudier. *From Mammies to Militants: Domestics in Black American Literature.* Philadelphia: Temple University Press, 1982.

hooks, bell. *Reel to Real: Race, Sex, and Class at the Movies.* New York: Routledge, 1996.

hooks, bell. *Black Looks: Race and Representation.* Boston, MA: South End Press, 1992.

Hopson, Mark C. *The Talking Drum: Exploring Black Communication and Critical Memory in Intercultural Communication Contexts.* Cresskill, NJ: Hampton Press, 2011.

Hull, Akasha Gloria. *Soul Talk: The New Spirituality of African American Women.* Rochester, VT: Inner Traditions International, 2001.

Izrael, Jimi. "In Defense of For Colored Girls." *NPR: Tell Me More.* November 12, 2010, http://www.npr.org/blogs/tellmemore/2010/11/12/131275640/in-defense-of-colored-girls.

*Jezebel Stereotype.* Jim Crow Museum of Racist Memorabilia. Accessed May 21, 2011, http://www.ferris.edu/htmls/news/jimcrow/jezebel/.

Jackson, II. Ronald L. and Mark C. Hopson, eds. *Masculinity in the Black Imagination: Politics of Communicating Race and Manhood.* New York: Peter Lang, 2011.

Lester, Neal. A. *Ntozake Shange: A Critical Study of the Plays.* New York: Garland, 1995.

Means Coleman, Robin. "Tyler Perry: The (Self-Appointed) Savior of Black Womanhood." In *Our Voices: Essays in Culture, Ethnicity and Communication*, edited by Alberto Gonzalez, Marsha Houston & Victoria Chen, 53–59. New York: Oxford, 2011.

Merc80, "Tyler Perry Versus . . . " *Merc80.com* (blog), http://merc80.com/2011/04/26/tyler-perry-versus/.

Milloy, Courtland. "For Black Men Who Have Considered Homicide After Watching Another Tyler Perry Movie." *The Washington Post.* November 8, 2010, http://www.washingtonpost.com/wp-dyn/content/article/2010/11/07/AR2010110704428.html?nav=emailpage.

Moyazb. "On #ForColoredGirls." *Crunk Feminist Collective* (blog), http://crunkfeministcollective.wordpress.com/2010/11/08/on-forcoloredgirls-spoiler-alert/.

Moynihan, Daniel Patrick. *The Negro Family: The Case for National Action.* Washington, DC: Government Printing Office, 1965.

Natisse, Kia M. "Tyler Perry Thumbs Nose at Critics with New 'Madea' Movie." *The Grio.* April 22, 2011, http://www.thegrio.com/entertainment/tyler-perry-thumbs-his-nose-at-critics-with-madeas-big-happy-family.php.

Neal, Mark Anthony. *New Black Man.* New York: Routledge, 2006.

Orbe, Mark P. and Mark C. Hopson. "Looking at the Front Door: Exploring Images of the Black Male on MTV's 'The Real World.'" In *Readings in Intercultural Contexts*: *Experiences and Contexts*, edited by Judith N. Martin, Thomas K. Nakayama, and Lisa A. Flores, 219–26. Boston, MA: McGraw Hill, 2002.

Perry, Tyler. Interview. *An Empire of His Own: Tyler Perry Beat the Odds to Become a Multihyphenate Cottage Industry by Refusing to Cede Creative Control. And He's Just Getting Started*, Matthew Belloni and Stephen Galloway, Hollywood Reporter. February 19, 2009.

Phillips, Layli, ed. *The Womanist Reader.* New York: Routledge, 2006.

RBoylorn. "A Return to Myself: A Delayed Response to For Colored Girls," *Crunk Feminist Collective* (blog), http://crunkfeministcollective.wordpress.com/2010/11/29/a-return-to-myself-a-delayed-response-to-for-colored-girls/.
*Sapphire Caricature*. Jim Crow Museum of Racist Memorabilia. Accessed May 21, 2011, http://www.ferris.edu/htmls/news/jimcrow/sapphire/.
Shange, Ntozake. *For Colored Girls Who Have Considered Suicide When the Rainbow is Enuf.* 1975. Reprint, New York: Scribner, 1997.
Shange, Ntozake. *For Colored Girls Who Have Considered Suicide When the Rainbow is Enuf.* 1975. Reprint, New York: Scribner, 2010.
Sheridf. "Tyler Perry Almost Walked Off Wid Alla my Stuff," *Crunk Feminist Collective* (blog), http://crunkfeministcollective.wordpress.com/2010/11/22/tyler-perry-almost-walked-off-wid-alla-my-stuff/.
Smith, Mychal Denzel. "Does Tyler Perry Have a Problem With Black Men?" *The Grio*. November 4, 2010, http://www.thegrio.com/entertainment/does-tyler-perry-have-a-problem-with-black-men.php.
West, Amber. "Metamorphic Rainbows: The Journey of Shange's For Colored Girls From Poetry to Television and Beyond." *Journal of Research on Women and Gender* 1 (2010): 191–208.
White, Armond. "For Oprah Winfrey Fans Who've Considered Victimhood When Too Many Coincidences are Enough." New York Press, http://nypress.com/for-oprah-winfrey-fans-whove-considered-victimhood-when-too-many-coincidences-are-enoughs/.
Yarbrough, Marilyn and Crystal Bennett. "Cassandra and the 'Sistahs': The Peculiar Treatment of African American Women in the Myth of Women as Liars." *Journal of Gender, Race, and Justice* 3, no. 2 (2000): 625–48.

*II*

# The Music Industry

*Chapter Six*

# Mother Appreciation Rap (MAR) as a Genre and Representation of Black Motherhood

## VaNatta S. Ford and Natasha R. Howard

Rap is a musical art form within the greater culture of hip hop that has great rhetorical value for both the rapper (also known as the MC) and the audience or receivers of the music. Geneva Smitherman writes, "Rap music is rooted in the Black Oral Tradition of tonal semantics, narrativising, signifation/signifyin,' the Dozens, Africanized syntax, and other communicative practices."[1] As one of hip hop cultures' four elements, rap music encompasses a vast range of subject matter artfully crafted over gritty drumbeats and raw baselines. In discussing the value of rap music, Michael Eric Dyson discusses that, "The best rappers are not interested in generating speech for its own sake, but in crafting superior rhetorical vehicles to articulate their distinct worldviews."[2]

One of the interesting traits of rap music is the fact that it cannot *all* be categorized the same way. Although numerous male and female rappers often use bravado to boast of their *sick* skills on the mic (microphone), how much money they have, or what expensive cars they drive, there is unquestionably a variety of subject matter that rap artists discuss in their music. Some MCs like Mos Def, Lupe Fiasco, Common, and the rap duo Dead Prez talk about Black history and social consciousness. Others like singer/rapper Lauryn Hill speak of their neighborhoods, how they grew up, and even their faith in God. In addition, another topic discussed by rap artists, which has garnered much research attention, is the role and significance of women.

Hip hop music is complex and multifaceted with many styles that have been both oppressive and encouraging. Thus, to think that all songs that discuss women are about misogyny would be incorrect. Yet this reflects the misguided notions of many outside of hip hop or urban culture.[3] It cannot be denied that many rap artists who are played in heavy rotation on radio stations across the United States obsessively talk about sex, money, dealing drugs, and even how women may fit into this lifestyle. However, there is a topic in rap music that *conscious* and *not-so-conscious* rappers seem to rhyme with passion and feeling—their love and appreciation for their mothers. Such a discussion of this important female figure in their life helps paint a picture of Black motherhood for rap music audiences. Although Black women may not be featured on the actual song discussing their roles as mothers, the way in which rappers discuss their own perceptions of these women serve as representations of Black American women.

The topic, or genre, in rap music presented for this analysis will be referred to as Mother Appreciation Rap. Though hip hop music can be easily pigeon-holed into a genre of misogyny and what Dyson refers to as "femiphobia," many rappers have emerged from this hole to talk about their appreciation for their mothers or other matriarchal figures that have positively impacted their lives.[4] Rappers such as the late Tupac Shakur, Jay-Z, Nas, Ghostface Killah, and Kanye West, to name a few, have all penned songs about their love and adoration for their mothers. Their songs were analyzed in order to assess how these rappers presented Black women as mothers.

The interesting aspect to how mothers and motherhood, in general, are discussed is that usually these narratives come from males, with few female rappers choosing to discuss their reproductive choices instead.[5] Additionally, these narratives have often run the spectrum from being cautionary tales of teenage motherhood/parenthood and unfavorable discussions of single mothers (often referred to as "baby mama drama" songs), to those that fit within the purposes of this study—mother appreciation. In particular, with regard to the songs that will be described in this analysis, mothers are equivocated to the Strong Black Woman archetype that has long existed within the Black community. Harris-Perry points out that the Strong Black Woman archetype is lauded for her dedication to "her own children, whether she has a male partner or not" and for her ability to carry on and not "require physical or economic protection from men."[6] These same qualities are seen in the lyrics from songs penned by rappers previously mentioned.

Additionally, the Strong Black Woman trope "is a deeply empowering symbol of endurance and hope. Her unassailable spirit is uplifting. Her courage in the face of seemingly insurmountable adversity emboldens black men and women when facing their own life challenges."[7] The key traits that are praised and are held up as the reasons these males adore their mothers are because of how their mothers seemingly fit within this complicated archetype. These descriptions run in staunch contrast to how younger women that are peers of these rappers are described in many other hip hop songs. Yet the basic commonality of these songs and the positive themes related to motherhood reflect a narrative indicative of a possible genre within hip hop music.

This analysis uses the descriptive form of generic criticism drawing on the work of Sonja Foss to discuss how a genre of Mother Appreciation Rap (hereafter referred to as MAR) exists among the songs "Hey Mama" (by Kanye West), "Dear Mama" (by Tupac), "All That I Got is You" (by Ghostface Killah and Mary J. Blige), "I Made It" (by Jay-Z), and "Dance" (by Nas).[8] These five songs were selected because they are by well known and respected rap artists who have large fan bases, sold numerous albums, and are considered by many as hip hop icons. This analysis will: (1) briefly describe generic criticism; (2) give a brief summary of each song chosen as part of this possible genre; (3) organize the rhetorical characteristics that can be seen or used in creating a MAR genre; and (4) explain why these songs make up a MAR genre and the implications and contradictions of there being such a genre in hip hop music. Examinations of these songs are significant and will add to existing research on this type of music because it will show that hip hop is not completely negative towards women but is also concerned with uplifting mother figures. Though female rappers have illustrated love for their mother figures in their music, this analysis specifically focuses on how male rappers view mother figures within their music.

## GENERIC CRITICISM

Each of the five songs selected share similar and divergent characteristics that seem to provide a genre where they fit. In the study of genres, Sharon Downey discusses that, ". . . discovering the recurrent elements of discourse which result from constraints imposed on a rhetor's response *is* genre analysis . . ."[9] Raymond Rodgers submits that, "The central assumption underlying genre criticism is basically essentialistic: by focusing upon the commonalities of discourse instead of the peculiarities, critics can move closer to grasping its essential nature."[10] This argument can be made for the existing genre of MAR. Since hip hop music is often viewed as misogynistically one-sided, showing that there are songs within this musical tradition that uplift women helps identify overlooked and underrepresented aspects of this musical form. Rodgers further reiterates this point by drawing on the work of Campbell and Jamieson stating: "The editors insisted initially that the justification for a generic claim is the understanding it produces rather than the ordered universe it creates, and the first criterion they set for generic criticism was that classification is justified only by the critical illumination it produces not by the neatness of a classificatory schema."[11] Downy draws from the work of Jackson Harrell and Will Linkugel as they assert that, "to impute a generic label on a group of discourses necessitates a description of its 'normative' factors," a determination of "what speeches participate in which genres," and an "application of [those] factors derived from generic description to other discourses."[12] Foss draws from each of the above-mentioned texts on generic criticism but breaks these examples down further into generic description, generic participation, and generic application.[13]

For the purposes of this study, generic description was used to analyze the selected songs. According to Foss generic description involves four steps: "(1) observing similarities in rhetorical responses to particular situations; (2) collecting artifacts that occur in similar situations; (3) analyzing the artifacts to discover if they share characteristics; and (4) formulating the organizing principle of the genre."[14]

Generic criticism is not new to the analysis of rap music. It has been previously used by Lacey Stein to examine rap music videos.[15] Though commonly used as a method of analyzing political speech, like in A. C. Carlson's work on John Quincy Adams speech, this method can also be used to effectively examine all aspects of hip hop culture, including rap music.[16] This examination of MAR as genre adds depth to the current discussion and literature on rap music by presenting an alternative dialogue of the discourse of rap music. In addition, it adds to the conversation on Black women who are presented in this historical and longstanding example of popular culture.

## SUMMARY OF SONGS

### "Hey Mama": Kanye West

West's song "Hey Mama" is off of his 2005 chart-topping sophomore album *Late Registration*. Tucked between more of his popular songs like "Touch the Sky," and "Gold Digger," "Hey Mama" is an ode to his mother's dedication, sacrifice, and hard work in raising and providing for him.[17] In the song, he rhymes about how his mother sacrificed to give him whatever he needed and even sometimes, things that he wanted. West also refers to his mother's unconditional love and support for him when he talks about the goals his mother had for him and how she supported him even when he chose his own path. West goes on to vow to give his mother everything she has always wanted, including a mansion, when he becomes successful.[18] West continues with his adoration by poetically paralleling his mother's grace and intelligence with that of notables like Maya Angelou and Nicky Giovanni. In the first verse of the song where he brings up the old gospel song "This Little Light of Mine" he even refers to his mother as the key force behind his spirit. The listener can easily get a sense that his mother is a very supportive figure in his life based on his heartfelt lyrics that are honest and passionately expressed in this song. He promises her, in the chorus, that he will eventually complete his education, a desire she had of him, and follows with a reaffirmation of his appreciation adding that he wants her to be proud of him.[19] This chorus solidifies West's love for his mother. Through his adoration and promise to give her a better life, "Hey Mama" is a perfect example of a son's love for his mother.[20]

## "Dear Mama": Tupac Shakur

In Tupac's song "Dear Mama" he talks about how much he appreciates his mother and praises her for her unconditional love, support, and consistent presence in his life.[21] He reflects on loving her unconditionally despite her flaws, as she did him, by admitting that she had not always been the best role model. In particular, he makes a reference to her past drug addiction, stating that even though she was a "crack fiend" she was still a "Black queen" signifying that though his mother had an addiction she was still admired and appreciated.[22] Tupac also expresses how much stress he caused his mother by going to jail, noting how hard it was for him to have her see him in a jail cell.[23] He then reflects on how his mother would spank him when he was younger and involved in activities that caused the police to chase him.[24]

Tupac's description of his mother also transcends to spiritual or religious terms when he refers to how, despite living in poverty, she was able to miraculously provide for them and always keep food on the table.[25] He, like West, emphasizes that no person could ever take his mother's place and that he appreciates her so much because of all she did to sacrifice for he and his sister. He additionally reflects his desire to keep her from feeling pain or hurt and wanting to take care of her—similar to the desires mentioned by West. His description of feeling pride about being able to pay her rent and send her a diamond necklace in the mail reflects his ending sentiment that although there is nothing he could do to pay her back, he appreciates and loves her.

## "All That I Got is You": Ghostface Killah ft. Mary J. Blige

Ghostface Killah's song "All That I Got is You" describes the harsh realities of a child (specifically Ghostface) living in the ghetto.[26] He speaks of his mother and grandmother as heroines who provided for him and his siblings as they lived in poverty. Though Ghostface's account of his childhood is daunting, there is a glimmer of hope as he narrates and thanks his mother for helping them to make it through the harsh conditions they faced. In the chorus, performed by Mary J. Blige (other versions by Takitha), he states his mother is all that he has and expresses his appreciation for being able to survive the bad times.[27] He is alluding to the idea that he would not have made it without his mother and grandmother, thus illustrating the gravity of their roles.

Ghostface reflects on seeing his mother cry about his father not being there and vows that, unlike his father, he will always be there for his mother. Despite how hard things were, he vows not to cry because he wanted to be strong for his mother. These lessons, he later reflects, helped shape him into the man he became. In the song he does wonder why his mother had so many children, but he also realizes the sacrifice that she made to provide for their family without the help of his father. He questions why his mother had so many children using the term "old Earth" to refer to his mother.[28] Ghostface's ending words to his verse illustrate the love that he has for his mother stating in his own unique way how much he loves her and how she brought him up.[29]

## "I Made It": Jay-Z

The song "I Made It" is from Jay-Z's ninth studio album *Kingdom Come*.[30] Jay-Z speaks about making it to the top of the music world and gaining the success that he never thought was possible to achieve, proclaiming to her that he had achieved the success he desired.[31] He rhymes with joy as he talks about how he is now a "made man" and able to provide for "at least three generations" because of his mother's role-modeling and dedication in his life.[32] In an interesting turn, Jay-Z also refers to how he became the man of the house because his father was not there. He states that, as a result, he acts like he is her husband even though he is just her son.[33] He revels in being able to take care of his mother and buy her things. He links his success to how she told him to not wait on anyone and to not be afraid to walk his own path.

He speaks very highly of his mother calling her "beautiful" and crediting her for renewing his relationship with his absentee father before his death.[34] Jay-Z lets his listeners know how much he appreciates his mother and will never forget her sacrifice. He states that she deserves praise for all she had done and describes his willingness and intentions to give her everything and anything that she has always wanted but was not able to get for herself.[35]

## "Dance": Nas

The song "Dance" written by celebrated emcee Nas, is a song dedicated to his late mother who died of breast cancer in April 2002.[36] He talks about the times they shared talking and laughing and how he wished he could go back in time just to have one more dance with her. In describing his mother, he talks about being thankful to have known a woman like her and prays that his future wife has at least one of her qualities.

Nas depicts his mother as an angel dressed in white looking down at him from heaven making sure that he is alright. He continues his description of her as a heavenly figure when he describes her death as "Jesus finally [getting] his bride."[37] He goes on to state that although he has accepted her death and how he envisions her finally happy and at peace, he wishes he could hear her voice again.[38] Nas' heartfelt dedication is somber but offers a ray of hope because he knows his mother is out of pain and in a better place. His last words on the song are a final declaration of his love, noting that despite her death she will always be with him.[39]

## ANALYSIS OF GENRE

Using Foss' four-step rubric, all of the songs presented were deconstructed to demonstrate qualities that can be classified as a MAR genre.[40] The four steps have been used to examine each of the songs in this analysis and are detailed below.

Step One: Similarities in rhetorical responses to particular situations:

- Each of the rappers speak very positively about their mothers or mother figures.
- All of the rappers have called women out of their names (bitch, ho, etc.) or have songs with misogynistic lyrics and or undertones (i.e., Jay-Z's *Girls, Girls, Girls* and *Money Cash Hoes*, Kanye's verses on *Lollipop Remix* and *Kinda Like a Big Deal,* Nas' *The Makings of a Perfect Bitch* and verse on the *Oochie Wally Remix*, Tupac's *How Do You Want It* and *I Get Around*, and Ghostface Killah's *Wildflower* and verse on *Ice Cream*).

Step Two: Collecting artifacts that occur in similar situations or constraints:

- All rappers listed were primarily raised by their mothers in single parent homes.
- Each of the rappers listed are Black American males.
- Most of the rappers were from lower socio-economic areas in the United States (urban areas).

Step Three: Analyzing the artifacts to discover if they share characteristics and/or differences:

- They see their mothers as queens, hardworking, providers, intelligent, supportive, dependable, caretakers, healers, irreplaceable, inspirational, and independent of a man's help.
- Their mothers deserve praise for all of their hard work in raising and caring for them.
- Each is very thankful that God gave them their mothers.

- Each promises their mothers that they do not have to work anymore (Jay-Z and Kanye West).
- The women are portrayed as being divine (miracle workers/healers).
- The women are described as being beautiful (but not based on outward physical appearance or standards but holistically).

Step Four: Formulating the organizing principle of the genre:

- The organizing principle that brings these five songs together is: complete respect and honor for their own or older matriarchal figures while maintaining minimal to significant dishonor, sexism, misogyny, and/or femiphobia for women in their own age groups and younger.

Examination of the lyrics "Hey Mama," "Dear Mama," "All That I Got is You," "I Made It," and "Dance," clearly shows that there is a place in hip hop for rappers to admire and verbally appreciate the mother figures in their lives.[41] It is evident that in each of the five songs mothers are depicted as saintly, reliable, resourceful, loving, and selfless figures that made positive impacts on the lives of their sons. This results in a positive presentation of Black women as mothers.

But from the same mouth, each of the rappers selected have participated and contributed in creating songs with misogynistic lyrics that devalue women other than their own mothers. In fact, an interesting contrast to mother appreciation raps, is that some of the most degrading lyrics produced by other male rappers, have been used to describe the young women with whom they have created children, also known as the Baby Mama. How can these same rappers uplift their own mothers but devalue women their own age and younger? According to Dyson,

> But for every paean to motherhood, there seem to be ten songs that insult, dismiss, harangue, and berate young black women who are lovers and mothers. The artists who draw such demeaning portraits of young women often ignore the contradiction that snares them: praising their mamas, slamming their baby mamas.[42]

The difference in the ways that rappers refer to their mothers and their baby mamas reflects a *good* woman/*bad* woman dichotomy that puts their mothers on one end of the spectrum as good and virtuous, but casts baby mamas in a role subject to shame and ridicule. While having children out of wedlock is not a new phenomenon in hip hop culture, the ways in which the younger generation of single mothers are regarded versus the ways previous generations of mothers have been described shows a marked difference.[43] As has been noted, each of the rappers within this genre was primarily raised in single-parent households by their mothers or mother figures, who they praise and refer to highly.

In stark contrast, however, are songs referring to younger mothers that are not as favorable. As Mark Anthony Neal pointed out "the baby mama" carries a negative connotation in the Black community.[44] While rappers refer to their mother figures as sources of unconditional love, younger single mothers are cast as *bad* mothers and described in terms that reflect disrespect, dislike, and sometimes hatred. Terms such as "baby mama drama" and descriptions of single mothers that stress out the fathers of their children and play into the role of the stereotypical Reagan-era *welfare* mothers are used with these younger mothers, thus casting them on the other end of the spectrum from the saintly mother figures featured in the MAR songs. Essentially, as Tia Tyree notes, when referring to baby mamas, "Black male rappers use language that reinforces negative Black female stereotypes and continues the historical misogynistic patterns commonly found in rap."[45]

It is obvious that many rappers who value their own mothers see little value and worth in other women making it acceptable to treat them like nothing more than sex objects worthy of men's ridicule. Out of the five rappers selected, Tupac Shakur is the only one that has been able to honor both younger and older women in some of his songs, though he has still participated in misogyny and sexism. In Tupac's song "Brenda's Got a Baby" he talks about the ills of teenage pregnancy by narrating a story about a young pregnant twelve-year-old named Brenda.[46] Throughout the song he talks about how teenage pregnancy affects the whole community while also addressing the issue of molestation of young girls. Tupac is able to transcend the *usual* misogynistic topics of rap music by showing many of the significant issues that face young women all over the world. In his song "Keep Ya Head Up" Tupac admonishes young women to keep their heads up even though life is tough and men don't respect and treat them right.[47] He makes specific mention of "sisters on welfare" stating that he cares about them and their well-being even if they feel no one else does.[48] He encourages them to not let themselves get down or believe in any negative talk that other men may direct at them.[49] He further advises them that if the man in their lives cannot respect them or really love them, then they should leave, implying that they are worthy of better treatment.[50] He clearly understands and empathizes with the plight that many women face. He is able to offer encouragement from a male's perspective to help them overcome the trials that they face.

It is hard to understand how Tupac can be so understanding and supportive of women's issues but also add fuel to the fire of sexism and misogyny with songs like "Fuck Friends" and "I Get Around."[51] In "Fuck Friends" he states how he "fucked your bitch" and then refers to what it is about him that attracts these women.[52] This type of juxtaposition is uncommon in mainstream hip hop music because a great majority of songs narrate women in unfavorable ways, making Tupac an exception in the hip hop world and within this genre of MAR.

It would seem that all of the rappers selected for the analysis believe in honoring and appreciating their mothers, showing that there is a possible genre of MAR and a positive representation of this group of Black women in rap music. However, these rappers have willingly made the decision to take part in patriarchy and sexism suggesting that respect for women stops at their mother figures. As stated previously the organizing principle that brings together "Hey Mama," "Dear Mama," "All That I Got is You," "I Made It," and "Dance," is their complete respect and honor for their own or older matriarchal figures while maintaining minimal to significant dishonor, sexism, misogyny, and/or femiphobia for women in their own age groups and younger.[53] Because of this detail, the five songs presented in this analysis illustrate that a genre of Mother Appreciation Rap does exist within hip hop music. The usage of generic description in this analysis to discuss the similarities and differences of these songs highlights the existence of a MAR genre and shows the variety of topics that are discussed within the genre of rap music. Whether speaking of the sacrifice that mothers make on a daily basis or how mothers continually work hard to provide for their families, a MAR genre is uplifting though contradictory to the ways in which most women are discussed within the confines of rap music.

This analysis contributes to the rhetorical theory because it shows hip hop music in a different light. Mother Appreciation Rap (MAR) helps listeners to view rappers as sensitive and caring and not solely concerned with the fast life and fame. MAR also brings more sensitive elements of humanity to the entire genre of hip hop, allowing rappers to uplift a segment of Black women by showing a variety of emotions that are not solely relegated to violence and sexual prowess. Since rap music is a major element of popular culture, examining how Black women are presented is crucial. While demeaning images and messages about Black women certainly still exist within rap music, the analysis reveals that Black women as mothers were presented in a favorable light when they were discussed by their children.

## NOTES

1. Geneva Smitherman, *Talkin That Talk: African American Language and Culture* (New York: Routledge, 2008).

2. Michael Eric Dyson, *Open Mike: Reflections on Philosophy, Race, Sex, Culture and Religion* (New York: Basic Civitas, 2003).

3. Layli Phillips, Kerri Reddick-Morgan, and Dionne Patricia Stephens, "Oppositional Consciousness within an Oppositional Realm: The Case of Feminism and Womanism in Rap and Hip-Hop 1976–2004," *The Journal of African American History* 90 no. 3 (2005): 253–77.

4. Michael Eric Dyson, *Know What I Mean?: Reflections on Hip-Hop* (New York: Basic Civitas, 2007).

5. Marlo David Azikwe, "More Than Baby Mamas: Black Mothers, and Hip-Hop Feminism" (2007). In *Home Girls Make Some Noise: Hip-Hop Feminism Anthology*, eds. Gwendolyn D. Pough, Elaine Richardson, Aisha Durham, and Rachel Raimist (Mira Loma, CA: Parker Publishing, 2005): 345–67.

6. Melissa Harris-Perry, *Sister Citizen* (New Haven, CT: Yale University Press, 2011).

7. Ibid., 215.

8. Sonya K. Foss, *Rhetorical Criticism: Exploration and Practice* (Long Grove, IL: Waveland, 2009); Kanye West and Donal Leace, "Hey Mama," on *Late Registration,* 2005, Hip-Hop Since 1978/Roc-A-Fella Records/Recordings, Compact disc; Tupac Shakur, Gregory Jacobs, and Ron Brooks, "I Get Around," on *Strictly 4 My N.I.G.G.A.Z,* 1993, Atlantic/Interscope Records, Compact disc; Dennis Coles and Mary J. Blige, "All That I Got is You," on *Ironman,* 1996, Razor Sharp/Epic Street/SME Records, Compact disc; Shawn Carter, "I Made It," on *Kingdom Come,* 2006, Roc-a-Fella Records/Def Jam Recordings, Compact disc; Nasir Jones, "Dance," on *God's Son, 2002,* Ill Will/Columbia Records, Compact disc.

9. Sharon D. Downey, "The Evolution of the Rhetorical Genre of Apologia" *Western Journal of Communication* 57 (1993): 42–64.

10. Raymond S. Rodgers, "Generic Tendencies in Majority and Non-Majority Supreme Court Opinions: The Case of Justice Douglas" *Communication Quarterly* 3 no. 3 (1982): 232–36.

11. Ibid; Quoted in Rodgers, 1982, 233.

12. Quoted in Downey, 1993, 44.

13. Foss, *Rhetorical Criticism: Exploration and Practice.*

14. Ibid., 141.

15. Lacey Stein, "An Uncommon Rap Music Video" in *Rhetorical Criticism*, ed. Sonya Foss (Longrove, IL: Waveland, 2009), 180–87.

16. A. C. Carlson, "John Quincy Adams' 'Amistad Address': Eloquence in a Generic Hybrid" *Western Journal of Speech Communication* 49 (1985): 14–26.

17. Kanye West, Justin Smith, Wasalu Muhammad Iaco, and Curtis Mayfield, "Touch the Sky," on *Late Registration,* 2005, Hip-Hop Since 1978/Roc-A-Fella Records/ Recordings, Compact disc; Kanye West, Ray Charles, and Renald Richard, "Gold Digger" on *Late Registration,* 2005, Hip-Hop Since 1978/Roc-A-Fella Records/Recordings, Compact disc; West and Leace, "Hey Mama."

18. Ibid.

19. Ibid.

20. Ibid.

21. Tupac Shakur and Tony Pizaro, "Dear Mama," on *Me Against the World*, 1995, Interscope Records, Compact Disc.

22. Ibid.

23. Ibid.

24. Ibid.

25. Ibid.

26. Coles and Blige, "All that I Got is You."

27. Ibid.

28. Ibid.

29. Ibid.

30. Carter, "I Made It."

31. Ibid.

32. Ibid.

33. Ibid.

34. Ibid.

35. Ibid.

36. Jones.

37. Ibid.

38. Ibid.

39. Ibid.
40. Foss, *Rhetorical Criticism: Exploration and Practice.*
41. West and Leace, "Hey Mama"; Tupac Shakur and Tony Pizaro, "Dear Mama," on *Me Against the World*, 1995, Interscope Records, Compact Disc; Coles and Blige, "All that I Got is You"; Carter, "I Made It"; Jones, "Dance."
42. Michael Eric Dyson, *Know What I Mean?: Reflections on Hip-Hop*, 137.
43. Tia C. M. Tyree, "Lovin' Momma and Hatin' on Baby Mama: A Comparison of Misogynistic and Stereotypical Representations in Songs about Rappers' Mothers and Baby Mamas" *Women and Language* 32, no. 2 (2009): 50–58.
44. Mark Anthony Neal, *Soul Babies: Black Popular Culture and the Post-Soul Aesthetic* (New York: Routledge, 1998).
45. Tyree, "Lovin' Momma and Hatin' on Baby Mama: A Comparison of Misogynistic and Stereotypical Representations in Songs about Rappers' Mothers and Baby Mamas," 56.
46. Tupac Shakur, "Brenda's Got a Baby," on *2Pacalypse Now*, 1991, Jive/Interscope Records, Compact Disc.
47. Shakur, "Keep Ya Head Up."
48. Ibid.
49. Ibid.
50. Ibid.
51. Tupac Shakur, "Fuck Friendz," on *Until the End of Time*, 2001, Amaru/Death Row/Interscope Records, Compact disc. Shakur, Jacobs, and Brooks, "I Get Around."
52. Shakur, "Fuck Friendz."
53. "West and Leace, "Hey Mama"; Shakur and Pizaro, "Dear Mama"; Coles and Blige, "All That I Got is You"; Carter, "I Made It"; Jones, "Dance."

# BIBLIOGRAPHY

Azikwe, Marlo David (2007). "More Than Baby Mamas: Black Mothers, and Hip-Hop Feminism." In *Home Girls Make Some Noise: Hip-hop Feminism Anthology*. Edited by Gwendolyn D. Pough, Elaine Richardson, Aisha Durham, and Rachel Raimist, 345–67. Mira Loma, CA: Parker Publishing, 2007.
Carlson, A. C. "John Quincy Adams' 'Amistad Address': Eloquence in a Generic Hybrid." *Western Journal of Speech Communication,* 49 (1985):14–26.
Carter, Shawn. "I Made It" on *Kingdom Come*. New York: Roc-a-Fella Records/Def Jam Recordings, 2006, Compact disc.
Coles, Dennis and Blige, Mary J. "All That I Got is You," on *Ironman.* New York: Razor Sharp/Epic Street/SME Records, 1996, Compact disc.
Downey, Sharon D. "The Evolution of the Rhetorical Genre of Apologia." *Western Journal of Communication,* 57 (1993): 42–64.
Dyson, Michael Eric. *Know What I Mean?: Reflections on Hip-hop.* New York: Basic Civitas, 2007.
Dyson, Michael Eric. *Open Mike: Reflections on Philosophy, Race, Sex, Culture and Religion.* New York: Basic Civitas, 2003.
Foss, Sonya K. *Rhetorical Criticism: Exploration and Practice.* Long Grove, IL: Waveland, 2009.
Harris-Perry, Melissa. *Sister Citizen*. New Haven, CT: Yale University Press, 2011.
Jones, Nasir. "Dance," on *God's Son.* New York: Ill Will/Columbia Records, 2002, Compact disc.
Neal, Mark Anthony. *Soul Babies: Black Popular Culture and the Post-Soul Aesthetic.* New York: Routledge, 1998.
Phillips, Layli, Reddick-Morgan, Kerri, and Stephens, Dionne Patricia. "Oppositional Consciousness within an Oppositional Realm: The Case of Feminism and Womanism in Rap and Hip-hop 1976-2004." *The Journal of African American History,* 90, no. 3 (2005): 253–77.

Rodgers, Raymond S. "Generic Tendencies in Majority and Non-Majority Supreme Court Opinions: The Case of Justice Douglas." *Communication Quarterly,* 3, no. 3 (1982): 232–36.

Shakur, Tupac. "Brenda's Got a Baby," on *2Pacalypse Now*. Santa Monica, CA: Jive/Interscope Records, 1991, Compact Disc.

Shakur, Tupac and Pizaro, Tony. "Dear Mama," on *Me Against the World*. Santa Monica, CA: Interscope Records, 1995, Compact Disc.

Shakur, Tupac. "Fuck Friendz," on *Until the End of Time*. Santa Monica, CA: Amaru/Death Row/Interscope Records, 2001, Compact disc.

Shakur, Tupac. "Keep Ya Head Up," on *Strictly 4 My N.I.G.G.A.Z.* Santa Monica, CA: Atlantic/Interscope Records, 1993, Compact disc.

Shakur, Tupac., Jacobs, Gregory, and Brooks, Ron. "I Get Around," on *Strictly 4 My N.I.G.G.A.Z.* Santa Monica, CA: Atlantic/Interscope Records, 1993, Compact disc.

Smitherman, Geneva. *Talkin That Talk: African American Language and Culture*. New York: Routledge, 1999.

Stein, Lacey. "An Uncommon Rap Music Video." In *Rhetorical Criticism*. Edited by Sonya Foss, 180–187. Longrove, IL: Waveland, 2009.

Tyree, Tia C. M. "Lovin' Momma and Hatin' on Baby Mama: A Comparison of Misogynistic and Stereotypical Representations in Songs about Rappers' Mothers and Baby Mamas." *Women and Language,* 32, no.2 (2009): 50–58.

West, Kanye and Leace, Donal. "Hey Mama," on *Late Registration.* New York: Hip-Hop Since 1978/Roc-A-Fella Records/Recordings, 2005, Compact disc.

*Chapter Seven*

# I Am Not My Sister's Keeper

*Shifting Themes in Female Rap Videos (2005–2011)*

Natasha R. Howard

The intersection of gender and rap music has always been a tenuous relationship. Nowhere is this more evident than in rap music videos. In general, since the advent of the music video, this genre of media has been critiqued for thematic content and images projected within them. Rap videos, however, have particularly come under attack from scholars, critics, and the viewing public for its violent and misogynistic images they have portrayed.[1] Politicians, scholars, and fans of the genre have voiced their disapproval of the images of women who are displayed as sexual objects to be conquered or performers featured solely for the enjoyment and amusement of men.[2] Part of this criticism is because increasingly music videos and mass media are becoming an area where youth are learning ideas about sexuality, gender roles, and relationship beliefs.[3] With the far-reaching implications that the themes and images within these videos have, they are a medium that continue to warrant analysis.

Primary research regarding rap music videos has tended to focus on those where the featured artist is male, and women only serve as objects of desire or background dancers.[4] Although women have always had some type of role within the rap music industry, they have always struggled to find their place within this male-dominated genre. Today, when one looks at the number of visible female images within hip hop music and hip hop videos, the number of those featured as artists, as opposed to dancers and models, is very small. Ideally rap music videos make up an arena where female artists can have a platform to artistically express their ideas and promote their images. However in reality, music companies control the images and messages that artists present. The themes and roles that female rappers present are subject to the trends of the industry and the music companies' beliefs of what will sell.[5] As a result, the "complex, often contradictory and multifaceted depictions of Black womanhood," as presented in the stories told by female Black rappers in rap videos, are often distorted.[6]

Despite the fact that music companies have so much control over music video content, audience members are not always aware of this power and control. There is still the potential for audiences to have the impression that artists control how they are presented in their videos, and that these representations are factual.[7] Therefore, it is important to investigate the themes within videos. As Cynthia Frisby and Jennifer Aubrey noted, "analyzing popular images of sexuality within the music video context contributes to an understanding of contemporary media messages, which may, ultimately contribute to how young people, especially girls and women, are socialized to see themselves."[8] Additionally, it is important to consider that videos are often used to artistically reinforce the songs they feature. Thus, one aspect of examining how Black women are presented by the music industry, in the music video form of media, is looking at the key themes within hip hop videos.

It has been established that hip hop culture has presented contemporary stereotypes regarding ideas of sexuality with regard to African-American women.[9] It has also been established that women are often exploited in rap videos when male artists are the featured performers.[10] However, not as much recent research has been conducted to establish if the same type of exploitation takes place in videos where women are the featured performers.[11] This research therefore focuses on music videos where the featured artist was a female.

Studies that have investigated the thematic content and images of female rappers' music videos have primarily examined artists and videos from the 1980s, 1990s, and the early part of the millennium. In addition, past scholars have established that there are three key themes common to most female rap songs and videos.[12] However, research has yet to be conducted to see if those same themes re-emerged in more current female rap songs and videos. As trends change in the music industry, it is important to examine if these same themes still exist within the videos of current female rappers and what, if any, different themes are featured in these videos. The aim of this study was to fill the gap in research.

To date, scholars have analyzed themes from various female rappers of past decades. However, there has not been much research examining themes pervasive in the videos of female rappers in the past decade, particularly those in the past seven years.[13] As such, this research looked at the videos of Black female rappers from major record labels that featured them as the primary artist (with only two other artists featured at maximum) between the time periods of January 1, 2005–December 31, 2011. Building off of the work of Layli Phillips, Kerri Reddick-Morgan, and Dionne Stephens, this study employed a thematic analysis, grounded in Black Feminist Thought and the Social Construction of Reality theory as the theoretical framework, to analyze the thematic images within music videos that feature female rappers as the featured artists.[14] In addition to a discussion of the themes presented, both new and old, implications and meaning of them are explored.

## HISTORY OF HIP HOP AND THE ROLE OF WOMEN

Throughout time music has served a major role within African-American culture. It has acted as both a socializing influence and an influential soundtrack to political movements, social phenomenon, and religion.[15] Rap music is no different. Indeed, "hip-hop's popularity and intelligibility across a number of spheres imbues it with undeniable potential for those hoping to reach young people, and particularly Black youth. Additionally . . . [it] provides sites of political disruption and subversion that also work to reinforce messages of resistance."[16] As such, investigation into the thematic content within rap music continues to be worth examining.

Many characteristics of rap are linked to the African and African-American traditions of oral storytelling and music-making.[17] In African and African-American societies, storytelling and speaking over drum beats were forms of entertainment. The stories and poetry performed incorporated rhetorical techniques such as call-and-response, chanting, and signifying, which are all aspects featured in rap music.[18] Predecessors to rap music can be found in numerous places from jazz musician Cab Calloway's "Minnie the Moocher" to the poetry of Gil Scott Heron and The Last Poets.[19] Historically rap music has been linked primarily to the blues and punk rock music. Because both originated from the 1970s in New York City by youth with similar rebellious and innovative attitude, punk music has been linked to rap music.[20] However, out of all the genres, rap music is most closely related to the blues because of their similar thematic content and creative expression. Similar to blues singers that sang about the realities of Black life in America, rap artists, who "value lyrical skill . . . provide a full assessment and critique of racism and sexism, while offering alternatives that explicitly explore social class as well as desire, emotion, power, and patriarchy."[21]

The similarities between female blues singers and female rappers, however, extend beyond rhetorical devices and thematic content. Historically, Black women's usage of rhetorical strategies were to create conversations designed to oppose and offer alternatives to negative representations of Black femininity in popular culture. The blues and rap music reflect this strategic use of rhetoric. The blues "provided a cultural space for community-building among working-class Black women, and was a space in which 'the coercions of bourgeois notions of sexual purity and true womanhood were absent.'"[22] Female rappers have been able to create that same type of community and use rap as an arena to re-define Black womanhood. Another commonality between blues and rap is their tendency to discuss different realities within their lyrics. Blues singers sang about "an identity that included working-class realities as well as one that suggested agency regarding sex, knowledge of both the [W]hite and [B]lack world's attitude and treatment of women, and complicity as well as critique of life for a [B]lack woman."[23] Along those same lines, rappers, particularly female rappers, used their music to represent a reality that is often not as talked about. Although their approaches may differ, in general "female rappers use rap music to develop and display their lyrical skills as well as present and challenge what it means to be a young [B]lack woman in America and the world, much like their blues foremothers did before them."[24]

Despite originating in Black communities, as rap music has grown and received more national attention, a large proportion of their buying audience today are White teenagers and young adults. Scholars propose that one reason for this is the idea that rap music is an urban genre for entertainment that allows outsiders to be *voyeurs* into the lives and realities of many Black people. As defined by Jennifer Lena, "the voyeuristic gaze is a learned mode of apperception that draws upon stereotypic notions of the 'other.' . . . the presumption is that members of the dominant group utilize the voyeuristic gaze to consume, understand, or authenticate images."[25] In particular, as Whitney Peoples explained, "mainstream rap music is most easily commodified because it represents ideas of [B]lackness that are in line with dominant racist and sexist ideologies; it has economic potential only because it works hand-in-hand with long established ideas about the sexual, social, and moral nature of [B]lack people."[26]

Based on the roles Black women have historically played within movements, it follows that in hip hop culture female rappers and other centrally featured performers are the women that have the most lasting impact to their female audiences.[27] However, as today's rap music becomes more commercialized and available to a more diverse consumer population, "Whiter audiences have coincided with less interest in the voices of Black women rappers in the past decade."[28] While there has never really been a time when the number of female rappers has been as plentiful as males, today the number of popular female rappers producing solo releases and videos is particularly low. It is within this climate of diminished female presence in rap music that this study examined the images and performances of Black womanhood presented within music videos.

## Thematic Content of Rap Music

According to Phillips, Reddick-Morgan, and Stephens female rappers have tended to create music that has addressed three key themes: "talking back to men and demanding respect for women, women's empowerment, self-help, and solidarity, and defense of [B]lack men to the larger society."[29] In particular, the first two themes are seen in songs that serve as examples of how hip hop is one of the few areas where everyday feminist and womanist concepts are seen applied in nonacademic *street* settings. By associating day-to-day issues and topics with themes of uplift, solidarity, self-love, and self-determination, they argue that many female rappers have sometimes unknowingly adapted feminist and womanist concepts to be applicable to their reality and culture. Examples of songs where women talk about men and their need to respect women include Salt-N-Pepa's "Tramp" and Queen Latifah's "U.N.I.T.Y." "Tramp" addressed the double-standard between men and women regarding sexuality. Queen Latifah's "U.N.I.T.Y." challenged the disrespectful treatment and language women often face and called for safer environments for women.[30]

The second theme Phillips, Reddick-Morgan, and Stephens discussed, is that of music with the self-empowerment, solidarity, and uplift theme.[31] Robin Roberts argues that Queen Latifah's "Ladies First" video is an exemplary feminist rap video, which she defines as one that "focuses on promoting women's importance that demands equal treatment for women, and that demonstrates the need for women to support each other."[32] The video itself features slides of historic African-American women such as Sojourner Truth, Angela Davis, and Harriet Tubman. In addition, Queen Latifah and rapper Monie Love are featured both dressed in red, black, and green military-like attire, as homage to the African National Congress. The video also features a group of other female rappers singing the chorus in unison. In general, the images serve to correlate with the overriding theme of overcoming sexism, racism, and striving to find a place for women in this struggle as a united front. Altogether, Roberts argues that the images and the verbal exchanges serve to create an African-American feminist message.[33]

## THEORETICAL FRAMEWORK

This study was grounded in two theoretical frameworks, Black Feminist Thought and the Social Construction of Reality. Using the components of both theories, this study was based on examining how images of Black women in the media are constructed, in order to interpret and discuss stereotypes and thematic content contained within them.

The effects of stereotypes in the media, including music videos, have long been debated by researchers.[34] In particular, entertainment media often typecast actors and performers based on factors such as their race, gender, and age under the premise that viewers will only accept certain images of groups of people due to stereotypes and preconceived notions they have of these groups.[35] However, the effect this can sometimes have is that audiences use these images to construct their ideals of groups of people.

The Social Construction of Reality theory asserts that "reality is socially constructed" and "intersubjective" in that it is shared with others.[36] The knowledge that we gain as humans is developed through our social interactions. In order to understand how this knowledge is developed and disseminated, it is necessary to examine the modes of our social interactions.

The media serve as institutions that inform social construction. In fact, Norman Denzin reported the portrayals of gender and sexual images have been found to be learned early in adolescence and transmitted through popular culture, namely the media.[37] Mike Brake also argued the media is one source where young girls often learn about femininity and womanhood.[38] Additionally, as Marci Littlefield argued, "the media serve as a system of racialization in that they have historically been used to perpetuate the dominant culture's perspective and create a public forum that defines and shapes ideas concerning race and ethnicity."[39]

Black Feminist Thought is a critical social theory that is composed of bodies of knowledge and practices which address issues and concerns African-American women face. As King explained, "Black feminist ideology fundamentally challenges the interstructure of the oppressions of racism, sexism, and classism both in the dominant society and within movements for liberation."[40] Although this theory asserts there is not one uniform experience of being an African-American woman, the intersection of these factors in the lives of African-American women creates oppression unique to this specific group.[41] Because of this shared oppression in the lives of Black women, the role of activism, and therefore the specific definition of Black Feminist Thought, is necessary.

Black Feminist Thought also asserts that the unique experiences Black women face, informed by the consciousness and knowledge of how the factors of race, class, sexuality, and gender interact to oppress, can lead to motivation for activism and work for social change.[42] Therefore, despite acknowledging their oppression, they do not believe in looking at Black women as victims, as this hastens the true goal of liberation.[43] Instead, Black feminists place value on sharing their personal narratives, recognizing the commonalities that can be found within this can lead to a growing consciousness and united effort to address the shared oppression Black women face.[44] Black Feminist Thought therefore encourages African-American women to create their own definitions of their identity, in opposition to the definitions that have been set by others.[45] "Because of its authority to shape perceptions of the world, global mass media circulate images of Black femininity and

Black masculinity and, in doing so, ideologies of race, gender, sexuality, and class."[46] Ultimately, Black Feminist Thought works to encourage African-American women to create new definitions of their vast identities that reflect their unique experiences in order to bring attention to and eventually fight the social injustices they may face.

Barbara Smith asserts that among other things, "Black feminism provides the theory that clarifies the nature of Black women's experiences . . ."[47] Under this premise, examining the work of Black female rappers is one way to examine the experiences of young Black women today. It is also a way to analyze and critique the images of Black womanhood that Black female entertainers in one genre of music are presenting. Patricia Hill Collins believes that in order to completely capture the experiences of Black women, one most examine and acknowledge poetry, music, and other art-forms that express the vast ranges of Black women's experiences.[48] As Angela Davis notes, "Any attempt . . . to understand in depth the evolution of women's consciousness within the Black community requires a serious examination of the music which has influenced them—particularly that which they themselves have created."[49]

## METHODOLOGY

This research dependeds on a number of key concepts. The first was the term rapper. Rap music is defined as "a form of rhymed storytelling accompanied by highly rhythmic, electronically based music."[50] A rapper is defined as a person that performs rap music. Within this study, the performers examined were female rappers who were appearing as the primary featured artist and not guest stars in duets or collaborations. In terms of the ethnicity of these female artists, all the artists examined were identified as having either an African-American or Caribbean background. For the purpose of this study, the term Black women was used to describe these artists and was defined as women of African descent, therefore encompassing the shared ancestry both of the African-American and Caribbean-American female rappers.

The rappers studied were all artists who released videos with major record label singles between the time of January 1, 2005–December 31, 2011. For the purposes of this study, a single was defined as any particularly popular song released by the artist that was used to represent a sample of their work. Additionally, a major record label was defined as any record label or affiliate that was covered under the Recording Industry Association of America (RIAA). The RIAA is the umbrella association that covers all intellectual property of artists affiliated with a record label that had a major distribution deal with one of the following major distribution companies: Warner Music Group, Universal Music Group, Sony/BMG, and Capitol/

EMI.[51] Therefore, artists under independent labels were not included in this study.

The sample consisted of videos of Black female rappers that were released to accompany major label singles between January 1, 2005, and December 31, 2011. By using a sample featuring only artists affiliated with major record labels, the goal was to analyze videos more likely to have been promoted and viewed by larger audiences, as they are financially promoted by major label record companies. Therefore, female rappers who are independent artists—artists that are not affiliated with a major record label—were not used in this study. Also, if an artist changed from a major record label to an independent label during the time span examined, only the videos produced under the major record label were analyzed. Additionally, because some rappers are known to both sing and rap in their songs, only songs where the song consisted primarily of rapping, regardless of whether there was singing in the chorus of the song, were included. Finally, since past studies have analyzed videos from female rappers through 2004 for various purposes, only videos released in the past six years were selected for this study.

In the music industry, artists often have musical collaborations with multiple artists who are featured in their videos. For example, often a female rapper will perform the key verses of the song, but another artist may be featured singing the chorus to the song. Also, duets and collaborations often take place, particularly in the case of artists that are affiliated with a group or fellow record label members. An example is with artist Nicki Minaj, who has collaborated on a number of songs with other artists. In order to ensure the videos studied were more focused on the individual performances of the specific Black female rap artist, the sample only allowed for videos that featured a maximum of one other artist. Additionally, the second artist could only be featured on the chorus or bridge of the song and not perform an entire verse.

In addition, in an effort to prohibit the narrative of one particular rapper from overshadowing those of others included in the study, no more than five videos per artist were examined in this study. As a result a total of thirty two videos (see table 7.2) were included in the sample for the study.

In order to begin this thematic analysis, each music video was viewed and coded to see if the following past themes, as noted by Phillips, Reddick-Morgan, and Stephens, were present in the work of female rap videos:[52]

1. Women talking back to men and demanding respect for all women. Images that were coded for this theme included those where Black women in the video were arguing or standing up to men in social settings and/or addressing the camera and performing lyrics relating to the topic of demanding respect. Also images where women were de-

fending themselves or other women against men were coded as correlating with this theme.
2. Women demonstrating empowerment, self-help, and solidarity. Images that were coded as representing this theme included those where Black women were working together, socially hanging out, interacting in a manner that implied friendship, and visibly offering assistance to each other or reaffirming each other. Although many of the videos included situations where the artist had female background dancers, these were not included unless there were scenarios where the artist and the background dancers were interacting in settings that implied an actual relationship or familiarity and did not involve choreography.
3. Women coming to the defense of Black men to the larger society. Images that were considered representative of this theme included those where Black women were helping men in their videos or addressing the camera while rapping lyrics related to defending Black men.

In addition to these themes, this study also examined whether any other emerging themes, outside of the three defined by Phillips, Reddick-Morgan, and Stephens, were revealed within the videos.[53]

After viewing the videos, I gathered all notes generated about the music video images and lyrics. Further analysis required the use of both an inductive and a deductive mode of analyzing the data. As such, a six-step process was applied. This six-step process allowed for the data to be analyzed deductively and inductively. The first step involved developing a list of themes to code for deductively. The second step involved testing the reliability of these pre-defined themes. The third step involved summarizing the collected data and identifying emerging initial themes. Next, additional notes on themes were taken for analysis. The gathered notes were then connected and organized into categories. Finally, all of the data, in both the predefined themes and emerging themes, were organized before they were interpreted.[54]

## RESULTS

In examining the thematic content for the videos, a number of findings were revealed (see table 7.1). First, some of the images and lyrics corresponded with more than one theme. Also, some of the videos did not correspond with any of the themes identified by Phillips, Reddick-Morgan, and Stephens. Additionally, some of the videos presented similar emerging themes outside of the ones that Phillips, Reddick-Morgan, and Stephens uncovered. All of the videos were coded based on the overall thematic and lyrical impressions that the videos communicated.

134     *Natasha R. Howard*

**Table 7.1. Themes Presented in Black Female Rapper Videos**

| Video Theme | Artist and Video /Song Name |
|---|---|
| Women Talking Back to Men and Demanding Respect for All Women | Lil' Mama—"Life"<br>Trina—"Here We Go" |
| Women's Empowerment, Self Help, and Solidarity | Ak'Sent—"Zingy"<br>Eve—"Tambourine"<br>Lil' Kim—"Lighter's Up"<br>Lil' Kim—"Whoa"<br>Missy Elliott—"We Run This"<br>Trina—"Here We Go"<br>Trina—"I Got a Thing For You"<br>Trina—"My Bitches"<br>Trina—"Single Again" |
| Women Coming to the Defense of Black Men to the Larger Society | N/A |
| New Theme—Bravado | Ak'Sent—"Losing Control"<br>Azealia Banks—"212"<br>Eve—"Tambourine"<br>Lil' Mama—"Lip Gloss"<br>Lil' Mama –"What It Is"<br>Nicki Minaj—"Did It On 'Em"<br>Nicki Minaj—"Massive Attack"<br>Remy Ma—"Conceited"<br>Rye Rye—"New Thing"<br>Rye Rye—"Sunshine"<br>Shawnna—"Damn"<br>Shawnna—"Gettin Some"<br>Trina—"Single Again"<br>Trina—"That's My Attitude" |
| New Theme—Love/Relationships/Intimacy | Ak'Sent—"All I Need"<br>Eve—"Give It To You"<br>Rye Rye—"Never Will Be Mine"<br>Nicki Minaj—"Right Thru Me"<br>Nicki Minaj—"Super Bass"<br>Trina—"Here We Go"<br>Trina—"I Got a Thing For You"<br>Trina—"Single Again" |

## Women Talking Back to Men and Demanding Respect for All Women

Out of the three prevailing themes that Phillips, Reddick-Morgan, and Stephens found in their study, only one remained as a common featured theme within the videos examined. The theme of women defending Black men against society was non-existent in the videos, and the theme of women talking back to Black men and demanding respect for women was only featured in two out of thirty-two videos. Even within these videos, the arguing depicted is that of individual women demanding respect for themselves and not for all women.

One example where women were depicted arguing with men for respect was a scene in the video for the song "L.I.F.E." by the artist Lil' Mama. This video featured three vignettes all related to social commentary about issues dealing with foster parenting, domestic violence, and broken families. Within each vignette, Lil' Mama is featured as a different character. In the first scene she is shown as one of eight foster children to an uninterested foster mother. The final scene shows Lil' Mama as a bystander on the sidewalk where a couple is arguing in front of a child. The man, who has a gym bag with him, appears to be leaving, as the woman is arguing and trying to get in the way while their child looks on. Neither of these scenes reflects the theme of women talking back to men, as it is actually the second vignette in the video that reflects this theme. As such, it is not the entire video that addresses this theme, then, but only one of the three.

In the second scene, Lil' Mama is depicted as a pregnant teenager who is in a physically abusive relationship with her boyfriend/child's father. In the scenes within this vignette you see her with a pregnant stomach walking home with groceries. During her walk, she is confronted by an angry young man that approaches her in a threatening way. His nonverbal behaviors, such as the angry look on his face, help to communicate the confrontation to the audience. From the lyrics, listeners are led to believe this is her child's father, and he is abusive towards her. The camera goes back and forth between two different images. The first image is of the two arguing and fighting on the sidewalk. The second image is of the pregnant female trying to talk to her mother inside their apartment, who she blames for not teaching her better about the types of men. This vignette ends with the boyfriend approaching her as though to embrace her. While it appears that she is going to let him embrace her, in the end she pushes him away and leaves. While she walks away, he is shown standing, covering his face and falling to his knees as though to cry. While the lyrics reflect her acceptance of this situation, the video reflects hope as she fights back against him.

In the second video, Trina's "Here We Go," a woman is shown arguing with a man as she demands his respect. This video is about a woman whose relationship is ending due to her finding out that her live-in boyfriend was unfaithful. The video begins with Trina seated at a dining room table on the phone leaving a voicemail message, presumably to her boyfriend, about how angry and fed up she is about their relationship. Future images reveal that the table had been set up for a romantic birthday dinner for him, as illustrated by the candles and birthday cake. As Trina begins the first verse of the song, she is depicted in the bedroom with her boyfriend arguing, and at times, physically pushing him. In the lyrics, Trina tells her boyfriend that she deserves better. She continues by chastising him for not appreciating her for everything she has done for him and expressing how she plans to move on.

As the video continues, Trina receives pictures that had been taken of her boyfriend with another woman. After, the video depicts movers taking boxes and other items from the house. A future scene shows Trina having a garage sale on her lawn. Since men are shown at the sale trying on male clothing, the audience can assume that she is selling all of the boyfriend's possessions. In the end of the video, after emptying out the house, Trina leaves and the boyfriend returns to find the house empty except for one envelope. As he opens the envelope, the audience sees it is full of the pictures of him cheating. This further communicates to the audience that Trina's actions were a result of his infidelity. Therefore, in addition to demanding her respect from the boyfriend, Trina exacts revenge and leaves him.

## Women's Empowerment, Self-Help, and Solidarity

The theme of women being empowered, showing solidarity and self-help was more common among the videos displayed. Nine of the thirty-two videos featured scenes or lyrics depicting women with their female friends as they shared advice or talked about spending time together. For example, in Trina's videos "I Got a Thing for You" and "Here We Go," the two singers who perform the chorus are both portrayed in the video as her friends. In the "Here We Go" video, as Trina is featured dealing with her boyfriend's infidelities, singer Kelly Rowland portrays the friend of Trina. Kelly is shown bringing Trina an envelope with pictures of Trina's boyfriend with another woman. Next, Kelly is shown comforting Trina by hugging her and pointing out things in the pictures. She is then side-by-side with Trina at the end of the video when the two get in the back of a limousine after emptying the house Trina had shared with her boyfriend. As the video ends, Kelly and Trina are shown laughing in the back of the limousine as it is revealed that the driver is actually the same woman in the photos that were taken of Trina's boyfriend. The idea implied is that all three women worked together to set up Trina's boyfriend.

A similar theme is expressed in Trina's video "I Got a Thing For You." While the video is about Trina having a crush on a man in her building, a friendship between singer Keyshia Cole, who sings the chorus for the song, is also implied. Images within the video depict Trina going to visit Keyshia's apartment, after seeing the male interest of the video in the lobby. While visiting Keyshia, she and Trina are seen laughing and talking to each other on the couch in a way that communicated their friendship.

Lil' Kim's video for "Whoa" similarly reflects female solidarity in terms of a friendship depicted between Lil' Kim and another woman in the video. The premise of this video is that Lil' Kim and two friends, one male and one female, are conducting a heist. The video begins with Lil' Kim being in a car with both friends preparing for their robbery. While in the car, her female friend expresses words of encouragement regarding her upcoming trip to jail and compliments her on her appearance. In addition to this scene, friendship is later referred to through lyrics in the song when Lil' Kim talks about her "team" and her "clique."

In a less direct way, friendship is also implied visually in the videos of Eve ("Tambourine"), Missy ("We Run This"), Lil' Kim ("Lighters Up"), and other videos by Trina ("My Bitches" and "Single Again"). For example, Trina's song "My Bitches," is dedicated to her female friends and the high regard she has for all of them. The video is comprised of images of Trina with a big group of women—her female crew—in an urban setting walking down the street while stopping to pose and dance. The chorus, which features Trina talking about how much she loves her girlfriend crew, who she refers to as *her* bitches, is accompanied with close-ups of the various friends, the size of which she mentions in the lyrics as being of at least twenty women.

Throughout Trina's lyrics, she also refers to all the things they have in common which make them desirable and special, despite the different occupations and backgrounds they all have.

Similarly, in other videos each of the female artists is seen at social events, whether hanging on a street corner, in an urban setting, or at parties with a group of female friends around her. Lil' Kim's video "Lighter's Up," is an example of this. The "Lighter's Up" video, which pays homage to Lil' Kim's hometown of Brooklyn, NY, depicts her in various urban backgrounds in Brooklyn. In some of these scenes, residents of the neighborhood are shown. Other scenes depict Lil' Kim either by herself or dancing and laughing with male and female friends. In particular, some of the scenes where she is with girlfriends feature fellow celebrities such as Mary J. Blige.

Eve's video for "Tambourine" similarly reflects this aspect of female solidarity. The video is full of images portraying Eve as a person of affluence with female maids and cooks serving her. Throughout the video, images are primarily focused on Eve by herself with jewels, clothing, and cars. However, at the end of the video Eve is pictured at a party where the same women that were portrayed as her maids in the beginning are now shown as her friends who are dancing and talking around her. Similarly, in the video for "Single Again," Trina is featured socializing with her girlfriends. Their presence implicates the friendship and solidarity they share. The video begins with images of Trina as a bride who walks away from her own wedding after a video of her fiancé kissing another woman is circulated through text message at her wedding. After running out on her wedding, she is next shown on vacation, lying poolside with girlfriends while eyeing the other men around her. Through the middle of the video, she is featured laughing and sipping on drinks with her friends while sitting poolside. At the end of the video, Trina enters a party and is seen talking and laughing with her friends, while she ignores her former fiancé who is also at the party. The socializing aspect of both the videos for "Tambourine" and "Single Again" implies a friendship and sort of female solidarity as these friends enjoy each other's company in various social settings.

Another example of female solidarity was in Missy's video, "We Run This." The theme of female solidarity in this video, however, was represented by the idea of teamwork. While much of the video features Missy either dancing by herself or dancing with a group of background dancers, alternate images feature her as a part of different teams. For example, the beginning of the video depicts Missy as a drum major with a marching band. Later in the video, Missy is depicted as being a part of a gymnastics team. Correlating with the song's inclusion on the soundtrack for the Disney Movie "Stick It," a movie about a gymnastics team, images from the film are also included. One particular scene from the movie features Missy's face photo-shopped onto the body of one of the athletes from the movie. In this particular scene, Missy completes a floor routine which results in the team winning. As the video goes off, Missy and the rest of the girls from the gymnastics team are on the Olympic podium having received their medals, while their coach, Olympic Gold Medalist gymnast Dominique Dawes, looks on with a smile of pride. This scene, with images of the girls cheering and celebrating their accomplishment, implies the idea of women working together, encouraging one another and being proud of each other.

A final aspect of the theme of women standing in solidarity was the references to female friends and friendships solely expressed through the lyrics of the songs and not with images. In her video for the song "Zingy," the artist Ak'Sent specifically uses the rhetorical method of call-and-response in her lyrics to ask the ladies in their audience if they could relate to the situation being discussed. She also mentions her friends, the activities, and possessions they like and the idea of having a *ladies' night*. Finally, she mentions a situation in which she remains loyal to a girlfriend by not accepting the advances from a man who had also tried to make a pass at her friend. While the images throughout the video feature Ak'Sent either dancing and posing by herself or with background dancers, her lyrics refer to her solidarity with her female friends and the women in the audience.

## NEW THEMES

While only eleven of the thirty-two videos from the analysis reflected the three themes Phillips, Reddick-Morgan, and Stephens found, some additional themes, emerged from this analysis. Each of these new themes was featured in eight or more of the videos. While none of these themes are new features in rap videos or music videos in general, their appearance in the most recent music videos from female rappers signifies a shift in terms of thematic storylines in their videos.

## Bravado

Fourteen of the thirty-two videos featured images and lyrics relating to the artists showing off or talking about their affluence, performance skills, or successful careers. In particular, videos that were considered to be related to their bravado often featured images of diamond and platinum jewelry, furs, images of them living in large houses, images of them being served by servants, or images of the artists driving, being driven in, or posing near big fancy cars. Examples of videos with visual images of bravado include those by Remy Ma ("Conceited"), Eve ("Tambourine"), Shawnna ("Getting Some" and "Damn"), Trina ("Single Again," "Here We Go," and "That's My Attitude"), and Nicki Minaj ("Massive Attack" and "Did It On 'Em").

In the videos for "Conceited," and "Tambourine," Remy Ma and Eve, respectively, are seen having servants work for them. The premise for the video "Conceited," is Remy Ma focusing on all the reasons she has to be conceited. As such, images reflect that she is living a high class life. For example, the video's opening scene features Remy Ma on her bed surrounded by servants, two of whom are fanning her with big palm leaves. As the video continues, some of the servants toss rose petals on the ground for her to walk on as she enters a room where her clothes and accessories are stored. The servants then parade clothing options for her. The images of servants are also present in "Tambourine" where Eve is depicted lounging in a chair while servants are shown picking out items for her to consider.

An additional example of bravado that is featured in the aforementioned videos, with the exception of "Massive Attack" and "Did It On 'Em" by Nicki Minaj, are camera stills of the women with diamond, gold, or platinum jewelry. In both "Conceited" and "Single Again," Remy Ma and Trina, respectively, are both featured in large rooms filled with clothes and accessories in the background.

In "Getting Some," "Damn," "Tambourine," and "Massive Attack," sports cars or large luxury automobiles are shown with the artist either driving them ("Damn"), being driven by others ("Massive Attack" and "Tambourine"), or lounging and posing near it ("Getting Some" and "Losing Control"). An additional aspect of bravado featured in videos with images of material items, are those where the primary settings featured are mansions, large houses, penthouse suites, or vacation locations. For example, the primary settings for the videos for "Conceited," "Here We Go," and "Tambourine" are all mansions. Trina's "Single Again" video and Shawnna's "Damn" video both feature the artists on vacation while lying on the beach in settings that imply expensive locales.

Another example of the bravado theme was where the lyrics, as well as some images, expressed the female's superiority to other rappers and other women, in general. Some of the common claims associated with this theme referred to their skills as rappers, their popularity with the opposite sex, the jealousy other females have towards them, references to their money, and general references to how great they are. All of these videos featured lyrical content related to the qualities and items they felt others should be envious of. Certain videos, however, also featured images where bystanders looked on with facial expressions implying envy and jealousy because of the amount of privilege the artist had.

Shawnna's video "Getting Some," is an example of this concept. The lyrics refer to how other women wish they were like her and men desired and wished they could be in a relationship with her. Similarly, images reflect bystanders looking on at her with envy. The video begins with images of a long line of women standing and waiting to enter a salon. Shawnna is then shown walking past this line and entering to get served before anyone else, while the women in line look on with dismay. Later, as she is sitting in the chair in the salon, the camera glances past some of the women standing in line so the audience can see them looking at her. These scenes are featured in between close-ups of her rapping while playing with her jewelry.

In a similar manner, Lil' Mama's video "Lip Gloss," features images of other girls looking at Lil' Mama in envy because of her popularity. Coupled with this imagery are her lyrics that tell the story of the power her lip gloss has on making everyone like her and want to be like her. In the beginning of the video when Lil' Mama puts on her magical lip gloss, all attention appears to be focused on her. As she appears in the school hallway, the guys and girls stop and point. Girls, who were once in the middle of a conversation, come up behind her and start dancing with her in the video. This communicates to the audience that she is suddenly popular. In a less direct way, Nicki Minaj's video for "Did It On 'Em" also features lyrical messages about her successful career, while stills of her in various magazines are also interwoven through the video. Amidst these images of her magazine covers and spreads is footage of her in concert performing with cheering fans in the audience. These images imply the success and popularity which she bragged about in her lyrics.

While the aforementioned videos each used an actual audience within the video to help communicate the bravado theme, such as bystanders and servants, some of the videos did not feature an actual audience. Instead, those videos relied on the song lyrics and other images to communicate the theme. For example, for Rye Rye's "Sunshine," "Bang," and "New Thing," the lyrics to all her songs refer to how great she and her friends are and how other people envy her skills, demeanor, and general persona. However, the settings of these videos are an urban basketball park, a club that appears to be in a warehouse, and a plain colored or patterned background screen, respectively. None of her videos include material items or images of people looking at her with envious expressions. The most that can be detected would be in the video for "Sunshine," where the video begins with images showing her riding her bicycle with a group of friends to a basketball park. Once there, Rye Rye climbs over a picnic table and pushes people out of the way. Later, she and her group of female friends begin dancing on the middle of the basketball court at the park. Throughout the video she is seen hanging with both groups of girls and guys while the lyrics in the background reaffirm her bravado as she mentions the attention she is receiving from the guys around her and her apathy towards it all. Images of material items or of others being envious of her status are not included in Rye Rye's videos.

This is similar to Azealia Banks' video for "212," a black-and-white video that primarily features images of Banks dancing with a friend or by herself while she performs her lyrics. The video does feature scenes with her talking, presumably to an opponent, mouthing lyrics about her prowess as a rapper and her superiority. Her opponent, however, does not seem to have a response and the video does not feature any other interactions or images.

## Love/Relationships/Intimacy

Eight of the videos analyzed featured themes relating to love, romantic relationships, and dating situations. In particular, three of these videos (Eve's "Give It To You," Nicki Minaj's "Right Thru Me," and Ak'Sent's "All I Need") featured lyrics about the artist being in a relationship with a man, with images also communicating their relationship. Eve's video for "Give It To You," for example, features rapper Sean Paul, who serves as her love interest and sings the chorus of the song. The video begins with Eve in her apartment. Upon receiving a call from her boyfriend, Eve is shown smiling and appearing happy. She is later shown looking out her apartment window for him, seemingly in anticipation for a date. After his arrival, the following scenes show her holding on to him as they ride his motorcycle to their destination and later, dance together. Towards the end of the video, Eve raps and performs on stage. While she is on stage dancing, she is looking directly at him. The way they interact as she raps, along with the lyrical content, suggest a romantic familiarity in terms of their use of touch and eye contact.

Similarly, Nicki Minaj's "Right Thru Me" depicts Nicki in an intimate relationship. The opening scene of the video features Nicki and her boyfriend arguing about her issues with him talking to another girl. After resolving this argument, further scenes throughout the video feature them in intimate scenarios. For example, they are featured holding each other while lying in bed.

In addition, Nicki is shown lying in bed with him while watching him sleep. However, other scenes depict the couple standing outside while arguing and later him embracing her before picking her up and carrying her off. Their interactions, as well as the lyrics that reflect her awe at how he is able to "see right thru" and understand her, reflect the theme of the couple being in a relationship.

Finally, Ak'Sent's video for "All I Need," demonstrates another example of a romantic relationship. The video opens with images of her looking up a spice cake recipe to make for her boyfriend. Images go back and forth between those of her interacting with him, talking to him on the phone, and preparing to get ready to go on a date, presumably with him. Amidst these images are the lyrics, which refer to her wanting to be "wifey" and expressing her love for him because of how he takes care of her. All three of these videos reflect images of the featured rappers involved in intimate love relationships.

Two other videos, however, reflected the end of relationships and the aftermath. For example, in Trina's video for "Here We Go," the storyline is also that of a relationship that is ending. The video begins with a scene reflecting her in an argument with her boyfriend in the bedroom as lyrics reflect how things in their relationship have changed. Next, there are images of her getting pictures of him cheating with another woman, followed by images of her packing up his things and clearing out the house. At the end of the video, he returns to find the house empty except for the envelope of the pictures of him cheating, as shown in previous images scattered throughout the video.

Trina's video for "Single Again" begins with the premise of Trina going on vacation after leaving her fiancé at the altar when she learned that he had been unfaithful. Lyrics refer to how perfect she thought the relationship was and how she plans to move on. The images show her looking at other men and relaxing with her friends. During the video, scenes depict the ex-fiancé trying to call Trina while she is lying in the sun. Eventually, she throws her phone into the swimming pool. Images at the end of the video show him trying to make eye contact and talk to her at a party while she ignores him.

Finally, two videos that dealt with the topic of love, relationships, and intimacy, focused on the artists being interested in a specific guy or type of guy. For example, in Nicki Minaj's video for "Super Bass," the lyrics and images depict her describing and interacting with a man that has qualities she desires. Images show her draped on a guy, caressing him, frolicking in a pink pond with him, and finally giving him a lap dance in the end. Close-up images feature different men and their body parts and facial features, which hint more towards attraction and desire for intimacy than love. However, Trina's video for "I Got a Thang For You," as mentioned earlier, tells the story of Trina's interest in a guy that lives in her building. Lyrics refer to how she is looking for more than a friend and how she wants to get to know him better. Images are shown of them locking eyes as she leaves the elevator headed to her friend's apartment. Further images show the guy coming to Trina's apartment door. Trina then lets him in and motions with her finger for him to come closer. He enters the apartment, they embrace, and he then unties her coat to reveal her wearing lingerie underneath. As they become more intimate with one another, the camera switches to another scene of her performing her lyrics with singer Keyshia Cole.

## DISCUSSION

This study sought to analyze the themes found in the music videos of Black female rappers from 2005–2011. Altogether, thirty-two videos from eleven artists were analyzed. The purpose of the study was to see how Black female rappers presented Black womanhood through the use of themes. I utilized the work of Phillips, Reddick-Morgan, and Stephens to analyze previously discovered themes from the music of Black female rappers.[55] The Social Construction of Reality theory and Black Feminist Thought were used as the theoretical frameworks in order to determine the possible implications these videos could have on their audiences and to provide context as to how the messages in these videos may apply to perceptions of Black womanhood. The findings were also compared to past representations of Black women in the media in order to ascertain the similarities and differences represented in the themes presented.

### No Unified Solidarity

Overall, the thematic content of female rappers' music videos has shifted since previous studies have examined this topic. Social commentary was found in only one of the videos, and themes related to women standing up in defense of Black men were not present. Additionally, images corresponding to the themes of women talking back to men and demanding respect for women, as well as those of female solidarity, were more often presented as individual situations and not as a general social call to the community. For example, videos with women talking back to men and demanding respect were one-on-one situations where the demand was for individual respect and not for women as a whole. The videos that represented aspects of this theme all involved the argument for respect being within domestic situations. In terms of a general social call for all men to respect women, this was not evident. Also, while many of the videos featured images that reflected female friendship, there were not any songs or videos where the key theme was championing all around sisterhood or female solidarity. In general, the images regarding this theme were more along the lines of reflecting interpersonal relationships between individual women. Onscreen depictions of friendship and loyalty between friends were shown, but the idea of overall female unity was not promoted.

While descriptions of female solidarity and demands for respect may have been themes from the past in female rap music, the images of isolated images of friendship and demands for respect are reflective of the climate in rap music today. In general record labels feel that female rappers are so risky financially that they are not willing to invest in an artist that they are not confident will be profitable. Therefore, producing music with social messages as a single, which may not sell, is not a risk they are able to take.

Similarly, as Ted Lucas pointed out, the risks associated with producing female rappers and guaranteeing a profit for them is such that they almost always have to be affiliated with a male rapper or crew, particularly in the beginning of their careers, if they want to see success.[56] Despite the fact that some of the artists featured in this study have not been associated with all-male crews, the level of visibility of those that have (i.e., Eve, Nikki Minaj, Lil Kim, and Trina) has been much higher than those who have not (Lil Mama, Azaelia Banks, Rye Rye, etc.) Many, such as Eve, Trina, and Lil Kim, have gone on to find independent success later on in their career. Yet, their origins started off with the task of proving they could attract both male and female audiences via their affiliation with an all-male crew. While female artists being a part of all-male crews is not a new concept, today's female rapper that is associated with an all-male crew seems to be in a precarious position of having to prove her allegiance with them first.

These shifting themes are reflective of a larger issue with regard to the messages in the work of Black female rappers. In a sense, due to commercialism and the need to appeal to wider audiences, the voice of the Black female rapper is muted today. As Hunter noted, "Black criminals sell; black intellectuals don't. Black women dancers sell; black women rappers don't."[57] The position of the Black female rapper therefore appears to be that if one wants to become successful, she cannot speak out too strongly. In the past, female rappers were able to talk about womanhood, solidarity, and dialogue with and about Black men on a larger scale (i.e., "Ladies First," by Queen Latifah, "Ladies Night," by Missy Elliott, Lil Kim, Angie Martinez, Left Eye, and Da Brat). Today, however, the Black female rapper is more concerned with being able to fit in and find a balance between appealing to both male and female fans. Because rap music audiences are continuously growing and becoming more global makes for an even more diverse audience that the Black female rapper needs to appeal to in order to become successful. As Rose noted:

> ... Rappers are not nearly as free to express outrage at racism, challenge government policies, speak out against the war, or identify whiteness as an

unfair advantage; these kinds of free expression are regularly discouraged or censored by the music industry so as to not offend white listeners, government officials, or mainstream institutions.[58]

The disappearance of the theme of women talking back in defense of Black men could also be related to this because themes that make strong statements, both about Black womanhood and Black solidarity, may alienate some audiences and their stereotypical perceptions of Black men and women.

The shifting of themes from being more universal to individualistic is also indicative of the Black female rapper's reliance on being part of an established all-male crew in order to secure a place in the music industry. Today's Black female rapper must show allegiance to the men she works with because she needs them to help shepherd her into the industry. As such, songs calling for men to respect all women or criticizing men for their behavior and lyrics are unlikely, because she needs these men. At the same time, the female rapper must maintain authenticity with her female audiences and be relatable to them. However, having female solidarity is not as much of a necessity for today's female rapper as having solidarity with a male crew. As a result, calls for solidarity among men and women have been exchanged for more individualistic representations. Instead of general calls demanding respect for Black men or calling for female solidarity, songs referring to individual friendships ("My Bitches," "Zingy," "We Run This," etc.) or describing specific men ("I Got a Thing For You," "Give It To You," "Right Thru Me," etc.) are made. These individualized themes may be less threatening. In the end, despite the ideal that Black Feminist Thought asserts about how the art of Black women can be representative of Black womanhood, in the current climate of rap music, the voice of Black womanhood has become distorted in some ways.

## Rap Love Songs

Although not a new theme, the relationships theme also symbolizes an interesting finding. The theme of relationships is generally common in music. But often within rap, the theme of relationships has not been as common. Love is generally seen as a *female* topic. With rap being a male-dominated genre and women often having to adopt a masculine demeanor in order to establish credibility, the topic of love has been more of one that is often downplayed in favor of sex. As Rose described, with the subject of love and relationships in rap:

> In contrast to male rappers that frame displays of hostility against women on the basis of past experiences where they had been taken advantage of or hurt by women, women [in hip-hop] frame themselves as emotionally, financially

independent, and sexually confident, sometimes in contrast to developing these qualities as a result of acquaintances with dishonest men.[59]

The emergence of the relationships, love, and intimacy as a theme in videos of the Black female rap artist reflects a vulnerability in them which therefore allows Black women to be seen in a different light. Historically, the idea of Black women as "passionate and emotional" has been used in a negative connotation as evidence of an ingrained hypersexuality used to exploit Black women.[60] Being presented as emotional and passionate within the confines of a relationship where genuine care is shown, without a discussion of material wealth to be gained, presents a different image of Black women to be observed.

## I'm the Best—But Is It Because I Have the Best?

The concept of bravado, which has long been a theme in rap music, is one major theme that was highlighted in many of the videos. The level of materialism, where the artists brag about their expensive lifestyles, their clothes, cars, and money, was previously a theme detected in videos from 1990s female rappers and seems to be continuing today as a part of the female bravado. Corresponding with this theme was the concept of materialism.[61] Many of the images featured the idea of financial and material wealth being the primary causes of the bravado displayed and referred to in the videos. A number of the videos featured incidences of bravado where, amidst the bragging lyrics, there were images of the women with expensive clothes, furs, jewelry, or cars. While rap music has long been accused of featuring materialistic images, many of these videos, particularly those depicting the women in mansions with servants and other luxuries, also accentuated the idea that being a diva and having success was equivalent to being rich and having material items.

Collins notes that "because rap revolves around self-promotion, female rappers are able to avoid accusations of being self-centered or narcissistic when they use the form to promote Black female power."[62] In this sense, it could be argued that by touting their accomplishments and their material items, they are showing their pride in having earned these items and other achievements. Thus, their use of bravado could be seen as female empowerment. Instead of talking about accruing wealth via use of their sexuality, illegal activity, or taking advantage of men, they present the idea that they have these things either from working hard or simply because they come from privilege. On the other hand, with material wealth appearing to have often been the symbol of success and the source of envy, it can also be argued that videos present a skewed image of female success and empowerment.

Table 7.2. Videos Examined (2005–2011)

| Artist | Name of Video and Year of Release |
|---|---|
| Ak'Sent | "Zingy" (2006)<br>"All I Need" (2006) |
| Azealia Banks | "212" (2011) |
| Eve | "Tambourine" (2007)<br>"Give it To You" (2007) |
| Lil' Kim | "Lighter's Up" (2005)<br>"Whoa" (2006) |
| Lil' Mama | "Lip Gloss" (2007)<br>"G Slide (Tour Bus)" (2008)<br>"What It Is" (2008)<br>"L.I.F.E." (2008) |
| Missy Elliott | "Lose Control" (2005)<br>"We Run This" (2006)<br>"Ching-A-Ling" (2009) |
| Nicki Minaj | "Massive Attack" (2010)<br>"Right Thru Me" (2010)<br>"Did It On 'Em" (2011)<br>"Super Bass" (2011)<br>"Fly" (2011) |
| Remy Ma | "Conceited" (2006)<br>"Whuteva" (2006) |
| Rye Rye | "Bang" (2009)<br>"Sunshine" (2010)<br>"Never Will Be Mine" (2011)<br>"New Thing" (2011) |
| Shawnna | "Damn" (2006)<br>"Gettin Some" (2006) |
| Trina | "Here We Go" (2005)<br>"Single Again" (2007)<br>"I Got a Thang For You" (2008)<br>"My Bitches" (2010)<br>"That's My Attitude" (2010) |

## Dancing Machine

An additional finding was the large number of videos featuring dancing with no accompanying storyline. While dancing has always been a feature of music videos, particularly within R&B and rap, the dancing was often done as part of the background. Within these videos, the message may have been linked to bravado, but the images all showcased the dancers and often did not correlate with the actual lyrics. The appearance of dancing and choreography as a theme in the videos of female rappers, reflects an aspect of the origin of hip hop. Although actual break-dancing was not featured in any of these videos, hip hop dance has always been important to the culture and a main component of hip hop. As such, the inclusion and focus of dance in the videos could almost be considered homage to the roots of hip hop.

## LIMITATIONS AND SUGGESTIONS FOR FUTURE RESEARCH

One of the primary limitations of the study is that many of the artists examined have not had videos out in the past few years. Because of the low number of Black female rappers with major label affiliations that have created videos in the past few years, an analysis of current videos featuring female rappers on singles for their own major label releases yielded a small sample size. What would be interesting, however, is to do a comparative analysis of the themes shown in videos of Black female rappers assigned to major record labels from the past year with those of Independent Black female rappers that have produced videos. Such a study could have the sample size chosen by a set number of views on YouTube, where videos from both independent and major label artists are featured. The sample could be based on each video having a certain number of views in order to be analyzed. The goal would be to assess if there are different and more diverse themes in the videos of Independent Black female rappers in comparison to those affiliated with major record labels.

Another idea for future research would be to extend the current study by examining media effects. Past videos have examined how the effects of rap music videos have influenced the sexual attitudes and beliefs of young men.[63] After examining the thematic content presented in the videos of Black female rappers, it would be interesting to see the effects of these same videos on the relationship ideals and self concepts of African-American young women. Past research has found that Black girls who identify with stereotypical images of Black women from music videos often are more aware and critical of their own appearance. Similarly, it would be interesting to research the effects of music videos featuring Black women as the primary artists on the perspectives of both teenage and young adult males and females of different ethnicities. As a result, analyzing the effects of the images of the most common themes today could possibly yield interesting results.

## NOTES

1. Tricia Rose, *Black Noise: Rap Music and Black Culture in Contemporary America* (Middletown: Wesleyan University Press, 1994).
2. Tricia Rose, *The Hip-Hop Wars: What We Talk About When We Talk About Hip-Hop—And Why it Matters* (New York: Basic Books, 2008).
3. Patricia Hill Collins, *Black Sexual Politics* (New York: Routledge, 2005).

4. Kate Conrad, Travis Dixon, and Yuanyuan Zhang, "Controversial Rap Themes, Gender Portrayals and Skin Tone Distortion: A Content Analysis of Rap Music Videos," *Journal of Broadcasting & Electronic Media* 53, no. 1 (2009): 134–56, doi: 10.1080/08838150802643795

5. Mako Fitts, "Drop it Like it's Hot: Culture Industry Laborers and Their Perspectives on Rap Music Video Production," *Meridians* 8, no. 1 (2008): 211–35; Fatimah N. Muhammad, "How to Not be 21st Century Venus Hottentot," in *Home Girls Make Some Noise: Hip-Hop Feminism Anthology*, eds. Gwendolyn D. Pough, Elaine Richardson, Aisha Durham, and Rachel Raimist (Mira Loma: Parker Publishing, 2005), 115–40; S. Craig Watkins, *Hip-Hop Matters: Politics, Pop Culture, and the Struggle For the Soul of a Movement* (Boston: Beacon Press, 2005).

6. Collins, *Black Sexual Politics*, 133.

7. Cynthia M. Frisby and Jennifer Stevens Aubrey, "Race and Genre in the Use of Sexual Objectification in Female Artists' Music Videos," *Howard Journal of Communications* 23, no. 1 (2012): 66–87.

8. Ibid, 20.

9. Scyatta A. Wallace et al., "Gold Diggers, Video Vixens, and Jezebels: Stereotype Images and Substance Use Among Urban African American Girls," *Journal of Women's Health* 20, no. 9 (2011): 1315–24.

10. Fitts, "Drop it Like it's Hot," 211–35; Rose, *Black Noise*; Rose, *The Hip-Hop Wars*; Watkins, *Hip-Hop Matters*.

11. Rose, *Black Noise;* Rose, *The Hip-Hop Wars.*

12. Layli Phillips, Kerri Reddick-Morgan, and Dionne Patricia Stephens, "Oppositional Consciousness within an Oppositional Realm: The Case of Feminism and Womanism in Rap and Hip-Hop 1976-2004," *The Journal of African American History* 90, no.3 (2005): 253–77.

13. Murali Balaji, "Owning Black Masculinity: The Intersection of Cultural Commodification and Self-Construction in Rap Music Videos," *Communication, Culture & Critique* 2 (2009): 21–38, doi: 10.1111/j.1753-9137.2008.01027; Rana A. Emerson "'Where My Girls At?': Negotiating Black Womanhood in Music Videos," *Gender and Society* 16, no. 1 (2002): 115–35; Robin Roberts, "Music Videos, Performance and Resistance: Feminist Rappers," *Journal of Popular Culture* 25, no. 2 (1991): 141–52; Robin Roberts, "'Ladies First': Queen Latifah's Afrocentric Feminist Music Video," *African American Review* 28, no. 2 (1994): 245–57.

14. Phillips, Reddick-Morgan, and Stephens, "Oppositional Consciousness within an Oppositional Realm," 253–77.

15. Marcyliena Morgan, "Hip-hop Women Shredding the Veil: Race and Class in Popular Feminist Identity," *The South Atlantic Quarterly* 104, no. 3 (2005): 424–44.

16. Whitney A. Peoples, "Under Construction: Identifying Foundations of Hip-Hop Feminism and Exploring Bridges Between Second-Wave and Hip-Hop Feminisms," *Meridians* 8, no. 1 (2008): 25.

17. Gwendolyn D. Pough, *Check it While I Wreck it: Black Womanhood, Hip-Hop Culture, and the Public Sphere* (Boston: Northeastern University Press, 2004).

18. Ibid; Levine, Lawrence W. *Black Culture and Black Consciousness: Afro-American Folk Thought From Slavery to Freedom.* (New York: Oxford University Press, 1977).

19. William Eric Perkins, "The Rap Attack: An Introduction," in *Droppin' Science: Critical Essays on Rap Music and Hip-Hop Culture.* ed. William Eric Perkins (Philadelphia: Temple University Press, 1996), 1–45.

20. Siobhan Brooks and Thomas Conroy, "Hip-Hop Culture in a Global Context: Interdisciplinary and Cross-Categorical Investigation," *American Behavioral Scientist* 55, no. 1 (2011): 3–8, doi:10.1177/0002764210381723.

21. Morgan, "Hip-hop Women Shredding the Veil," 435.

22. Collins, *Black Sexual Politics,* 73.

23. Morgan, "Hip-hop Women Shredding the Veil," 434.

24. Ibid, 427.

25. Jennifer C. Lena, "Voyeurism and Resistance in Rap Music Videos," *Communication and Critical/Cultural Studies* 5, no. 3 (2008): 264–79.

26. Whitney Peoples, "Under Construction," 24.

27. Muhammad, "How to Not be 21st Century Venus Hottentot," 115–40.
28. Margaret Hunter, "Shake it Baby, Shake it: Consumption and the New Gender Relation in Hip-Hop," *Sociological Perspectives* 54, no. 1 (2011): 15–36.
29. Phillips, Reddick-Morgan, and Stephens, "Oppositional ConsciousnessWithin an Oppositional Realm," 261.
30. Ibid, 262–65.
31. Ibid.
32. Roberts, "Ladies First," 245.
33. Ibid.
34. John C. Besley, "Media Use and Human Values," *Journalism and Mass Communication Quarterly* 85, no. 2 (2008): 311–30; Tara M. Emmers-Sommer et al., "Love, Suspense, Sex, and Violence: Men's and Women's Film Predilections, Exposure to Sexually Violent Media, and Their Relationship to Rape Myth Acceptance," *Sex Roles*, 55 (2006): 311–20, doi:10.1007/s11199-006-9085-0; Su-Lin Gan, Dolf Zillmann, and Michael Mitrook, "Stereotyping Effect of Black Women's Sexual Rap on White Audiences," *Basic and Applied Social Psychology* 19, no. 3 (1997): 381–99; LeeAnn Kahlor and Dan Morrison, "Television Viewing and Rape Myth Acceptance Among College Women," *Sex Roles* 56 (2007): 729–39, doi:10/1007/s11199-007-9232-2; Michelle E. Kistler and Moon J. Lee, "Does Exposure to Sexual Hip-Hop Music Videos Influence the Sexual Attitudes of College Students," *Mass Communication and Society* 13 (2010): 67–86, doi:10.1080/15205430902865336; Shani H. Peterson et al., "Images of Sexual Stereotypes in Rap Videos and the Health of African-American Female Adolescents," *Journal of Women's Health* 16, no. 8 (2007): 1157–64, doi:10.1089/jwh.2007.0429; Jacob S. Turner, "Sex and the Spectacle of Music Videos: An Examination of the Portrayal of Race and Sexuality in Music Videos," *Sex Roles* 64 (2011): 173–91, doi: 10.1007/s11199-010-9766-6; Cara Wallis, "Performing Gender: A Content Analysis of Gender Display in Music Videos," *Sex Roles* 64 (2011): 160–72, doi:10.1007/s11199-010-9814-2; Yuanyan Zhang, Travis L. Dixon, and Kate Conrad, "Rap Music Videos and African American Women's Body Image: The Moderating Role of Ethnic Identity," *Journal of Communication* 59 (2009): 262–78, doi:10.1111/j.1460-2466.2009.01415; Zhang, Laura E. Miller, and Kristen Harrison, "The Relationship Between Exposure to Sexual Music Videos and Young Adults' Sexual Attitudes," *Journal of Broadcasting & Electronic Media* 52, no. 3 (2008): 368–86, doi: 10.1080/08838150802205462.
35. Paul M. Lester and Susan D. Ross, "Images That Injure: An Introduction," in *Images That Injure: Pictorial Stereotypes in the Media,* eds. P. M. Lester and S. D. Ross (Westport: Praeger Publishers, 2003), 1–4.
36. Peter L. Berger and Thomas Luckmann, *The Social Construction of Reality* (Garden City: Anchor Books, 1966), 1, 23.
37. Norman K. Denzin, *Symbolic Interactionism and Cultural Studies: The Politics of Interpretation* (Cambridge: Blackwell, 1992).
38. Mike Brake, *Comparative Youth Culture: The Sociology of Youth Cultures and Youth Subcultures in America, Britain, and Canada* (London: Routledge and Kegan Paul, 1985).
39. Marci Bounds Littlefield, "The Media as a System of Racialization: Exploring Images of African American Women and the New Racism," *American Behavioral Scientist* 51, no. 5 (2008): 677, doi: 10.1177/0002764207307747.
40. Deborah K. King, "Multiple Jeopardy, Multiple Consciousness: The Context of Black Feminist Ideology," in *Words of Fire: An Anthology of African-American Feminist Thought*, ed. Beverly Guy-Sheftall (New York: New Press, 1995), 312.
41. Ibid.
42. Ibid.
43. Ibid.
44. The Combahee River Collective, "A Black Feminist Statement," in *Words of Fire: An Anthology of African-American Feminist Thought,* ed. Beverly Guy-Sheftall (New York: New Press, 1995), 233.
45. Ibid.
46. Collins, *Black Sexual Politics*, 122.

47. Barbara Smith, "Some Home Truths on the Contemporary Black Feminist Movement," in *Words of Fire: An Anthology of African-American Feminist Thought,* ed. Bevery Guy-Sheftall (New York: New Press, 1995), 262.
48. Patricia Hill Collins, *Black Feminist Thought* (New York: Routledge, 2009).
49. Angela Y. Davis, "Black Women and Music: A Historical Legacy of Struggle," in *Black Feminist Cultural Criticism,* ed. Jacqueline Bobo (Malden: Blackwell Publishers, 1990), 217.
50. Rose, *Black Noise*, 2.
51. Recording Industry Association of America http://www.riaa.com/aboutus.php?content_selector=about-whowe-are-riaa.
52. Phillips, Reddick-Morgan, and Stephens, "Oppositional Consciousness Within an Oppositional Realm," 253–77.
53. Ibid.
54. Jennifer Fereday and Eimear Muir-Cochrane, "Demonstrating Rigor Using Thematic Analysis: A Hybrid Approach of Inductive and Deductive Coding and Theme Development," *International Journal of Qualitative Methods* 5, no. 1 (2006): 80–92.
55. Phillips, Reddick-Morgan, and Stephens, "Oppositional Consciousness within an Oppositional Realm," 253–77.
56. Ted Lucas, "Still a Man's World for Female Rappers," *Billboard,* April 1, 2006.
57. Margaret Hunter, "Shake it Baby, Shake it: Consumption and the New Gender Relation in Hip-Hop," *Sociological Perspectives* 54, no. 1 (2011): 31.
58. Rose, *The Hip-Hop Wars*, 155.
59. Rose, *Black Noise*, 174.
60. Collins, *Black Feminist Thought.*
61. Watkins, *Hip-Hop Matters.*
62. Collins, *Black Sexual Politics*, 133.
63. Jennifer Stevens Aubrey, K. Megan Hopper, and Wanjiru G. Mbure, "Check That Body! The Effects of Sexually Objectifying Music Videos on College Men's Sexual Beliefs," *Journal of Broadcasting & Electronic Media* 55, no. 3 (2011): 360–79; Yaphet Bryant, "Relationships between Exposure to Rap Music Videos and Attitudes toward Relationships among African American Youth," *Journal of Black Psychology* 34, no. 3 (2008): 356–80; Peterson et al., "Images of Sexual Stereotypes in Rap Videos and the Health of African-American Female Adolescents."

# BIBLIOGRAPHY

Aubrey, Jennifer Stevens, K. Megan Hopper, and Wanjiru Mbure. "Check That Body! The Effects of Sexually Objectifying Music Videos on College Men's Sexual Beliefs." *Journal of Broadcasting & Electronic Media* 55, no.3 (2011): 360–79.

Balaji, Murali. "Owning Black Masculinity: The Intersection of Cultural Commodification and Self-Construction in Rap Music Videos." *Communication, Culture & Critique* 2 (2009): 21–38. doi: 10.1111/j.1753-9137.2008.01027.x

Berger, Peter L., and Thomas Luckmann. *The Social Construction of Reality.* Garden City: Anchor Books, 1966.

Besley, John C. "Media Use and Human Values." *Journalism and Mass Communication Quarterly* 85, no. 2 (2008): 311–30.

Brake, Mike. *Comparative Youth Culture: The Sociology of Youth Cultures and Youth Subcultures in America, Britain, and Canada.* London: Routledge and Kegan Paul, 1985.

Brooks, Siobhan, and Thomas Conroy. "Hip-Hop Culture in a Global Context: Interdisciplinary and Cross-Categorical Investigation." *American Behavioral Scientist* 55, no. 1 (2011): 3–8. doi:10.1177/0002764210381723.

Bryant, Yaphet. "Relationships Between Exposure to Rap Music Videos and Attitudes Toward Relationships Among African American Youth." *Journal of Black Psychology* 34, no. 3 (2008): 356–80.

Collins, Patricia Hill. *Black Feminist Thought.* New York: Routledge, 2009.

Collins, Patricia Hill. *Black Sexual Politics.* New York: Routledge, 2005.

Conrad, Kate, Travis Dixon, and Yuanyuan Zhang. "Controversial Rap Themes, Gender Portrayals and Skin Tone Distortion: A Content Analysis of Rap Music Videos." *Journal of Broadcasting & Electronic Media* 53, no. 1 (2009): 134–56. doi:10.1080/08838150802643795.

Davis, Angela Y. "Black Women and Music: A Historical Legacy of Struggle." In *Black Feminist Cultural Criticism.* Edited by Jacqueline Bobo. Malden: Blackwell Publishers, 1990, 217.

Denzin, Norman K. *Symbolic Interactionism and Cultural Studies: The Politics of Interpretation.* Cambridge: Blackwell, 1992.

Emerson, Rana A. "'Where My Girls At?': Negotiating Black Womanhood in Music Videos." *Gender and Society* 16, no. 1 (2002): 115–35.

Emmers-Sommer, Tara M., Perry Pauley, Alesia Hanzal, and Laura Triplett. "Love, Suspense, Sex, and Violence: Men's and Women's Film Predilections, Exposure to Sexually Violent Media, and Their Relationship to Rape Myth Acceptance." *Sex Roles* 55 (2006): 311–20. doi:10.1007/s11199-006-9085-0.

Fereday, Jennifer, and Eimear Muir-Cochrane. "Demonstrating Rigor Using Thematic Analysis: A Hybrid Approach of Inductive and Deductive Coding and Theme Development." *International Journal of Qualitative Methods* 5, no. 1 (2006): 80–92.

Fitts, Mako. "Drop it Like it's Hot: Culture Industry Laborers and Their Perspectives on Rap Music Video Production." *Meridians* 8, no. 1 (2008): 211–35.

Frisby, Cynthia M., and Jennifer Stevens Aubrey. "Race and Genre in the Use of Sexual Objectification in Female Artists' Music Videos." *Howard Journal of Communications* 23, no. 1 (2012): 66–87.

Gan, Su-Lin, Dolf Zillmann, and Michael Mitrook. "Stereotyping Effect of Black Women's Sexual Rap on White Audiences." *Basic and Applied Social Psychology* 19, no. 3 (1997): 381–99.

Hunter, Margaret. "Shake it Baby, Shake it: Consumption and the New Gender Relation in Hip-Hop." *Sociological Perspectives* 54, no. 1 (2011): 15–36.

Kahlor, LeeAnn, and Dan Morrison. "Television Viewing and Rape Myth Acceptance Among College Women." *Sex Roles* 56 (2007): 729–39. doi:10/1007/s11199-007-9232-2.

King, Deborah K. "Multiple Jeopardy, Multiple Consciousness: The Context of Black Feminist Ideology." In *Words of Fire: An Anthology of African-American Feminist Thought.* Edited by Beverly Guy-Sheftall. New York: New Press, 1995, 294–317.

Kistler, Michelle E., and Moon J. Lee. "Does Exposure to Sexual Hip-Hop Music Videos Influence the Sexual Attitudes of College Students?" *Mass Communication and Society* 13 (2010): 67–86. doi:10.1080/15205430902865336.

Lena, Jennifer C. "Voyeurism and Resistance in Rap Music Videos." *Communication and Critical/Cultural Studies* 5, no. 3 (2008): 264–79.

Lester, Paul M., and Susan D. Ross. "Images That Injure: An Introduction." In *Images That Injure:Pictorial Stereotypes in the Media.* Edited by Paul M. Lester and Susan D. Ross. Westport: Praeger Publishers, 2003, 1–4.

Levine, Lawrence W. *Black Culture and Black Consciousness: Afro-American Folk Thought From Slavery to Freedom.* New York: Oxford University Press, 1977.

Littlefield, Marci Bounds. "The Media as a System of Racialization: Exploring Images of African American Women and the New Racism." *American Behavioral Scientist* 51, no. 5 (2008): 675–85. doi:10.1177/0002764207307747.

Lucas, Ted. "Still a Man's World for Female Rappers." Billboard, April 1, 2006.

Morgan, Marcyliena. "Hip-hop Women Shredding the Veil: Race and Class in Popular Feminist Identity." *The South Atlantic Quarterly* 104, no. 3 (2005): 424–44.

Muhammad, Fatimah N. "How to Not be 21st Century Venus Hottentot." In *Home Girls Make Some Noise: Hip-Hop Feminism Anthology.* Edited by Gwendolyn D. Pough, Elaine Richardson, Aisha Durham, and Rachel Raimist. Mira Loma: Parker Publishing, 2005, 115–40.

Peoples, Whitney A. "Under Construction: Identifying Foundations of Hip-Hop Feminism and Exploring Bridges Between Second-Wave and Hip-Hop Feminisms." *Meridians* 8, no. 1 (2008): 19–52.

Perkins, William Eric "The Rap Attack: An Introduction." In *Droppin' Science: Critical Essays on Rap Music and Hip-Hop Culture.* Edited by William Eric Perkins. Philadelphia: Temple University Press, 1996, 1–45.

Peterson, Shani H., Gina M. Wingood, Ralph J. DiClemente, Kathy Harrington, and Susan Davies. "Images of Sexual Stereotypes in Rap Videos and the Health of African-American Female Adolescents." *Journal of Women's Health* 16, no. 8 (2007): 1157–64. doi:10.1089/jwh.2007.0429.

Phillips, Layli, Kerri Reddick-Morgan, and Dionn Patricia Stephens. "Oppositional Consciousness within an Oppositional Realm: The Case of Feminism and Womanism in Rap and Hip-Hop 1976-2004." *The Journal of African American History* 90, no. 3 (2005): 253–77.

Pough, Gwendolyn D. *Check it While I Wreck it: Black Womanhood, Hip-Hop Culture, and the Public Sphere.* Boston: Northeastern University Press, 2004.

Recording Industry Association of America, 2012. www.riaa.com/aboutus.php?content_selector=about-who-we-are-riaa.

Roberts, Robin. "'Ladies First': Queen Latifah's Afrocentric Feminist Music Video." *African American Review* 28, no. 2 (1994): 245–57.

Roberts, Robin. "Music Videos, Performance and Resistance: Feminist Rappers." *Journal of Popular Culture* 25, no. 2 (1991): 141–52.

Rose, Tricia. *Black Noise: Rap Music and Black Culture in Contemporary America.* Middletown: Wesleyan University Press, 1994.

Rose, Tricia. *The Hip-Hop Wars: What We Talk About When We Talk About Hip-Hop—And Why it Matters.* New York: Basic Books, 2008.

Smith, Barbara. "Some Home Truths on the Contemporary Black Feminist Movement." In *Words of Fire: An Anthology of African-American Feminist Thought.* Edited by Beverly Guy-Sheftall. New York: New Press, 1995, 254–67.

The Combahee River Collective. "A Black Feminist Statement." In *Words of Fire: An Anthology of African-American Feminist Thought.* Edited by Beverly Guy-Sheftall. New York: New Press, 1995, 232–40.

Turner, Jacob S. "Sex and the Spectacle of Music Videos: An Examination of the Portrayal of Race and Sexuality in Music Videos." *Sex Roles* 64 (2011): 173–91. doi:10.1007/s11199-010-9766-6.

Wallace, Scyatta A., Tiffany G. Townsend, Marcia Y. Glasgow, and Mary Jan Ojie. "Gold Diggers, Video Vixens, and Jezebels: Stereotype Images and Substance Use Among Urban African American Girls." *Journal of Women's Health* 20, no. 9 (2011): 1315–24.

Wallis, Cara. "Performing Gender: A Content Analysis of Gender Display in Music Videos." *Sex Roles* 64 (2011): 160–72. doi:10.1007/s11199-010-9814-2.

Watkins, S. Craig. *Hip-Hop Matters: Politics, Pop Culture, and the Struggle For the Soul of a Movement.* Boston: Beacon Press, 2005.

Zhang, Yuanyan, Travis L. Dixon, and Kate Conrad. "Rap Music Videos and African American Women's Body Image: The Moderating Role of Ethnic Identity." *Journal of Communication* 59 (2009): 262–78. doi:10.1111/j.1460-2466.2009.01415.x.

Zhang, Yuanyuan, Laura E. Miller, and Kristen Harrison. "The Relationship between Exposure to Sexual Music Videos and Young Adults' Sexual Attitudes." *Journal of Broadcasting & Electronic Media* 52, no. 3 (2008): 368–86. doi:10.1080/08838150802205462.

*Chapter Eight*

# "Bey Feminism" vs. Black Feminism

## *A Critical Conversation on Word-of-Mouth Advertisement of* Beyoncé's Visual Album

## Elizabeth Y. Whittington and Mackenzie Jordan

The purpose of this chapter is to analyze how advertisement plays a role in the representation of Black women in popular culture. Critical academic scholars have long been concerned with how Black women are portrayed in traditional forms of advertisements such as magazines, television, and commercials.[1] In this work, we have decided to take a different perspective. Social media has provided an avenue for consumers to receive and respond to information in a more interactive forum. It is no longer productive to see the general customer as only a consumer of the media since they can now voice their opinion and ultimately have an influence on the perception of the topic. Because of this, we were intrigued by the idea of what would happen if social media were the sole means of advertisement for an album. There is no better representation of this than the December 2013 release of the *Beyoncé Visual Album*.[2] Through her artistry, we will not only explore the power of social media as an advertisement tool but, also, how Beyoncé Knowles-Carter reinscribes feminist sensibilities in her music which impact popular culture. At this intersection of advertisement, digital (social) media, and music, we will explore how the *Queen Bey* seems to navigate through these various aspects within a pop cultural paradigm.

Beyoncé Knowles-Carter is a Grammy award winning, multiplatinum selling artist. Originally a member of the group Destiny's Child, Beyoncé chose to venture away from the group to establish herself as a solo artist with her first album *Dangerously in Love* in Summer 2003.[3] Since that time, Beyoncé has established herself as one of the best entertainers of this generation. Beyoncé continued to push the bar in the industry in 2013 when she released *Beyoncé: The Visual Album* with no notice, no prior press coverage, and by using social media as her sole means of advertisement for the album.[4] Word of mouth played an important role in the sales of the album, which skyrocketed to the top of the charts during the first week of sales. Several factors played a role in the sales of this album including the "voice" of the consumer and blogs. The blogs became a pivotal part of not only the success of the album, but also a substantial form of advertisement. This chapter will analyze five blogs in the context of feminist representations of Black women in popular culture. Looking at this unique and previously untapped form of advertisement, we will explore the future of feminism as it is seen in the ivory tower in comparison with how it is seen by the everyday Black woman consumer.

On December 13, at midnight, Beyoncé Knowles-Carter released a secret album no one knew she was working on.[5] I (Elizabeth) remember getting ready to leave the state where I currently hold a faculty position to fly home for the holidays. I opened my Instagram account and there was a video posted by Beyoncé (or the people who manage her account) that started with a black screen that kept flashing the word Beyoncé in pink letters, several clips (that I would soon realize were from the videos included in the album), and the last image again in pink letters *available now*. Underneath the video was the word *Surprise!*

Beyoncé had done what no artist has ever done. She released an album with fourteen tracks and seventeen videos without a record label and without any of the public knowing.[6] She had no advertising of this album before she released it. This was not the only surprise about her album. For many, this was Beyoncé's debut as a self-proclaimed feminist. In many feminist circles her track titled "***Flawless," featuring the voice of celebrated Nigerian writer and feminist Chimamanda Ngozi Adichie, was evidence that she finally claimed feminism.[7] Since this album has been released, feminists across America have been debating this form of feminism Beyoncé proclaims, and whether or not it is really feminism.

The following chapter seeks to explore the difference between traditional or *Ivory Tower* Black feminism and Beyoncé's feminism or Bey Feminism (a term that we coined for the purpose of naming this brand of feminism). The Ivory Tower is a term used by academicians to describe the American institution of higher education. The term refers to the elitism that is evident within the academy (universities and colleges) that forms a barrier to many who do not attend these institutions. Many feel the term seeks to segregate groups of individuals of those who are attaining or have attained a degree and those that do not. Merriam-Webster's Dictionary states the Ivory Tower is "a place or situation in which people make and discuss theories about problems (such as poverty and racism) without having any experience with those problems."[8] For the sake of this chapter, the term refers to all of the abovementioned descriptions as a word to describe an institution of higher education that has an elitist attitude towards those that do not obtain passage through the halls of academia.

We argue that Bey Feminism is attractive to the everyday Black woman for several reasons, and assisted in the advertisement of her album once it was released. Every day Black women are embracing Bey Feminism as a way of "negotiating, co-creating, reinforcing, and challenging" their identities as Black women in American society.[9] First, we will discuss traditional Black feminism. Second, we present a brief history of Bey Feminism and its appeal to the everyday Black woman. Third, we provide an analysis of the blogs that appeared after the album was released. Last, we present a discussion of what Bey Feminism means to the world of Black feminism and the everyday Black woman.

## THEORETICAL FRAMEWORK

### Black Feminism

Patricia Hills Collins outlines four principles as the core of understanding Black feminism:

1. Racism, sexism, and classism are interlocking systems of oppression.
2. We must maintain a humanist vision that will not accept any amount of human oppression.
3. We must define ourselves and give voice to the everyday Black woman and everyday experience.
4. We must operate from the standpoint that Black women are unique and our experiences are unique.[10]

Collins states that Black feminism is a critical social theory that "aims to empower African-American women within the context of social injustice sustained by intersecting oppressions."[11] Black feminist thought is situated around knowledge and the importance of knowledge "to empower oppressed people."[12] Within Black feminism, there is this double bind of recognizing the oppressive nature of the Black community and its patriarchal ways, but also knowing the value of the community and the supportive nature of Black women to that community.[13]

It is a consciousness that first caused the development of Black feminism because traditional or dominant feminism wanted Black women to focus on their gender oppression, while the Black liberation movement (or Black men) wanted Black women to focus on their racial oppression.[14] This argument began with the Combahee River Collective, a group of Black women feminists and lesbians that sought to fight for the rights of Black women. They realized no one was going to fight for their rights but them. They sought to end oppression through their own identity recognition understanding that before anyone else can free them they must free themselves. They recognized the unique struggle of being both Black and female and the need to examine the multiple layers of Black women and work within the community to help end the oppression.[15] However, for the Black woman there is not a choice, we cannot separate our blackness from our femaleness, and for many Black women there come other intersections of their identity that they cannot separate such as class, sexuality, and/or religion. With the rise of more Black women achieving degrees than in years past, Black feminist scholarship has expanded and resides mainly in the realm of Black educated women or women who have the access to this scholarship. Next we will examine the history of how Bey Feminism came into being.

## Bey Feminism

Since Beyoncé's debut in the music industry with the group Destiny's Child, there have been references to the subject of Beyoncé and feminism.[16] The song "Independent Woman" from the *Charlie's Angels* movie soundtrack became an anthem for female empowerment and fashioned a spiral of events that put Beyoncé in the center of many conversations on modern-day feminism.[17] Unlike many other artist in popular culture, Beyoncé has not shied away from her feminist label and self-describes her views to *The Daily Mail UK* as follows:

> I think I am a feminist, in a way. It's not something I consciously decided I was going to be; perhaps it's because I grew up in a singing group with other women, and that was so helpful to me. It kept me out of so much trouble and out of bad relationships. My friendships with my girls are just so much a part of me that there are things I am never going to do that would upset that bond. I never want to betray that friendship, because I love being a woman and I love being a friend to other women.[18]

The definition of feminism that Beyoncé presented in the above quote is in many ways distinguishable from the definitions that are found in the academy. The debate on what the definition of feminism should look like has been going on for decades. Some believe that feminism should be broad and encompass many different perspectives; others feel that feminism should be specific and detailed.[19] For the purpose of this chapter, we will explore a few of the definitions that are being used. Cellestine Ware states, "radical feminism is working for the eradication of domination and elitism in all human relationships. This would make self-determination the ultimate good and require the downfall of society as we know it today."[20]

Many definitions of the early days of feminism involved looking at political issues such as women's rights to vote, support for women's businesses, end to sexism against women in various societal institutions such as the workplace, universities, sports, etc., an examination of welfare reform, and stricter laws against rape and sexual assault against women.[21] Barbara Berg defines feminism as "a broad movement embracing numerous phases of woman's emancipation."[22] This definition focuses more on the personal freedoms of women to be able to choose what brand of feminism they want to embody. The context is more abstract. bell hooks discusses one way to define feminism as a struggle to eradicate the ideology of domination that permeates Western culture on various levels, as well as a commitment to reorganizing society so that the self-development of people can take precedence over imperialism, economic expansion, and material desires.[23] This definition however lays a burden on all women who would call themselves a feminist to be politically minded on the issues that are going on within their society. The definition that we accept and use as a model for the rest of this chapter states:

> Feminism is the struggle to end sexist oppression. Its aim is not to benefit solely any specific group of women, any particular race or class of women. It does not privilege women over men. It has the power to transform in a meaningful way all our lives. Most importantly, feminism is neither a lifestyle nor a ready-made identity or role one can step into.[24]

With the different varieties of feminism throughout the years, it is not surprising the amount of criticism Beyoncé has received with branding her own version. However, the amount of controversy that has followed Beyoncé's decision to associate with feminism motivated us to give her grassroots style of feminism the unique title of Bey Feminism. The term is derived from one of Beyoncé's nicknames Queen Bey (pronounced Bee). This is not a term that Beyoncé uses but one in which we felt could embody her brand of feminism that she claims. Although she does admit to having some issues with the word feminism, she does exemplify the characteristics in many of the actions that she has taken throughout her life and career.[25] For example, since her first solo tour, Beyoncé has maintained an all female band that she consciously put together to inspire more women to play music.[26] As her career flourished, she also made the decision to relinquish her father Matthew Knowles from his long time role of manager in order to have the opportunity to be financially independent from men, which she believes creates long-term power.[27] In terms of her personal life, it is alleged in some media outlets that Beyoncé and her husband, hip hop artist Jay-Z (Shawn Carter), hyphenated their names to Knowles-Carter to honor her family name since her father has no sons.[28]

The biggest platform, in which Beyoncé has expressed her thoughts on women's equality, is in her music. In her song "If I were a Boy," Beyoncé takes the conversation of gender roles head on as she discusses the stereotypes of behaviors that are deemed acceptable in the context of relationships.[29] In the song, she sings about how by switching genders she would be better able to understand how to love a girl because she has been a girl and by doing that it would make her a better man for that girl.[30] These lyrics show her consciousness of the different behaviors and expectations that are put on genders, in particular women. Her song "Run the World (Girls)" is an anthem for women to stand up and realize their influence and strength.[31] In addition to the aforementioned lyrics, "Single Ladies (Put A Ring on It)," is a track that sings about women respecting themselves outside of a relationship, "Diva," is a female empowering song that encourages women to work hard for what they want in life, "Pretty Hurts," is a track about societal requirements of beauty in society and how they should not define a woman's beauty, "Me, Myself and I," is a track about learning from the consequences of a boyfriend who is unfaithful, and "Grown Woman" is a track about being an adult woman who is in control of her life and what she wants to get out of it.[32] As illustrated all these songs have themes extremely applicable to feminist related concepts.

Throughout the years, there have been many critics of Beyoncé's version of feminism. Some believe that she is inauthentic in her cause and is using feminism and women's issues only as a means to sell albums.[33] Another concern with Beyoncé's style of feminism is her over-sexualized figure. Beyoncé not only performs frequently in leotards, but also has dressed in extremely revealing outfits on magazine covers and in various music videos. Critics believe this shows a lack of confidence that does not provide a good example for other woman in terms of body image.[34] Although Beyoncé has moments of female empowerment in her lyrics, she has also shown some mannerisms that make some believe she is overly "submissive" to her man. Her 2013 tour The Mrs. Carter Show caused some to believe that she could only find her identity as wife to her husband Jay-Z.[35]

Beyoncé also has some controversial songs about submissiveness including "Cater 2 U," "Naughty Girl," "Blow," and "Partition," which have themes centered on the physical pleasure of a man and being sexually pleasured by a man.[36] As one blogger, Robin Boylorn discusses, perhaps positioning one's self as sexually confident and knowing how to both give and receive pleasure should be something that Black women should embrace and not let the dominant discourse continue to silence Black women's sexuality.[37] The backlash Beyoncé has received from these songs as being too sexual or too risqué, Boylorn discusses in the context of sex positive messages. She explains that much can be gained from these songs and how embracing one's sexuality should also be part of the feminist dialogue.[38] It is hard for some to see how Beyoncé can define herself as independent while on the same album positioning her body as the center of a man's desires. Regardless of perspective, Beyoncé's history with popular culture and feminism created a discourse that was an instrumental part of the conversation through the first few weeks of her album sales.

The goal of this chapter is to elaborate on the conversations surrounding Beyoncé's album. Many Black feminists, and other feminists across the country, argue that the singer's actions are not feminist. However, through an analysis of blog commentary and discussion we will illustrate how Beyoncé, in fact, launched her own brand of feminism. Furthermore, our discussion illustrates how Beyoncé presents herself as a Black woman in the music industry. Readers will see the intersectionality of music, social media, and advertising. Perhaps a different construct of understanding what Black feminism is, and what Beyoncé is trying to achieve, is a better alternative to discussions of feminism versus anti-feminism. We will view Beyoncé's feminist landscape through the perspective of a self-proclaiming Black feminist, and the other author's perspective as an anti-labeling Black female (the second author does not accept the label of Black feminist). The next section is an overview of some of the comments from various blog posts after the release of Beyoncé's album, along with commentary from her mini documentaries on her vision for the album, also released after the album.

## THE CONVERSATION

The first blog discussed is titled "The Problem with Beyhive Bottom Bitch Feminism" from the site *Real Colored Girls*. The article begins by defining *bottom bitch* from the perspective of Pimp Theory, a term used in the blog that discusses the dichotomy between a pimp and a hoe. The Pimp is the man who controls and provides protection for his female prostitutes or his hoes. The definition of bottom bitch states:

> the one in the whores' hierarchy who rides hardest for her man. She's the rock of every hustler economy and her primary occupation is keeping other ho's in check and gettin' that money. She isn't trying to elevate the status of her sister ho's. She isn't looking to transform pimp culture. The bottom bitch is a token who is allowed symbolic power, which she uses to discipline, advocate for, represent and advance the domain of the stable. In pop culture, she represents the trope of the chosen black female, loyal to her man and complicit in her own commodification.[39]

The blog continues to discuss how Beyoncé is a bottom bitch with the use of her husband's rap lyrics in the song "Drunk in Love" specifically referencing the violence of how he is going to treat her.[40] In the song Jay-Z compares himself to Mike Tyson and Ike Turner; two men who were accused of physical abuse and rape and Tyson was convicted of rape in 1992. They go on to discuss how Beyoncé is silencing the voice of Black women through her lyrics in songs such as "***Flawless" by telling women, or rather "bitches," to "bow" before her.[41] However, they do mention that they welcome a discussion on this Beyhive bottom bitch feminism, but in the same moment consider that:

> This does not replace nor is it even in the realm of the critical work of black women writers and artists across the discursive spectrum, as some folks have proclaimed across social media. As womanists and black feminists, we have a responsibility to bring it with our cultural work which we will infuse, at all times, with an ethic of care and responsibilities.[42]

This critique silences Beyoncé's voice by asserting that she is not a part of the critical discourse of *real* Black feminists. This is disturbing because it reads to some that unless the formal script of Black feminism is followed there is an inherent problem with that belief.

Though I (Elizabeth) do not agree with some of the rap lines and lyrics in "Drunk in Love," I do recognize the impact of the discourse for the everyday Black woman who listens to Beyoncé.[43] I hear Jay-Z's rap lyrics differently; as a possible attempt to separate himself from Mike Tyson and Ike Turner through his lyrical metaphors of *beating it up* and *eating cake*. Immediately after he mentions their names he raps about his *niceness*, which could be read that he is not like these men, but instead chooses to be creative with how he describes his coital skills. Instead of *beating it up*, meaning to inflict physical violence on his wife, alternatively in the hip hop vernacular it is referred to as having an intense sexual encounter. Jay-Z's usage of the term *cake* is used to describe a woman's buttocks. Instead of those lines representing a connection to justifying physical violence and rape against a woman it refers to various sexual activities between two consenting adults. As a woman who does not self identify as a critical feminist, I (Mackenzie) understand the artistry in the music as it relates to the everyday Black woman. As I write this, it is important to note that I do not condone domestic violence in any form nor do I believe they are situations to be taken lightly. Much of hip hop music is built on clever analogies and in this context; I believe that is where Jay-Z was trying to go with his lyrics. Throughout his rap, Jay-Z talks about how they are drunk, trash talking, and then engage in rough sex. Some argue that the lyrics of this song are damaging to our youth and their self-image. I refute this logic, as youth should not be listening to a song with such graphic, sexual content in any instance. Beyoncé gave the song an adult rating for a reason and anyone of maturity should be able to understand the figurative meaning behind these lyrics, even if they do not agree.

The traditional view of Black feminism is not being heard by the everyday Black woman because it appears as if women in the academy have taken ownership of what it means to be a Black feminist. To be more frank, women who do not reside in the walls of academia or do not view the world with a similar critical lens are, at times, the outliers of traditional Black feminism. Beyoncé states in her own exploration of videos about feminism, "I was scrolling through videos about feminism on YouTube and I ran across this video of this incredible Nigerian author Chimamanda Adichie. Everything she said is exactly how I feel."[44] She goes on to insert the quote by Adichie, "We raise girls to see each other as competitors not for jobs or accomplishments which I think can be a good thing, but for the attention of man."[45] Before watching this video and hearing the clip, I wonder how many Black women (outside of the academy) wanted to be a feminist or knew anything about Chimamanda Adichie?

It would seem that Black feminism sometimes fails to reach the very women it seeks to help empower, and that is where the problem lies. However, Bey Feminism is reaching them, and giving them a voice that is far too often silenced by every level of society. Beyoncé's tentative verbal acceptance of feminism has been one that people have grabbed on to, and held her to standards that she herself has never claimed as her own. What Beyoncé represents publically does not seem to add up to how she is privately. This contradicts feminist perspectives such as bell hooks' discussion of how the personal is political, and there can be no separation between one's public self and private self since it is all part of the whole representation of a woman.[46] She agrees with the empowerment of women and equality for all, but she has never said she would limit her sexuality or her performance of her gender.

People (mainly feminists) have boxed Beyoncé into a prototype of feminism because of progressive behaviors such as hiring an all female band when she goes on tour and sampling a feminist writer's words in a song. But, none of these examples signify a verbal declaration that she is a certain *type* of feminist. Instead of focusing entirely on problematic aspects of what we contend as Bey Feminism, why not focus on what it is accomplishing in communities of everyday Black women? Beyoncé says that her message for this album is "finding the beauty in imperfection."[47] How many Black women can relate to feeling imperfect and never correlating that with dominant beauty standards? Black feminists should ask these hard questions of the Black female community. The history of Black feminism was "traditionally such women [who] were blues singers, poets, autobiographers, storytellers, and orators validated by every day Black women as experts on a Black women's standpoint."[48] Beyoncé is part of a long line of Black women who used their voice to articulate how they felt as a Black women, and to give other Black women power through their messages.

The next blog "On Defending Beyoncé: Black Feminists, White Feminists and the Line in the Sand" is from the Black Girl Dangerous website written by Mia McKenzie.[49] McKenzie starts off with a discussion of the many Black feminists that have now declared Beyoncé a real feminist by quoting Mikki Kendall from the *Guardian*. Kendall states:

> This album makes it clear that her feminism isn't academic; isn't about waves, or labels. It simply is a part of her as much as anything else in her life. She's pro-woman without being anti-man, and she wants the world to know that you can be feminist on a personal level without sacrificing emotions, friendships or fun.[50]

McKenzie, agreeing with Kendall, goes on to once again claim Beyoncé as a feminist with imperfections and flaws as all feminists have, but she is still a feminist nonetheless. In her blog, McKenzie also brings up Jay-Z's anti-feminist and anti-woman lyrics. Although she goes on to say that claiming herself as a feminist is something that she rarely does, her ideals and what she works for leans more towards feminist values.[51]

Although her position is valid, this is McKenzie's opinion not Beyoncé's. Throughout her post, there are some contradictions on what she is arguing. Although she claims Beyoncé's album is her *feminist* album, Beyoncé has never said that this is what her album should be labeled. She argues that maybe two or three songs fit a feminist mold but not the whole album. McKenzie then argues that there is no one, two, or even five ways to be a feminist, but one cannot call herself (or himself) a feminist if they support the glorification of domestic violence (which she is arguing Beyoncé does by allowing her husband's lyrics to be included in her album).[52] McKenzie apparently makes many justifications of what is and what is not feminism in her blog, even though she says there is no perfect way to be a feminist.[53] She makes the judgment call of how anti-feminist she believes Beyoncé to be, although *we* (Black women) must defend Beyoncé against White women since it's our responsibility to defend the entire Black race. However, we cannot do so at the expense of allowing Beyoncé a pass on the problematic areas featured in her album. McKenzie goes on to state:

> What I'm not here for is pretending that Beyoncé is some champion of black feminism as some kind of "up yours" to white women, especially if it means ignoring seriously problematic things. Frankly, I think we can do a whole lot better than that. I think—I hope—we can defend Beyoncé in all the legitimate ways there are to do so (and there are many) without losing our sense of what black feminism really is, in all of its complexities, and what it's really *not* (see again: Ike Turner). I hope—I really hope—we can *love* Beyoncé and stand up for her without giving her, or ourselves, or anyone else, a pass.[54]

In Narayan's article on non-western feminism, she concurs with McKenzie's argument about feminism.[55] Narayan states:

> If nonwestern feminists talk about the value of women's experiences in terms totally different from those of traditional discourse, the difference is likely to be drowned out by the louder and more powerful voice of the traditional discourse, which will then claim that "what those feminists say" vindicates its views that the roles and experiences it assigns to women have value and that women should stick to those rules.[56]

In other words, the traditional voice of feminism continues to marginalize the voice of alternate feminist perspectives that differ from traditional ideas because they do not have that same lived experience. This traditional brand of feminism tends to overshadow the lived experiences of Black women leaving them without a place or a voice within the dominant discourse of feminist rhetoric. This sheds light on the backlash of Bey Feminism, and how McKenzie, although wanting to support Beyoncé, does not appreciate her brand of feminism because of the patriarchal aspects (or imperfections) within it. Although, interestingly, she argues that there is no perfect brand of feminism. What if, among Black feminists, we are doing to each other what White feminists have done towards Black women? That is to say, labeling any feminism that does not fit what is defined as traditional Black feminism as not having a place at all. McKenzie's last statement in this discussion, "But it should not happen at the expense of a black feminism that includes keeping our critical lens focused, not just on white women and others who would seek to tear us down, but also on our idols and ourselves" highlights this idea that all Black women should be able to see things through a critical lens.[57] In my experience (Elizabeth) viewing the world with a critical lens was acquired in graduate school. I did not learn what it meant to view issues critically, until someone gave me the tools through various books, journal articles, and challenging class discussion. Some Black women may not have these critical tools unless they come through the walls of academia.

Another blog (NPR radio) entry that provided critical commentary on Beyoncé's project is titled, "Feminists Everywhere React to Beyoncé's Latest" by Bilal Qureshi.[58] Qureshi begins to explain the interest that drew many Black feminists into listening to the album. Qureshi discusses how numerous social media outlets were brimming with news about the album, which drew a lot of attention.[59] The word of mouth advertisement really had many people downloading the album, which ended with 617,000 albums sold in three days.[60] Qureshi shares commentary from several feminist writers, going back and forth with their thoughts on whether the album portrays Beyoncé as a feminist, once and for all.[61] One of these commentators, Tanya Steele, a filmmaker, states "I saw her in pornographic poses . . . I couldn't understand what black feminists were looking at . . . it was just another tired example of a woman performing for men."[62] Anna Holmes, founder of Jezebel, a website focused on women's issues, states, "We don't often see women in bodysuits writhing around on cars except when—I don't know, it's *Maxim* magazine, so it does feel like a performance for the benefit of men."[63] Another critique from Professor Brittney Cooper, who studies Black feminism, says, "Beyoncé's videos aren't degrading. Instead, the singer empowers women of color. I think it's risqué, but I think she's asking us to think about what it means for black women to be sexual on our own terms."[64] These are just three of the comments from various feminists cited in the blog. The commentary goes back and forth on how they rate Beyoncé's feminism. At the end of the piece, Qureshi plays Beyoncé's "Grown Woman" where she sings about being "grown" and having the agency to do what she wants to do.[65] This is the draw for the everyday Black woman. To have a space to embrace the many parts of themselves, but still be able to embody equality. It is about accepting all the parts of what it means to be a Black woman, which is unique from White womanhood, because of how we conceptualize who we are within the Black community, the Black family, our work, and how the world perceives us.

The *Crunk Feminist Collective* blog "Five Reasons I'm Here for Beyoncé, The Feminist" begins with controversy by arguing that Beyoncé is a "bad bitch" for releasing her album in such a unique fashion.[66] The blogger defends her right to call Beyoncé the *b* word stating that marginalized groups should have the right to self define. The remainder of the blog is spent giving supporting arguments on how Beyoncé should be considered a feminist. Her first claim is that Beyoncé calls herself a feminist, and that even though her feminism may be complicated it should not be dismissed.[67] Secondly, she goes on to assert that telling, "bitches to bow down" as she does in the song "***Flawless" is sometimes necessary.[68] She states that people should come to a conversation with appropriate rationale and that women should not be so inclined to take everyone's opinions so seriously.[69]

Next, the article takes academic feminism head on by stating that it is not the only type of feminism that should be acknowledged. She believes that the level of education and the ability to articulate an eloquent argument should not be the standard qualifications for feminism.[70] People can accept that our ancestors who were feminist did not have a formal education, but have a hard time accepting Beyoncé's homegrown type of feminism. I (Mackenzie) whole-heartedly believe this point. If critical scholars are the only ones who can define the qualifications of feminism than we may be losing the message in the Ivory Tower. Feminism should be relatable and easy for the everyday woman to implement into her everyday routine. It is not a book chapter or an academic journal that is going to help women gain equal pay but instead, the voices of everyday women who live the message (see writings from bell hooks, Audre Lourde, June Jordan, and Alice Walker). The blogger also commends Beyoncé for making an attempt to figure out her relationship with feminism, when others are not even willing to use the term.[71]

From my (Elizabeth) point of view, feminism is intrinsic and is expressed in a variety of meaningful ways relevant to personal experience. This ties into the blogger's last point that feminism is not an exclusive nightclub that requires a list for entry.[72] Instead of spending time trying to figure out who is allowed to call himself or herself a feminist, they should focus on more ways to allow feminism to be relatable to women outside of the Ivory Tower. Individuals need a space for feminism to be intriguing without the threat of ridicule, so that people can learn to embrace the concept as part of their everyday existence.

The last article/blog analyzed is titled, "Beyoncé Serenades Teenage Boys and Black Feminists" by Tanya Steele.[73] This article is unique from the others, in that it focuses on the visual aspect of the Beyoncé's album. As previously mentioned, Beyoncé released a music video with every song on the CD, which is unprecedented in the industry. Steele starts by discussing her perspective on how visual images are essential to marketing and album sales in this country.[74] She argues that despite the empowering lyrics that are expressed in her music, Beyoncé counteracts her words by using visual images that are sexually oppressive.[75] From her perspective, Beyoncé had to continue to sell sex visually, in spite of her lyrics, because she was ultimately interested in the album sales. To appease this conflict of interest, Beyoncé spent much of her time in the videos in revealing clothing, which she felt was predominately a reflection of the American patriarchal society.[76] Steele takes issue with this even in the video for the song "***Flawless."[77] She further explains that Beyoncé still exposes body parts to the camera, which incidentally makes her go against one of the feminist ideals of sexual oppression.[78] She believes that Black feminists should not worry about the opinions of other races, but be quicker to speak freely about qualms in Black female sexual expressions. Steele finds that the overarching problem is not Beyoncé showing off her body, but the fact that patriarchy in this country requires that to sell albums.[79] For Steele, having agency over one's own body is great but that does not create an excuse to contradict the lyrics of the music that is written.

I (Mackenzie) understand the argument of female bodies being on display for men's pleasure, and that women should work to push past the traditional constraints of this objectification being the norm. However, who makes the decision on whether someone is showing skin to stay within patriarchy or to break free of the reins that it holds? There takes a certain level of vulnerability for someone to feel confident enough to put his or her body on display. I disagree that a woman being comfortable and having control over her sexuality, is something that should *automatically* be considered oppressive or misogynistic. There are various points on the album where Beyoncé overtly expresses how she enjoys her sexuality and that it is her choice on how she displays it. I do not automatically believe that because a woman likes to please, or look good for her man, that she cannot be a feminist. For an individual to have a blanket definition of what is seen as oppressive seems limited and narrow-minded.

## DISCUSSION AND CONCLUSION

This chapter analyzed the feminist-consumer-rhetoric that emerged as a result of the spontaneous release of the *Beyoncé Visual Album*.[80] Throughout this chapter we sought to explore Beyoncé's version of feminism by coining the term "Bey Feminism" in comparison to traditional Black feminism. We argue that today's version of Black feminism is not reaching the diverse populations of women that Beyoncé is able to reach. There is a great debate among Black women (and many other feminists) about the impact of Beyoncé's self-titled album, to the world of Black feminism. Instead of dissecting all of the things *wrong* or *right* with the albums lyrics and videos, we start a discussion about her appeal to the everyday Black woman and why they are drawn to her brand of feminism. What does this say about the community of Black women? Black feminists need to stop separating themselves from Bey Feminism because that separates them from the struggles, and successes, that many Black women feel Beyoncé embodies. This is not necessarily from a class perspective, but from the working (career) woman who is a wife (or a baby mama as her husband affectionately refers to her) and a mother.

Also, Beyoncé has always been a firm believer in the friendship and strong ties that are needed among Black women. She cherishes these friendships as helping her to become the woman she is today. This is at the heart of the Black female community and sheds more light on loving, than intellectually stimulating or critically evaluating. In her book *All about Love*, bell hooks discusses the importance of love and reaching people through love in order to activate change to the status quo.[81] Instead of arguing about Bey Feminism, Black feminists need to examine its appeal and possibly replicate it in a way that still deals with the oppressive nature of patriarchy, but does not lose sight of the importance of relationship. A strong bond between women can help to sustain and create outlets for activism to challenge the discrepancies within the community that keep Black women in oppressive states. We will not be able to correct these issues by silencing the voices that are reaching the everyday Black woman. And a major voice that is reaching and resonating with everyday Black women happens to be Beyoncé's. As consumers become more involved in blogging, they will play a pivotal role in drawing attention to artists and albums. We set out to show that the face of music promotion is changing by demonstrating how vital conversations can emerge and engage the everyday person. In the case of Beyoncé, Black feminism took center stage, starting a conversation that should be acknowledged and continued.

We hope to have adequately summarized what is happening in the community of millennial Black feminists and encourage more conversations around feminism. It is the conversations and the relationships built through these discussions that can help continue the discourse around Black feminism. Such conversations are also extremely vital in order for Black Feminist scholars to continue to reach others who may not receive the messages in the form of books or articles. It is not the label that matters, but the acceptance of a common goal to allow the validation of women's experiences and voice, and the ending of sexist oppression.

## NOTES

1. Jannette L. Dates and William Barlow, *Split Image: African Americans in the Media* (2nd ed) (Washington, DC: Howard University Press, 1993); Shawna V. Hudson, "Re-creational Television: The Paradox of Change and Continuity Within Stereotypical Iconography, *Sociological Inquiry,* 68, no. 2 (1998): 242–57; Dionne P. Stephens and Layli D. Phillips, "Freaks, Gold Diggers, Divas, and Dykes: The Sociohistorical Development of Adolescent African American Women's Sexual Scripts." *Sexuality & Culture* 7, no. 1 (2003): 3–49; Juanita J. Covert and Travis L. Dixon, "A Changing View: Representation and Effects of the Portrayal of Women of Color in Mainstream Women's Magazines," *Communication Research* 35, no. 2 (2008): 232–256.
2. Beyoncé Knowles. *Beyoncé the Visual Album,* Columbia Records, 2013, compact disc.
3. Beyoncé Knowles. *Dangerously in Love,* Columbia Records, 2003, compact disc.
4. Rob Sheffield, "Beyoncé," *Rolling Stones*, last modified December 14, 2013, http://www.rollingstone.com/music/albumreviews/beyonce-20131214.
5. Ibid.
6. Ibid.
7. See Mikki Kendall's writing for the *Guardian*, see Britney Cooper's writing for the *Salon*, and see Christina Coleman's writing for *Global Grind*.
8. "Ivory Tower," Merriam-Webster.com, accessed March 24, 2014, http://www.merriam-webster.com/dictionary/ivory tower.
9. Judith Martin, "Understanding Whiteness in the United States," in *Intercultural Communication: A Reader* (14th ed.), edited by Larry A. Samovar, Richard E. Porter, Edwin R. McDaniel, and Carolyn Sexton Roy (Boston: Cengage Learning, 2015), 77.
10. Patricia Hill Collins, *Black feminist thought: Knowledge, consciousness and the politics of empowerment* (New York: Wadsworth Publishing Company, 2000).
11. Hill Collins, *Black feminist thought,* 22.
12. Ibid.
13. Uma Narayan, "The Project of Feminist Epistemology: Perspectives from a Non-Western Feminist," in *Feminist Theory Reader: Local and Global Perspectives,* edited by Carole McCann and Seung-kyung Kim (New York: Routledge, 2003), 370–78.
14. The Combahee River Collective. "A Black Feminist Statement." In *Feminist Theory Reader: Local and Global Perspectives,* edited by Carole McCann and Seung-kyung Kim (New York: Routledge, 2003), 116–22.
15. The Combahee River Collective, 2003.
16. Angelina Murphy. "14 Songs that Empower Women." *Fem Magazine*, last modified November 16, 2013, http://femmagazine.com/?p=4509.

17. Beyoncé Knowles, Kelly Rowland, Sam Barnes, Jean-Claude Olivier, and Cory Rooney. "Independent Women," movie soundtrack for *Charlie's Angels*, performed by Destiny's Child, Columbia Records, 2000, compact disc.

18. Jane Gordon, "Beyoncé: The multi-talented star reveals what she is planning next." *Mail Online*, last modified August 15, 2010, http://www.dailymail.co.uk/home/you/article-1301838/Beyonc--The-multi-talented-star-reveals-planning-next.html.

19. bell hooks, *Feminist Theory: From Margin to Center*, 2nd edition (Cambridge, MA, South End Press Classics, 2000).

20. Ibid., 20.

21. Ibid.

22. Ibid., 25.

23. Ibid., 26.

24. Ibid., 28.

25. Elisa Lipsky-Karasz, "Beyoncé's Baby Love," *Harpers Bazaar*, September 2011.

26. Jorge Rivas. "But What about Beyoncé's Band?" *Colorlines*, last modified February 4, 2013, http://colorlines.com/archives/2013/02/but_what_about_beyonces_band.html.

27. *Beyoncé: Life Is But A Dream*, directed by Ed Burke, Beyoncé Knowles, & Ilan Y. Benatar, 2013, New York: HBO Network and Parkwood Entertainment, 2013. DVD.

28. "Beyoncé Knowles' name change," *Boston Globe*, last modified December 23, 2009. http://www.boston.com/ae/celebrity/articles/2009/12/23/beyonce_knowles_name_change/.

29. B. C. Jean and Toby Gad, "If I Were a Boy," performed by Beyoncé, *I Am . . . Sasha Fierce*, 2008, Columbia Records, compact disc.

30. Ibid.

31. Terius "The Dream" Nash, Beyoncé Knowles, Wesley Pentz, David Taylor, Adidja Palmer, and Nick van de Wall, "Run the World (Girls)" performed by Beyoncé, *4*, 2011, Columbia Records, compact disc.

32. Christopher "Tricky" Stewart, Terius "The Dream" Nash, Thaddis Harrell, Beyoncé Knowles, "Single Ladies," performed by Beyoncé, *I Am...Sasha Fierce*, 2008, Columbia Records, compact disc; Beyoncé Knowles, Shondrae "Bangladesh" Crawford, and Sean Garrett, "Diva," performed by Beyoncé, *I Am...Sasha Fierce*, 2008, Columbia Records, compact disc; Joshua Coleman, Sia Furler, Bobby Long, Beyoncé Knowles, "Pretty Hurts," performed by Beyoncé, *Beyoncé*, 2013, Columbia Records, compact disc; Terius "The Dream" Nash and Beyoncé Knowles, "Grown Woman," performed by Beyoncé, *Beyoncé*, 2013, Columbia Records, compact disc.

33. Anushay Hossain, "Is Beyoncé A Feminist Just For Record Sales?" *Forbes.com*, last modified January 29, 2014, http://www.forbes.com/sites/worldviews/2014/01/29/is-beyonce-being-a-feminist-just-for-record-sales-2/.

34. Tanya Steele, "'Beyoncé' Serenades Teenage Boys & Black Feminists," (blog), *Indiewire*, last modified December 16, 2013, http://blogs.indiewire.com/shadowandact/beyonce-serenades-teenage-boys-black-feminists.

35. Aisha Harris, "Who Runs the World? Husbands?" *Slate*, last modified February 4, 2013, http://www.slate.com/blogs/browbeat/2013/02/04/beyonc_s_mrs_carter_show_world_tour_why_use_her_married_name.html.

36. Rodney Jerkins, Beyoncé Knowles, Ricky Lewis, Kelly Rowland, Robert Waller, and Michelle Williams, "Cater 2 U," performed by Destiny's Child, *Destiny Fulfilled*, 2005, Columbia Records, compact disc; Beyoncé Knowles, Scott Storch, Robert Waller, Angela Beyoncé, Pete Bellotte, Giorgio Moroder, and Donna Summer, "Naughty Girl," performed by Beyoncé, *Dangerously In Love*, 2004, Columbia Records, compact disc; Beyoncé Knowles, Pharrell Williams, James Fauntleroy, Timothy Mosley, Jerome Harmon, and Justin Timberlake, "Blow," performed by Beyoncé, *Beyoncé*, 2013, Columbia Records, compact disc; Terius "The Dream" Nash, Beyoncé Knowles, Justin Timberlake, Timothy Mosley, Jerome Harmon, Dwane Weir, and Mike Dean, "Partition," performed by Beyoncé, *Beyoncé*, 2013, Columbia Records, compact disc.

37. Robin Boylorn "Pleasure Principles: 5 Lessons about Sex from Beyoncé," (blog) *Crunk Feminist Collective*, last modified March 24, 2014, http://www.crunkfeministcollective.com/2014/03/24/pleasure-principles-5-lessons-about-sex-from-beyonce/.

38. Ibid.
39. Christa Bell and Mako Fitts Ward, "The Problem with Beyhive Bottom Bitch Feminism," (blog), *Real Colored Girls*, last modified December 15, 2013, http://realcoloredgirls.wordpress.com/2013/12/15/the-problem-with-beyhive-bottom-bitch-feminism/.
40. Beyoncé Knowles, Noel Fisher, Shawn Carter, Andre Eric Proctor, Rasool Diaz, Brian Soko, Timothy Mosley, and Jerome Harmon, "Drunk in Love," performed by Beyoncé featuring Jay Z, *Beyoncé,* 2013, Columbia Records, compact disc (hereafter cited as "Drunk in Love").
41. Beyoncé Knowles, Terius "The Dream" Nash, Chauncey Hollis, and Rey Reel, "***Flawless," performed by Beyoncé Knowles featuring Chimamanda Ngozi Adichie, *Beyoncé,* 2013, Columbia Records, compact disc.
42. Christa Bell and Mako Fitts Ward, "The Problem with Beyhive Bottom Bitch Feminism."
43. "Drunk in Love."
44. "'Self-Titled' Part 2. Imperfection," December 17, 2013, video clip, accessed March 28, 2014, YouTube, http://www.youtube.com/watch?v=cIv1z6n3Xxo.
45. "***Flawless."
46. bell hooks, *Feminist Theory: From Margin to Center, 2nd Edition* (Cambridge, MA: South End Press, 2000).
47. "'Self-Titled' Part I. The Visual Album," December 13, 2013, video clip, accessed March 28, 2014, YouTube, https://www.youtube.com/watch?v=IcN6Ke2V-rQ.
48. Hill Collins, *Black Feminist Thought,* 221–28.
49. Mia McKenzie, "On Defending Beyoncé: Black feminists, White feminists, and the Line in the Sand," (blog), *Black Girl Dangerous*, last modified December 16, 2013, http://www.blackgirldangerous.org/2013/12/defending-beyonce-black-feminists-white-feminists-line-sand/.
50. Ibid.
51. Ibid.
52. Ibid.
53. Ibid.
54. Ibid.
55. Uma Narayan, "The Project of Feminist Epistemology," 370–78.
56. Ibid., 374.
57. McKenzie, "On Defending Beyoncé."
58. Bilal Quershi, "Feminists Everywhere React to Beyoncé's Latest," (blog), *NPR.org*, last modified December 19, 2013, http://www.npr.org/blogs/therecord/2013/12/19/255527290/feminists-everywhere-react-to-beyonc-slatest?utm_content=socialflow&utm_campaign=nprfacebook&utm_source=npr&utm_medium=facebook.
59. Ibid.
60. Ibid.
61. Ibid.
62. Ibid.
63. Ibid.
64. Ibid.
65. Ibid.
66. "5 Reasons I'm Here for Beyoncé', the Feminist," (blog), *Crunk Feminist Collective*, last modified December 13, 2013, http://www.crunkfeministcollective.com/2013/12/13/5-reasons-im-here-for-beyonce-the-feminist/.
67. Ibid.
68. Ibid.
69. Ibid.
70. Ibid.
71. Ibid.
72. Ibid.

73. Tanya Steele, "'Beyoncé' Serenades Teenage Boys & Black Feminists," (blog), *Indiewire*, last modified December 16, 2013, http://blogs.indiewire.com/shadowandact/beyonce-serenades-teenage-boys-black-feminists.
74. Ibid.
75. Ibid.
76. Ibid.
77. Ibid.
78. Ibid.
79. Ibid
80. Beyoncé Knowles. *Beyoncé the Visual Album.*
81. bell hooks, *All about love: New visions* (New York: Harper Perennial, 2000).

# BIBLIOGRAPHY

"5 Reasons I'm Here for Beyoncé,' the Feminist." (blog). *Crunk Feminist Collective*. Last modified December 13, 2013. http://www.crunkfeministcollective.com/2013/12/13/5-reasons-im-here-for-beyonce-the-feminist/.
Bell, Christa, and Mako Fitts Ward. "The Problem with Beyhive Bottom Bitch Feminism." (blog). *Real Colored Girls*. Last modified December 15, 2013. http://realcoloredgirls.wordpress.com/2013/12/15/the-problem-with-beyhive-bottom-bitch-feminism/.
"Beyoncé Knowles' name change," *Boston Globe*, last modified December 23, 2009. http://www.boston.com/ae/celebrity/articles/2009/12/23/beyonce_knowles_name_change/.
*Beyoncé: Life Is But A Dream*. Directed by Ed Burke, Beyoncé Knowles, & Ilan Y. Benatar. 2013. New York: HBO Network and Parkwood Entertainment, 2013. DVD.
Boylorn, Robin. "Pleasure Principles: 5 Lessons about Sex from Beyoncé." (blog). *Crunk Feminist Collective*. Last modified March 24, 2014. http://www.crunkfeministcollective.com/2014/03/24/pleasure-principles-5-lessons-about-sex-from-beyonce/.
Coleman, Joshua, Sia Furler, Bobby Long, and Beyoncé Knowles. "Pretty Hurts." Performed by Beyoncé. *Beyoncé the Visual Album*. 2013. Columbia Records, compact disc.
Collins, Patricia Hill. *Black feminist thought: Knowledge, consciousness and the politics of empowerment*. New York: Wadsworth Publishing Company, 2000.
Covert, Juanita J., and Travis L. Dixon. "A Changing View: Representation and Effects of the Portrayal of Women of Color in Mainstream Women's Magazines." *Communication Research* 35, no. 2 (2008): 232–56.
Dates, Jannette L., and William Barlow. *Split Image: African Americans in the Media* (2nd ed). Washington, DC: Howard University Press, 1993.
Gordon, Jane, "Beyoncé: The multi-talented star reveals what she is planning next." *Mail Online*. Last modified August 15, 2010. http://www.dailymail.co.uk/home/you/article-1301838/Beyonc--The-multi-talented-star-reveals-planning-next.html.
Harris, Aisha. "Who Runs the World? Husbands?" *Slate*. Last modified February 4, 2013. http://www.slate.com/blogs/browbeat/2013/02/04/beyonc_s_mrs_carter_show_world_tour_why_use_her_married_name.html.
hooks, bell. *All about love: New visions*. New York: Harper Perennial, 2000.
hooks, bell. *Feminist Theory: From Margin to Center*. Cambridge, MA: South End Press, 2000.
Hossain, Anushay. "Is Beyonce A Feminist Just For Record Sales?" *Forbes.com*. Last modified January 29, 2014. http://www.forbes.com/sites/worldviews/2014/01/29/is-beyonce-being-a-feminist-just-for-record-sales-2/.
Hudson, Shawna V. "Re-creational Television: The Paradox of Change and Continuity Within Stereotypical Iconography. *Sociological Inquiry*, 68, no. 2 (1998): 242–57.
"Ivory Tower." Merriam-Webster.com. Accessed March 24, 2014. http://www.merriam-webster.com/dictionary/ivory tower.
Jean, B. C., and Toby Gad. "If I Were a Boy." Performed by Beyoncé. *I Am...Sasha Fierce*. 2008. Columbia Records, compact disc.

Jerkins, Rodney, Beyoncé Knowles, Ricky Lewis, Kelly Rowland, Robert Waller, and Michelle Williams. "Cater 2 U." Performed by Destiny's Child. *Destiny Fulfilled.* 2005. Columbia Records, compact disc.

Knowles, Beyoncé. *Beyoncé the Visual Album.* Columbia Records, 2013, compact disc.

Knowles, Beyoncé, Kelly Rowland, Sam Barnes, Jean-Claude Olivier, and Cory Rooney. "Independent Women." Performed by Destiny's Child. In *Charlie's Angels* movie. 2000. Columbia Records, compact disc.

Knowles, Beyoncé, Noel Fisher, Shawn Carter, Andre Eric Proctor, Rasool Diaz, Brian Soko, Timothy Mosley, and Jerome Harmon. "Drunk in Love." Performed by Beyoncé featuring Jay Z. *Beyoncé the Visual Album.* 2013. Columbia Records, compact disc.

Knowles, Beyoncé, Pharrell Williams, James Fauntleroy, Timothy Mosley, Jerome Harmon, and Justin Timberlake. "Blow." Performed by Beyoncé. *Beyoncé the Visual Album.* 2013. Columbia Records, compact disc.

Knowles, Beyoncé, Scott Storch, and Robert Waller. "Me, Myself, and I." Performed by Beyoncé. *Dangerously in Love.* 2003. Columbia Records, compact disc.

Knowles, Beyoncé, Scott Storch, Robert Waller, Angela Beyoncé, Pete Bellotte, Giorgio Moroder, and Donna Summer. "Naughty Girl." Performed by Beyoncé. *Dangerously In Love.* 2004. Columbia Records, compact disc.

Knowles, Beyoncé, Shondrae "Bangladesh" Crawford, and Sean Garrett. "Diva." Performed by Beyoncé. *I Am...Sasha Fierce.* 2008. Columbia Records, compact disc.

Lipsky-Karasz, Elisa. "Beyoncé's Baby Love." *Harpers Bazaar*, September 2011.

Martin, Judith. "Understanding Whiteness in the United States." In *Intercultural Communication: A Reader* (14th ed.), edited by Larry A. Samovar, Richard E. Porter, Edwin R. McDaniel, and Carolyn Sexton Roy, 76–84. Boston: Cengage Learning, 2015.

McKenzie, Mia. "On Defending Beyoncé: Black feminists, White feminists, and the Line in the Sand." (blog). *Black Girl Dangerous.* Last modified December 16, 2013. http://www.blackgirldangerous.org/2013/12/defending-beyonce-black-feminists-white-feminists-line-sand/.

Murphy, Angelina. "14 Songs that Empower Women." *Fem Magazine.* Last modified November 16, 2013. http://femmagazine.com/?p=4509.

Narayan, Uma. "The Project of Feminist Epistemology: Perspectives from a Non-Western Feminist." In *Feminist Theory Reader: Local and Global Perspectives,* edited by Carole McCann and Seung-kyung Kim, 370–378. New York: Routledge, 2003.

Nash, Terius. "The Dream" and Beyoncé Knowles. "Grown Woman." Performed by Beyoncé. *Beyoncé the Visual Album.* 2013. Columbia Records, compact disc.

Nash, Terius. "The Dream," Beyoncé Knowles, Justin Timberlake, Timothy Mosley, Jerome Harmon, Dwane Weir, and Mike Dean. "Partition." Performed by Beyoncé. *Beyoncé the Visual Album.* 2013. Columbia Records, compact disc.

Nash, Terius. "The Dream," Beyoncé Knowles, Wesley Pentz, David Taylor, Adidja Palmer, and Nick van de Wall. "Run the World (Girls)." Performed by Beyoncé. *4.* 2011. Columbia Record, compact disc.

Quershi, Bilal. "Feminists Everywhere React to Beyoncé's Latest." (blog). *NPR.org.* Last modified December 19, 2013. http://www.npr.org/blogs/therecord/2013/12/19/255527290/feminists-everywhere-react-to-beyonc-slatest?utm_content=socialflow&utm_campaign=nprfacebook&utm_source=npr&utm_medium=facebook.

Rivas, Jorge. "But What about Beyoncé's Band?" *Colorlines.* Last modified February 4, 2013. http://colorlines.com/archives/2013/02/but_what_about_beyonces_band.html.

"'Self-Titled' Part 2. Imperfection." December 17, 2013. Video clip. Accessed March 28, 2014. YouTube. *www.YouTube.com,* http://www.youtube.com/watch?v=cIv1z6n3Xxo.

"'Self-Titled' Part 1. The Visual Album." December 13, 2013. Video clip. Accessed March 28, 2014. YouTube. *www.YouTube.com,* https://www.youtube.com/watch?v=IcN6Ke2V-rQ.

Sheffield, Rob. "Beyoncé." *Rolling Stones.* Last modified December 14, 2013. http://www.rollingstone.com/music/albumreviews/beyonce-20131214.

Steele, Tanya. "'Beyoncé' Serenades Teenage Boys & Black Feminists." (blog). *Indiewire.* Last modified December 16, 2013. http://blogs.indiewire.com/shadowandact/beyonce-serenades-teenage-boys-black-feminists.

Stephens, Dionne P. and Layli D. Phillips. "Freaks, Gold Diggers, Divas, and Dykes: The Sociohistorical Development of Adolescent African American Women's Sexual Scripts." *Sexuality & Culture* 7, no. 1 (2003): 3–49.

Stewart, Christopher "Tricky," Terius "The Dream" Nash, Thaddis Harrell, and Beyoncé Knowles. "Single Ladies (Put a Ring on It)." Performed by Beyoncé. *I Am . . . Sasha Fierce.* 2008, Columbia Records, compact disc.

The Combahee River Collective. "A Black Feminist Statement." In *Feminist Theory Reader: Local and Global Perspectives,* edited by Carole McCann and Seung-kyung Kim. New York: Routledge, 2003.

Wallace, Tracey. "Beyoncé has turned Feminism into an All-Powerful Marketing Tool." (blog). *PolicyMic.* Last modified January 14, 2014. http://www.policymic.com/articles/79007/beyonce-has-turned-feminism-into-an-all-powerful-marketing-tool.

Weiner, Sophie. "Beyoncé's Most Feminist Moments." *Flavorwire.* Last modified February 5, 2013. http://flavorwire.com/369101/beyonces-1most-feminist-moments/7/.

*Chapter Nine*

# Black Women and Gender Violence

*Lil' Wayne's "How to Love" as Progressive Hip Hop*

Joshua Daniel Phillips and Rachel Alicia Griffin

In *The Will to Change: Men, Masculinity, and Love*, bell hooks[1] identifies popular culture as "a powerful vehicle for teaching the art of the possible. Enlightened men must claim it as the space of their public voice and create a progressive popular culture that will teach men how to connect with others, how to communicate, how to love."[2] In agreement with hooks,[3] we also believe that acknowledging progressive popular culture created by men is key—even when it emerges from hip hop artists, such as Lil' Wayne, who consistently spout hypermasculine, misogynistic, and homophobic lyrics in exchange for commercialized popularity and profit. As critical scholars deeply invested in anti-gender violence activism, we understand that positioning Lil' Wayne as an *enlightened* hip hop artist feels disingenuous given the prevalence and glorification of violence against women in his music. However ignoring "How to Love,"[4] solely because Lil' Wayne performs it, feels equally disingenuous since we interpret the song as the most progressive representation in contemporary hip hop to emerge from a Black male artist that calls attention to men's violence against Black women.[5]

Utilizing a Black feminist lens,[6] in tune with hip hop feminism,[7] we illuminate "How to Love"[8] as a progressive song that not only narrates how Black women's lives are impacted by gender violence but also humanizes Black women beyond the confines of negative caricatures. Our endeavor forefronts the rich complexity of hip hop and hip hop artists, and also highlights mainstream hip hop as a means to confront and challenge the dehumanization of Black women. First, we discuss hip hop as a vehicle for resistant empowerment with a mindful eye toward the commercialization of the industry. Second, we detail how sexism consistently anchors rappers' representations of womanhood and compare these representations to more progressive representations of Black women. Next, we define Black feminist thought (BFT) and then employ BFT, infused with the insight of hip hop feminists, to deconstruct "How to Love"[9] and reveal how the song productively challenges negative caricatures of Black femininity. Lastly, we underscore the potential of Black male hip hop artists to intentionally humanize Black women despite the commercial tendency to collapse themselves and Black women back into negative caricatures.

## THE ROOTS OF HIP HOP AS RESISTANCE AND CONTEMPORARY COMMERCIALIZATION

The foundation of hip hop can be traced back to the 1970s and 1980s when "deindustrialization and new trends in urban planning destroyed impoverished black and Latino/a neighborhoods."[10] Such trends strategically devastated low-income communities of color that could not absorb the economic swing toward privatization and gentrification that resulted in severe reductions in government programs intended to aid systemically marginalized communities.[11] Absent a formal political platform for low-income communities of color to voice their struggles and advocate for their needs, hip hop offered an artistic means to express the angering disenfranchisement many felt. Narrating the resistant roots of hip hop, Woods[12] says "the hip hop generation rose from the devastation of the state's war against black revolutionaries to carry on the tradition of irreverence and creative artistry."[13] In this context, hip hop quickly garnered traction as a means for young people to critique political policies, practices, and systems that were ignoring their needs, erasing their realities, and silencing their voices.[14]

As the lyrical movement steadily grew in popularity, the racial and socioeconomic demographics of the artists and consumers began to fragment. Additionally, the commitment to political resistance became vulnerable to White corporatization. In short, once it became clear that hip hop artists, Black males in particular, could garner substantial profit via their craft, the predominantly White owned and controlled mainstream music industry invested in producing and disseminating hip hop to mass audiences.[15] The onset of the early hip hop movement being commercially hijacked is typically dated back to 1972 when The Harvard Report, commissioned by Columbia Records, indicated that the Black music market was profitable.[16] Capitalizing on this market provided a means for music corporations, largely owned and controlled by Whites, to sell predominantly Black music to White consumers. Ironically, White corporatization also led to the music industry selling hip hop back to the communities of color from which it had emerged. Therefore hip hop was, in effect, commercially colonized by the very policies, practices, and systems it initially resisted and, subsequently, much of hip hop's political edge was surrendered in exchange for mainstream consumption.[17]

Ripening hip hop for mainstream consumption required that both the music and artists became palatable to White audiences.[18] For Black males, this meant (and continues to mean) strategically maintaining White fascination with stereotypical characterizations of *authentic* Black culture, as to not disrupt the profitability of hip hop's image. In essence, the predominantly White owned and controlled industry, alongside Black male industry artists, peddles music to the predominantly White fan base that reinforces racist and sexist caricatures of Black culture as violent, dangerous, and sexually deviant.[19] Such practices legitimate the status quo and undermine Black liberation; addressing gangsta rap specifically, Johnnetta B. Cole and Beverly Guy-Sheftall[20] offer:

> Angry young men hurling epithets at their homeboys and female counterparts, and hypnotic songs and videos depicting mindless violence, conspicuous material excess, and hostile sexism may be closer to representing New Jack stereotypes of Black buffoonery than paving the way to Black progress.[21]

From this vantage point, hip hop is argued to offer a wellspring of opportunity for young, predominantly White males to appropriate hip hop (e.g., music, language, dance, etc.) without being accountable to its resistant roots or conscious of its potential for critical cultural commentary.[22]

Popular and academic critics alike have lodged a long list of complaints against commercialized hip hop ranging from a lack of political mobilization to anti-intellectualism to nihilism to hyper-sexualized pathology.[23] While we agree with the aforementioned critiques, we are troubled by the common default to criminalize the genre in its entirety by drawing attention to appalling lyrics and offensive imagery without recognizing hip hop's potential for and actualization of progressive cultural commentary. This is not to imply that commercialized hip hop is undeserving of negative critique—it certainly is. However, of equal importance are critiques of hip hop that acknowledge, for better and for worse, the intellectual contributions of Black male artists.[24] Surprisingly, given Lil' Wayne's amassed success over two decades which includes four Grammy awards[25] and surpassing Elvis Presley's Billboard Hot 100 record with 109 hits as a solo artist,[26] few scholarly outlets have centered his music.[27] Aligning with scholars who position hip hop as pedagogical,[28] in the next section we center representations of sexism, Black femininity, and gender violence in hip hop to further contextualize the significance of "How to Love."[29]

## REPRESENTATIONS OF SEXISM AND GENDER VIOLENCE IN HIP HOP

To fairly address the prevalence of sexism in hip hop, it is important to recognize that hip hop does not exist in a cultural vacuum.[30] More specifically, the hypermasculine expressions of patriarchal posturing, objectification, and violence found within hip hop mirrors U.S. American society at large.[31] Therefore, while it is essential to critique the reproduction of sexism by Black male artists, it is also important to remember their immersion in a commercialized industry and society that necessitates the reproduction of patriarchal ideology in exchange for power and profit. This acknowledgement does not negate the culpability of Black male artists whose success is, in part, founded on the denigration of all women and Black women in particular, but it does contextualize the racist and sexist roots of U.S. American culture that permeate multiple genres of music.

Numerous popular and academic critics, and even artists themselves, have critiqued contemporary hip hop's continuous assault on women that vacillates among an endless stream of references to women as *bitches* and *tricks*, the sexual exploitation and violation of female bodies, and femicide.[32] According to Craig Watkins,[33] "the most tragic aspect of hip hop's lust for the libido was the elaboration of an imagination that viewed women as cheap, consumable, and dispensable."[34] Turning toward representations of Black women, given the (mis)perception of hip hop as "the face of Black America in the world today,"[35] Michael Eric Dyson[36] parallels the Black female body in contemporary hip hop to the Black women sold atop slave auction blocks as does West[37] in a chapter provocatively titled, "Still on the Auction Block: The (S)exploitation of Black Adolescent Girls in Rap(e) Music and Hip-Hop Culture." As such, the hypersexualized Black female body in contemporary hip hop can be understood as a chronological extension of the commodification of Black women during slavery.

Absent literal enslavement, the simultaneously sexist and racist commodification of Black women in hip hop commonly manifests in alignment with sex work situating Black women as strippers, dancers, and prostitutes for the pleasure of men.[38] Additionally, the gamut of hip hop lyrics and music videos glorify "transactional sex"[39] which entails Black women being *rewarded* for sexual favors via material goods (e.g., designer clothes, cars, etc.); reproduce colorism by privileging light-skinned Black women with White European facial features and hair texture; naturalize humiliation of the Black female body by depicting Black women as "atomized body parts"[40] and mere objects to be fucked/fucked with; and normalize men's violence against Black women.[41] Recording and performing since he was eleven years old,[42] Lil' Wayne has taken part in the commodification of Black femininity via hip hop for the majority of his life.

As a talented lyricist, Lil' Wayne has been marketed and now markets himself as a hardened Black male who came up in the Dirty South. His hypermasculine persona has been strengthened by his 2010 stint in prison for felony weapons charges,[43] alongside a wealth of songs from multiple albums that testify to his violent deeds, sexual prowess, and self-proclaimed freedom to disrespect and dominate women (e.g., "Mrs. Officer,"[44] "We Be Steady Mobbin',"[45] "Right Above It,"[46] etc.). The pervasive sexism that characterizes commercialized hip hop at large and Lil' Wayne's gangsta rap, makes it difficult to describe either as anything more than a hypersexualized mélange steeped in the systemized degradation of Black women. However, although rare, there are a handful of mainstream Black male artists who have released songs that progressively address the violence that Black women endure most often at the hands of Black men. Tupac, Ludacris, and, most recently, Lil' Wayne serve as three examples of Black male rappers who have been criticized for their rampantly misogynistic lyrics and music videos but who have also lyrically embraced the struggles, power, and beauty of Black women.

We situate Tupac, Ludacris, and Lil' Wayne as paradoxical hip hop artists in that their music both reproduces and contests negative caricatures of Black girls and women. For example, in "Lie to Kick It,"[47] Tupac dedicates the song to Mike Tyson who was convicted of raping a Black woman named Desiree Washington. The opening lines of the song even go so far as to indicate that a woman should not even call a man unless she is willing to have sex with him. Nonetheless, Tupac is also remembered for "Keep Ya Head Up"[48] and "Dear Mama";[49] both of which narrate the harsh realities of Black women who suffer at the mercy of poverty, addiction, and violent Black men. Similarly, Ludacris raps about having "hoes" in multiple locations in his song "Area Codes"[50] but also featured Mary J. Blige in "Runaway Love"[51] to narrate the trauma young girls experience fleeing abusive and painful circumstances. Like Tupac and Ludacris, Lil' Wayne has spouted ample sexist dehumanization via his lyrics which are often visually partnered with Black women in his music videos. For example, in "Mrs. Officer"[52] Lil' Wayne sexually dominates a Black female police officer and likens having sex with her to the beating of Rodney King, which mirrors the common practice in hip hop of establishing male authority and superiority via the sexual conquest of Black women.

As Tricia Rose[53] reminds us, "if you want to find openly celebrated sexism against black women, there is no richer contemporary source than commercial, mainstream hip-hop." Taken as a staple of his music, the degradation imparted on Black women via Lil' Wayne is impossible to defend from a feminist perspective. However, like many Black male hip hop artists who narrate their respect for Black women in their lives despite their music, Lil' Wayne is complicated—especially when "How to Love" became part of his musical repertoire. To fully appreciate "How to Love"[54] as a severe departure from Lil' Wayne's norm, in the section that follows, we position Black feminist thought[55] in alignment with hip hop feminism[56] to guide our critique.

## BLACK FEMINIST THOUGHT AND HIP HOP FEMINISM

Working at the intersections of racist and sexist oppression, Black feminist thought (BFT) operates as a "critical social theory" for Black women, which aims to "find ways to escape from, survive in, and/or oppose prevailing social and economic injustice."[57] Focused on the intersectional, systemic oppressions that Black women endure, BFT illuminates how Black women experience racial oppression differently from their Black male counterparts and gender oppression differently from their White female counterparts; this approach is key because the interests of Black women are often discounted when race *or* gender are leveraged as concerns rather than race *and* gender.[58] Termed intersectionality by Kimberlè Crenshaw,[59] a Black feminist framework highlights the nuances of how race and gender simultaneously influence representations of Black femininity. Additional core commitments of BFT central to the critique of popular culture include: underscoring the relevance of historical marginalization, exposing harmful politics of respectability, heightening self-definition and self-determination, denouncing negative caricatures of Black womanhood, and promoting critically conscious consumption of popular culture.[60]

Sharing BFT's core commitments, hip hop feminism (HHF) is equally as concerned with the empowerment of Black women and seeks "to combine feminism and hip-hop in politically meaningful ways."[61] Generally speaking, hip hop feminism can be understood "as a continuation—though a disruptive one—of second-wave black feminism."[62] More specifically, HHF fosters a critical response to the sexist exploitation of Black women in commercial hip hop while simultaneously situating hip hop, and Black women's relationships to the genre, as complex and ambivalent.[63] Emotively articulating her need for HHF beyond the confines of BFT, Joan Morgan[64] says,

> Racism and the will to survive it creates a sense of intra-racial loyalty that makes it impossible for black women to turn our backs on black men—even in their ugliest and most sexist of moments. I needed a feminism that would allow us to continue loving ourselves *and* the brothers who hurt us without letting race loyalty buy us early tombstones.[65]

Following Morgan's lead, HHF allows hip hop feminists to "refuse easy and essentialist political stances about what is right or wrong and who or what gets to be called a feminist."[66]

Via the embrace of ambivalence, HHF does not sacrifice the potential of hip hop or artists to participate in the liberation of Black women—despite the gendered degradation deeply embedded in the commercial genre.[67] Of particular importance is HHF's allowance for scholars to acknowledge and celebrate progressive representations of Black womanhood rather than limiting feminist engagement with hip hop to critiques of sexism, misogyny, and patriarchy.[68] Suturing BFT and HHF together allows us to theorize "How to Love"[69] as a progressive hip hop song without romanticizing Lil' Wayne or dissuading further critique of hip hop.

In the analysis of "How to Love"[70] that follows, we are specifically concerned with how Lil' Wayne confronts Black men's violence against Black women while contextualizing and challenging the Jezebel as a controlling image of Black womanhood rooted in the social institution of slavery. According to Patricia Hill Collins the Jezebel,[71] and more contemporary manifestations of the Jezebel including the Gold Digger, Hoochie, and Freak, is key in the contemporary objectification, exploitation, and domination of Black women. Linked to sexual scripts of hypersexuality, promiscuity, and sexual deviance,[72] Black women reductively cast as Jezebels are depicted as deserving of their pain; therefore, those who harm Black women are excused from culpability.[73] Driven by the joint concerns of BFT and HHF with controlling imagery and HHF's emphasis on the progressive potential of hip hop, our analysis is guided by the following questions:

1. How does "How to Love" challenge the normalization of Black men's violence against Black women?
2. What does "How to Love" teach us about Black girls and women?

## "HOW TO LOVE" AS PROGRESSIVE HIP HOP

### Highlighting Black Men's Violence against Black Women

The protagonist in the music video, played by Chanta Patton, begins her life as an unwanted pregnancy set to be aborted before her mother cries in the music video, "I changed my mind. I can't do this. No! I can't do this!"[74] and then struggles off the operating table to flee the hospital. As the music fades in, the audience is then shown an image of the protagonist as a baby strapped into a car-seat on a living room floor. In the background, her mother is being abused by a Black male, presumably her father, while Lil' Wayne raps about the multiple men who have abused this young woman her entire life and made it impossible for her to understand the meaning of love. Focused on the absence of love, coupled with the images of domestic violence and the protagonist's mother trying to comfort her, Lil' Wayne's lyrics signal the systemically influenced trajectory of this young Black girl's life.

In the next scene, Lil' Wayne sutures the abovementioned message with an image of the protagonist as a toddler visiting her father in jail. Via the camera's angle, we watch her closely as she places her hand on the plexiglass to meet his followed by her mother angrily slamming the phone down and carrying her away, while her father pounds on the window. We interpret this scene as a testament to how healthy relationships with Black men, or the lack thereof, can impact multiple generations of Black women. In this instance, both the protagonist and her mother are impacted by her father's abuse and incarceration—both of which are beyond their control.

In the absence of her father, the girl grows up with a single mother who continues to have abusive Black male intimate partners. The audience knows this to be true when, as an adolescent, the video depicts the protagonist being sexually violated by her mother's partner while her mother sleeps, perhaps passed out given the beer bottles on the coffee table, in the background. This early and coercive sexual violation is paired with Lil' Wayne rapping about the young woman's feelings of insecurity and worthlessness despite her beauty. Threaded throughout images of her teenage years and young adulthood, the audience understands that she engages in relationships and sexual relations with the only type of Black men she's ever known—"crooks" who hurt, abuse, and exploit her. For example, she is approached on the steps at school by a Black male wearing a wifebeater, similar to the one her childhood attacker wore. Of equal importance, when he kisses her, he does so with his hand possessively gripping her throat. Soon after, indicating the cyclic effect of domestic and sexual violence, we learn that she too has become a young mother with two young children who are also shown to be fatherless.

Of importance to underscore is how the story told thus far in "How to Love"[75] aligns with Black feminist advocacy against gender violence.[76] More specifically, given that most gender violence is intraracial,[77] Lil' Wayne exposes the culpability of Black men in the consequential pain that Black women endure. We interpret his decision to do so as progressive given the strength of what Russell-Brown refers to as "Black protectionism"[78] which, in the context of Black men's violence against Black women, prioritizes racism at the expense of addressing sexism. Such practices, in turn, shield Black male attackers at the expense of their Black female survivors and victims.

Rather than masking or dismissing the violent and hurtful roles that some Black men can and do play in the lives of Black women, Lil' Wayne opts to center gender violence as an issue within the Black community. Signaling the seriousness of "How to Love"[79] just after its release, he says "I can tell you that I've never had a single like it, and it's an amazing song. It's an amazing song."[80] Similarly the director of the music video, Chris Robinson, does not shy away from gender violence as a Black issue. In an MTV interview he states, "I have a daughter, Wayne has a daughter, and he really wanted to tell the story" followed by "We were talking about statistics of abuse in our community. We were talking about really telling this story for every young woman in the world."[81] In this regard, we interpret that Robinson and Lil' Wayne made conscious decisions to depict Black women's experiences with gender violence at the hands of Black men—despite the complexity of doing so given the historical criminalization of Black men as a collective.[82]

## Contextualizing and Questioning the Jezebel

In addition to centering Black men's violence against Black women, "How to Love"[83] also addresses the underlying politics of the Jezebel as a controlling image utilized to degrade Black girls and women. More specifically, Lil' Wayne utilizes imagery of the protagonist as a stripper, prostitute, addict, and young single mother to narrate how her life came to be as it is and to humanize her experiences. Signaling the Jezebel, such imagery is oftentimes naturalized as how Black women choose to move through the world. However, when coupled with Lil' Wayne's lyrics, communicated via a solemn and compassionate tone, the Jezebel as innate is brought into question. For example, the climax of the music video depicts the Black female protagonist as a stripper prostituting herself out to patrons after performing on stage. Illuminated by Black feminist thought (BFT), the key distinction between Lil' Wayne's representation of the Black female stripper/prostitute versus Jezebel imagery is that he troubles the assumption of her agency and culpability. More specifically, most representations of strippers and prostitutes in popular culture ignore the systemic pulse of their profession, whereas "How to Love"[84] illustrates how the protagonist's reality is informed by factors rooted in systemic oppression that are beyond her control.

Questioning the assumption of her agency to be/become a sex worker which denaturalizes her *decision* to do so, the lyrics of "How to Love" craft a narrative that juxtaposes her youthful hopes and dreams with the bleak opportunities that *life* has created for her. Ergo, being a sex worker was not a life decision this woman made on her own. Instead, her circumstances reflect the negative choices made by others. Through this narrative, the audience is encouraged to empathize with the possibility that Black women who are sex workers had hurtful experiences that placed their dreams beyond reach. Thus, despite a Black woman's desire for self-determination as a means to imagine and pursue her hopes and dreams,[85] at the intersections of racism, sexism, and classism, Black women who turn to sex work may do so for lack of other options. Watching the video, we see the protagonist's small children just before she cringes through a gulp of alcohol, interpreted as liquid courage prior to getting on stage. As she gulps, we see a close up of her saddened eyes that indicate she would have chosen a different path in life had she had access to the agency to do so.

In this vein, "How to Love" contextualizes the representation of the Jezebel as a Black woman who is impacted by her past experiences and culturally afforded few opportunities for success outside of sexual exploitation.[86] Therefore, Lil' Wayne helps the audience understand how her difficult reality came to be by offering a rare glimpse into a Black woman's life from birth to adulthood. However, his narration of her experiences and subsequent critique of society's ease casting her away as a Jezebel does not end there. Rather, he explicitly positions himself as someone who cares for her when he briefly appears behind her just after her client leaves money on the nightstand. Reaching out to her, he seems to momentarily bring her comfort although she can't see him.

As the video shifts toward the next scene, Lil' Wayne returns to the chorus and once again highlights how abusive men have made it impossible for the protagonist to understand the meaning of love.[87] On the closing note of the chorus, the music comes to an abrupt halt and the young woman is in the same doctor's office where her mother once attempted to abort her. In the music video, we witness their conversation. The doctor states,

Doctor: Your blood test came up positive.

Protagonist: What? Positive for what?

Doctor: HIV[88]

As her mother tries to quiet her shrieks and sobs, the image cuts away and the protagonist is shown running through the same hospital corridors her mother ran through several years ago.

While the lyrics and images that have been discussed so far are painful to address, we feel they work in concordance with Black feminist efforts to deconstruct how Black women are negatively scripted as Jezebels. Thus, as shown in the music video, the contextual factors that influence Black women's lives are indicative of Black women's limited agency and the extreme difficulty of breaking cyclic violence and thriving, opposed to merely surviving. Yet as powerful as the first half of the music video is, the second half helps the audience imagine how different cultural circumstances, coupled with heightened self-definition and self-determination,[89] can positively shape Black women's lives. Explaining their creative approach to producing the music video, Robinson says, "The concept is more a narrative. It's a story about two paths in someone's life and how one small choice that you make can affect your whole life."[90]

## Reimagining the Realities of Black Women

The connection between contextualizing and challenging the Jezebel as a controlling image and the need to reimagine Black women's lives is not lost on Lil' Wayne. For him, the consideration of love was key to this song. In an MTV interview about "How to Love"[91] he says, "A lot of women don't know how to love because there's deep reasons for them not knowing how to love. . . . And what I mean by deep reasons is deep and dark reasons."[92] Exploring this sentiment via BFT, we return to Collins'[93] assessment that representations of Black women do not typically purport the realities of Black women's pain nor are Black women, due to the strength of controlling images, typically included in the realm of mediated representations of victimhood. Additionally, for many Black women to speak out about the violence and "deep reasons" that inform their difficulty loving themselves and others, sexism would have to be accounted for equally alongside racism. Furthermore, Black women who embody characteristics of the Jezebel oftentimes find themselves victimized by the politics of respectability that police Black women's sexuality.

"[P]olitics of respectability" emerged during the early 1900s and emphasized virtue, morality, and purity among Black women in alignment with Christian ideology.[94] Given the historical context, the politics of respectability were embodied by Black women to argue against systemic subordination. However, inadvertently, respectability manifests in contemporary society as a means to police Black female sexuality since the ideological underpinnings of respectability necessitate sexual "surveillance, control, and repression."[95] Black women deemed respectable in accordance with dominant ideology are often regarded as *ladies* and *queens* while those who are not are negated as *bitches* and *whores*.[96] Challenging this sexist and racist dichotomy, Lil' Wayne explicitly honors the Black female protagonist at arguably her lowest moment having just been diagnosed with HIV. Thus, as she runs from the hospital and her diagnosis, the audience can hear Lil' Wayne rapping about her beauty and value as well as telling the young woman that she is worthy of love.[97] Just after this moment in the song, we watch the protagonist's experiences rewind right before our eyes as Lil' Wayne seizes an opportunity to reimagine her life absent the violence of Black men.

With Lil' Wayne testifying to the protagonist's beauty and value as her life rewinds, the music video and lyrics work together to communicate unconditional love—despite the worst of life's circumstances and the protagonist having fallen short of respectability according to dominant ideology. To this end, Lil' Wayne is not dehumanizing, marginalizing, or blaming the protagonist as a Black woman who has encountered domestic violence, sexual assault, single-motherhood, stripping, prostituting, and HIV. Instead, he empathetically communicates compassion which is antithetical to the majority of his music and the mainstream hip hop industry. Literally extending his compassion into her world, opposed to ending the narrative with her diagnosis, Lil' Wayne uses the second half of the video to imagine the life circumstances in which the protagonist could exercise her agency beyond the confines of the Jezebel caricature. As such, she is empowered to create her own path via self-determination rather than her trajectory being destined in accordance with racism and sexism.

This new journey begins with the protagonist's mother leaving her abusive father and moving in with her grandmother. This depiction is incredibly significant given the importance of early intervention in the cycle of domestic violence and the signified strength of three generations of Black women under one roof. In this context, you have Black mothers protecting their daughters and Black women encouraging self-esteem and self-worth among each other. In addition, rather than visiting her father in prison, the young woman is shown as a flower girl in her mother's wedding. This particular image is important for two reasons. First, it sharply contrasts with earlier images of abuse and abandonment to provide a representation of what committed, healthy love can look like. Second, this image provides a redemptive representation of Black masculinity—far from the protagonist's abusive and then absent father, the man who sexually assaulted her as an adolescent, the young man who gripped her neck on the steps, and the john who gave her HIV. While a majority of the video situates the protagonist's negative experiences at the hands of violent Black men, latter images showcase a Black man who unconditionally loves Black women.

By genuinely loving his stepdaughter, her stepfather sets an example for what the protagonist should expect from men and, in turn, she is shown having high self-esteem and high expectations of herself and her Black male suitor. With this new understanding of how to love, she is afforded the agency and opportunity to define her identity through her intelligence and talents rather than being reduced to her sexuality. Bringing this reality to life, the music video depicts her excelling in high school, enrolling in cosmetology school, and graduating. A culminating image, accompanied by Lil' Wayne repeating "how to love,"[98] shows the protagonist smiling in her cap and gown with her mother and grandmother on either side. This scene offers an empowering alternative to the previous depiction of her despondently clad in a bra, panties, and stilettos with sad eyes and smeared make-up. In the final scene of the music video, the audience returns to the hospital room for a third time where the protagonist and her mother are awaiting test results.

Doctor: I have here the results of your test. It looks like you're pregnant.

Nurse: Congratulations.

Protagonist: Thank you. Thank you.

Doctor: Good luck you two.

Protagonist (to mother): Oh my gosh. I'm pregnant. Thank you. Just thank you for being there for me and teaching me how to love.[99]

These final moments in "How to Love"[100] are crucial from a Black feminist perspective since the protagonist was ultimately empowered to make her own decisions about her sexuality and she learned how to love over the course of her life by being genuinely loved. Taken in its entirety, Lil' Wayne utilizes the lyrics and music video to encourage his audience to understand that circumstances beyond the control of Black women can influence the trajectory of their lives. Likewise, he importantly draws sharp distinctions between what love is (i.e., respect, compassion, etc.) versus what it is not (i.e., abuse, exploitation, etc.). In essence, when provided love and support, Black women can empower themselves and rise above stereotyped imagery. In this regard, the protagonist at the end of the video serves as an amplified representation of Black womanhood that cannot be confined to the sexualized caricatures typically reserved for Black women in hip hop. To us, Lil' Wayne's use of "How to Love"[101] to highlight Black men's violence against Black women as consequential, contextualizes and questions the Jezebel caricature and thus reimagines the realities of Black women in hip hop.

## LIL' WAYNE AND HIP HOP AS PARADOXICAL

Creating a space for one Black woman's positive trajectory to be seen and celebrated in hip hop surely does not excuse Lil' Wayne's reliance on sexism, misogyny, and homophobia in the bulk of his music. However, via Black feminist thought (BFT) and hip hop feminism (HHF), there are undeniable ways that "How to Love"[102] humanizes Black women. Aligning ourselves with Jenkins' assertion that "Hip-hop has never been perfect. But it is not all worthless,"[103] we believe that through "How to Love"[104] Lil' Wayne meaningfully expands the repertoire of representations of Black women in hip hop. However as demonstrated by his televised performance at the 2011 MTV Video Music Awards, split between "How to Love"[105] and "John (If I Die Today),"[106] one song is not enough to transform an artist or an industry.

Lil' Wayne's performance begins with the lyrics of "How to Love" rapped in a sentimental cadence that includes an invitation to sing along. Then, removing his sunglasses as if to more deeply connect, he uses the lyrics to remind young women of their beauty and value.[107] At the end of this verse, rather than dedicating the entirety of his stage time to "How to Love," at just over two minutes into his performance he removes his hat and white t-shirt, puts his sunglasses back on and screams, "Ladies and Gentlemen my name is Lil' Wayne!"[108] At this moment, the stage comes newly alive with bright lights, forceful drums and guitars, and a screeching opening to "John (If I Die Today)."[109] The gravity of changes to Lil' Wayne's persona, accomplished in mere seconds, coupled with his self-introduction mid-performance communicates to the audience that he is now showcasing his more genuine, erratic self by playing off his last line of "How to Love," to communicate that he is not an average artist.[110]

In this context, BFT and HHF beckon us to highlight Lil' Wayne's apparent insincerity toward the progressive potential of "How to Love"[111] in that he had the choice to fully perform the song in front of millions worldwide without "John (If I Die Today)"[112] but chose "Black buffoonery"[113] and misogyny instead. Feeling duped, it seems that what we perceived as an opportunity to emotively connect with the audience by removing his sunglasses, while underscoring the significance of Black women via the song, was really a move to make it easier to strip off his t-shirt and strut to his usual beat of hypermasculinity.

In sharp contrast to the first half, during the second part of his performance Lil' Wayne equates a female sex partner with a dog and graphically narrates his aggressive and lewd sexual contact with her.[114] Intensifying his hypermasculine persona, his performance is frenzied and he struts the stage and chest-bumps with male audience members. Then, he ends his stage time by briefly stroking a guitar before throwing it down in a fit of discontent. From a feminist perspective, it is abysmally clear that Lil' Wayne reverted back to his customary practice of establishing his male authority and superiority via the sexual conquest of a Black woman. Confirming our interpretation, in the music video a Black female dancer is shown performing in a fenced cage and scantily clad in spiked leather.[115]

Rather than arguing that all of "How to Love's"[116] progressive potential is undermined by Lil' Wayne's 2011 MTV Video Music Awards performance, we instead want to underscore the complex and ambivalent relationship that many Black women have with hip hop. While scholars and activists alike may feel paralyzed by the depravity of songs such as "John (If I Die Today),"[117] it is vital to address hip hop as a pedagogical force in our culture. Therefore, we must highlight songs like "How to Love"[118] that offer critical cultural commentary on sexism, misogyny, and patriarchy as "progressive popular culture."[119] Surely such songs do not offer a definitive answer to commercial hip hop's extensive degradation of women, nor does one song signify the transformation of an artist or the industry. However, taken together, "How to Love,"[120] "Runaway Love,"[121] "Keep Ya Head Up,"[122] and "Dear Mama"[123] certainly highlight the progressive capabilities of Black male artists and signal progressive possibility from within the industry itself.

## NOTES

1. bell hooks, *The Will to Change: Men, Masculinity, and Love* (New York, NY: Atria Books, 2004).
2. Ibid., 134.
3. Ibid.
4. Dwayne Carter Jr., Marcus J. Boyd, Noel Fisher, Lanelle Seymore Quintez, Jermaine A. Preyan, and LaMar Seymour, "How to Love," *Tha Carter IV*, Young Money Entertainment, compact disc, 001554802, 2011.
5. Due to copyright and fair use restrictions, we suggest that readers independently access the music video and song lyrics of "How to Love" to inform their understanding of our argument.
6. Patricia Hill Collins, *Black Feminist Thought: Knowledge, Consciousness, and the Politics of Empowerment*, 3rd ed. (New York, NY: Routledge, 2009).
7. Joan Morgan, *When Chickenheads Come Home to Roost: A Hip-Hop Feminist Breaks it Down* (New York, NY: Simon and Schuster, 1999).
8. Carter, et al., "How to Love."
9. Ibid.
10. Michael P. Jefferies, *Thug Life: Race, Gender, and the Meaning of Hip-Hop* (Chicago, IL: University of Chicago Press, 2011), 1.
11. Jefferies, *Thug Life*; Manning Marable, *How Capitalism Underdeveloped Black America* (Boston, MA: South End Press, 2000).
12. Tryon P. Woods, "'Beat It Like a Cop': The Erotic Cultural Politics of Punishment in the Era of Postracialism," *Social Text* 31 (2013).
13. Ibid., 29.
14. M. K. Asante, *It's Bigger than Hip Hop: The Rise of the Post-Hip-Hop Generation* (New York, NY: St. Martin's Press, 2008); Jefferies, *Thug Life*.
15. Whitney A. Peoples, "'Under Construction': Identifying Foundations of Hip-Hop Feminism and Exploring Bridges between Black Second-Wave and Hip-Hop Feminisms," *Meridians: Feminism, Race, and Transnationalism* 8 (2008); Guillermo Rebollo-Gil and Amanda Moras, "Black Women and Black Men in Hip Hop Music: Misogyny, Violence and the Negotiation of (White-Owned) Space," *Journal of Popular Culture* 45 (2012); Tricia Rose, *Black Noise: Rap Music and Black Culture in Contemporary America* (Hanover, NH: University Press of New England, 1994).
16. Jefferies, *Thug Life*.
17. Rose, *Black Noise*; Tricia Rose, *The Hip Hop Wars: What We Talk about When We Talk about Hip Hop—And Why It Matters* (New York, NY: Basic Civitas Books, 2008); Toby S. Jenkins, "A Beautiful Mind: Black Male Intellectual Identity and Hip-Hop Culture," *Journal of Black Studies* 42 (2011); S. Craig Watkins, *Hip Hop Matters: Politics, Pop Culture, and the Struggle for the Soul of a Movement* (Boston, MA: Beacon Press, 2005).
18. Bakari Kitwana, *Why White Kids Love Hip-Hop: Wanksta, Wiggers, Wannabes, and the New Reality of Race in America* (New York, NY: Basic Civitas Books, 2005); Rebollo-Gil and Moras, "Black Women"; Watkins, *Matters*.
19. Kitwana, *Why White*; Rose, *Hip Hop Wars*; Watkins, *Matters*.
20. Johnnetta Betsch Cole and Beverly Guy-Sheftall, *Gender Talk: The Struggle for Women's Equality in African American Communities* (New York, NY: Ballantine Books, 2003).
21. Ibid., 193.
22. Kitwana, *Why White*; Watkins, *Matters*.
23. John McWhorter, "How Hip-hop Holds Blacks Back," *City Journal*, 2003, http://www.city-journal.org/html/13_3_how_hip_hop.html; Rose, *Hip Hop Wars*; Tricia Rose, "Jay-Z—Dropping the Word 'Bitch' Doesn't Begin to Cover It," *The Guardian*, 2012, http://www.theguardian.com/commentisfree/2012/jan/17/jay-z-bitch-rapper-hip-hop; Liza Weisstuch, "Sexism in Rap Sparks Black Magazine to Say, 'Enough!'" *The Christian Science Monitor*, 2005, http://www.csmonitor.com/2005/0112/p11s01-almp.html.
24. Jenkins, "Beautiful Mind."

25. Ben Sisario, "Three Acts Win Big at Grammy's," *The New York Times* (February 8, 2009), http://www.nytimes.com/2009/02/09/arts/music/09grammy.html?_r=0.

26. CNN, "Lil' Wayne Passes Elvis Presley's Hot 100 Record," September 27, 2012, http://marquee.blogs.cnn.com/2012/09/27/lil-wayne-passes-elvis-presleys-hot-100-record/.

27. Woods, "'Beat It'"; Sharon Lauricella and Matthew Alexander, "Voice from Rikers: Spirituality in Hip Hop Artist Lil' Wayne's Prison Blog," *Journal of Religion and Popular Culture* 24 (2012).

28. Ruth Nicole Brown and Chamara Jewel Kwakye, *Wish To Live: The Hip-Hop Feminism Pedagogy Reader* (New York, NY: Peter Lang Publishing, 2012); Marc Lamont Hill, *Beats, Rhymes, and Classroom Life: Hip-Hop Pedagogy and the Politics of Identity* (New York, NY: Teachers College Press, 2009).

29. Carter, et al., "How to Love."

30. Rebollo-Gil and Moras, "Black Women."

31. Woods, "'Beat It.'"

32. Cole and Guy-Sheftall, *Gender Talk*; Rose, *Black Noise*; Rose, *Hip Hop Wars*; Rose, "Jay-Z"; PBS, "Tavis Smiley: Examining Hip-Hop Culture," 2012, http://www.pbs.org/wnet/tavissmiley/features/examining-hip-hop-culture/; Mychal Denzel Smith, "Rap's Long History of 'Conscious' Condescension to Women," *The Atlantic*, 2012, http://www.theatlantic.com/entertainment/archive/2012/08/raps-long-history-of-conscious-condescension-to-women/261651/.

33. Watkins, *Matters*.

34. Ibid., 211.

35. Greg Tate, "Hiphop Turns 30: Whatcha Celebratin' for?" in *That's the Joint!: The Hip Hop Studies Reader*, 2nd ed., eds. Murray Forman and Mark Anthony Neal, 64–67 (New York, NY: Routledge, 2012), 65.

36. Michael Eric Dyson, *Know What I Mean?: Reflections on Hip Hop* (New York, NY: Basic Civitas Books, 2007).

37. Carolyn M. West, "Still on the Auction Block: The (S)exploitation of Black Adolescent Girls in Rap(e) Music and Hip-Hop Culture," in *The Sexualization of Childhood*, ed. Sharna Olfman, 89–102 (Westport, CT: Praeger, 2009).

38. Margaret Hunter and Kathleen Soto, "Women of Color in Hip Hop: The Pornographic Gaze," *Race, Gender, and Class* 16 (2009).

39. West, "Auction Block," 95.

40. Cole and Guy-Sheftall, *Gender Talk*, 195.

41. Cole and Guy-Sheftall, *Gender Talk*; Kimberlè Williams Crenshaw, "Beyond Racism and Misogyny: Black Feminism and 2 Live Crew," in *Words that Wound: Critical Race Theory, Assaultive Speech, and the First Amendment*, eds. Mari J. Matsuda, Charles R. Lawrence, Richard Delgado, and Kimberlè Williams Crenshaw, 111–45 (Boulder, CO: Westview Press, 1993); Hunter and Soto, "Pornographic Gaze"; West, "Auction Block."

42. Claire Hoffman, "Lil Wayne," *Gentlemen's Quarterly*, November 2011, 159–60.

43. Haroon Siddique, "Rapper Lil Wayne Begins One-Year Prison Term," *The Guardian*, March 9, 2010, http://www.theguardian.com/world/2010/mar/09/rapper-lil-wayne-prison-rikers-island.

44. Curtis Stewart, Dwayne Carter, Jr., Darius Harrison, Robert Wilson, "Mrs. Officer," *Tha Carter III*, Cash Money Records, compact disc, 001197702, 2008.

45. Daniel Johnson, Dwayne Carter Jr., and Radric Davis, "Steady Mobbin'," *We Are Young Money*, Young Money Entertainment, compact disc, 001379502, 2009.

46. Daniel Johnson, Dwayne Carter, Jr., and Aubrey Graham, "Right Above It," *I Am Not A Human Being*, Young Money Entertainment, compact disc, 001500200, 2010.

47. Tupac Shakur, "Lie to Kick It," *R U Still Down? (Remember Me)*, Interscope Records, compact disc, 41628, 1997.

48. Tupac Shakur, "Keep Ya Head Up," *Strictly 4 My N.I.G.G.A.Z.*, Interscope Records, compact disc, 41634, 1993.

49. Tupac Shakur, "Dear Mama," *Me Against the World*, Interscope Records, compact disc, 42636, 1995.

50. Christopher Brian Bridges, Billy Nichols, Phalon Anton Alexander, and Nathaniel D. Hale, "Area Codes," *Word of Mouf*, Def Jam Records, compact disc, 586446, 2001.

51. Jamal F. Jones, Christopher B. Bridges, Keri L. Hilson, Douglas L. Davis, and Richard M. L. Walters, "Runaway Love," *Release Therapy*, Def Jam Records, compact disc, 000722401, 2006.

52. Curtis Stewart, Dwayne Carter Jr., Darius Harrison, Robert Wilson, *Mrs. Officer*.

53. Rose, "Jay-Z."

54. Carter, et al., *How to Love*.

55. Collins, *Black Feminist Thought*.

56. Morgan, *Home to Roost*.

57. Collins, *Black Feminist Thought*, 11.

58. Collins, *Black Feminist Thought*.

59. Kimberlè Williams Crenshaw, "Mapping the Margins: Intersectionality, Identity Politics, and Violence against Women of Color," *Stanford Law Review* 43 (1991).

60. Cole and Guy-Sheftall, *Gender Talk*; Collins, *Black Feminist Thought*; Rachel Alicia Griffin, "I AM an Angry Black Woman: Black Feminist Autoethnography, Voice, and Resistance," *Women's Studies in Communication* 35 (2012); bell hooks, *Black Looks: Race and Representation* (Boston, MA: South End Press, 1992).

61. Gwendolyn D. Pough, "Do the Ladies Run This . . . ?: Some Thoughts on Hip-Hop Feminism," in *Catching a Wave: Reclaiming Feminism for the 21st Century*, eds. Rory Dicker and Alison Piepmeier, 232–43 (Boston, MA: Northeastern University Press, 2003), 238.

62. Peoples, "'Under Construction,'" 22.

63. Aisha Durham, Brittney C. Cooper, and Susana M. Morris, "The Stage Hip-Hop Feminism Built: A New Directions Essay," *Signs: Journal of Women in Culture and Society* 38 (2013); Morgan, *Home to Roost*; Peoples, "'Under Construction.'"

64. Morgan, *Home to Roost*.

65. Ibid., 36.

66. Durham, Cooper, and Morris, "The Stage," 723.

67. Morgan, *Home to Roost*; Peoples, "'Under Construction.'"

68. Morgan, *Home to Roost*; Peoples, "'Under Construction'"; Pough, "Do the Ladies."

69. Carter, et al., "How to Love."

70. Ibid.

71. Collins, *Black Feminist Thought*.

72. Ibid.; bell hooks, *Ain't I A Woman: Black Women and Feminism* (Boston, MA: South End, 1981).

73. Jody Freeman, "The Disciplinary Function of Rape's Representation: Lessons from the Kennedy Smith and Tyson Trials," *Law and Social Inquiry* 18 (1993); Rachel Alicia Griffin, "Gender Violence and the Black Female Body: The Enduring Significance of 'Crazy' Mike Tyson," *Howard Journal of Communications* 24 (2012).

74. LilWayneVEVO, *Lil Wayne—How to Love (Shazam Version)*, music video, 5 min., 22 sec., August 24, 2011, http://www.youtube.com/watch?v=y8Gf4-eT3w0.

75. Ibid.

76. Patricia Hill Collins, "The Tie that Binds: Race, Gender, and US Violence," *Ethnic and Racial Studies* 21 (1998); Angela Y. Davis, *Violence Against Women and the Ongoing Challenge to Racism* (Albany, NY: Kitchen Table: Women of Color Press, 1985); Griffin, "Gender Violence."

77. Thema Bryant-Davis, "Breaking the Silence: The Role of Progressive Black Men in the Fight Against Sexual Assault," in *Progressive Black Masculinities*, ed. Athena D. Mutua, 245–61 (New York, NY: Routledge, 2006).

78. Katheryn Russell-Brown, *Protecting Our Own: Race, Crime, and African Americans* (Lanham, MD: Rowman & Littlefield, 2006), 100.

79. Carter, et al., "How to Love."

80. Rob Markman, "Lil Wayne Says New Single 'How To Love' Gives Him 'Goose Bumps,'" *MTV*, May 27, 2011, http://www.mtv.com/news/articles/1664772/lil-wayne-how-to-love.jhtml.

81. Rob Markman, "Lil Wayne's 'How to Love' Video 'Harsh' But 'Real,'" *MTV*, August 24, 2011, http://www.mtv.com/news/articles/1669637/lil-wanye-how-to-love-director.jhtml.

82. Suzanne Enck-Wanzer, "All's Fair in Love and Sport: Black Masculinity and Domestic Violence in the News," *Communication and Critical/Cultural Studies* 6 (2009); Ronald L. Jackson, *Scripting the Black Masculine Body: Identity, Discourse, and Racial Politics in Popular Media* (New York, NY: State University of New York Press, 2006).

83. Carter, et al., "How to Love."

84. Ibid.

85. Collins, *Black Feminist Thought*.

86. Our intentions are not to label all sex work as exploitive but rather we perceive sex work as exploitive in this instance based upon the actor's facial expressions, behaviors, and disposition in the music video.

87. Carter, et al., "How to Love."

88. LilWayneVEVO, *Lil Wayne—How to Love (Shazam Version)*.

89. Collins, *Black Feminist Thought*.

90. Markman, "'Harsh' But 'Real'."

91. Carter, et al., "How to Love."

92. Rob Markman, "Lil Wayne's Carter IV 'Totally Done," *MTV*, July 11, 2011, http://www.mtv.com/news/articles/1667052/lil-wayne-tha-carter-iv.jhtml.

93. Collins, *Black Feminist Thought*.

94. Evelyn Brooks Higginbotham, *Righteous Discontent: The Women's Movement in the Black Baptist Church, 1880–1920* (Cambridge, MA: Harvard University Press, 1993), 186.

95. Durham, Cooper, and Morris, "The Stage," 724.

96. Ibid.

97. Carter, et al., "How to Love."

98. Ibid.

99. LilWayneVEVO, *Lil Wayne—How to Love (Shazam Version)*.

100. Carter, et al., "How to Love."

101. Ibid.

102. Ibid.

103. Jenkins, "Beautiful Mind," 1232.

104. Carter, et al., "How to Love."

105. Ibid.

106. Dwayne Carter, Jr., "John (If I Die Today)," *Tha Carter IV*, Young Money Entertainment, compact disc, 2768141, 2011.

107. jairo zamora, *Lil Wayne VMA MTV 2011*, music video, 4 min., 15 sec., June 2012, http://http://vimeo.com/43767178

108. Ibid.

109. Carter, "John."

110. zamora, *Lil Wayne*.

111. Carter, et al., "How to Love."

112. Carter, "John."

113. Cole and Guy-Sheftall, *Gender Talk*, 193.

114. zamora, *Lil Wayne*.

115. LilWayneVEVO, *Lil Wayne – John (Explicit) ft. Rick Ross*, music video, 5 min., 1 sec., May 12, 2011, https://www.youtube.com/watch?v=3fumBcKC6RE.

116. Carter, et al., "How to Love."

117. Carter, "John."

118. Carter, et al., "How to Love."

119. hooks, *The Will*, 134.

120. Carter, et al., "How to Love."

121. Jones, et al., "Runaway Love."

122. Shakur, "Keep Ya Head Up."

123. Shakur, "Dear Mama."

# BIBLIOGRAPHY

Asante, M. K. *It's Bigger than Hip Hop: The Rise of the Post-Hip-Hop Generation*. New York, NY: St. Martin's Press, 2008.

Bridges, Christopher Brian, Billy Nichols, Phalon Anton Alexander, and Nathaniel D. Hale. "Area Codes." *Word of Mouf*. Def Jam Records. Compact Disc. 586446, 2001.

Brown, Ruth Nicole, and Chamara Jewel Kwakye. *Wish to Live: The Hip-Hop Feminism Pedagogy Reader*. New York, NY: Peter Lang Publishing, 2012.

Bryant-Davis, Thema. "Breaking the Silence: The Role of Progressive Black Men in the Fight against Sexual Assault." In *Progressive Black Masculinities*, edited by Athena D. Mutua, 245–61. New York, NY: Routledge, 2006.

Carter, Jr., Dwayne. "John (If I Die Today)." *Tha Carter IV*. Young Money Entertainment. Compact Disc. 001554802, 2011.

Carter, Jr., Dwayne, Marcus J. Boyd, Noel Fisher, Lanelle Seymore Quintez, Jermaine A Preyan, and LaMar Seymour. "How to Love." *Tha Carter IV*. Young Money Entertainment. Compact Disc. 001554802, 2011.

CNN. "Lil' Wayne Passes Elvis Presley's Hot 100 Record." September 27, 2012. http://marquee.blogs.cnn.com/2012/09/27/lil-wayne-passes-elvis-presleys-hot-100-record/.

Cole, Johnnetta Betsch, and Beverly Guy-Sheftall. *Gender Talk: The Struggle for Women's Equality in African American Communities*. New York, NY: Ballantine Books, 2003.

Collins, Patricia Hill. "The Tie that Binds: Race, Gender, and US Violence." *Ethnic and Racial Studies* 21, no. 5 (1998): 917–38.

———. *Black Feminist Thought: Knowledge, Consciousness, and the Politics of Empowerment*. 3rd ed. New York, NY: Routledge, 2009.

Crenshaw, Kimberlè Williams. "Mapping the Margins: Intersectionality, Identity Politics, and Violence against Women of Color." *Stanford Law Review* 43, no. 6 (1991): 1241–99.

———. "Beyond Racism and Misogyny: Black Feminism and 2 Live Crew." In *Words that Wound: Critical Race Theory, Assaultive Speech, and the First Amendment*, edited by Mari J. Matsuda, Charles R. Lawrence, Richard Delgado, and Kimberlè Williams Crenshaw, 111–145. Boulder, CO: Westview Press, 1993.

Davis, Angela Y. *Violence against Women and the Ongoing Challenge to Racism*. Albany, NY: Kitchen Table: Women of Color Press, 1985.

Durham, Aisha, Brittney C. Cooper, and Susana M. Morris. "The Stage Hip-Hop Feminism Built: A New Directions Essay." *Signs: Journal of Women in Culture and Society* 38, no. 3 (2013): 721–37.

Dyson, Michael Eric. *Know What I Mean?: Reflections on Hip Hop*. New York, NY: Basic Civitas Books, 2007.

Enck-Wanzer, Suzanne. "All's Fair in Love and Sport: Black Masculinity and Domestic Violence in the News." *Communication and Critical/Cultural Studies* 6, no. 1 (2009): 1–18.

Freeman, Jody. "The Disciplinary Function of Rape's Representation: Lessons from the Kennedy Smith and Tyson Trials." *Law and Social Inquiry* 18, no. 3 (1993): 517–46.

Griffin, Rachel Alicia. "I AM an Angry Black Woman: Black Feminist Autoethnography, Voice, and Resistance," *Women's Studies in Communication* 35, no. 2 (2012): 138–57.

———. "Gender Violence and the Black Female Body: The Enduring Significance of 'Crazy' Mike Tyson." *Howard Journal of Communications* 24 (2012): 71–94.

Higginbotham, Evelyn Brooks. *Righteous Discontent: The Women's Movement in the Black Baptist Church, 1880–1920*. Cambridge, MA: Harvard University Press, 1993.

Hill, Marc Lamont. *Beats, Rhymes, and Classroom Life: Hip-Hop Pedagogy and the Politics of Identity*. New York, NY: Teachers College Press, 2009.

Hoffman, Claire. "Lil Wayne." *Gentlemen's Quarterly* (November 2011): 159–60.

hooks, bell. *Ain't I a Woman: Black Women and Feminism*. Boston, MA: South End Press, 1981.

———. *Black Looks: Race and Representation*. Boston, MA: South End Press, 1992.

———. *The Will to Change: Men, Masculinity, and Love*. New York, NY: Atria Books, 2004.

Hunter, Margaret and Kathleen Soto. "Women of Color in Hip Hop: The Pornographic Gaze." *Race, Gender, and Class* 16, no. 1/2 (2009): 170–91.

Jackson, Ronald L. *Scripting the Black Masculine Body: Identity, Discourse, and Racial Politics in Popular Media.* New York, NY: State University of New York Press, 2006.

Jefferies, Michael P. *Thug Life: Race, Gender, and the Meaning of Hip-Hop.* Chicago, IL: University of Chicago Press, 2011.

Jenkins, Toby S. "A Beautiful Mind: Black Male Intellectual Identity and Hip-Hop Culture." *Journal of Black Studies* 42, no. 8 (2011): 1231–51.

Johnson, Daniel, Dwayne Carter Jr., and Radric Davis. "Steady Mobbin'." *We Are Young Money.* Young Money Entertainment. Compact Disc. 001379502, 2009.

Johnson, Daniel, Dwayne Carter Jr., and Aubrey D. Graham. "Right Above It." *I Am Not A Human Being.* Young Money Entertainment. Compact Disc. 001500200, 2010.

Jones, Jamal F., Christopher B. Bridges, Keri L. Hilson, Douglas L. Davis, and Richard M. L. Walters. "Runaway Love." *Release Therapy.* Def Jam Records. Compact Disc. 000722401, 2006.

Kitwana, Bakari. *Why White Kids Love Hip-Hop: Wankstas, Wiggers, Wannabes, and the New Reality of Race in America.* New York, NY: Basic Civitas Books, 2005.

Lauricella, Sharon, and Matthew Alexander. "Voice from Rikers: Spirituality in Hip Hop Artist Lil' Wayne's Prison Blog." *Journal of Religion and Popular Culture* 24, no.1 (2012): 15–28.

*Lil Wayne—How to Love (Shazam Version).* YouTube Video. 5:22, posted by "LilWayneVEVO." August 24, 2011, http://www.youtube.com/watch?v=y8Gf4-eT3w0.

*Lil Wayne—John (Explicit) ft. Rick Ross.* YouTube Video. 5:01, posted by "LilWayneVEVO." May 12, 2011, http://www.youtube.com/watch?v=3fumBcKC6RE.

*Lil Wayne VMA MTV 2011.* Vimeo Video. 4:15, posted by "jairo zamora." June 2012, http://vimeo.com/43767178.

Marable, Manning. *How Capitalism Underdeveloped Black America.* Boston, MA: South End Press, 2000.

Markman, Rob. "Lil Wayne's Carter IV 'Totally Done.'" *MTV.* July 11, 2011. http://www.mtv.com/news/articles/1667052/lil-wayne-tha-carter-iv.jhtml.

———. "Lil Wayne Drops Deep Messages in 'How to Love' Video." *MTV.* August 24, 2011. http://www.mtv.com/news/articles/1669574/lil-wayne-how-to-love-music-video.jhtml.

———. "Lil Wayne's 'How to Love' Video 'Harsh' But 'Real'. *MTV.* August 24, 2011. http://www.mtv.com/news/articles/1669637/lil-wanye-how-to-love-director.jhtml.

———. "Lil Wayne Says New Single 'How to Love' Gives Him 'Goose Bumps.'" *MTV.* May 27, 2011. http://www.mtv.com/news/articles/1664772/lil-wayne-how-to-love.jhtml.

McWhorter, John H. "How Hip-hop Holds Blacks Back" *City Journal.* 2003. http://www.city-journal.org/html/13_3_how_hip_hop.html.

Morgan, Joan. *When Chickenheads Come Home to Roost: A Hip-Hop Feminist Breaks it Down.* New York, NY: Simon and Schuster, 1999.

PBS. "Tavis Smiley: Examining Hip-Hop Culture." 2012. http://www.pbs.org/wnet/tavissmiley/features/examining-hip-hop-culture/.

Peoples, Whitney A. "'Under Construction': Identifying Foundations of Hip-Hop Feminism and Exploring Bridges between Black Second-Wave and Hip-Hop Feminisms." *Meridians: Feminism, Race, and Transnationalism* 8, no. 1 (2008): 19–52.

Pough, Gwendolyn D. "Do the Ladies Run This…?: Some Thoughts on Hip-Hop Feminism." In *Catching a Wave: Reclaiming Feminism for the 21 st Century,* edited by Rory Dicker and Alison Piepmeier, 232-43. Boston, MA: Northeastern University Press, 2003.

Rebollo-Gil, Guillermo and Amanda Moras. "Black Women and Black Men in Hip Hop Music: Misogyny, Violence and the Negotiation of (White-Owned) Space." *Journal of Popular Culture* 45, no. 1 (2012): 118–32.

Rose, Tricia. *Black Noise: Rap Music and Black Culture in Contemporary America.* Hanover, NH: University Press of New England, 1994.

———. *The Hip Hop Wars: What We Talk about When We Talk about Hip Hop—And Why It Matters.* New York, NY: Basic Civitas Books, 2008.

———. "Jay-Z—Dropping the Word 'Bitch' Doesn't Begin to Cover It." *The Guardian,* 2012. http://www.theguardian.com/commentisfree/2012/jan/17/jay-z-bitch-rapper-hip-hop.

Russell-Brown, Katheryn. *Protecting Our Own: Race, Crime, and African Americans*. Lanham, MD: Rowman and Littlefield, 2006.

Shakur, Tupac. "Keep Ya Head Up." *Strictly 4 My N.I.G.G.A.Z*. Interscope Records. Compact Disc. 41634, 1993.

———. "Dear Mama." *Me Against the World*. Interscope Records. Compact Disc. 41636, 1995.

———. "Lie to Kick It." *R U Still Down? (Remember Me)*. Interscope Records. Compact Disc. 41628, 1997.

Siddique, Haroon. "Rapper Lil Wayne Begins One-Year Prison Term." *The Guardian*, March 9, 2010. http://www.theguardian.com/world/2010/mar/09/rapper-lil-wayne-prison-rikers-island.

Sisario, Ben. "Three Acts Win Big at Grammy's." *The New York Times,* February 8, 2009. http://www.nytimes.com/2009/02/09/arts/music/09grammy.html?_r=0.

Smith, Mychal Denzel. "Rap's Long History of 'Conscious' Condescension to Women." *The Atlantic*, 2012. http://www.theatlantic.com/entertainment/archive/2012/08/raps-long-history-of-conscious-condescension-to-women/261651/.

Stewart, Curtis, Dwayne Carter Jr., Darius Harrison, Robert Wilson. "Mrs. Officer." *Tha Carter III*. Cash Money Records. Compact Disc. 001197702, 2008.

Tate, Greg. "Hiphop Turns 30: Whatcha Celebratin' for?" In *That's the Joint!: The Hip Hop Studies Reader*. 2nd ed, edited by Murray Forman and Mark Anthony Neal, 64–7. New York, NY: Routledge, 2012.

Watkins, S. Craig. *Hip Hop Matters: Politics, Pop Culture, and the Struggle for the Soul of a Movement*. Boston, MA: Beacon Press, 2005.

Weisstuch, Liza. Sexism in Rap Sparks Black Magazine to Say, 'Enough!,'." *The Christian Science Monitor*, 2005. http://www.csmonitor.com/2005/0112/p11s01-almp.html.

West, Carolyn M. "Still on the Auction Block: The (S)exploitation of Black Adolescent Girls in Rap(e) Music and Hip-Hop Culture." In *The Sexualization of Childhood*, edited by Sharna Olfman, 89-102. Westport, CT: Praeger, 2009.

Woods, Tryon P. "'Beat It Like a Cop': The Erotic Cultural Politics of Punishment in the Era of Postracialism." *Social Text* 31, no. 1 (2013): 21–41.

*III*

# Advertising, Print, and Digital Media

*Chapter Ten*

# Apparitions of the Past and Obscure Visions for the Future

*Stereotypes of Black Women and Advertising during a Paradigm Shift*

Joanna L. Jenkins

Since 2006 there has been a resurgence of stereotypes of Black women within advertising. Recently, these cornerstones of American visual rhetoric have been used to advertise a plethora of ideas and products ranging from fast food, ice cream, and hygienic supplies to family vacations, insurance, and cosmetics.[1] At first glance this abundance of stereotypes appears to be a startling contradiction considering the groundbreaking achievements that Black women have accomplished within recent decades. However, careful observation has revealed that stereotypical imagery is not only highly anticipated but also a natural occurrence during revolutionary times such as these.

A paradigm shift in advertising is underway. During these times of great change a critical juncture now exists. Previous lines of demarcation and structural norms have begun to erode leading to power redistribution. During this transitional period, opportunities to shape the future and create new systems of empowerment are presented. Along with potential achievements, heightened levels of boldness and conservatism also characterize these times. While innovators break new ground, those who seek to maintain the status quo will often launch tactical reprisals that are empirical or rhetorical in nature. Despite dissension, opportunities for extraordinary achievements abound. More focus must be placed upon awareness of such opportunities in order to promote their potential. Such is the goal of this chapter.

It is important to note that this chapter is most particularly concerned with stereotypes of Black women and advertising during a paradigm shift. Stereotypes of Black women have long since been an essential element of empirical and rhetorical attacks. Due to negativity associated with stereotypes, it is easy to understand controversies that may surround their resurgence. However, lucidity surrounding these matters may not only fortify progressive efforts towards achievement but also mitigate misguided attempts. Far too often skepticism surrounding the perceived ability of society to change obscures visions for the future. Truth surrounding apparitions often reveals that they do not exist at all. Although startling in appearance, a deeper gaze affirms that they are a natural precursor to extraordinary change.

This discussion conceptualizes advertising as an institution in order to demonstrate how stereotypes of Black women impact individuals, society, and historical circumstances. Conceptualizations of advertising that are limited in scope often fail to demonstrate the ubiquitous nature of advertising and may diminish its collective impact. In this chapter a range of examples are discussed to authenticate the power of advertising and elevate the conversation surrounding its roles and functions. Following a brief survey of contemporary advertising as it relates to paradigmic shifts, a chronicle of stereotypes of Black women in advertising is offered. This chronicle will be traced from the seventeenth to the twenty-first centuries to reveal how patterns have persisted over time. To conclude, this chapter will offer insights for navigating through complexity during a period of great transition.

## ADVERTISING

As a basis for this discussion, a comprehensive meaning of advertising must be ascertained. Advertising is a deeply pervasive and powerful force that encompasses ideology, industry, and execution. It is most commonly defined as paid, non-personal communication delivered through various media from identifiable corporations, nonprofit organizations, or individuals who desire to inform or persuade a particular audience.[2] As an industry, advertising is defined as the systematic aggregate of manufacturing or technically productive enterprises that use persuasive communications to promote the sale of specific commodities, ideas, or services.[3]

In its early stages, advertising was primarily intended to provide information about economic goods and services. However, under modern conditions, advertising expanded and assumed broad and noneconomic roles and functions.[4] During the wave of the industrial revolution characterized by Electronification of industrial systems, mass production, and mass communications technology, Charles Peirce, semiotician, philosopher, and scientist, stated the following, "Let an institution be created which shall have for its object to keep correct doctrines before the attention of the people, to reiterate them perpetually, and to teach them to the young; having at the same time power to prevent contrary doctrines from being taught, advocated, or expressed."[5]

Peirce's works affirmed that institutions were implemented by society to uphold authority and preserve order. Accordingly, institutions widely perpetuate information through levels that include structural norms and individuals. Within a society all knowledge is derived from either authority or reason. Whatever is deduced by reason depends ultimately on standards that have been derived from authority.[6] Thus, the perception of Black women is largely determined by norms that have been established through advertising. Such norms manifest as stereotypes, which are often incongruent with reality, leading to negative and erroneous perceptions of Black women.

The extent of advertising's influence is largely accomplished through its inextricable relationship with popular culture. In the 1920s monumental growth within society, the economy, and industry led to enormous prosperity for advertising. In what was known as "The Roaring Twenties" consumerism expanded exponentially through media, celebrity, lifestyle, and technology. Undoubtedly, advertising and popular culture fused and formed a singular authoritative discipline.[7] This relationship created a ubiquitous channel to disseminate standards of normalcy and cultivate ideals while remaining deeply entrenched at the pulse of culture.

Another important factor to consider involving advertising lies within its relationship to mass media. Advertising established the tradition of creating content that would be the most appealing to wide audiences. This concept, and derived practices, gave birth to the term mass media, which described the ability of media to attract large audiences to whom advertisers could directly target their messaging.[8] Consequently, media are often reliant upon advertising for their revenue. Content must appeal to the audiences of advertisers in order to be successful.

As this practice has evolved over the years, mass media developed content and messaging that would attract the largest audiences and excluded content and messaging that could offend or alienate viewers. Practices such as these reinforce advertising's ability to convey messaging and imagery that uphold social standards of influence and value formation. As a result, advertising proliferates portrayals of people of color, such as Black women, that reflect the perceived values and norms of general market audiences. Within advertising, general market audiences usually consist of consumers who have the most spending power and influence. For years, general market audiences have been largely Caucasian and/or male. As a result, the history of advertising reflects once widely held racist practices and prejudicial beliefs of Caucasian majority audiences rather than reality or perspectives of people of color.

This is of particular importance as it relates to Black women. Their specific history of commodification, oppression, and social construction has contributed to widespread stereotypical depictions within advertising. Thus, the broad use of integrated advertising techniques, which include product placement, sponsorship, branded entertainment, and IMC (Integrated Marketing Communications), creates confusion and fosters growing complexities. In the contemporary media environment, it is difficult to determine distinctions between advertisements, such as commercials, and media content, such as television programming. The lines of demarcation have become increasingly blurred. With a comprehensive understanding of advertising, as it relates specifically to Black woman, contemporary situational dramas and reality television programming could easily be perceived as advertisements that reinforce and widely proliferate stereotypes of Black women. These areas will be expanded upon subsequently in our discussion. However, now it is important to address the paradigm shift in advertising as to connect the former with the latter.

## ADVERTISING AND PARADIGM SHIFTS

As with any major discipline, advertising experienced highs and lows. Nonetheless, a period of recognized achievement began in the 1960s. During these times advertising experience a period of significant change that facilitated growth in numerous directions. Advocates of creative expression surged to the forefront of advertising, while cultural shifts in America were reflected in the workplace and advertising executions. Although short lived, these shifts sparked an era in advertising known as the creative revolution. However, despite growth and global expansion, advertising began a descent into a state of crisis by the 1980s, which signaled an impending paradigm shift.[9] In a state of crisis, anomalies accumulate to a point at which productivity becomes impossible to sustain. Weaknesses in the current paradigm are revealed and the transition towards a paradigm shift ensues.

Although major strides in advertising occurred in the 1980s, they were also a period of tremendous difficulty as well. America had been deeply entrenched in consumer culture for nearly a century. Accordingly, markets began to mature and become overly saturated. Expenditures peaked in 1984 and trended downward since that time.[10] Revolutionary advances in technology, which eventually resulted in the democratization of information, overhauled advertising's business and commerce practices along with its longstanding structural relationships. Other severe problems during these times included polarized audiences, internal conflicts, factions, and ineffective tactics.

By the close of the 1980s, the American public, particularly youth culture, had grown tired of advertising and weary of its tactics. Generation X—those born between 1956 and 1980—became nearly immune to the strategies and tactics used by the advertising industry. Such a small, yet diverse, cohort posed a problem for advertisers. As a result, advertising struggled to reach this audience.[11] Traditional advertising strategies and tactics failed to counteract the norms surrounding this youth market. Hence, lifestyle and cultural integration became popular advertising strategies. Widespread emulation of hip-hop and urban culture was used to advertise numerous brands and products including soft drinks, cars, and fast food.

Difficulties for advertising were further compounded by radical change. In 1992 the rise of Internet created a global mass communications phenomenon. The Internet altered nearly every facet of advertising from its agency environment, strategies, and practices to its markets, consumer audiences, and underlying business principles. Despite attempts to leverage the Internet, it was a relatively young medium and therefore largely in flux. By 2000, Internet frenzy came to a grisly halt with the dot.com bust. According to the Internet Advertising Bureau, after soaring to rates of 150 percent, advertising Internet spending tumbled to a negative 6.5 percent in one quarter alone.[12]

At the close of catastrophe, the Internet remained along with a promise of a new mass audience. The dot.com bubble left behind a well-equipped commercial infrastructure that had the capacity to sustain global networks. Fiber optic channels, ethanol plants, and web-hosting facilities had been developed. Additionally, models for potential success were provided by several companies, including Google, Amazon, and eBay.[13]

The dot.com bust ushered in a period of rapid change and uncertainty for advertising. From chat rooms and blogs to social networks and mobile devices, the Internet continuously reshaped and redefined media. Advertising struggled in a media environment that appeared to no longer be receptive to its governing paradigm. The days of absolute persuasion that resulted in influence, predictability, and control had been replaced by interactivity and feedback. Brands and products were beginning to become the result of co-creations with new and interactive consumer audiences.

By these times the general market had undergone considerable change as well. Significant shifts in America's demographic and generational landscape occurred. U.S. census data revealed that 1 in every 3 Americans is a person of color, adults over the age of sixty-five constitute the fastest growing population segment, and specialty markets driven by female buying power comprise 84 percent of the U.S. population.[14] Contemporary African American markets have become trendsetters and influencers within the global community. Black women are now the primary decision makers in their households and businesses, which has made them a coveted target market. This group also wields tremendous spending power. Moreover, the American public is largely interactive and increasingly disloyal to brands and products. The largest population segments, Boomers and Millennials, are diverse, participatory, and deeply engaged with media.[15]

Major shifts such as these have resulted in a contemporary environment characterized by change. The extent of these rapid transitions has contributed to a state of crisis, which has led to a paradigm shift in advertising. The decisive markers of a paradigm shift are often difficult to pinpoint. A paradigm shift begins with blurring. This intermingling intensifies complexity. Consequently, a new paradigm can emerge in an infinitesimal state before crisis has matured or before the new paradigm has the ability to be recognized universally. As a result, both paradigm shifts and revolutions can often be invisible.[16] It is imperative to encourage discourse regarding this matter. As previously stated, advertising ranks among the most powerful educational forces in the world. It has the capacity to empower communities and individuals through a proliferation of positive imagery and messaging. During this malleable state, it is imperative to increase awareness and promote opportunities that accompany change.

## COMPLEXITIES AND CONTRADICTIONS

It is necessary to understand the complexity of crisis that accompanies a paradigm shift. It is within this complexity that the capacity for understanding and the ability to influence problem solving occurs. The paradigm shift in advertising is largely attributed to the impact of triadic convergence. Triadic convergence is a multifaceted, ever changing, and complex phenomenon. This dynamic force is comprised of the sophisticated intermingling of media, technology, and culture. Intermingling is characterized by the constant mutative and adaptive synergy achieved between these three forces. Triadic convergence is shaped and shifts in correspondence with the central locus of power within the triad.[17]

In the 1980s, former chairman of the Columbia Broadcasting System (CBS) William Paley affirmed the powerful presence of convergence. Paley stated that while corporations were overly focused on their specific areas of media interest, they largely ignored the extent to which they were being drawn together by the vast revolution in Electronification.[18] As lines of demarcation began to erode, media conglomerates maneuvered to command entire areas of entertainment. Specific delineations between media and media devices blurred and were sometimes eradicated. Revolution was ushered in through technological innovations that allowed pulses of electromagnetic energy to embody and convey messages. Electronification facilitated the near seamless flow of content across channels. A central electrical environment was created in which content and information could be stored, manipulated, distributed, shared, and presented.[19] Electronification, which has largely caused convergence, contributed to an upset in normative structures, roles, and relationships. Previous boundaries have dissolved and power has been dispersed amongst larger audiences.

It is important to understand the causes and meanings associated with paradigm shifts because they often characterize revolution. As it relates to advertising, an extremely lucrative global institution, change may be greatly resisted due to the desire to maintain the status quo and normative power structures. Advertising is also subject to simplified patterns of technological determinism, which inhibits its ability to respond to shifts caused by technology in a timely manner. As a result, advertising may behave as a constraint on change and appear futile as technology matures. Moreover, the contemporary advertising environment is highly characterized by conglomerate monopolies. Corporate giants often embrace convergence strategies as a way to leverage their position and power. Convergence creates profitable methods to sell content directly to audiences while renewing consumer loyalty through seemingly customized distribution channels, which often benefit conglomerates because of their vast ownership.

Although convergence contributes to methods that benefit the status quo, it also produces opportunities to redistribute power. This is particularly evident as it relates to Black women. Over the years, the role of Black women in advertising has been elevated, due to power redistribution, from product to audience to producer. In an environment in which former products are now highly coveted target audiences and powerful content producers significant upheaval will ensue. Resultantly, competing interests, tactical decisions, obscure direction, erratic outcomes, and unprecedented disruptions will characterize these times. A great deal of tension and confusion will emerge as the old collides with the new.[20]

Response to change is demonstrated in distinct ways. There are those that will remain unaware or choose to ignore issues and opportunities. There will also be those who seek avenues of innovation and progress in order to leverage opportunities that accompany change. Lastly, there are those that will continually refute change in order to maintain the status quo.[21] This is of particular importance as it relates to this discussion. Stereotypes in advertising have long since been used as tools in propagandistic attacks against Black women to perpetuate ideals that keep them in marginalized positions. Therefore, stereotypes are a natural component of rhetorical attacks launched to refute change.

Increased attention surrounding these matters is needed in order to create awareness. Although failing, the established paradigm has the natural tendency to suppress change and refute alternatives, which could inhibit positive outcomes that accompany change. To reiterate, new paradigms may appear to be invisible and/or emerge in an infinitesimal state prior to being accepted in consensus. This period of uncertain transition has no conclusive delineation. Nonetheless, it is within the intersection of this complexity and contradiction that extraordinary possibilities lie dormant waiting for discovery.

These are some of the ways that paradigm shifts in advertising have an impact, both specifically and generally. In order to specifically apply these concepts to stereotypes of Black women a broad historical discussion is also required. The following section will trace stereotypes of Black women in advertising from the seventeenth to the twenty-first centuries.

## STEREOTYPES OF BLACK WOMEN AND ADVERTISING

The paradigm shift in advertising has created an opportunity to redistribute power. This is of particular importance to those who have historically been powerless. In the complex intersection between race and gender Black women have resided along the margins as an undervalued, disempowered, and ignored community. In support of this unique intersection, the four basic principles of Black feminism are incorporated to increase the specificity and relevance of this discussion.[22]

1. Racism, sexism, and classism are interlocking systems of oppression.
2. We must maintain a humanist vision that will not accept any amount of human oppression.
3. We must define ourselves and give voice to the everyday Black woman and everyday experiences.
4. We must operate from the standpoint that Black women are unique and our experiences are unique.

Generally, images of Black people can be categorized into three images: the dependable, yet conniving, slave figure; the native who is both dignified and savage; and the clown or entertainer whose existence is defined by how well they amuse the White majority.[23] Relating more specifically, mainstream imagery of Black women is generally detrimental and stereotypical.[24] According to Robin M. Coleman and Emily Chivers Yochim,

> A stereotype is defined as a conventional, formulaic, oversimplified concept, opinion, or belief. It describes the promotion of an unvarying depiction of a group that, in a media context, has come to be associated with negative portrayals. However, as a concept, *stereotype* is particularly reliant on discourses that actively signify that which is a present and identifiable, constructed image. A stereotype, then, is quite adept at drawing our attention to how individuals and groups are presented, but the concept may not function as well in capturing the meanings associated with absence, omission, or even an inclusion that is not so obviously problematic.[25]

To explore stereotypes of Black women in advertising we begin with their origins. Black women first appeared in advertising throughout the seventeenth century as products and commodities to be bought, raffled, and sold. Advertisements, which emphasized the skills and attributes of slaves, primarily appeared in newspapers and as posters and handbills. Objectifying imagery such as this continued well into the nineteenth century through advertisements used in the capture of runaway slaves. In addition to skills and desirable attributes, these advertisements emphasized physical characteristics of slaves and monetary sums that were offered in exchange for human value.

Black women in advertisements were generally referred to as wenches, a term synonymous with a prostitute or a sexually promiscuous woman. Such terminology reinforced stereotypical misconceptions associated with Black women regarding lewd sexual conduct and excessive child bearing. Although the Black female slave experience has not received widespread historical attention, research has revealed that the plight of enslaved Black women was often more arduous, difficult, and restricted than that of their male counterparts.[26] The labor of Black female slaves was most often equal to that of men, and child bearing and rearing compounded hardship. Black women received heinous punishments regardless of infirmity, pregnancy, or motherhood. In fact, the children of Black female slaves were often deliberately leveraged as a tactic to disempower and manipulate women.[27] Moreover, the sexual exploitation and abuse of Black women by White men was rampant, which was a stark contrast with the stereotypical imagery of Black women portrayed in advertising during these times.

By the close of the nineteenth century imagery of Black women in advertising began to shift. Within society and advertising, Black women existed in a state of uncertainty. Although their roles as slaves had been altered neither their identity nor future had been clearly defined. Despite watersheds in history, including the Emancipation Proclamation (1863) and Thirteenth Amendment (1865), which took strides to abolish slavery in America, Black people did not gain freedom and equality. In some cases, already horrendous conditions were exacerbated. Black people struggled through abject poverty, psychological terror, and rampant racial violence. Legislation and social cues, including Black Codes and Jim Crow, resurrected the atrocities of slavery that many hoped would end following the Civil War (1861–1865) During Reconstruction, (1865–1870s) and well after, Black people continued to suffer. The Civil War did not end slavery, but rather affirmed the direction of the nation. America's future rested upon harnessing industrial systems of production.

In a period of toxic divergence America struggled to reconcile incompatible ideals. Nevertheless, the momentum of the Industrial Revolution swept through the nation. Increased mechanization contributed to widespread fervor surrounding consumption and lifestyle. Robust consumer audiences emerged as advertising gained momentum through its fusion with popular culture. However, below the surface of change, vengeful and racist beliefs were ever present. Advertising, largely due to its interwoven practices with culture and the economy, became a vastitude that reflected America's vile and gaping wounds.

As advertising prospered, imagery of Black people proliferated and became a mainstay. Most often imagery depicted offensive and demeaning stereotypes. Physical features were highly exaggerated including bulging eyes, protruding lips, and carnivorous teeth. Defaming racial slurs and humiliating language was used to reinforce derogatory imagery.[28]

Marginalized and disempowered conceptualizations of the Black female experience perpetuated within society were transferred to advertising. Black females were often characterized as Pickaninny, Auntie, and Mammy.[29] Pickaninnies are racial caricatures of Black children. In such depictions young Black girls appeared wild, ignorant, and unkempt. Pickaninnies were often moderately clothed, sexualized, disheveled, and dirty. This representation suggested neglectful parenting and indirect burdens placed upon civilized society and lifestyle. In advertising Pickaninnies were often the target of violence, cruel humor and animal bait. In an advertisement for the product "Pickaninny Brand Peanut Butter," a Black girl was referred to as a "dainty morsel" for alligator bait.[30] Aunties and Mammies, which will be expanded upon further in this discussion, were featured in advertisements as maids, docile caretakers, and humble servants.

Advertising cards epitomized such imagery and stereotypes during the Reconstruction and the Post-Reconstruction era in America. Black females were used within stereotypical binary portrayals to construct ideal conceptualizations of gender, race, domesticity and consumerism. Typically through juxtaposition, Black females appeared in mirrored pairings with Caucasian females in inferior position as servants, laborers, and primitives. These depictions were contemporaneous representations of class positioning, civility, and commodification within a broad social construct.[31]

Stereotypes in advertising were embedded within society through imagery and messaging as well as behavior. Not only were advertising cards used to increase public acceptance of advertising and promote commercial products, advertising cards were collected and arranged within scrapbooks by children and adolescents. Advertising promoted this practice among youth audiences and it became an extremely popular cultural pastime. In addition to accomplishing their goal of public acceptance of advertising, this activity also created a context to understand normative values associated with consumerism, gender roles, and womanhood in America.[32]

Like advertising cards, the advertising industry also used poster stamps, as a tool to foster public acceptance of advertising. Also known as advertising stamps, poster stamps were used with a number of products ranging from food and insurance to clothing and tobacco. It was the norm to receive postal items with an image of a Black female as a Pickaninny or Auntie.[33] Stereotypes were also ingrained within a range of other advertisements including posters, packaging, collectibles, and paraphernalia.

In addition to visual representations, stereotypes were a fundamental underpinning of advertising concepts, positioning, and strategies throughout the nineteenth century as well. Themes surrounding the appearance of Black women in advertising concepts and strategies included self-hate, filth, inferiority, worthlessness, frivolity, and servitude. In a Campbell's soup advertisement, which appeared in the *Christian Herald* during the early 1900s, a Black woman appears in the background of the composition preparing soup for a small Caucasian girl.[34] Although the advertisement is black and white, the Black woman is heavily inked leaving little to no ability to determine any facial features. She is smiling. Her white teeth are gleaming but her head is lowered and her eyes are not visible. Overweight and matronly, she is dressed in an apron and head kerchief. Depicted as a Mammy derivative, this Black woman is a devout caretaker to a young White girl. However, the body copy of the advertisement reveals deeper meanings. The Black woman is referred to as an *artful minx* who will do anything to have *her fill* of tempting and satisfying meals. Mothers are urged to be mindful of the *physical welfare* of their children.[35]

Stereotypical imagery and derogative conceptualizations of Black women have been woven into mainstream culture through advertising. As this institution expanded its influence and reach, negative depictions continued to proliferate. Pickaninnies, Aunties, and Mammies became an essential communication tool used in visual rhetoric, semiotics, and American culture. Symbolism and messaging associated with these stereotypes have been exemplified within brand extensions, product attributes, folklore, slogans, and widespread conceptual framework.

One of the most readily apparent examples of this is found within the advertising strategy involving the use of Aunt Jemima. For over a century, Aunt Jemima has existed as a highly recognizable and influential trademark and stereotype of Black women used in advertising. In terms of physical appearance, Aunt Jemima was depicted in absolute contrast with the American standard of beauty. In traditional depictions she had very dark skin, broad features, and was obese. Aunt Jemima was portrayed as matronly and asexual with a pleasant disposition. She wore a red bandanna, also known as a chignon, in which her hair was rolled to the back of her head. Original advertising involving Aunt Jemima revolved around a fictitious plantation and incorporated exaggerated copy that bastardized the English language. Although some perceived Aunt Jemima as a symbol of Southern hospitality, this trademark was also viewed as a symbol that was reminiscent of slavery.

Pearl Milling Company developed the Aunt Jemima icon, based on content from a popular blackface minstrel show. The inspiring performance featured a New Orleans style cakewalk and a popular song titled "Old Aunt Jemima." Minstrels dressed in aprons and red bandannas while performing the song. Chris L. Rutt, co-owner of Pearl Milling Company, decided to leverage the name and likeness used in the popular minstrel show. In 1890 Aunt Jemima was registered as the name and trademark for Pearl Milling's newest product, instant pancake mix.[36] Creators believed the iconic use of Aunt Jemima, which is a derivative of the Mammy stereotype, would resonate with American housewives through connotations of trusted convenient servitude.

In addition to housewives, advertisers sought to appease general market audiences, namely those in the South. It was a known axiom that Southern Caucasian markets were not tolerant of progressive or positive imagery of Black people. Advertisers were concerned about alienating consumers and diminishing sales. Southern communities boycotted brands and corporations that associated with Black Americans or Black issues.[37]

Despite support, Black communities voiced discontent. Research affirming dissension within the Black community surrounding the use of stereotypes such as Aunt Jemima can be traced back to the 1920s. In response to advertisements featuring Aunt Jemima, Black women of varied socio-economic backgrounds stated that the use of the image would prevent them from purchasing the product. They expressed discontent stating that the image was not an accurate depiction of Black women and was an obvious and negative reference to slavery. The discontent expressed by Black women regarding their negative portrayals in advertising was largely ignored.[38] In fact, advertisers recruited Black women to assist in the proliferation of Aunt Jemima.

Black women were cast in advertisements to personify the trademark for the product and brand. Although fictitious, a historical narrative was created for Aunt Jemima that evolved into a promotional strategy. This strategy featured folklore, songs, product demonstrations, personal appearances, celebrity endorsements, branded entertainment, cartoons, souvenirs, and other collateral, including dolls and paraphernalia. Nancy Green, a former slave and cook, was cast as the original Aunt Jemima. Upon her death, five Black women were cast as featured trademarks until the decision to use an illustration was implemented many decades later.[39]

Like advertising, Aunt Jemima continued to thrive from the nineteenth well into the twentieth century. Although it experienced the pendulum of ups and downs, there was an undercurrent of overall prosperity. Although relatively short lived, in the 1960s advertising began to experience an era of change known as the Creative Revolution. During these times social justice movements and technological advancements helped push the barometer for change forward. In the 1960s, America elected its youngest president: John

F. Kennedy, space exploration strengthened America's role as a global leader, television experienced explosive growth, and Martin Luther King Jr. spearheaded movements for social equality and civil rights. Although, advertising reflected aspects of change experienced by the nation, it mirrored the tension experienced during times of transition as well.

Advertising began to implement radically different creative tactics and strategies. Diversified imagery was used in advertisements, in many cases for the first time, which included Native Americans, Jewish Americans, and gender pluralism. Additionally, advertising began to depict more authentic representations and conceptualizations of foreign markets and youth culture, while addressing previously taboo topics including sexuality and drug use.

Despite progress, exploitive depictions or virtual absence continued to characterize imagery of Black women in advertising. During these times there were many social advances but few extended directly to Black women, which authenticates claims of continued exclusion and stereotypical depictions. Even in issues concerning communities that would seem to have significant impact on Black women, which include Civil Rights and Gender Pluralism, the experiences of everyday Black women were still largely ignored. Under the tenets of Black feminism this is of concern.

In the particular case of Aunt Jemima, by the 1960s, the brand and product grew to become a breakfast category leader. Despite dissension expressed by Black women, Aunt Jemima elicited such positive brand lift and equity that it was able to expand its product line to include items such as waffles, syrup, sandwiches, and other breakfast foods.

The prevalence of concern regarding stereotypes of Black women was further exacerbated with strides in communication technology. The explosive growth of color television and its rise towards media dominance created the potential opportunity for restrictions based on skin tone variance and facial features to occur. There were concerns over the perpetuation of monolithic standards of beauty as well as well as the continued proliferation of stereotypes.[40]

Critics argued that the frequent and repetitive nature of advertising commercial messaging intensified feelings of Black inferiority and subordinate cultural positioning. There was an increased demand for accurate and dignified portrayals of Black people in advertising. Some advertising critics contended that progress would most likely occur through change within advertising agencies and employment opportunities. During the 1960s advocacy groups requested that advertisers and advertising agencies incorporate positive imagery of Black people into their campaigns and take steps towards a more diversified workforce.[41]

Such issues were addressed through the Kerner Report, which was published in 1968. The Kerner Commission concluded that a mass medium dominated by Whites would be unable to effectively communicate with a diverse audience. Therefore, the report recommended that positive Black imagery appear more frequently in advertising. However, progress took time to achieve. Four years after recommendations issued in the Kerner report, the Congressional Black Caucus issued the following statements:

1. The social and occupational progress of Black people is being hindered by the negative stereotypes appearing on television.
2. Negative stereotypes teach self-hate and consequently destructive self-images to Black people,
3. Negative stereotypes create and reinforce the myth of white superiority. [42]

According to an AAAA (American Association for Advertising Agencies) study conducted from 1970–1974, minority employment within 38 of advertising's top agencies increased from 8.9 percent to 9.9 percent.[43] However in 1975, the AAAA reported that African Americans were experiencing increased tensions within agencies and being denied positions of executive leadership. In fact, African Americans within leadership positions at advertising agencies decreased from 4.6 percent to 4.2 percent from 1970–1974.[44] Winthrop James, a Black advertising executive, declared that integration efforts had led to a degree of self-deception within the advertising industry. Accordingly, many Black Americans filed employment discrimination charges against most of the top advertising agencies during the 1970s.[45]

By the 1980s, although some progress had been achieved, there was still no widespread attention placed upon the Black female experience in advertising. Generally, trends in advertising began to shift toward brands and status. Accordingly, invigorated stereotypes surrounding Black people emerged which depicted professional athletes and entertainers. Advertising often featured Black male *super stars* including comedian Bill Cosby, athlete Michael Jordan, and entertainer Michael Jackson. Although these icons had the ability to heavily influence massive popular culture audiences, their widespread usage contributed to the void of the experience of everyday Black women in advertising.

Hooks argued that Black women have experienced condemnation as they are often relegated to controlling, sexually wanton representations in mass media.[46] In the 1990s a framework was developed to specifically address the stereotypes of Black women. The framework consisted of four dominant archetypes, which include the Mammy, the Matriarch, the Sexual Siren, and the Welfare Queen. Advertising proliferates stereotypes at both macro and micro levels. Therefore, examples of stereotypes of Black women in advertising are highly impactful in a wide range of depictions including brand strategies, target audiences, pop culture, and iconic visual imagery.

In the stereotypical category of Mammy the Black woman is characterized as a loyal domestic servant. Patricia Hill-Collins posits that this image was "created to justify the economic exploitation of house slaves and sustained to explain Black women's long-standing restriction to domestic service; the mammy image represents the normative yardstick used to evaluate all Black women's behavior."[47] As previously discussed, this depiction is readily apparent within advertising through the brand strategy, trademark, and characterization of Aunt Jemima. For nearly 125 years, Aunt Jemima has demonstrated the fortitude and massive influence of stereotypical depictions in advertising. Despite the dissension and metamorphosis of this image, the acceptance of Mammy stereotypes symbolizes complexities surrounding the identity and perception of Black women as well as their collective power within American society.

The next stereotypical category is that of the Matriarch. She is represented by the image of the Black woman as a mother within the Black home. The Matriarch is often depicted as controlling, aggressive, and emasculating. Collins suggests that the matriarch is "central to interlocking systems of race, gender, and class oppression."[48] The continual portrayal of Black women as Matriarchs indirectly suggests that Black women are solely responsible for the success or failure of Black children. This perspective diverts attention from resource disparities that affect Black families and suggests that anyone can rise from poverty if he or she only received good values at home.[49]

The stereotypical category of the Matriarch is demonstrated through advertising strategies that emphasize and frequently target Black mothers. Although strategy is not always readily apparent within creative executions, strategy largely influences aspects of advertising that include content, casting, and media buys. Strategies are often embedded within the internal construction of target audiences and creative briefs, which are largely informed by strategic research. Leading strategic marketing researchers have urged advertising agencies, brands, and advertisers to maximize their ROI (return on investments) and increase their market share by targeting Black mothers. In support of their strategies, popular marketing researchers affirm that Black women have tremendous spending power and are more likely to be primary decision makers in their households, particularly in the areas of travel, finances, real estate, home electronics, and automobiles.[50] Although this strategy may indeed be financially profitable, it contributes to stereotypical portrayals and negative social outcomes.

The third stereotypical category is that of the sexual siren. She represents portrayals of the Black women as a hyper sexualized and an uncaring bitch or whore. Collins suggests that Jezebel is "central in this nexus of elite White male images of Black womanhood because efforts to control Black women's sexuality lie at the heart of Black women's oppression."[51] This imagery of Black women was fostered during slavery to excuse the sexual abuse they endured. The widespread popularity and acceptance of this stereotype within advertising is revealed through the abundance of celebrity endorsements and sponsorships by the influential and highly sexualized popular culture icons, including Rihanna and Nicki Minaj.[52] Although Robyn (Rihanna) Fenty may be very different from her projected pop-culture persona, the social construction of Rihanna is a near perfect depiction of a jezebel. The music, attire, imagery, styling, lyrics, and content that promote Rihanna exude sex and a callous defiant attitude. The desire to perpetuate such characteristics is affirmed by her widespread acceptance and influence. As a brand ambassador, muse, and spokesperson, Rihanna has secured millions of dollars through relationships with premiere brands and products including Mac Cosmetics, River Island, Budweiser, Armani, Gucci, Alexander Wang, Balmain, Reb'l Fleu, Nivea, Vita Coco, Nike, Covergirl, Secret, and Kodak.[53]

The fourth stereotypical category is that of the Welfare Queen.[54] This stereotypical archetype is a contemporary depiction of the breeder stereotype perpetuated during slavery. This depiction rationalizes the primary use of Black women to breed slaves. In the contemporary stereotype welfare mothers are depicted as feral breeders that have no desire to work and are supported through government assistance. This portrayal of Black women positions them as a burden to society and an economic liability to the economy. It also indirectly justifies desires and efforts to restrict the fertility of Black women. Derivatives of the welfare queen stereotype can be seen through the iconic visual imagery of Black women in health care advertising and media imagery, particularly as it relates to the bias embedded in portrayals of pregnant drug users.[55]

Melissa Harris-Perry sophisticates these archetypes through incorporating cognitive theoretical framework and physiological responses to reveal further oppressive conditions experienced by Black women due to stereotypes. She discusses the trope, *Strong Black Woman*, within the contemporary examination of stereotypes of Black women.[56] Once considered a dignified aspirational image used to uplift, this depiction has become a shackle of oppression. Under this stereotype Black women are expected to be strong, selfless, resilient, and excel regardless of resource disparity or debilitating social constructs. This is detrimental because infallible strength is virtually impossible to maintain. The stereotype, Strong Black Woman, creates unhealthy expectations of achievement and endurance for Black women. Moreover, it contributes to obscurity surrounding the truth of the actual lived experiences of Black women. Without an accurate depiction of reality, many of the ills that affect Black women may be ignored or disregarded.

Advertising depictions of the Strong Black Woman are apparent in character narratives that are developed to resonate with Black women. As stated, Black women have become a targeted demographic due to the perceived ability to generate profitable ROI. Adaptations of the Strong Black Woman in advertising are visible within leading and supporting roles, which feature Black women in television programming, movies, commercials, and branded entertainment. A classic example of this stereotype is demonstrated in the United Way commercial that features a young Black girl, Kianna.[57] The visual depicts Kianna valiantly running through a villainized and stereotypical urban ghetto. A summary of the voiceover suggests that every day, Kianna has to run past drug dealers on her way to school. It goes on to state that the United Way salutes girls like Kianna. Although heroic, this execution infers that superseding reality is ideal and readily achievable with courage. Moreover, it contributes to repudiation of urban communities and the disavowal of harsh conditions that Black females endure.

Harris-Perry suggests that the proliferation of categorical stereotypes within the mass media has created a field of visual perception for Black women that is skewed and off kilter. Moreover, the stigma and shame experienced as a result of stereotypes thwart the ability of Black women to engage in authentic experiences with themselves and the socially constructed world around them. Oppressive conditions disempower Black women and force them to engage in negotiated relationships within a convoluted environment that offers little distinction between what is real and what is illusory. The ubiquitous presence of advertising creates a virtually inescapable web of complexity that undermines mental dexterity and health. Additionally, stereotypes have contributed to a number of physiological responses and physical conditions in Black women that have resulted in a multitude of infirmities including diabetes, stress disorders, weight gain, heart disease, hardening of the arteries, and immune system dysfunction.[58]

## LOOKING TOWARD THE FUTURE OF ADVERTISING

Although these frameworks aid in the discussion of stereotypes of Black women and advertising, further attention is sorely needed. Advertising is a complex institution of tremendous influence. It is an evolving phenomenon. Stereotypes of Black women and advertising warrant further examination from both macro and micro vantage points. This will help develop understandings of broad perspectives and intricate nuances of lived experiences. Within the intricacies of complexity the unique experience of Black women may be propelled towards the public sphere.

In the 1970s the Black women of the Combahee River Collective affirmed the power associated with the potential liberation of Black women.[59] They suggested that the freedom of Black women would lead to the freedom of virtually all oppressed communities. This was largely due to the fact that they believed the freedom of Black women would be accompanied by dissolution of powerful systems of oppression.

Nearly a half a century later, a condition exists that has the potential to liberate Black women from psychological and societal barriers. The paradigm shift in advertising has created an opportunity to help redefine and shape one of the most powerful institutions in the world. Through this opportunity positive and empowering depictions of Black women can be created to replace derogatory stereotypes in advertising. Over time, the proliferation of progressive depictions may counteract the toxicity advertising has proliferated. As a result of positive and accurate visual rhetoric and messaging, progressive shifts may occur in standards of normalcy, societal values, health, identity construction, and race relations worldwide.

As it stands today, large numbers of Black women have been empowered. Black women are more educated, more economically successful, and hold more executive positions than in previous times. Black women have become powerful producers and stakeholders in advertising. Christian Norman, a Black woman, is executive editor of the *Huffington Post's Black Voices*. As a former MTV president, Norman is a known expert for blending serious content and entertainment. She is expected to make strides among leading advertising brands concerning the perception of multi-cultural markets and multi-cultural advertising budgets. Additionally, a commissioner of the FCC (Federal Communications Commission), a government agency that regulates advertising and broadcast communications, is Mignon Clyburn, a Black woman. Clyburn has an extremely impressive track record as a staunch advocate of consumer rights and defender of public interest. Prior to her role as commissioner, Clyburn co-owned and operated a newspaper that focused primarily on issues affecting the Black community.

The general market has also shifted, which has led to increased opportunities and empowerment. Black women have become a highly coveted target audience. Not only are they a highly influential community, but Black women also have tremendous spending power. In terms of influence, Black women's standards of normalcy have led to shifts in beauty, fashion, entrepreneurism, and business.[60] Advertisers must be respectful and responsive to shifts if they wish to succeed. New advertising strategies that incorporate co-creation and peer-to-peer communications have been developed to respond to shifts and avoid stereotyping. Brands are increasingly using real people, often bloggers and social media influencers, to endorse their products, increase shareability, and build consumer trust.

The future of advertising is heavily dependent upon its ability to create content that will engage and resonate with contemporary audiences. L'Oréal, the cosmetic beauty brand, has become an exemplar in this area through creating engaging content using participatory strategies.[61] Their advertising incorporates a YouTube channel, which features content by diverse beauty experts. Luvs, made by Proctor & Gamble, has also employed similar tactics in their advertising.[62] The diaper brand has used insights from bloggers to demonstrate accurate depictions of motherhood. Brands are making the effort to connect with modern audiences to attain longevity and continued success. Consequently, if consumers demand the dissolution of stereotypes of Black women, many advertisers and will comply.

Technological advances have also increased opportunities for empowerment. The Internet has become a forum for communities to mobilize their collective voices to support causes they care about, increase philanthropy, and use consumerism for good. Recently, a powerful Internet community, comprised mostly of women, caused the demise of a brand after the brand pulled funding for breast cancer screenings from Planned Parenthood.[63] Advertising has become increasingly participatory. As a result, advertisers are being held accountable for their choices in real time. Communities that are empowered and interactive can create positive change and significant impact.

Online groups, including Rewind and Reframe[64] have created platforms to give young women the opportunity to blog and take action against sexist and racist media content. Rewind and Reframe urges females to demand more from advertisers and artists that breach broadcast advertising codes, which include unjustified depictions of sex, nudity, offensive language, and images which condone or encourage harmful discriminatory behavior, treatment, or prejudice. Young girls have contended that stereotypes have contributed to confusion and inappropriate behavior in their lives. In these forums young girls have expressed pressures surrounding sex, identity, race, and beauty that they have experienced due to stereotypes, particularly the Jezebel.

As communities have become increasingly interactive and held advertisers accountable for offensive stereotypes, advantageous results have occurred. These results have included retractions, public apologies, cancelations, and decision reversals. Summer's Eve, a feminine care company, removed controversial commercials from their website and YouTube, following pressure from critics. The campaign, which featured talking hand puppets personifying women's vaginas, was perceived as stereotypical, racially insensitive, and highly offensive. One commercial in particular, featured a Black woman's character, which was heavily criticized due to stereotypical language, content, delivery, and excessive attitudinal connotations. Although the campaign's creator stated that the advertisements were intended to be relatable rather than stereotypical, controversy continued to mount. Advertisers believed that the criticism began to overshadow the message and goal of the larger campaign. Critics pressured the company to not only pull the advertisements from the Internet but to issue a statement as well. A public relations executive affirmed that the decision to remove the advertisements was to acknowledge the backlash and move forward to focus on the company's greater mission.[65]

Opportunities for progress and extraordinary accomplishments abound. Potential paths to great achievement have been made available to Black women through shifts in executive leadership, general market audiences, and technological advances. Critical dialogue to create awareness concerning these opportunities is essential during this timely juncture. The following section will provide further insights surrounding this discussion.

## INSIGHTS FOR STEREOTYPES OF BLACK WOMEN AND ADVERTISING

As previously stated, a paradigm shift in advertising indicates a critical juncture in which traditional practices may be replaced with fresh ideas and new methods. Within contemporary advertising, Black women now have the opportunity to create and demand positive and diverse portrayals of Black women, and their experiences, to widespread audiences. However, within this new environment there will be power struggles and a collision of past ideals with future aspirations. Significant disruption occurs within an environment in which former products are now highly coveted target audiences as well as powerful leaders and content producers. To navigate through unchartered complexity, critical insights are offered. To increase specificity, a survey of contemporary advertising along with a relevant synthesis of stereotypes of Black women in advertising were triangulated with the four basic principles of Black feminism. Listed below are some of the most critical insights.

- During a time of a paradigm shift, claims to embrace change will be as readily apparent as attempts to renounce change in order to maintain the status quo. Stereotypes of Black women are lucrative, effective, and deeply entrenched within society and individual psyches. Thus, there may be increased usage of stereotypical imagery during these times.
- Increased awareness regarding stereotypes of Black women in advertising is needed to help safeguard against further widespread proliferation. History has revealed that when a new medium gains widespread momentum, advertising has consistently shifted its most lucrative practices and content from the old media to the new media. For example, when television surpassed radio as the dominant media much of radio's content and practices were transferred to television. Thus, stereotypes of Black women may become increasingly rampant on the Internet and within IMC (Integrated Marketing Communication) solutions.

Moreover, the Internet is a relatively new medium. Therefore, profuse stereotypes of Black women on the Internet may be largely unregulated. A lack of regulation may lead to even more proliferation of stereotypes and negative future practices. Widespread stereotypes of Black women on the Internet not only contribute to negative perceptions of Black women and the physical, physiological, and psychological implications that accompany erroneous beliefs, but they may also overshadow new possibilities. An abundance of stereotypes on the Internet may give users the impression that nothing has changed. A lack of awareness and understanding may decrease the potential to leverage opportunities presented by change.

- Increased options have promoted the strategic use of transmediality and IMC (Integrated Marketing Communication) advertising tactics. Multiple media formats and the Internet may be widely used to disseminate advertisements across various platforms. These strategies may be motivated by economic profit, which benefits consumers and conglomerations rather than citizens. In a consumer driven culture it is critical that the value of humanity and democratic rights are not inherently motivated by consumerism. Although Black women have made economic strides, a considerable amount of Black women are a part of working class or impoverished communities. Advertising transmediality and IMC may result in diminished rights for Black women due to geographic locations and/or economic spending patterns.
- Market segmentation driven by consumerism often parallels broader debates concerning civil rights and Black empowerment. In particular regard to advertising, strategies of economic separatism devolved into forms of market segmentation that operate under the control of multinational media conglomerates.[66] Thus, the increased conglomeration within advertising and media may result in worsened conditions concerning civil rights and Black female empowerment. The slated merger of advertising's second- and third-largest communications companies will create an industry behemoth with nearly $23 billion in revenue. Half of all advertising agencies will be consolidated in one company. It is estimated that the Publicis Omnicom Group, which will finalize by the close of 2014, will control 40 percent of U.S. media buying and 20 percent of the global market.[67]
- The need for privacy amongst Black women will be exacerbated in an era propelled by the acquisition of information and widespread transmediality. Due to their history of commodification, Black Women live under heightened scrutiny. As members of a stigmatized group Black women, regardless of stature or income, contend with the reality of hypervisibility.[68] This situation may be exacerbated as advertising conglomerates expand and proliferate the usage of data mining tactics.

Lastly, it is important to stress that advertising is a deeply human institution. Much of advertising is created by people to resonate with people. Thus, by its very nature advertising is deeply complex, yet malleable. As demonstrated through this discussion, advertising can be used to reflect perverse horrors and atrocities. Advertising can also be used to shape, uplift, and empower. During a paradigm shift a window of opportunity is presented to help create the future. This critical juncture is accompanied by boundless opportunities and power redistribution. Awareness and critical dialogue will decrease the possibility that the vision for the future is obscured by apparitions of the past. Communities are urged to harness interactive capabilities and seize opportunities that have been presented through change.

## NOTES

1. Sheri Parks, *Fierce Angels: The Strong Black Woman in American Life and Culture* (New York: One World/Ballantine Books, 2010).
2. Roxanne Hovland and Joyce Marie Wolburg, *Advertising, Society, and Consumer Culture* (Armonk: M. E. Sharpe, 2010).
3. Marcel Danesi, *Popular Culture: Introductory Perspectives* (Lanham: Rowman & Littlefield, 2012).
4. James W. Carey, "Advertising: An Institutional Approach," in *The Role of Advertising in Society*, eds. Charles H. Sandage and Vernon Fryburger (Homewood: Richard D. Irwin, Inc. 1960), 3–17.
5. Charles S. Peirce and Cornelis de Waal, *Illustrations of the Logic of Science* (Open Court, 2014).
6. Ibid.
7. Timothy D. Taylor, "Advertising and the Conquest of Culture," *Social Semiotics* 19, no. 4 (2009): 405–25.
8. Clint C. Wilson II, Félix Gutiérrez, and Lena M. Chao, *Racism, Sexism, and the Media: The Rise of Class Communication in Multicultural America* (Thousand Oaks: Sage Publications, 2003).
9. Thomas S. Kuhn, *The Structure of Scientific Revolutions* (Chicago: University of Chicago Press, 1970).
10. Roland T. Rust and Richard W. Oliver, "The Death of Advertising," *Journal of Advertising* 23, no. 4 (1994): 71–77.
11. Jeff Gordinier, *X Saves The World: How Generation X Got the Shaft But Can Still Keep Everything from Sucking* (New York: Viking, 2008).
12. Hovland and Wolburg, *Advertising, Society, and Consumer Culture*.
13. Phil Simon and Mitch Joel, *The Age of the Platform: How Amazon, Apple, Facebook, and Google Have Redefined Business* (Las Vegas: Motion Publishing, 2011).
14. Tom Altstiel and Jean Grow, *Advertising Creative: Strategy, Copy and Design* (Los Angeles: SAGE, 2012).
15. Hovland and Wolburg, *Advertising, Society, and Consumer Culture*.
16. Kuhn, *The Structure of Scientific Revolutions*.
17. Joanna Jenkins, "The Convergence Crisis: The Impact of Convergence on Advertising" (PhD diss., Howard University, 2013).
18. Ithiel de Sola Pool, *Technologies of Freedom* (Cambridge, MA: Belknap Press, 1983).
19. Ibid.
20. Henry Jenkins, *Convergence Culture: Where Old and New Media Collide* (New York: New York University Press, 2006).
21. Kuhn, *The Structure of Scientific Revolutions*.
22. Patricia Hill Collins, *Black Feminist Thought: Knowledge, Consciousness, and the Politics of Empowerment* (New York: Routledge, 1991).
23. Jennifer B. Woodard and Teresa Mastin, "Black Womanhood: Essence and Its Treatment of Stereotypical Images of Black Women," *Journal of Black Studies* 36, no. 2 (2005): 264–81.
24. Robin R. Means Coleman and Emily Chivers Yochim, "The Symbolic Annihilation of Race: A Review of the 'Blackness' Literature," *African American Research Perspectives* 12 (2008): 1–12.

25. Ibid., 2.
26. Marilyn Kern-Foxworth, *Aunt Jemima, Uncle Ben, and Rastus: Blacks in Advertising, Yesterday, Today, and Tomorrow* (Westport: Greenwood Press, 1994).
27. Ibid.
28. Ibid.
29. Ibid.
30. Ibid.
31. Marilyn Maness Mehaffy, "Advertising Race/Racing Advertising: The Feminine Consumer 1876–1900," *Advertising: Critical Readings* 4 (2010): 253.
32. Ibid.
33. Kern-Foxworth, *Aunt Jemima, Uncle Ben, and Rastus.*
34. Ibid.
35. Ibid.
36. Ibid.
37. Ibid.
38. Ibid.
39. Ibid.
40. Means Coleman and Chivers Yochim, *The Symbolic Annihilation of Race.*
41. Wilson, Gutiérrez, and Chao, *Racism, Sexism, and the Media.*
42. Kern-Foxworth, *Aunt Jemima, Uncle Ben, and Rastus.*
43. Stephen R. Fox, *The Mirror Makers* (Champaign: Illini Books, 1997).
44. Ibid.
45. Ibid.
46. bell hooks, *Black Looks: Race and Representation* (Boston: South End Press, 1992).
47. Collins, *Black Feminist Thought*, 71.
48. Ibid., 74.
49. Ibid.
50. Pepper Miller and Herb Kemp, *What's Black About It: Insights to Increase Your Share of a Changing African-American Market* (Ithaca: Paramount Market Pub., 2005).
51. Collins, *Black Feminist Thought*, 77.
52. Emma Bazillian, "Pepsi Nicki Minaj and Billions of Frozen Humans Star in the Brand's First Global Campaign," *Adweek*, May 10, 2012, accessed February 1, 2014, http://www.adweek.com/news/advertising-branding/ad-day-pepsi-140206.
53. Dorothy Pomerantz, "Oprah Winfrey Regains No. 1 Slot On Forbes 2013 List Of The Most Powerful Celebrities," *Forbes*, June 2013, accessed February 1, 2014, http://www.forbes.com/profile/rihanna/.
54. Hill Collins, *Black Feminist Thought*, 77.
55. Kristen W. Springer, "The Race and Class Privilege of Motherhood: The New York Times Presentations of Pregnant Drug-Using Women," *Sociological Forum* 25, no. 3 (2010): 476–99.
56. Melissa V. Harris-Perry, *Sister Citizen: Shame, Stereotypes, and Black Women in America* (New Haven: Yale University Press, 2011).
57. Ibid.
58. Ibid.
59. Ibid.
60. Miller and Kemp, *What's Black About It.*
61. David Gianatasio, The Courage to Advertise without Female Stereotypes: How Brands Like Huggies, Tide and Target Go Beyond the Clichés, *Ad Week*, February 25, 2013, accessed February 1, 2014, http://www.adweek.com/news/advertising-branding/courage-advertise-without-female-stereotypes-147484.
62. Ibid.
63. Lisa Belkin, Babes No More: Mom and Dad Bloggers are Coming of Age as Their Virtual Communities Prove to be Powerful Indeed, *Ad Week*, February 27, 2012, accessed February 1, 2014, http://www.adweek.com/news/advertising-branding/babes-no-more-138511.
64. http://www.rewindreframe.org.

65. Tim Nudd, Summer's Eve Pulls Controversial Talking-Vagina Videos. The online clips had been accused of being racially stereotypical, *Ad Week*, July 27, 2011, accessed February 1, 2014, http://www.adweek.com/news/advertising-branding/summers-eve-pulls-controversial-talking-vagina-videos-133714.

66. Oscar H. Gandy Jr., *Coming to Terms with Chance Engaging Rational Discrimination and Cumulative Disadvantage* (Farnham: Ashgate, 2009).

67. Alexandra Bruell, Publicis Omnicom Merger Passes Antitrust Test in U.S., *Advertising Age*, November 1, 2013, accessed February 1, 2014, http://adage.com/article/agency-news/publicis-omnicom-merger-passes-antitrust-test-u-s/245074/.

68. Harris-Perry, *Sister Citizen: Shame, Stereotypes, and Black women in America.*

# BIBLIOGRAPHY

Alstiel, Tom, and Jean Grow. *Advertising Creative: Strategy, Copy, and Design*. Los Angeles: SAGE, 2012.

Carey, James W. "Advertising: An institutional approach." In *The Role of Advertising in Society*, edited by Charles H. Sandage & Vernon Fryburger, 3–17. Homewood: Richard D. Irwin, Inc., 1960.

Coleman, Robin R. M., and Emily C. Yochim. "The Symbolic Annihilation of Race: A Review of the 'Blackness' Literature." *African American Research Perspectives* 12 (2008), 1–12.

Collins, Patricia H. *Black Feminist Thought: Knowledge, Consciousness, and the Politics of Empowerment*. New York: Routledge, 1991.

Danesi, Marcel. *Popular Culture: Introductory Perspectives*. Lanham: Rowman & Littlefield, 2012.

de Sola Pool, Ithiel. *Technologies of Freedom*. Cambridge, MA: Belknap Press, 1983.

Fox, Stephen R. *The Mirror Makers*. Champaign: Illini Books, 1997.

Gandy Jr., Oscar H. *Coming to Terms with Chance Engaging Rational Discrimination and Cumulative Disadvantage*. Farnham: Ashgate, 2009.

Gordinier, Jeff. *X Saves The World: How Generation X Got the Shaft But Can Still Keep Everything from Sucking*. New York: Viking, 2008.

Harris-Perry, Melissa V. *Sister Citizen: Shame, Stereotypes, and Black Women in America*. New Haven: Yale University Press, 2011.

hooks, bell. *Black Looks: Race and Representation*. Boston: South End Press, 1992.

Hovland, Roxanne, and Joyce Marie Wolburg. *Advertising, Society, and Consumer Culture*. Armonk: M. E. Sharpe, 2010.

Jenkins, Henry. *Convergence Culture: Where Old and New Media Collide*. New York: New York University Press, 2006.

Jenkins, Joanna. "The Convergence Crisis: The Impact of Convergence on Advertising." PhD Diss., Howard University, 2013.

Kern-Foxworth, Marilyn. *Aunt Jemima, Uncle Ben, and Rastus: Blacks in Advertising, Yesterday, Today, and Tomorrow*. Westport: Greenwood Press, 1994.

Kuhn, Thomas S. *The Structure of Scientific Revolutions*. Chicago: University of Chicago Press, 1970.

Mehaffy, Marilyn, M. "Advertising Race/Racing Advertising: The Feminine Consumer 1876–1900." *Advertising: Critical Readings* 4 (2010), 253.

Miller, Pepper, and Herb Kemp. *What's Black About It: Insights to Increase Your Share of a Changing African-American Market*. Ithaca: Paramount Market Publishing, 2005.

Parks, Sheri. *Fierce Angels: The Strong Black Woman in American Life and Culture*. New York: One World/Ballantine Books, 2010.

Peirce, Charles, and Cornelis de Waal. *Illustrations of the Logic of Science*, Open Court, 2014.

Rust, Roland T., and Richard W. Oliver. "The Death of Advertising." *Journal of Advertising* 23, no. 4 (1994), 71–77.

Simon, Phil, and Mitch Joel. *The Age of the Platform: How Amazon, Apple, Facebook, and Google Have Redefined Business*. Las Vegas: Motion Publishing, 2011.

Springer, Kristen W. "The Race and Class Privilege of Motherhood: *The New York Times* Presentations of Pregnant Drug-Using Women." *Sociological Forum* 25, no. 3 (2010), 476–99.

Taylor, Timothy D. "Advertising and the Conquest of Culture." *Social Semiotics* 19, no. 4 (2009): 405–25.

Wilson, Clint C., Félix Gutiérrez, and Lena M. Chao. *Racism, Sexism, and the Media: The Rise of Class Communication in Multicultural America*, 3rd edition. Thousand Oaks: Sage Publications, 2003.

Woodard, Jennifer B., and Teresa Mastin. "Black Womanhood: Essence and its Treatment of Stereotypical Images of Black Women." *Journal of Black Studies* 36, no. 2 (2005), 264–81.

*Chapter Eleven*

# Writing (about) the Black Female Body

*An Exploration of Skin Color Politics in Advertising within* Ebony *and* Essence

Simone Puff

In her first novel *The Bluest Eye,* Toni Morrison called physical beauty "[p]robably . . . [one of the two] most destructive ideas in the history of human thought."[1] While ostensibly a destructive notion for everyone, throughout the book we see how extraordinarily damaging dominant ideas of beauty are for those who society puts on the *margins,* in this case Black women. The Black female body in the United States has been a space of contestation always and everywhere, not just in fiction. As beauty was—and, to a certain extent, continues to be—defined by a White European standard, the Black female body is often regarded as lacking and deficient. This is, of course, fruitful ground for advertising, which has been targeting Black women with emotional messages to pretend "that intangibles like love, popularity, and beauty themselves could be bought."[2] This is still the case today, perhaps even more so than in the past, with an ever-increasing attempt to commodify beauty, something which Cornel West called, an "ever-expanding market culture that puts everything and everyone up for sale."[3]

The following is an exploratory study that looks at selected advertisements for skin care products in the Black-oriented monthly magazines *Ebony* and *Essence.* The aim of this analysis is to establish subtle recurring themes and tropes that contradict messages of celebrating Black beauty in all their shades, something both magazines are known to allegedly promote with their mission statements. *Essence,* for example, wants to "help Black women feel as beautiful as they are" and *Ebony* claims that it "ignites conversation, promotes empowerment and celebrates aspiration."[4] For this study a random sample of advertisements for creams and serums, which promise some type of change in skin tone and which appeared in the two periodicals between February 2011 and February 2014, were selected for closer inspection. They were carefully examined for any hidden ideological undertones that would perpetuate the discourse of a light-skinned ideal of beauty. Contrasting these twenty-first century sales pitches for skin tone creams with some of their ad campaigns from the 1950s and 1960s further exposes that, while the language may be different in terms of explicitness, the racial subtext and the ultimate message to Black women is still the same: Only "if you're light you're (truly) alright," to play on a well-known, yet hurtful, adage. This ultimately purports the idea of lighter skin tone serving as a form of what Margaret Hunter calls "racial capital,"[5] a fact that possibly informs some Black women's choice to keep using these types of products.

Such a study of contemporary expressions of colorism in Black media is important because it reveals the values that are still placed on light skin color in the twenty-first century, which are essentially values that stem from ideals and norms of the dominant White society. It is these ideals that continue to define Black women's lives, with even Black-oriented media perpetuating covert messages of *light still being right*. Before going into detail with the analysis, however, this study needs some socio-historical context and a little bit of history on the development of the discourse of skin color in the Black media. This background will show that the significance of skin color politics in the Black community can be traced all the way back to the country's colonial days of slavery.

## THE MEANING OF *BLACK* ON THE BLACK FEMALE BODY: A SOCIO-HISTORICAL CONTEXT

In the United States—and in many other parts of the Western world—the dominant White society has always regarded the Black female body in direct opposition to their views of the White female body. It is, to use a metaphor by artist Lorraine O'Grady, as if the female body in the West were a coin: "[i]t has an obverse and a reverse: on the one side, it is white; on the other, not-white or, prototypically, black . . . White is what woman is; not-white (and the stereotypes not-white gathers in) is what she had better not be."[6] Because Black and White have been historically defined as binary opposites, the meaning of a Black female body is contingent on what it means to be a White woman. If the seventeenth-century Anglo Americans who colonized the New World used White womanhood to signify femininity, purity, and chastity, then Black womanhood had to be defined as oppositional to those characteristics and thereby *Othered*. This is in line with Jacques Derrida's concept of non-neutral binary oppositions, with one category being dominant and the other subjugated.[7] As a consequence, the "Othering" of Black female bodies led to what Patricia Hill Collins called "ideological justification for race, gender, and class oppression."[8]

The intersection of different forms of oppression[9] has always been most intense for dark-skinned Black women who bear the brunt of negative stereotypes in a society that orients itself along a type of *pigmentocracy*. This rank-ordering along skin color gradations awards people with White or light skin with the most privileges and, conversely, *punishes* people with dark black skin with the most disadvantages. As a result of the effects of racial discrimination by Whites, this rank-ordering eventually also developed within communities of color, creating a form of intra-racial discrimination—today widely known as colorism.

While certainly not unique to the United States,[10] in the United States colorism is said to be as old as slavery. White slave masters would habitually differentiate between their darker-skinned slaves, whom they would send out to work in the fields, and their lighter-skinned slaves, whom they would allow to work closer to the house. This differentiation between so-called "house negroes" and "field negroes," as detailed in accounts by, for example, Lawrence Graham[11] and E. Franklin Frazier,[12] can be seen as the foundation for intra-racial hierarchies based on skin color. Slaves soon realized that their lighter skin often served as an advantage over their darker-skinned brethren, because in the eyes of racist White slave owners they were seen as less threatening. To Whites they also looked less African, and—in line with scientific racist logic of the day—were therefore regarded as more intelligent, allegedly having White blood coursing through their veins.[13]

During times of slavery light-skinned Black women were also seen as the most prized beauties among Black female slaves and were often sold as concubines to White men at so-called "quadroon balls."[14] Once slavery was abolished, this favoring of lighter-skinned African Americans, particularly of women, continued. In an early piece on the politics of the significance of skin color (and hair) in Black communities, Margo Okazawa-Rey, Tracy Robinson, and Janie Victoria Ward determine that "racism and sexism . . . gave birth to color consciousness in the black community and maintain it today."[15] Detailed accounts of the development of colorism throughout U.S. history can be found, for example, in works by Evelyn Nakano Glenn, Kimberly Norwood, as well as Kathy Russell-Cole, Midge Wilson, and Ronald Hall.[16]

Essentially, White and light skin served as the gold standard of beauty until the Black is Beautiful movement of the late 1960s. But even this communal effort to see dark skin and other Afrocentric features as new ideals of beauty was ephemeral. With this effort fading so did the message of dark skin being considered equally beautiful, and—once more—gave way to *Black get back*. Society has definitely become more inclusive of embracing different forms and hues of African-American beauty today, yet those on the dark-skinned end of the spectrum still continue to be underrepresented as models for female beauty. As Margaret Hunter argues, "[t]rue femininity is still defined in relation to whiteness,"[17] and light skin continues to serve as a veritable form of currency. This is why Black women are, to this day, often more affected by this intra-racial color hierarchy than Black men.[18] Like any other form of discrimination, colorism results in a lot of emotional pain that exists on both ends of the color spectrum. While dark skin color is often derided with hurtful language and not regarded as beautiful, the slurs that light-skinned people often have to endure for "not being Black enough" or for being "sellouts" are also harmful to people's perception of self.[19]

Colorism does not just result in emotional pain, however. The material effect of such a hierarchy which favors light-skinned African Americans is noticeable in all areas of life: Sociological studies have continuously presented correlations between light skin tone and more success, not only professionally but also in the realm of interpersonal relationships.[20] Additionally, studies reveal that darker skin increases chances of being racially profiled and even goes so far as to potentially result in a longer prison sentence when convicted by a jury.[21] Based on all these real-life consequences that have not seen any substantial improvements throughout the years, scholars today agree that colorism will continue to exist as long as racism exists.

Being the "crazy aunt in the attic of racism," as a *Washington Post* journalist once provocatively called it,[22] colorism can thus not be eradicated unless a discussion also centers on larger issues: institutional racism, the commodification of a White Eurocentric standard of beauty, and White privilege. In other words, people must acknowledge the tangible benefits that light skin brings to people who either have light skin or are able to purchase it. This is what Margaret Hunter means when she refers to "racial capital," which acts as transforming light skin tone "into social capital (social networks), symbolic capital (esteem or status), or even economic capital (high-paying job or promotion)."[23] Problematizing these issues in public is one step in the right direction, which is why it is essential that colorism is no longer regarded as the taboo issue it once was.

## FROM TABOO TO TOP OF THE AGENDA: SKIN COLOR POLITICS IN PUBLIC DISCOURSE

Until recently, colorism was a word that some saw as too much of a taboo to be publicly uttered. As Joy Bennett Kinnon claims in her feature article on the significance of skin color in the April 2000 issue of *Ebony*, it was "whispered softly in clubs and coffee bars, at poetry slams and casinos, at church fellowship and funeral repasts. It is the family secret that won't go away."[24] Now this "family secret" seems to finally be out in the open, and is featured regularly in public media discourse, alongside the discourse of institutional racism, where it belongs. Today the discussion of what Marita Golden called "African Americans' pernicious, persistent dirty little secret"[25] is no longer considered as "airing dirty laundry." This is a result of numerous books on the issue, people having frank debates about skin color politics online, and, most recently, the widely-publicized film *Dark Girls*.[26] As a documentary it features a range of Black women giving candid testimonials on being dark-skinned in America.[27] Together with several studies on colorism and its impacts that were published simultaneously, a somewhat permanent public platform for the discourse on colorism has been created, at least for the time being.

In years past, Black periodicals like *Ebony* and *Essence* sometimes wrote about the "issue" or "problem" of skin color in the Black community.[28] For the most part, however, they were only following large-scale discursive events which highlighted the complexities of skin color politics. Among these were, for example, the election of light-skinned Vanessa Williams as the first African-American woman to be crowned Miss America in 1984, or the release of movies, such as Spike Lee's *School Daze* (1992), which openly, if satirically, confronted colorism on campuses of HBCUs.[29] At the end of the first decade of the twenty-first century, however, it seems that large-scale discursive changes in American society ushered a renewed and continuing interest in discussions of colorism.

Among those discursive changes is certainly the prominence of dark-hued Michelle Obama as a powerful First Lady and icon of beauty in the White House. Alongside that, there is a somewhat renewed general public consciousness about what *Black is Beautiful* means in the twenty-first century. This includes the recent natural-hair movement[30] and other Black consciousness movements, such as the commercially-driven "My Black Is Beautiful" campaign, which was kick-started by Procter & Gamble in 2007.[31] Additionally there are "grassroots" online communities, such as the blog *For Harriet*, which was launched in 2010, that promised to "engage in candid, revelatory dialogue about the beauty and complexity of Black womanhood."[32]

The issue of colorism is still a heated one that generates a lot of debate and emotion among Black people along the entire *color continuum*. Hence it is only logical that the more traditional Black media outlets such as *Ebony* and *Essence* have jumped on the bandwagon and seized the opportunity to engage in a regular dialogue on skin color politics in the Black community. One of the first Black media outlets to launch an outright campaign against what one could call the *war on colorism*, was *Essence* magazine. In September 2011 then editor-in-chief Constance C. R. White promoted a public discussion, stating in her debut editorial that "[i]t's time to move beyond our own divisive attitudes and embrace the glorious range and beauty of our skin tones."[33] This was followed by several articles on skin color politics in subsequent print issues, and even more coverage of colorism on the magazine's website *Essence.com*.[34]

*Ebony* quickly followed suit in October 2011 with print and online coverage of the film documentary *Dark Girls*, an online interview with colorism scholar Yaba Blay, and other online stories pertaining to skin color politics and colorism.[35] With more and more readers embracing modern technology, the magazine even held its "weekly Twitter convo" on colorism in February 2013: "#Ebony chat—Colorism: The Struggle Continues."[36] This generated numerous Twitter confessions about how deep-seated the issue still is among people of African descent. Of course, the discussion also reflected the often atrocious comments that the *hashtag wars* between #teamlightskin and #teamdarkskin created on other social media, as well. In short, it seems like a healing process has begun, with colorism having moved from taboo to top of the agenda. In March 2014 the conversation was once again fueled, this time by actress Lupita Nyong'o's appearance in the national spotlight upon winning an Academy Award for Best Supporting Actress for her performance in *12 Years a Slave*. This renewed focus on colorism was provoked in part because Nyong'o, who is dark-skinned, openly spoke about limited definitions of Black beauty and her own difficulties and self-doubts related to her dark skin tone early in her life.[37]

Discussions about the necessity to rid the larger society of narrowly-defined White beauty ideals and subsequently the Black society of colorist practices and "colonized mindsets"[38] are positive and important. This holds particularly true in light of recent controversies on celebrity-marketed skin bleaching products, such as Jamaican dancehall artist Vybz Kartel's Cake Soap,[39] or the skin lightening cream Whitenicious, which was created and is advertised by the Nigerian-Cameroonian pop singer Dencia. The products are not just in Africa but also in the United States.[40] Those controversies and celebrity publicity stunts aside, the now often purported message that all hues of skin should be considered equally beautiful falls short when—upon skimming the pages of either *Ebony* or *Essence*—the attentive reader still has a chance of stumbling over ads that feature skin lightening products. The following analysis looks at selected advertisements from these two magazines that are oriented to Black audiences. Despite many messages proclaiming self-love on their editorial pages, some of the magazines' ads continue to promote lightening creams. In the twenty-first century, they do so with the use of different terminology and less frequently than in previous decades.

## BLEACH—FADE—GLOW: SKIN LIGHTENING ADVERTISEMENTS IN *EBONY* AND *ESSENCE*

In the past, skin bleaching advertisements in Black periodicals were numerous and frequent. Language was explicit in devaluing dark skin and Black (female) beauty.[41] Today, advertisements for skin lightening products are harder to find, but this has more to do with the different coded language used than with the disappearance of the products. Also, a decrease in advertisements does not necessarily mean that the products are not used anymore. The figures cited vary, but some statistics estimate the world's skin bleaching market to be worth more than $5.6 billion, a figure which is expected to rise continually over the next few years.[42]

Today, the largest increase of skin bleaching sales is in countries in Asia, Africa, and the Middle East. In these countries cosmetics companies still often advertise their skin lightening products with the words *whitening*, or *lightening*. Such labels are no longer common in the United States where the products are now mostly called *fade* creams, *eventone* creams, *dark spot correctors*, or *dark spot removers*. Fashion Fair Cosmetics's Vantex Skin Bleaching Crème is a prominent exception. It continues to be sold with the label *bleaching cream* to this day and was advertised as such in *Ebony* until 2006. But even Fashion Fair Cosmetics recently revamped and expanded its product line and is now offering an additional product called "Vantex True Tone Dark Spot Corrector (with natural skin brightener)," perhaps to target a different group of customers.[43] Generally speaking, the marketing as dark spot correctors is, I claim, mostly a result of the complex history of race in the United States. It created a highly sensitive awareness for anything that would sound, to Black people like, *wanting* to be White and thereby *selling out*.

Already during the rallying cries for *Black is Beautiful* of the 1960s, companies, if only momentarily, had to adjust and tone down their language. If not, they could lose customers who may fear continuing to buy *bleaching* and *skin-lightening* creams would risk their *race loyalty*. This was reflected in the ads found in *Ebony* and *Essence* during that time.[44] After the 1960s some of the language was resumed to once again promote products that would *lighten and brighten* skin complexion. A 1992 report by the Department of Consumer Affairs of the City of New York pointed out, however, a gradual linguistic change from *skin bleaching* and *skin lightening* cream to *skin tone evener*. This was "perhaps under the belief that some potential users do not want to be reminded what the product really does is lighten the skin."[45] On the other hand, changed language is also contingent on the fact that the Food and Drug Administration (FDA) issued new regulations about which claims were legitimate and which were not with regards to the advertisements' promise to customers.[46]

As mentioned before, today the most prominent creams and lotions on the market bear creatively subdued names, such as *fade* creams and *dark spot correctors*. I consider these to be examples of twenty-first century euphemisms used in an attempt to cover up the products' original intent and usage.[47] When looking at the products advertised in *Ebony* and *Essence* today, one can differentiate between two categories. On the one hand are the more traditional "race products,"[48] which are distributed by companies that exclusively target African-American female customers. Well-known examples for this first category in the business of skin care products are Nadinola, Ambi, and, to a certain extent, Palmer's, which all established their own lines of skin bleaching creams in the early and mid-twentieth century. Palmer's also targets a White female audience, particularly with its cocoa butter products. But advertisements from the 1950s and 1960s in *Ebony* show that the corporation specifically geared some of its products to African Americans before many other mainstream cosmetics companies did.[49]

The other group of skin tone correcting creams has only been around for a few years in the first decade of the twenty-first century. These are products promoted by high-end mainstream cosmetics companies such as Clinique, Estée Lauder, and Lancôme. These *skin tone correctors* that have been advertised in *Ebony* and *Essence* since the early 2010s are all simultaneously marketed to women of all ethnicities. This is often showcased by ads that feature multiple women of different ethnicities when published in mainstream and ethnic magazines, or just the Black model in some of the spreads that are printed in *Ebony* and *Essence*, all while still including a reference to the larger multiracial target group.

At the same time, the older and more traditional *race products,* such as Ambi and Palmer's, continue to carry skin lightening cream products which are, once in a while at least, still advertised in *Ebony* and *Essence*. Despite bearing different names that avoid any obvious association with the labels *bleaching* and *lightening,* I argue that they remain *colorist* in their undertones of lighter being better. Supporting arguments for this claim are three-fold: First, the products now advertised under different names contain more or less the same ingredients as in years past, most importantly the active bleaching agent hydroquinone (HQ).

Second, cosmetics companies have already once successfully tried to mask their products with language that fit the political tone and discourse of the time. This was particularly noticeable in the 1960s with J. Strickland & Co., which sells Nadinola skin bleaching cream. The company tried to sell its product to socially and politically conscious Black female customers who could no longer allow themselves to be caught with a bleaching cream in hand. Possibly for fear of losing business, the company then ran an ad campaign that was titled "Black is Beautiful," advertising a line of creams which "brings out the natural beauty of your complexion" with "a smooth, glowing skin tone that's even all over."[50] Although until 1965 the product was still called *skin brightener,* in this 1968 ad the different brands were simply referred to as Ultra Nadinola, Deluxe Nadinola, and Original Nadinola, thereby avoiding the descriptions of *bleaching, lightening,* and *brightening.* That way the company was probably hoping to make it less offensive to Black customers, or rather, to make the same product marketable in disguise.

Third, these product lines that once were explicitly labeled as skin bleaching creams, Ambi and Palmer's, for example,[51] have achieved a name for themselves. In other words, they have name recognition and are known to be only marketed to African-American women. As Maya Angelou remarked in a 1995 article in *Ebony*: "Companies created and sold Nadinola face cream so that Black women could lighten their complexion and reflect what was thought of as the beauty of White women."[52] The long-standing reputation of these brands is reason enough why some African-American women, who see such ads today, will be reminded of the products' original intent, particularly if the audience happens to be older.

In addition to the above-mentioned arguments, which indicate little actual change, it is vital to keep in mind common strategies used in advertising. One such strategy is explained by sociolinguist Fern Johnson in her study on verbal and visual codes in advertising: "The logic of advertising relies heavily on ellipsis and inference, or the omission of items necessary to complete the text."[53] Such implied meanings, as Johnson asserts, are understood "in a cultural, ideologically coded context and left unarticulated, and must be inferred by the cultural reader."[54] The Black female cultural reader of twenty-first-century *fade cream* advertisements is thus likely to infer these racial undertones, precisely because these are the same brands that were explicitly labeled as skin bleaching and skin lightening creams in the past. Mere synonyms and euphemisms do not strip the products of their original meaning. This claim is supported by a quote by Lisa Jones, daughter of the poets Hettie Jones and Amiri Baraka. She writes about "the pain, the wounds, [and] the subtext that these products carry with them," regardless of whether they come with the label "fade cream . . . skin-tone cream, bleaching cream, [or] skin whitener."[55] Or, as Margaret Hunter argues, "cosmetics corporations invent ever more ways to convince women of color that 'their black is beautiful' while reminding them that 'white is right.'"[56] The claim is that something is still wrong with Black skin, which Black women can fix by using these products to make their skin *brighter* and more *even.* A simple purchase can *fade* what is unattractive, which in essence, is too much color.

One such example is the brand Ambi, which is, to this day, one of the most well-known cosmetics brands designed exclusively for Black skin. Due to the company's history and active focus on *bleaching,* later *lightening,* and now *fade* creams, it has also become a household name for attempts to sidestep the Black physicality. In so doing racial capital is attained by engaging in practices that would make skin lighter and brighter. The brand's name by itself seems to be a play on the prefix meaning both, thus evoking words like *ambiguity*. Such a connotation would be fitting to the semantic field that the brand could be toying with: Ambiguity, for one, calls forth an association with racial ambiguity, which is the term used to describe those that cannot be clearly labeled visually with regards to their racial or ethnic background. This, of course, is a desired outcome of skin bleaching, if one assumes that one goal could be to racially "pass," thereby engage in what I elsewhere referred to as "modern acts of racial passing."[57]

In recent years Ambi emphasized a message to customers, which ostensibly affirms an explicit love of self and body. In 2006, for example, ads printed in *Ebony* and *Essence* asserted this with the statement, "We know you love your natural skin tone. It's the dark spots you don't love."[58] How, then, is this product different from earlier times? It is the same Ambi Fade Cream that contains the bleaching agent hydroquinone and that was advertised to more or less explicitly lighten people's skin up until the 1990s. The answer, I contend, is that there is no difference other than one in semantics in order to mask the racial undertones of the product.

A quick look into Merriam-Webster's online dictionary suffices to find clues for what these undertones communicate. The verb "to fade" is described, among other things, as "to disappear gradually [and] to become less bright: to lose color."[59] Hearing the word *fade* cream, therefore, inevitably evokes connotations with attaining lighter skin. Based on the history of the product these connotations do not just mean fading any dark spots or marks, but it reminds people of a past when it was still politically correct to speak of *skin bleaching* and *skin lightening*. For that reason, the discourse permeating Ambi's *fade cream* is still the same in 2013 as it was in previous years: It is implied that there is something wrong with Black women's skin which needs to be fixed and Ambi has the solution that helps Black women fix it. This discourse of repair is now cleverly interwoven with the discourse of (racial) authenticity, by playing on Black women's self-confidence and love for their true and "natural" selves, which should not be threatened by using a "fade" cream.

In a campaign that was launched in 2011, Ambi products are promoted with different shots of the face and body of a "racially authentic" brown-skinned woman and the slogans playing with the words "glow" ("You Glow, Girl")[60] and "flawless." A full-page ad in the June 2013 issues of both *Ebony* and *Essence*, for instance, is titled Simply Flawless. The language of the body of the ad then reads like this: "Achieving flawless skin is as easy as 1, 2, 3. CLEANSE—MOISTURIZE—TREAT. AMBI designed a skincare regime to treat skin discoloration and dark marks without changing natural skin tone. THE COLOR OF FLAWLESS SKIN."[61] As the fade cream is advertised together with a cleanser and a moisturizer, this three-step procedure implies that using the fade cream should be part of every Black woman's daily beauty routine. The disclaimer, without *changing* natural skin tone, comes almost as an after-thought.

Not all customers believe this pretension, however. On the blogging platform *Statigram* an attentive *Ebony* reader posted a picture with a self-made visual juxtaposition of a 1959 Nadinola bleaching cream ad and this 2013 advertisement for Ambi. The tagline read: "You can change the language, but the colonization of our bodies remains the same," and was followed by the Twitter hashtag "#BlackGirlPain."[62] The colonization this reader refers to can be linked with what bell hooks and others have called the "colonization of the mind."[63] One outcome of said colonization is the normalization of the White body and the need for Black bodies to be approximated to this norm. It could be said that the disclaimer functions merely to protect the company from criticism for selling what essentially is still a skin lightening cream. The disclaimer is, of course, also oxymoronic: How, if the product allegedly works to make dark marks go away, would this not lighten one's overall complexion if applied all over one's face? Moreover, the combination of the ad for a fade cream with that for a cleanser and a moisturizer—products that are always applied over one's entire face—invites the interpretation that the fade cream should also be used in the same way.

Just like Ambi, Palmer's continues to advertise its Skin Success Eventone products in *Ebony* and *Essence*. In the past these ads also often featured racially ambiguous women and, of course, included more explicit language. In the August 1966 issue of *Ebony*, for example, a quarter-page ad for Palmer's Skin Success Cream shows a light-skinned woman with European facial features who smiles from the picture next to the directive "Enjoy the light side of life." The body of the ad promises that the cream "tones the shades of your skin for that natural, fairer, clearer loveliness."[64] By comparison, vertical banners in the 2012 March and August issues of *Ebony* showcase a dark-skinned model below the statement "Palmer's works. I'm the proof." This is another parallel to Ambi, where today's *fade cream* is also marketed with dark-skinned women in the advertisements. The visual message thus is one that highlights Black beauty in its darker shades, foregrounding the use of the product to fade dark spots, as the testimonial below the photograph reads: "I had dark spots and a dull complexion. With Palmer's I saw a difference right away and now my skin is clear and even.—Lauren W."[65] While it is unclear if the model in the ad is the same person who gave this review, the body of the ad informs the reader of the product's potential that "can help give you brighter, clearer skin."[66] This produces another, competing narrative which draws on language that suggests skin brightening. It should perhaps also remind of the product's history as a skin lightening cream in the past. The 2012 advertisement offers a variety of four products that the potential customer can choose from: a fade cream, a fade milk, the ultra fade serum, and a complexion soap. The repeated use of the word fade is reminiscent of language from the past, drawing on the idea that what should fade is, of course, skin color, not limited to any dark spots or discolorations. This should be achieved with the same chemical lightening agent used in the past because just like Ambi, Palmer's Skin Success Eventone products still contain hydroquinone in the two-percent concentration that is legal for over-the-counter products today.

Unlike the two aforementioned *race products,* more recent products by high-end mainstream cosmetics companies do not contain hydroquinone. Their direction at women of all ethnicities also seems to go against an obvious racial message. Yet upon a close reading of the visual and verbal codes, this racial message is there, even though it is cleverly hidden between the lines. An advertising campaign for Estée Lauder's Even Skintone Illuminator, which was launched in 2011, features a Black, a White, and an Asian woman to emphasize the product's intended appeal to all ethnicities. In order to specifically highlight the cream's relevance to Black audiences, however, the June 2011 issue of *Essence* pictures just the Puerto Rican model, Joan Smalls, who is photographed to advertise the product.[67] The body of the ad states that the cream is "[p]roven gentle and effective for all ethnicities." This is in line with the suggestions on what to use it for, which are dermatological problems that women regardless of racial or ethnic background may possibly want to treat (e.g. acne marks, discolorations, dark spots, and uneven skin tone). At the same time the product is called Skintone Illuminator. One dictionary definition of "to illuminate" is "to supply (something) with light," thereby clearly invoking a reference to lightening and brightening.[68] While this message is not at all racial for White women, as their skin is already light, for Black women this seems to include yet another subtle hidden agenda and imply the potential for achieving lighter skin with this product.

Lancôme's Dreamtone Skin Tone Correcting Serum, which was introduced to the market in 2013, is even more indirect with its message. It also features a multi-racial cast of three women (one White, one Black, and one who appears biracial) in a double-page-spread for the product.[69] The slogan boasts for the serum to be "the next generation of dark spot correction," and features three different types of the same product, which are customized according to *fair, medium,* and *dark* skin tone. The correcting serum itself features the slogan "ultimate dark spot corrector / beautiful skin tone creator" on the bottle.[70] The second part of this claim is particularly interesting. Creating a skin tone implies that it was not there before, and this, I would read, is a way to discretely state that using this product does not merely speak to the discourse of repairing and restoring what was once there, but also to the discourse of creating something new. In other words, the skin tone you had before using the product is seen as less beautiful than the skin tone you will have after you apply the correcting serum.

This, by implication, is the skin tone of your dreams, as the product's name Dreamtone suggests. Again the underlying message for Black women is that society still values lighter skin as more beautiful, and this product will help "create" that beautiful skin tone. What is undesirable for some customers may be just the dark spots, but for others it may be dark skin all over. Again, the product's claim that it lightens darker parts also indicates that it can potentially lighten more if applied to larger areas of the face and body.

Clinique's Even Better Clinical Dark Spot Corrector, which has been around since 2010, takes a slightly different visual path with its advertisement campaign. One of the ads features two light-brown eggs, one with visible dark spots and one without, next to a bottle of the product. The headline states that the "dark spot corrector" has "[t]he power to even skin tone with results equal to a leading prescription agent," which is an implicit reference to hydroquinone (HQ).[71] Of course, this is not as readily known to White Americans, who had little use for skin bleaching creams in the past and have only become a target group for these "spot correctors" since the twenty-first century. White women are often told that skin tone correctors could make age spots or sun spots disappear, which are typically seen as a sign of advanced age. Advertising skin tone correctors to White women thus mainly draws on discourses of youth and health, rather than anything else. Therefore, White women are not likely to know of a leading prescription agent, as is indicated in the advertising copy. Consequently, when marketing a *safe* alternative, this seems to be covertly designed to appeal to African-American customers who either have a known intolerance for HQ, which they obviously would only know from previous use of skin lighteners, or who are otherwise aware of the risks of the bleaching agent.

Clinique claims its product is also recommended to be used "comfortably, long term." This is one more hint that an implied goal of using the product is to permanently achieve a change in one's complexion. It is not just a onetime removal of the spots and marks the corrector is allegedly targeted to eliminate. An ad printed in the February 2012 issue of *Essence* featured a double-spread for the Clinique Even Better Clinical Dark Spot Corrector together with Clinique Even Better Make-Up. While at first the ad claims to be intended for visibly reducing dark spots, a few lines later the advertising body reads, "Even Better Makeup creates that uniform, nearly perfect look instantly. And over time, helps brighten skin, too." Talking about bright skin, then, is not at all subtle in the sense that it is a common synonym for the word *light* skin. Therefore, what other intention could this claim have than to lure readers into believing that the product would also lighten their skin tone? It is implied that you can use the product for whatever you like and feel comfortable with the results, whether it is merely getting rid of a few dark spots or lightening your complexion overall. Clinique thereby achieves a double benefit: The brand may attract those who merely want to get rid of a few dark spots without implying that they are purchasing a skin lightening cream, and it may also succeed in convincing those who seek a skin lightener to have found what they were looking for by using covert language. What better way of tapping into multiple consumer groups than that?

## BLACK SKIN, WHITE CREAMS? SOME CLARIFICATIONS

Dermatological research shows that Black women suffer from skin problems such as hyperpigmentation and discoloration at a higher rate than White women.[72] It is therefore obvious that they are an important target group for creams and concoctions which promise to fade dark spots and other discolorations. In other words, there is a distinction between someone's wish to get rid of isolated, unwanted dark marks or trying to lighten one's skin tone overall. This distinction between skin lightening (skin bleaching) and skin evening (correcting dark spots) was pointed out by a reader's online response to an article on skin lightening:

> Please stop confuses [sic] skin lightening creams with tone correcting/skin evening creams. . . . Women of color, due to high melanin content, live with hyper-pigmentation. This means that a dark spot left from one little popped pimple is highly visible & can take up to a year to fade. Tone correction creams speed up that process. While there are women who use creams to lighten their skin overall, the vast majority of . . . products . . . are simply used by women seeking to even out their complexions, not obliterate their racial identity.[73]

As can be seen from this comment, the reason for why African-American women and other women of color choose to buy skin fade creams or skin tone correctors may have nothing to do with wanting lighter skin color overall.

Therefore, I am not suggesting that these products cannot or are not used to merely eliminate a scar or a dark spot on someone's skin. My claim is, however, that the messages these cosmetics companies are sending out with their ads are contradictory and possibly intentionally ambiguous. Such messages diminish the claim that all shades of Black skin are equally beautiful. Aesthetics of the body are culturally determined and still orient themselves along the lines of a European White norm. Therefore, as Hunter argues, "[s]kin bleaching practices that whiten or lighten the skin are responses to hegemonic cultural norms that idealize white beauty."[74] It is these hegemonic norms that continue to exist, which is something that cosmetics companies have been taking advantage of by trying to sell more *racial capital,* in this case lighter skin.

## CONCLUSION

Colorism and the significance of skin color politics in the Black community in the United States have become a frequent topic of discussion in the early twenty-first century. The issue is no longer considered a taboo topic and is openly addressed in Black and—increasingly—also in mainstream media, which is clearly a sign of progress. Moreover, *Ebony* and *Essence* as the two leading Black periodicals in the United States are continuously celebrating Black beauty in all its shades in their editorial content. For the most part, this celebration of Blackness also extends into the advertising content found in the magazines. Campaigns highlighting the beauty of Black skin meet with campaigns for natural hair care products, which are all signs for a social climate that allows for embracing Blackness in all its shapes, shades, and forms. Nevertheless, both magazines continue to accept advertisements for skin lightening products. While they do not appear as regularly as up until the end of the twentieth century, these ads surface in irregular intervals. This, I argue, supersedes and torpedoes any positive image campaigns, as ads for skin tone creams send out ambiguous messages in the twenty-first century. Their intent is couched in euphemistic language to seemingly hide the products' underlying purpose of lightening one's skin tone. Therefore, these ads undermine messages of self-love and a celebration of the Black beauty aesthetic and once again favor an aesthetic that orients itself towards an ideal of *light is right*.

A cursory glance at skin tone ads in *Ebony* and *Essence* in the years between early 2011 and early 2014 suggests two concurrent developments: On the one hand, long-established older "race products"[75] by the likes of Ambi and Palmer's are slowly fading—pun intended—to the background. They remain on the market, which alludes to their continued popularity, but are less frequently advertised in Black-oriented magazines. When they are advertised, however, their long-standing name recognition in the Black community likely suffices to remind potential consumers of their original intent, regardless of which euphemistic language is used. Using more *politically correct* terms such as *fade creams,* instead of calling them *skin lighteners,* therefore merely serves the purpose of making sure the products do not offend racially conscious customers and readers, and thereby minimizes public backlash for promoting a White or light-skinned beauty ideal.

While these older products appear less regularly in Black magazines, new skin care products targeted to all ethnicities have increasingly taken up advertising space in *Ebony* and *Essence*. This suggests an intensified desire to commodify Black beauty on behalf of large-scale multinational cosmetics companies and their realization that tapping into the African American consumer market is a lucrative enterprise. Such products are promoted by blending language of the past to *brighten* skin tones (Clinique's Dark Spot Corrector) with more recent covert claims for the products to *illuminate* (Estée Lauder's Even Skintone Illuminator) and "create" the skin tone of your dreams (Lancôme's Dreamtone Skin Tone Correcting Serum).

My exploratory analysis of selected skin cream advertisements reveals a significant trend that high-end mainstream companies such as Clinique, Estée Lauder, and Lancôme now are all promoting skin tone correctors in *Ebony* and *Essence*. These companies evidently see a new market which is created, on the one hand, by the mass-marketed striving for flawless beauty among women, regardless of racial or ethnic background, in Western capitalist societies. On the other hand, the companies try to gain appeal for their products by nurturing deep-seated notions among Black women that there is something wrong with Black skin, which has to be *corrected*. While the ads appear as not racially charged on the surface level, they carry implicit racial undertones, which make the message to Black female customers a slightly different one than the message to their White female counterparts. What looks like progress with regards to the message of the ads may just be a form of adjustment to appeal to a twenty-first century Black female audience. Therefore, one could speak with the voice of Toni Morrison's narrator Claudia Breedlove from *The Bluest Eye* and claim that, "the change was adjustment without improvement."[76] Ultimately, real improvement would mean a world in which light skin tone is no longer considered "racial capital" with material benefits for those who have it, and for those who use skin lightening products as a means to get it.

## NOTES

1. Toni Morrison, *The Bluest Eye* (London: Vintage, 1999), 95.

2. Susannah Walker, *Style & Status: Selling Beauty to African American Women, 1920–1975* (Lexington: University Press of Kentucky, 2007), 6.

3. Cornel West, *Race Matters*, 2nd Vintage Books ed. (New York: Vintage Books, 2001), xvi.

4. See the mission statements by *Essence* and *Ebony*: "About Essence Magazine," *Essence.com*, accessed February 18, 2014, http://www.essence.com/about/magazine; "About Ebony," *Ebony.com*, accessed February 18, 2014, http://www.ebony.com/about-ebony #axzz2s3ncsMkU.

5. Margaret Hunter, "Buying Racial Capital: Skin-Bleaching and Cosmetic Surgery in a Globalized World," *The Journal of Pan African Studies* 4, no. 4 (2011).

6. Lorraine O'Grady, "Olympia's Maid: Reclaiming Female Subjectivity," in *The Feminism and Visual Culture Reader*, ed. Amelia Jones (New York: Routledge, 2003), 174.

7. Qtd. in Stuart Hall, *Representation: Cultural Representations and Signifying Practices, Culture, Media, and Identities* (London: SAGE in association with the Open University, 1997), 235.

8. Patricia Hill Collins, *Black Feminist Thought: Knowledge, Consciousness, and the Politics of Empowerment*, Rev. 10th anniversary ed. (New York: Routledge, 2000), 70.

9. For early writings on intersectionality theory see Kimberle Crenshaw, "Mapping the Margins: Intersectionality, Identity Politics, and Violence against Women of Color," *Stanford Law Review* 43, no. 6 (1991), 1241–99.

10. Colorism is an issue for people of color globally and a rising number of studies reveal its persisting effects on people in African countries, India, and the Caribbean. Even within the United States colorism affects diverse racial groups. Apart from African Americans it is also an issue among Latino/a Americans and in Asian-American communities. See Edward Eric Telles, *Race in Another America: The Significance of Skin Color in Brazil* (Princeton: Princeton University Press, 2004); Joanne L. Rondilla and Paul R. Spickard, *Is Lighter Better? Skin Tone Discrimination among Asian Americans* (Lanham: Rowman & Littlefield, 2007).

11. Lawrence Graham, *Our Kind of People: Inside America's Black Upper Class* (New York: Harper Collins, 1999), 20.

12. Edward Franklin Frazier, *The Negro in the United States* (New York: Macmillan Co., 1949).

13. Kathy Russell-Cole, Midge Wilson, and Ronald E. Hall, *The Color Complex: The Politics of Skin Color in a New Millennium*, Rev. ed. (New York: Anchor Books, 2013), 56.

14. Obiagele Lake, *Blue Veins and Kinky Hair: Naming and Color Consciousness in African America* (Westport, CT: Praeger, 2003).

15. Margo Okazawa-Rey, Tracy Robinson, and Janie Victoria Ward, "Black Women and the Politics of Skin Color and Hair," *Women's Studies Quarterly* 14, no. 1/2 (1986): 13.

16. Evelyn Nakano Glenn, ed. *Shades of Difference: Why Skin Color Matters* (Stanford: Stanford University Press, 2009); Kimberly Jade Norwood, ed., *Color Matters: Skin Tone Bias and the Myth of a Postracial America* (New York: Taylor & Francis, 2014); Russell-Cole, Wilson, and Hall, *The Color Complex: The Politics of Skin Color in a New Millennium*.

17. Margaret L. Hunter, *Race, Gender, and the Politics of Skin Tone* (New York: Routledge, 2005), 77.

18. Ibid., 69.

19. See Marita Golden, *Don't Play in the Sun: One Woman's Journey through the Color Complex* (New York: Doubleday, 2004), 65; Hunter, *Race, Gender, and the Politics of Skin Tone*, 101; JeffriAnne Wilder, "Revisiting 'Color Names and Color Notions': A Contemporary Examination of the Language and Attitudes of Skin Color among Young Black Women," *Journal of Black Studies* 41, no. 1 (2010): 196.

20. See Ronald Hall, *An Historical Analysis of Skin Color Discrimination in America: Victimism among Victim Group Populations* (New York: Springer, 2009); Cedric Herring, Verna Keith, and Hayward Derrick Horton, eds., *Skin Deep: How Race and Complexion Matter in the "Color-Blind" Era* (Urbana, Ill.: University of Illinois Press, 2004); Russell-Cole, Wilson, and Hall, *The Color Complex: The Politics of Skin Color in a New Millennium*.

21. Jill Viglione, Lance Hannon, and Robert DeFina, "The Impact of Light Skin on Prison Time for Black Female Offenders," *Social Science Journal* 48, no. 1 (2011): 250–58.

22. DeNeen L. Brown, "Through the Past, Darkly; The Legacy of Colorism Reflects Wounds of Racism that Are More than Skin-Deep," *Washington Post*, July 12, 2009, E.1.

23. Hunter, "Buying Racial Capital: Skin-Bleaching and Cosmetic Surgery in a Globalized World," 145.

24. Joy Bennett Kinnon, "Is Skin Color Still an Issue in Black America?" *Ebony*, April 2000, 52.

25. Golden, *Don't Play in the Sun: One Woman's Journey through the Color Complex*, 7.

26. *Dark Girls*, directed by D. Channsin Berry and Bill Duke (2011; RLJ Entertainment, 2013), DVD.

27. The independently produced film was first aired on Oprah's television channel *OWN* in 2013, after having gone on a screening tour across the United States. It received considerable media attention and praise, not in the least by the TV mogul Oprah herself.

28. See, for example, "Is Skin Color Still a Problem in Black America?" *Ebony*, December 1984, 66–70; "Why Skin Color Suddenly Is a Big Issue Again," *Ebony*, March 1992, 120–22; Joy Bennett Kinnon, "Is Skin Color Still an Issue in Black America?" 52–56.

29. See Simone Puff, "What's in a Shade? The Significance of Skin Color in *Ebony* Magazine" (PhD diss., Alpen-Adria Universitaet Klagenfurt, Austria, 2012), 175–80.

30. See Ayana D. Byrd and Lori L. Tharps, *Hair Story: Untangling the Roots of Black Hair in America*, Second revised and updated ed. (New York: St. Martin's Press, 2014); Antonia

Opiah, "the changing business of black hair," *un-ruly.com*, posted January 23, 2014, accessed February 20, 2014, http://un-ruly.com/the-changing-business-of-black-hair/.

31. Jack Neff, "My Black Is Beautiful," *Advertising Age*, August 27, 2007, accessed February 20, 2014, http://adage.com/article/news/black-beautiful/120091.

32. Kimberly N. Foster, "Mission Statement," *For Harriet*, accessed February 15, 2003, http://www.forharriet.com/p/about.html.

33. Constance C. R. White, "Color Trends," *Essence*, September 2011, 42.

34. See Denene Millner, "Color Struck," *Essence*, December 2011, 134–39. Two articles online are, for example, "The Write or Die Chick" and "Dark Girls, Light Girls—Most Brown Girls Have a Colorism Story," *Essence.com*, January 31, 2012, accessed February 15, 2014, http://www.essence.com/2012/01/31/the-write-or-die-chick-dark-girls-light-girls-most-brown-girls-have-a-colorism-story; Silvia Obell, "Essence Poll: Have You Experienced Colorism?," *Essence.com*, January 10, 2014, accessed February 15, 2014, http://www.essence.com/2014/01/10/essence-poll-how-have-you-experienced-colorism.

35. Kelley L. Carter, "Dark Girls: A New Documentary by Bill Duke," *Ebony*, October 2011, 36; Akiba Solomon, "'Dark Girls' Does the Right Thing," *Ebony.com*, January 30, 2012, accessed February 14, 2014, http://www.ebony.com/entertainment-culture/dark-girls-does-the-right-thing#.Uy6aF4WAmHc; Chris Williams, "Colorism: The War at Home. Interview with Dr. Yaba Blay," *Ebony.com*, February 20, 2013, accessed February 14, 2014, http://www.ebony.com/news-views/colorism-the-war-at-home-405#axzz2wlwccewu.

36. "#Ebonychat—Colorism: The Struggle Continues," *Ebony.com*, February 21, 2013, accessed February 14, 2014, http://www.ebony.com/discuss/news-views/ebonychat-colorism-the-struggle-continues-452#axzz2wlwccewu.

37. For a transcript of the speech see "Lupita Nyong'o Delivers Moving 'Black Women in Hollywood' Acceptance Speech," *Essence.com*, February 28, 2014, accessed March 15, 2014, http://www.essence.com/2014/02/27/lupita-nyongo-delivers-moving-black-women-hollywood-acceptance-speech.

38. bell hooks, *Teaching Critical Thinking: Practical Wisdom* (New York: Routledge, 2010), 25.

39. Lanre Bakare, "Is Skin Bleaching in Danger of Becoming a Trend among Men?" *The Guardian*, September 7, 2010, accessed February 10, 2014, http://www.guardian.co.uk/fashion/fashion-blog/2011/sep/07/skin-bleaching-whitening-vybz-kartel.

40. Yaba Blay, "Dencia Wants to Set the Record Straight on Whitenicious," *Ebony.com*. February 3, 2014, accessed February 15, 2014, http://www.ebony.com/entertainment-culture/dencia-wants-to-set-the-record-straight-on-whitenicious-interview-453#axzz2sOThrhDb.

41. See Walker, *Style & Status: Selling Beauty to African American Women, 1920-1975*.

42. Russell-Cole, Wilson, and Hall, *The Color Complex: The Politics of Skin Color in a New Millennium*, 71.

43. See "Vantex True Tone Dark Spot Corrector," *Fashionfair.com*, accessed February 10, 2014, http://shop.fashionfair.com/ProductDetails.asp?ProductCode=0051.

44. Walker, *Style & Status: Selling Beauty to African American Women, 1920–1975*, 177–78.

45. Mark Green, "A Study in Hype and Risk: The Marketing of Skin Bleaches," ed. City of New York Department of Consumer Affairs (1992), 9.

46. Ibid., 8.

47. Simone Puff, "Colors in Conflict: Light Vs. Dark Reloaded; or, the Commodification of (Black) Beauty," in *Cultures in Conflict / Conflicting Cultures*, eds. Christina Ljungberg and Mario Klarer, *Spell: Swiss Papers in English Language and Literature* (Tübingen: Narr, 2013), 165.

48. Joan Jacobs Brumberg, *The Body Project: An Intimate History of American Girls* (New York: Random House, 1997), 79.

49. Palmer's should not be confused with a skin bleaching brand long known as Dr. Fred Palmer (now called Dr. Fred Summit), which also sells a variety of skin lightening creams to a Black target group, but no longer advertises in *Ebony* or *Essence*. In contrast to Palmer's, which has adopted different more euphemistic language for its products a while ago, the cream

by Dr. Fred Summit is still labeled "Skin Whitener Tone and Bleach Cream" and is sold, for example, at Walmart, CVS, and Walgreens.

50. Walker, *Style & Status: Selling Beauty to African American Women, 1920–1975*, 177–78.

51. Other well-known brands are Nadinola, Artra, Vantex, and Porcelana, but while these continue to be readily available in drug stores, cosmetics sections of department stores, and—of course—online, they are not currently running large-scale new advertising campaigns and have also not done so in at least a few years.

52. Maya Angelou, "Then Ebony Arrived," *Ebony*, November 1995, 43.

53. Fern L. Johnson, *Imaging in Advertising: Verbal and Visual Codes of Commerce* (New York: Routledge, 2008), 2.

54. Ibid.

55. Lisa Jones, *Bulletproof Diva: Tales of Race, Sex, and Hair* (New York: Anchor Books, 1994), 154.

56. Hunter, "Buying Racial Capital: Skin-Bleaching and Cosmetic Surgery in a Globalized World," 156.

57. Simone Puff, "Modern Acts of Passing: How Stereotypes Make African American Women Yearn for 'Lightness' in the Twenty-First Century," in *From Theory to Practice 2012: Proceedings of the Fourth International Conference on Anglophone Studies*, ed. Gregory Jason Bell, Katarína Nemčoková, and Bartosz Wójcik (Zlín, Czech Republic: Tomas Bata University, 2013), 187–98.

58. Ambi, "Ambi Fade Cream," *Ebony*, March 2006, 131; "Ambi Fade Cream," *Essence*, January 2006, 45.

59. "fade," *Merriam-Webster*, accessed February 15, 2014, http://www.merriam-webster.com/dictionary/fade.

60. Ambi, "You Glow, Girl," *Essence*, November 2010, 52.

61. Ambi, "Simply Flawless," *Essence*, June 2013, 39.

62. kiryat, "#Ebony Magazine Ads," *Statigram*, July 7, 2013, accessed January 18, 2014, http://statigr.am/p/494812682649271688_22727750#/detail/494812682649271688_22727750.

63. hooks, *Teaching Critical Thinking: Practical Wisdom*, 26.

64. Palmer's, "Palmer's Skin Success Cream," *Ebony*, August 1966, 143. This ad also explicitly highlights the product's major bleaching ingredient of the time: ammoniated mercury, which was determined a major health risk and banned by the FDA in 1990 and was then replaced by hydroquinone.

65. Palmer's, "Palmer's Skin Success Cream," *Ebony*, March 2012, 84.

66. Ibid.

67. Estée Lauder, "Even Skintone Illuminator," *Essence*, June 2011, 1.

68. "illluminate," *Merriam-Webster*, accessed February 10, 2014, http://www.merriam-webster.com/dictionary/illuminate.

69. Lancôme, "Dreamtone Skin Tone Correcting Serum," *Essence*, February 2014, 3–4.

70. Ibid.

71. Clinique, "High-Powered Couple," *Essence*, February 2012, 1–2.

72. Erica C. Davis and Valerie D. Callender, "Postinflammatory Hyperpigmentation: A Review of the Epidemiology, Clinical Features, and Treatment Options in Skin of Color," *The Journal of Clinical and Aesthetic Dermatology* 3, no. 7 (2010): 20–31.

73. "doit2julia!" comment in Jenna Sauers, "P&G Backs 'Black Is Beautiful' Doc, Sells Skin-Lightening Cream," *Jezebel*, April 19, 2013, 7:22 p.m., accessed February 15, 2014, http://jezebel.com/p-g-backs-black-is-beautiful-doc-sells-skin-lighteni-476509650.

74. Hunter, "Buying Racial Capital: Skin-Bleaching and Cosmetic Surgery in a Globalized World," 157.

75. Brumberg, *The Body Project: An Intimate History of American Girls*, 79.

76. Morrison, *The Bluest Eye*, 16.

# BIBLIOGRAPHY

"About Ebony." *Ebony.com.* Accessed February 18, 2014. http://www.ebony.com/about-ebony#axzz2s3ncsMkU.

"About Essence Magazine." *Essence.com.* Accessed February 18, 2014. http://www.essence.com/about/magazine.

Ambi. "Ambi Fade Cream." *Essence*, January 2006, 45.

———. "Ambi Fade Cream." *Ebony*, March 2006, 131.

———. "Simply Flawless." *Essence*, June 2013, 39.

———. "You Glow, Girl." *Essence*, November 2010, 53.

Angelou, Maya. "Then Ebony Arrived." *Ebony*, November 1995, 42–43.

Bakare, Lanre. "Is Skin Bleaching in Danger of Becoming a Trend among Men?" *The Guardian*. September 7, 2010, Accessed February 10, 2014. http://www.guardian.co.uk/fashion/fashion-blog/2011/sep/07/skin-bleaching-whitening-vybz-kartel.

Bennett Kinnon, Joy. "Is Skin Color Still an Issue in Black America?" *Ebony*, April 2000, 52–56.

Blay, Yaba. "Dencia Wants to Set the Record Straight on Whitenicious." *Ebony.com.* February 3, 2014. Accessed February 15, 2014. http://www.ebony.com/entertainment-culture/dencia-wants-to-set-the-record-straight-on-whitenicious-interview-453#axzz2sOThrhDb.

Brown, DeNeen L. "Through the Past, Darkly; The Legacy of Colorism Reflects Wounds of Racism that Are More than Skin-Deep." *Washington Post*, July 12, 2009, E.1.

Brumberg, Joan Jacobs. *The Body Project: An Intimate History of American Girls*. New York: Random House, 1997.

Byrd, Ayana D., and Lori L. Tharps. *Hair Story: Untangling the Roots of Black Hair in America*. Second revised and updated ed. New York: St. Martin's Press, 2014.

Carter, Kelley L. "Dark Girls: A New Documentary by Bill Duke." *Ebony*, October 2011, 36.

Clinique. "High-Powered Couple." *Essence*, February 2012, 1–2.

Collins, Patricia Hill. *Black Feminist Thought: Knowledge, Consciousness, and the Politics of Empowerment*. Rev. 10th anniversary ed. New York: Routledge, 2000.

Crenshaw, Kimberle. "Mapping the Margins: Intersectionality, Identity Politics, and Violence against Women of Color." *Stanford Law Review* 43, no. 6 (1991): 1241–99.

*Dark Girls*. Directed by D. Channsin Berry and Bill Duke: 2011. RLJ Entertainment, 2013. DVD.

Davis, Erica C., and Valerie D. Callender. "Postinflammatory Hyperpigmentation: A Review of the Epidemiology, Clinical Features, and Treatment Options in Skin of Color." *The Journal of Clinical and Aesthetic Dermatology* 3, no. 7 (2010): 20–31.

"#Ebonychat - Colorism: The Struggle Continues." *Ebony.com.* February 21, 2013. Accessed February 14, 2014. http://www.ebony.com/discuss/news-views/ebonychat-colorism-the-struggle-continues-452#axzz2wlwccewu.

Estée Lauder. "Even Skintone Illuminator." *Essence*, June 2011, 1.

"fade." *Merriam-Webster*. Accessed February 15, 2014. http://www.merriam-webster.com/dictionary/fade.

Foster, Kimberly N. "Mission Statement." *For Harriet*. Accessed February 15, 2013. http://www.forharriet.com/p/about.html.

Frazier, Edward Franklin. *The Negro in the United States*. New York: Macmillan Co., 1949.

Glenn, Evelyn Nakano, ed. *Shades of Difference: Why Skin Color Matters*. Stanford: Stanford University Press, 2009.

Golden, Marita. *Don't Play in the Sun: One Woman's Journey through the Color Complex*. New York: Doubleday, 2004.

Graham, Lawrence. *Our Kind of People: Inside America's Black Upper Class*. New York: Harper Collins, 1999.

Green, Mark. "A Study in Hype and Risk: The Marketing of Skin Bleaches." Edited by City of New York Department of Consumer Affairs, 1992.

Hall, Ronald. *An Historical Analysis of Skin Color Discrimination in America: Victimism among Victim Group Populations*. New York: Springer, 2009.

Hall, Stuart. *Representation: Cultural Representations and Signifying Practices*. Culture, Media, and Identities. London: SAGE in association with the Open University, 1997.
Herring, Cedric, Verna Keith, and Hayward Derrick Horton, eds. *Skin Deep: How Race and Complexion Matter in the "Color-Blind" Era*. Urbana, IL: University of Illinois Press, 2004.
hooks, bell. *Teaching Critical Thinking: Practical Wisdom*. New York: Routledge, 2010.
Hunter, Margaret. "Buying Racial Capital: Skin-Bleaching and Cosmetic Surgery in a Globalized World." *The Journal of Pan African Studies* 4, no. 4 (2011): 142–64.
Hunter, Margaret L. *Race, Gender, and the Politics of Skin Tone*. New York: Routledge, 2005.
"illluminate." *Merriam-Webster*. Accessed February 10, 2014. http://www.merriam-webster.com/dictionary/illuminate.
"Is Skin Color Still a Problem in Black America?" *Ebony*, December 1984, 66–70.
Johnson, Fern L. *Imaging in Advertising: Verbal and Visual Codes of Commerce*. New York: Routledge, 2008.
Jones, Lisa. *Bulletproof Diva: Tales of Race, Sex, and Hair*. New York: Anchor Books, 1994.
kiryat. "#Ebony Magazine Ads." *Statigram*. July 7, 2013, Accessed January 18, 2014. http://statigr.am/p/494812682649271688_22727750#/detail/494812682649271688_22727750.
Lake, Obiagele. *Blue Veins and Kinky Hair: Naming and Color Consciousness in African America*. Westport, CT: Praeger, 2003.
Lancôme. "Dreamtone Skin Tone Correcting Serum." *Essence*, February 2014, 3–4.
"Lupita Nyong'o Delivers Moving 'Black Women in Hollywood' Acceptance Speech." *Essence.com*. February 28, 2014. Accessed March 15, 2014. http://www.essence.com/2014/02/27/lupita-nyongo-delivers-moving-black-women-hollywood-acceptance-speech.
Millner, Denene. "Color Struck." *Essence*, December 2011, 134–39.
Morrison, Toni. *The Bluest Eye*. London: Vintage, 1999. 1970.
Neff, Jack. "My Black Is Beautiful." *Advertising Age*. August 27, 2007. Accessed February 20, 2014. http://adage.com/article/news/black-beautiful/120091.
Norwood, Kimberly Jade, ed. *Color Matters: Skin Tone Bias and the Myth of a Postracial America*. New Directions in American History. New York: Taylor & Francis, 2014.
O'Grady, Lorraine. "Olympia's Maid: Reclaiming Female Subjectivity." In *The Feminism and Visual Culture Reader*, edited by Amelia Jones, 174–87. New York: Routledge, 2003.
Obell, Silvia. "Essence Poll: Have You Experienced Colorism?" *Essence.com*. January 10, 2014. Accessed February 15, 2014. http://www.essence.com/2014/01/10/essence-poll-how-have-you-experienced-colorism.
Okazawa-Rey, Margo, Tracy Robinson, and Janie Victoria Ward. "Black Women and the Politics of Skin Color and Hair." *Women's Studies Quarterly* 14, no. 1/2 (1986): 13–14.
Opiah, Antonia. "the changing business of black hair," *un-ruly.com*. Posted January 23, 2014. Accessed February 20, 2014, http://un-ruly.com/the-changing-business-of-black-hair/.
Palmer's. "Palmer's Skin Success Cream." *Ebony*, August 1966, 143.
———. "Palmer's Skin Success Cream." *Ebony*, March 2012, 84.
Puff, Simone. "Colors in Conflict: Light Vs. Dark Reloaded; or, the Commodification of (Black) Beauty." In *Cultures in Conflict / Conflicting Cultures*, edited by Christina Ljungberg and Mario Klarer. Spell: Swiss Papers in English Language and Literature 159-76. Tübingen: Narr, 2013.
———. "Modern Acts of Passing: How Stereotypes Make African American Women Yearn for 'Lightness' in the Twenty-First Century." In *From Theory to Practice 2012: Proceedings of the Fourth International Conference on Anglophone Studies*, edited by Gregory Jason Bell, Katarína Nemčoková, and Bartosz Wójcik, 187-98. Zlin, Czech Republic: Tomas Bata University, 2013.
———. "What's in a Shade? The Significance of Skin Color in *Ebony* Magazine." PhD diss., Alpen-Adria Universitaet Klagenfurt, Austria, 2012.
Rondilla, Joanne L., and Paul R. Spickard. *Is Lighter Better? Skin-Tone Discrimination among Asian Americans*. Lanham: Rowman & Littlefield, 2007.
Russell-Cole, Kathy, Midge Wilson, and Ronald E. Hall. *The Color Complex: The Politics of Skin Color in a New Millennium*. Rev. ed. New York: Anchor Books, 2013.

Sauers, Jenna. "P&G Backs 'Black Is Beautiful' Doc, Sells Skin-Lightening Cream." *Jezebel* (2014). Comment by "doit2julia!" April 19, 2013, 7:22 p.m. Accessed February 15, 2014. http://jezebel.com/p-g-backs-black-is-beautiful-doc-sells-skin-lighteni-476509650.

Solomon, Akiba. "'Dark Girls' Does the Right Thing." *Ebony.com*. January 30, 2012. Accessed February 14, 2014. http://www.ebony.com/entertainment-culture/dark-girls-does-the-right-thing#.Uy6aF4WAmHc.

The Write or Die Chick. "Dark Girls, Light Girls—Most Brown Girls Have a Colorism Story." *Essence.com* (2012). January 31, 2012. Accessed February 15, 2014. http://www.essence.com/2012/01/31/the-write-or-die-chick-dark-girls-light-girls-most-brown-girls-have-a-colorism-story.

Telles, Edward Eric. *Race in Another America: The Significance of Skin Color in Brazil*. Princeton: Princeton University Press, 2004.

Vantex. "Vantex True Tone Dark Spot Corrector." *Fashionfair.com*. Accessed February 10, 2014. http://shop.fashionfair.com/ProductDetails.asp?ProductCode=0051.

Viglione, Jill, Lance Hannon, and Robert DeFina. "The Impact of Light Skin on Prison Time for Black Female Offenders." *Social Science Journal* 48, no. 1 (2011): 250–58.

Walker, Susannah. *Style & Status: Selling Beauty to African American Women, 1920–1975*. Lexington: University Press of Kentucky, 2007.

West, Cornel. *Race Matters*. 2nd Vintage Books ed. New York: Vintage Books, 2001. 1993.

White, Constance C. R. "Color Trends." *Essence*, September 2011, 5.

"Why Skin Color Suddenly Is a Big Issue Again." *Ebony*, March 1992, 120–22.

Wilder, JeffriAnne. "Revisiting 'Color Names and Color Notions': A Contemporary Examination of the Language and Attitudes of Skin Color among Young Black Women." *Journal of Black Studies* 41, no. 1 (September 1, 2010): 184–206.

Williams, Chris. "Colorism: The War at Home. Interview with Dr. Yaba Blay." *Ebony.com*. February 20, 2013. Accessed February 14, 2014. http://www.ebony.com/news-views/colorism-the-war-at-home-405#axzz2wlwccewu.

*Chapter Twelve*

# Black Millennial Women as Digital Entrepreneurs

*A New Lane on the Information Superhighway*

Alexa A. Harris

An investigation of young Black women business owners with careers launched via the digital space revealed similarities with their brands and journeys to success. The creation of a genre called Black Millennial Women Digital Entrepreneurs (or BMW DoErs) was formed to highlight shared characteristics of the group. The women are labeled Digital Entrepreneurs because of their ability to turn online activity into a successful business. Because of an increase of Black Millennial women using the Internet as a platform to start organizations and express themselves creatively, it was not only important to study the demographic, but to note connections they have with previous generations.

Historically, griots were members of African tribes with the sacred role of sharing stories to preserve traditions. Often, elders bearing the torch of knowledge used artistic expressions to inspire a village.[1] However, the gift of wisdom was not limited to selected leaders of a community. If one reflects on the communication dynamics of Black women, it is evident the demographic has been equipped with the gift of storytelling. Whether using quilts during slavery or participating in *kitchen table talk*, sharing stories serves as a guide for some and as therapy, inspiration, and encouragement for others. It is also one of the unique aspects of sisterhood.

In *Honey Hush*, Daryl Cumber Dance uses a lens of humor to explore the unique features of Black women's stories. She identified a range of topics including: the power and strength of a Black woman, self-denigrating tales, problems with husband and lovers, the Black church, motherly advice, Black women's physical image, courtship and good loving, dealing with a racist and sexist America, the Civil Rights Movement, and integration.[2] These themes continue through an array of platforms with the Millennial generation, especially the digital space.[3] Black Millennial women, in particular, have used blogs, music, and web shows to share their perspectives, which has often led to large audiences and innovative careers. After examining three Black Millennial Women (BMW), who creatively used social media to share stories, interesting links were identified between the entrepreneurial careers of writer Natasha Eubanks, singer Janelle Monae Robinson, and web-show creator, Issa Rae.

## MILLENNIALS

Before delving into the careers of the three BMW DoErs selected for this study, it is important to examine the similarity they have in age. All the women are members of the Millennial generation. A growing number of marketing and research firms, scholars, and consulting agencies have conducted research on different generations and the defining characteristics of their culture. As of late, the Millennial generation has received much attention. Paul Taylor and Scott Keeter have done a great deal of research on members of this generation, often referred to as "Millennials,"

> Generation names are the handiwork of popular culture. Some are drawn from historic events; others from rapid social or demographic change; others from a big turn in the calendar. . . . The Millennial generation falls into the third category. The label refers to those born after 1980-the first generation to come of age in the new millennium.[4]

It is important to identify characteristics of Millennials in order to fully understand connections among Black women, entrepreneurship, and the digital space.

The trailblazing generation and crop of "80s and 90s babies" is the most multicultural generation America has experienced. Only about 6-in-10 Millennials (61 percent) are non-Hispanic Whites.[5] According to Taylor and Keeter's study, "Millennials-the American teens, twenty [and early thirty]-something's are making the passage into adulthood at the start of the new millennium-have begun to forge theirs: confident, self-expressive, liberal, upbeat and open to change."[6]

### Gender and the Workforce

Millennials have broken traditional gender norms in many arenas, particularly in higher education and the workplace. Taylor and Keeter found, "Millennial women surpass Millennial men in the share graduating from or attending college. This reversal of traditional patterns first occurred among Generation X. In the Boomer and Silent generations, men exceeded women in college attendance and graduation rates."[7] Because of the shift in more women graduating college and starting careers, America can expect a change in the workforce. Lisa Orrell has done a great deal of research about Millennials, particularly with a keen lens on gender in the workplace. She notes,

> One other thing employers need to note about Millennial Chicks: They don't expect to have to "earn" a male colleague's respect because they are "women." Millennial Chicks were raised to believe they are equal to men, and will expect to be treated as such the minute they walk through your doors. These women will not hesitate to demand it if you don't offer it.[8]

Moreover, analyses have shown Millennials of both genders greatly value family and friends over careers in the workplace. Orrell found, "these young adults value the good life like their parents do, but are not willing to sacrifice time with family and friends to achieve it."[9] As this generation rises through the ranks of the corporate ladder, it will be interesting to see if changes in gender inequities in wages, maternity leave, and vacation policies will take place in organizations.

Additionally, this perspective has played a role in the rise of interest in entrepreneurship among Millennials. The Kauffman Foundation conducted a poll about Millennials and entrepreneurship and found 63 percent of African American and 64 percent of Latino Millennials want to start their own companies.[10] Veteran entrepreneur, Jack Nadel wrote an article in the *Huffington Post* about the reasons Millennials should start their own businesses with unaffordable housing, unemployment rates, and other social ills topping the list.[11] Nadel also mentioned the advantages of the Internet and other digital tools that make it easier to get a new business up and running, especially in comparison to starting a business thirty years ago.

## Millennials and Technology

Millennials believe the key distinctive difference between their generation and others is their technology use.[12] T. J. Becker of the *Chicago Tribune* wrote, "The greatest hallmark of the Millennium Generation is its comfort with technology. Although Generation Xers are computer savvy, Millennials are technologically precocious, growing up with a rattle in one hand and a mouse in the other."[13] Scott Beale, author of *The Millennial Manifesto*, shares Becker's sentiments. As a Millennial, he compared the digital savviness of the two generations by sharing,

> When Gen Xers were still buying records and tapes, we were asking for CD players and video game systems with computer chips powerful enough to operate foreign countries' missile systems. Most of us have never used a manual or even an electric typewriter.
>
> We apply to college using computer disks and keep photo albums with digital cameras. Millennials are pre-teens on cell phones and organized students with Palm Pilots.[14]

As a result, the Millennial generation touts technological entrepreneurs like Mark Zuckerberg, the Harvard University dropout and billionaire that created the social networking website, Facebook.[15] Before the site's popularity, some Millennials had already been exposed to virtual interactions with others through social media websites such as College Club, Black Planet, Life Journal, Myspace, and chat rooms.

Elana J. Hendler, a Millennial entrepreneur, noted her generation has learned key business principles from online activities. She posits,

> Since we've participated in the evolution of social media, we naturally understand that when we're building a brand, we're building a community. Communities are not about products. Communities are about values, and millennial entrepreneurs are empowered by technology to use our products as a vehicle to communicate our values and express ourselves. That's not to say that we are devoid of capitalist pursuits, but rather we hope that financial gains and success are achieved as a result of authentic self-expression, not a strategic initiative. Millennial entrepreneurs don't just want to start businesses, they also want to start movements, raise awareness and express their personalities at the same time.[16]

While technology usage is a unifying characteristic of Millennials, Orrell also examined usage differences between those who have attended college in comparison to those who did not.[17] From her research, Orrell found, Millennials that attended college, "use social networking sites, watch and post video online, connect to the Internet wirelessly, and send and receive text messages more than those who did not attend college."[18] Once these practices have become instilled in Millennials, their workplace performance is altered as well. The technological habits of Millennials often cause friction in the workplace as they join members of other generations, who utilize traditional communication methods to complete daily tasks.[19]

## Social Networking and Millennials

Despite an array of similarities between members of the Millennial generation, there are also a vast amount of differences. Race, class, gender, and even the birth year of Millennials (those born in the 1980s versus the 1990s) have impacted the psyche of generation members. The same holds true with Internet usage. Taylor and Keeter discovered,

> Younger Millennials are more likely than their older counterparts to use social networking sites and to visit them more often. About eight-in-ten (81 percent) 18–24 year olds have created their own social networking profile, compared with 66 percent of those ages 25 to 29. Similarly, 58 percent of young Millennial social networking users visit the sites they use most often at least daily, compared with 48 percent of older Millennials.[20]

They also found racial differences among the percentages of Millennials that have created a social networking of web profiles. Eighty-three percent of White Millennials are more likely to have created such a profile while only 71 percent of Blacks and 52 percent of Latinos would do the same.[21] Despite these differences, "Blacks are more likely to use these sites multiple times a day (45 percent vs. 25 percent of whites)," which makes it imperative to further examine Black Millennial online communication dynamics.[22] Additionally, differences have been found with gender and social networking as 33 percent more women than men (24 percent), "visit a social networking site several times a day."[23] These statistics can easily make one wonder the roles culture, gender, community, and connectivity play in Black women exchanging information on the Internet.

## Black Millennials

This study connected race, gender, age, and cyberspace in a way that shines light on an underrepresented group. Studying Black Millennial women (referred to hereafter as BMW) challenges the ideas of scholars, such as Orrell, who have a multicultural utopian perspective about the Millennial generation.[24] In other words, they believe that because there are more citizens of color in this generation than previous ones, the history, race, and class of Millennials do not impact their experiences. If this were true, Tatum would not have written *Why are All the Black Kids Sitting Together in the Cafeteria* at the turn of the "new millennium."[25] Furthermore, if race were not an issue in the study of Millennials, Asian Americans would have been included in the Pew's American Life Project on Millennials. However, because Asian Americans only made up 5 percent of the participants, their answers were excluded from the outcomes of the study.[26] Consequently, because Caucasians appear to be the largest racial group in the Millennial generation, many of the Pew research group's outcomes reflected a White perspective. As a result, various areas of American life are ignored as Whites are used as representatives of the entire generation. Notable findings were disregarded in areas such as religion and teenage pregnancy, where there are different realities for Black people in the Millennial generation.

The Applied Research Center conducted a study with 16 focus groups of African American, Latino, Asian, and White Millennials.[27] They found an array of facts that would dispel myths about Millennials living in a *post racial* society due to the election of a Black president. Specifically, Multicultural Millennials believe racism continues to be a major social ill in American society, especially with employment, public school, criminal justice, healthcare, and immigration systems.

In her text, *Black Still Matters in Marketing*, Pepper Miller makes a similar assertion about people ignoring *difference* within the Millennial generation. Miller explained, "Many marketers believe that growing up in the age of 'post-racial' America . . . this group [Millennials] will eliminate the need to speak to different segments and groups."[28] Her organization, The Hunter-Miller Group, and other marketing experts with a focus on multicultural communities, have taken note of the lack of attention placed on multicultural members of the Millennial Generation.[29] As professionals of color, they tackle the tough questions others choose to ignore. Some of the differences between Black Millennials and others in the generation include placing more value on community service and also experiencing higher rates of unemployment.

Black Millennials grew up with a cultural lens, despite not being a part of major groundbreaking events like the Civil Rights Movement. W. E. B. Dubois' double consciousness ideal of recognizing two identities as Black and American is still present in an array of institutions and daily activities. This was especially evident with the popular culture Black Millennals were exposed to while being raised in the 1980s and 1990s. It was the first time in television history cable networks were formed with programming specifically catered to young and multicultural demographics.[30] Gone were the days youngsters had to countdown to Saturday mornings for cartoons or the "Thank Goodness It's Friday (TGIF)" programming block to view television.[31] Instead, Black Millennials with cable access were introduced to Nickelodeon and Black Entertainment Television (BET). From shows like BET's *Teen Summit* and Nickelodeon's *All That, Gullah Gullah Island*, and *My Brother and Me*, Black Millennials saw cable television shows with casts that looked just like them.

Additionally, Black Millennials born in the 1980s were exposed to diverse families, relationships, and representations of race, class, and sexual orientation. Broadcast networks aired shows showing an array of family and community dynamics, such as: *227* (NBC), *The Cosby Show* (NBC), *Family Matters* (ABC), *The Fresh Prince of Bel-Air* (NBC), *Full House* (ABC), *Ghostwriter* (PBS), *Gilmore Girls* (WB/CW), *Hangin' With Mr. Cooper* (ABC), *Married With Children* (FOX), *Moesha* (UPN), *Roseanne* (ABC), *Sister Sister* (ABC/WB), *South Central* (FOX), *The Wayans Brothers* (WB), *and Will and Grace* (NBC).[32] Viewing these shows as children and teenagers exposed Black Millennials to worlds beyond those represented in previous decades through images of *The Brady Bunch* (ABC), *Good Times* (CBS), *Sanford and Son* (NBC), and *All in The Family* (CBS). By understanding potential age, social climate, and popular culture influences in the lives of BMW DoErs, it is now imperative to obtain a glimpse of those who have accomplished similar professional feats before their time.

## A CLOSER LOOK AT "HER" STORY: PIONEERING BLACK WOMEN ENTREPRENEURS

This study is one of the first and few of its kind to focus specifically on Black Millennial women as entrepreneurs in the digital space. Prior to this text, my dissertation research compared communication dynamics of a BMW blogger and previous Black rhetorical studies.[33] However, in that study the focus was on language and not the business model of the blogosphere. Other scholars have studied women and marginalized communities on the Internet, but with a special lens to crafting, diaries, Greek life, politics, or sex blogs.[34] Similar to the way the feminist movement was not representative of the needs and experiences of Black women in America, previous research on women and social media has not included the unique perspective and experiences of Black women.

However, Black women and entrepreneurship is not a new phenomenon. Women like Madame CeCee McCarty, who in 1848 was worth $150,000 because of her work in the dry goods business, paved the way for those seeking job independence.[35] At the same time, others, like Madame C. J. Walker, the first Black woman millionaire, blazed a trail for many to follow in the hair and beauty industries.[36] From their stories, Black women have learned to capitalize off their gifts and talents. This legacy is carried on today through contemporary entrepreneurs like Lisa Price of Carol's Daughters hair care products and millions of Black women salon owners. Additionally, cosmetic line proprietors like supermodel Iman, and restaurateurs like B. Smith have turned their passions into profit. The same holds true for Black women entrepreneurs in the arts and entertainment.

### Black Women in the Arts

Early rhetors such as Phyllis Wheatley, Harriet E. Wilson, Hannah Bond, Ida B. Wells, Sojourner Truth, and Anna Julia Cooper set a foundation for Black women to speak their truths. Novelists and poets such as Maya Angelou, Toni Cade Bambara, Octavia Butler, Gwendolyn Brooks, Gloria Wade-Gayles, Terry McMillian, and Toni Morrison carried their torches with published works in the twentieth century, many of which even became films.[37] An array of Black women journalists such as Joyce Davis, Demetria Lucas, and Susan Taylor have gone from writing for magazines, working as editors, and owning blogs to publishing books. Other Black women have created their own publishing companies, such as Jamie Foster Brown (*Sister to Sister* magazine) and Karen Hunter (Karen Hunter Publishing) to provide an outlet for others. These women have provided platforms for Black women to connect, celebrate accomplishments, offer advice, and share experiences and perspectives.

The same remains true for women in the music industry. Talented Black women artists like rapper, singer, songwriter, and record producer Melissa (Missy) Elliott created her own record label, The Goldmind, Inc. While entertainment attorneys protect the rights of musicians, such as Jo-na A. Williams who started The Artist Empowerment Firm, veteran Black women music executives, such as Sylvia Rhone began Vested In Culture, a record label for fresh, emerging talent. Additionally *momagers*, or mothers who have also worn the hats of manager for their children in the spotlight, have started their own talent management companies. Sonja Norwood (mother of singer, Brandy) and Jonetta Patton (mother of singer, Usher) are just two examples of Black women who have made such a transition. Other Black women in the music industry have done the same while also venturing into an array of other business endeavors. For example, singer, songwriter, and reality and web-show starlet Kandi Burruss added television producer, store-owner, play-writer, and intimate toy line owner to her repertoire.

Oprah Winfrey's Harpo studios blazed a new trail for Black women in the television arena. Not only did the world become introduced to a Black woman in front of the camera, Winfrey also called the shots behind the scenes. In contemporary times, the door she opened can be seen in an array of television and film companies owned by Black women (many of which will be mentioned below). Winfrey also created her OWN television network.

Winfrey is not the only Black woman that can call herself an entertainment mogul. Cathy Hughes created a media empire with Radio One and TV One. Model, talk show host, and author Tyra Banks merged her talent and passion to help young women with her company, Bankable Productions. Her media organization created one of the most popular and longest running, international reality television show franchises to date, *America's Top Model* to launch the careers of young adults aspiring to follow in her footsteps.

Banks and Hughes are not alone in their class of contemporary Black women in entertainment that have mixed creativity and business savvy to form lucrative careers. Rapper, singer, actress, and two-time talk show host, Queen Latifah created the Flavor Unit production company, which is responsible for an array of television and film projects. Additionally, another talk show host, Wendy Williams Hunter, has followed suit with her production company, Wendy Williams Productions.

However, Black women, as production company owners, have not been limited to models, musicians, rappers, and veteran journalists. Black women writers and producers of fiction programming have also formed their own production companies with shows distributed on broadcast television networks. Yvette Lee Bowser's Sisterlee Productions is credited for the first sitcom to air on television created by a Black woman, *Living Single*. Additionally, Shonda Rhimes' production company, Shondaland, is responsible for an array of primetime hits on ABC, such as *Grey's Anatomy*, *Private Practice*, and *Scandal*.

Other Black women have spread their wings from the television arena with major investments in leisure and entertainment industries, such as sports franchises. Shelia Johnson, co-founder of Black Entertainment Network (BET), made history when she became the first Black woman to serve as owner or partner in three professional sports franchises, The Washington Capitals (NHL), the Washington Wizards (NBA), and the Washington Mystics (WNBA). Additionally, Johnson owns Salamander Hospitality, a company with luxury resorts and vacation getaways. Johnson is not the only Black woman with a career path in both television and sports arenas. Paula Madison, former executive vice president and chief diversity officer of NBC Universal, co-founded the Africa Channel and has held shares in the WNBA's Los Angeles Sparks team.

## INNOVATIVE BMW DOERS

### Young, Black, and Fabulous Storyteller: Natasha Eubanks, Writer

Natasha Eubanks' blog, TheYBF, which stands for "the Young, Black, and Fabulous" serves as an interesting artifact to investigate Black Millennial women entrepreneurs in the digital space. With an average of "15 million page views a month" and $1 million in revenue during 2009, Eubanks' blog is not just an online magazine, but also a media empire.[38]

Eubanks, a self-described "celebrity gossip and entertainment news fan" started the site June 29, 2005.[39] While working as a hostess at an Olive Garden restaurant and waiting for law school to start in the fall, she realized no magazines or blogs were featuring photos or articles about Black celebrities. Eubanks would visit "20 plus blogs and never see mention of a Black celeb," she told Kim Elle.[40] After contacting online media outlets, like Pink is the New Blog about including more Black celebrities in their sites and getting no reply, she took matters into her own hands by creating TheYBF.[41]

After enduring Hurricane Katrina in August of 2005, Eubanks, a New Orleans native, stopped blogging for two weeks.[42] She only decided to resume writing on her blog after numerous e-mails were sent from readers, encouraging her through the difficult time. Eubanks told *Black Enterprise* magazine she realized, "people want this, people need this, and people actually love it. And there's still nothing really like it, so I have to keep doing it."[43] Instead of returning to law school for her second year, Eubanks decided to put her plans of becoming a lobbyist on hold in order to work on TheYBF full time.[44] In an interview with Caroline Clark for *Black Enterprise* magazine, she also disclosed she had applied for numerous jobs and received no offers.[45] Additionally, she noted it helped her realize failure would not be an option with her new endeavor.[46] Eubanks purchased a web server, began posting more frequently, and watched her website grow.

Two of the most interesting features of Eubank's blog are the diversity of topics featured and the unique *ybf* vocabulary, or rhetoric, she has created to coincide with each story. As a pop culture critic and wordsmith, she created a lexicon with words like *foolywang*, which refers to someone or a situation that is a bit out of the ordinary or foolish. Synonyms for *foolywang* are slang terms such as "a hot mess," or "crazy." Smitherman-Donaldson defined "crazy" in the Black vernacular as a word describing "any action that is unconventional or non-conformist, whether political action or not."[47] The majority of *foolywang* stories featured on the site are chastising celebrities, in a sense, about irresponsible behavior. A mix of creative language, slang, signifyin', call and response, and other African-American rhetorical traditions are reflected on the site.[48] Many of her posts are gathered from around the web. Eubanks also includes links from other online sources for her stories, including websites for CNN, Instagram, TMX, Twitter, and YouTube.

TheYBF promotes various products from their sponsors through advertisements, sweepstakes, giveaways, and co-sponsoring events. During the 2010 *Essence* Music Festival in New Orleans, for example, TheYBF supported an event with Carol's Daughter's Hair Care line for Black women.[49] While on the scene for the event, TheYBF had a live blog feed documenting every moment of the affair, which included Black celebrities and hundreds of fans in attendance. Furthermore, Eubanks has featured contests on TheYBF, such as a $1,000 shopping spree for clothing by Rachel Roy, a fashion designer who is also a woman of color.[50] While it is evident that many of the sponsors of Eubank's site are specifically targeting Black women with their products, other companies, such as WalMart, MetLife, and Macy's, have also jumped on board to advertise on her site. In 2009, TheYBF earned $1 million in revenue, 90 percent coming from advertisers striving to reach Eubank's "niche audience."[51]

Eubanks noted it is not always easy obtaining top dollar from advertisers. Sometimes she has to fight for her demographic when corporations strive to not provide adequate compensation for marketing to her audience. "I have to remind them we are the purchasers of their products, the shoes, the handbags, it is the buying power of Black women, my readers are who you want, so there is no reason you should not compensate accordingly," Eubanks shared during an interview with *Black Enterprise*.[52] Because of Eubanks' accomplishments with TheYBF, she was featured on the January 2010 cover of *Black Enterprise* magazine, which named her as a leader in "the new generation of risk-takers and dealmakers."[53]

## A Journey to Metropolis: Janelle Monae Robinson, Singer

Janelle Monae Robinson is a BMW with the power to use music to connect generations. With a fan base ranging from music legend Prince to First Lady Michelle Obama, the Kansas City, Kansas native "defies every label," genre, or category one may try to place her.[54] Robinson is in a class of her own, which is why her unique rise to stardom came from a healthy mix of traditional hard work and determination, merged with a side of digital media.

The talented songstress began her professional career bellowing soulful melodies on college campuses of the Atlanta University Center and other venues around Georgia's capital city, which is known for breaking contemporary musical legends.[55] Robinson pounded the pavement and sold copies of her music on CDs that she pressed on her own. The starlet created her own record label, Wondaland Arts Society, and released music around college campuses, through her website, and social media sites such as Myspace.[56] Her demo, *Janelle Monae: The Audition,* shared a collection of personal experiences and inspirational melodies about a variety of themes, such as her journey to not conform to the expectations of others while striving to live her dreams.

Robinson completed all of these great feats while living in a boarding house with six young women in Atlanta and working at Office Depot.[57] One day, Robinson lost her job because she was using her work computer to thank fans for their support. Her experience getting fired served as inspiration for one of her songs, "Lettin' Go." After rapper Big Boi of the hip hop group, Outkast, heard her sing at an open mic night, he began working to help her dreams become reality.[58] She appeared on some of his songs, including a few on the *Idlewild* movie soundtrack with Outkast. Big Boi also placed her song "Lettin' Go" on his *Got Purp Vol. 2* compilation album.[59]

Music mogul Sean "Puffy" Combs listened to Robinson's music on her myspace.com page.[60] Upon hearing one of her songs, "Violet Stars Happy Hunting!" he contacted her with interests in helping promote her music.[61] Combs visited Atlanta to watch Robinson perform.[62] Blown away by her powerful concert, he met with Robinson and shared his delight with her work. He also explained his willingness to help with promotion and distribution of her music so more listeners could be exposed to her artistic movement. Prior to meeting Combs, Robinson had plans to release her music through myspace.com as she had done before. Her album, *Metropolis*, was inspired by the 1927 German Sci-Fi film by Fritz Lang.[63] On it, she created a futuristic world with "androids," which were used as metaphors in songs to tackle issues of injustice marginalized groups face in society.[64]

Before signing paperwork to begin a partnership with Combs' Bad Boy Entertainment and Atlantic Records, Robinson asked them to read a list of her core values and *The Big Moo* by Seth Godin.[65] It was imperative for potential partners to be on the same page with her vision and goals. This also set the tone for them to understand who she was as an artist, what she stood for, and the importance of staying true to her image and craft.

Robinson values her integrity, faith in God, and passion to be an inspiration for young women *and* members of her hometown in Kansas. Because of her authenticity, consistency, and determination to "leave it all on the stage after every performance," she has gained much acclaim and respect, not only from fans, but industry colleagues, mentors, and world leaders.[66] Both Big Boi and Sean (Puffy) Combs admitted to not wanting to interfere with Robinson's artistry. Instead, they encouraged her to freely express creativity and vision on her own terms.

Additionally, musical icons, such as Prince, contacted her to celebrate her artistry and business savvy. He invited her for a jam session at his house and shared his admiration for anyone who had the bravery to enter the music industry and tell Sean Combs what to do.[67] Combs, a self-proclaimed "control freak," was at a turning point in his career, striving to be more open to the ideas of others.[68] Prince also invited Robinson to join him on tour. Similarly, singer Erykah Badu reached out to encourage Robinson, and was the first female artist to invite Robinson to join her on tour. Badu serves as a mentor and "big sister" to Robinson.[69] Both Prince and Badu were collaborators on her latest album, *The Electric Lady*. The connection these artists share with Robinson is a fearlessness of experimental and conceptual art forms. They also to tell stories through metaphors, inspire audiences, and speak to social ills through music.

Corporations also noticed the high moral standard Robinson set for herself—to portray genuine images all while inspiring and encouraging the next generation. Cover Girl cosmetics and Sonos wireless speakers are just a few of the many organizations that hired Robinson for advertising campaigns to represent their brands.[70] Additionally, she has been invited to grace an array of prestigious stages with her electrifying, one of a kind performance style—from the 2011 Nobel Peace Prize Celebration in Oslo Norway, to the East Room in the White House.[71]

With a loyal following of college students, and the powerful role of social media, Robinson has sustained a strong fan base over the years. She continues to give back to her fans and stays true to her "social media roots." The full versions of all of her songs from throughout her career, including her last album, are available for their listening pleasure on Myspace.[72]

## Awkward Black Girl: Issa Rae, Web Series Creator

Issa Rae channeled her experiences of being "socially awkward," Black, and female into a successful web series entitled, *The Misadventures of Awkward Black Girl*, or *ABG*.[73] The BMW realized mainstream television and film ignored telling stories about women like her. So, she took matters in her own hands by creating, writing, producing, directing, and starring in a web show series. The main character, *J*, represents the antithesis of one-dimensional Black women often seen in media. She also serves as an oxymoron for stereotypical characters reflecting women of color. Rae used YouTube as her distribution platform.

The web show was created with friends that donated their time and talent on the weekends. This included Tracey Oliver, an aspiring television writer Rae met as a student at Stanford University.[74] The two had previously worked together on a series of creative projects while in college, including a soap opera style show about daily life as a Black student at Stanford.[75]

Resonating with over a million viewers, *ABG* raised over $44,000 for production from audience members and show supporters.[76] Kickstarter, a social media fundraising website, served as the platform to receive the green light of financing many people of color are often denied from Hollywood studios. After receiving much acclaim for the show from several different media outlets, Rae also began experiencing offers and attention from entertainment heavyweights.[77] Famed music producer, Pharrell Williams, applauded Rae's work and paid for the second season of the show.[78] Additionally, he distributed the show through his YouTube channel, *I Am Other*.[79] The goal of Williams' network is to show a diverse array of talent from people "outside the norm," in which case Rae's unique perspective on Black womanhood fits the bill.

Additionally, broadcast television show creator and producer, Shonda Rhimes, had a meeting with Rae to learn about her additional show ideas. The two developed a show entitled, *I Hate LA Dudes* and pitched it to ABC.[80] While it did not get picked up by the network, Rae speaks highly in interviews about the great learning experience she had working with Rhimes.[81] Currently, Rae is working with veteran writer, actor, and television producer, Larry Wilmore, on a deal with HBO to bring a show in the spirit of *ABG* to the small screen.[82] However, others have reached out to Rae, and were not so lucky as she declined offers that did not complement her vision, allow her creative control, or allow her to keep the rights to her show.

## ANALYZING BMW DOERS WITH GENERIC DESCRIPTION

Generic criticism was used as the method of study for this rhetorical analysis. It served as the best way to identify and define the genre, or group, of Black

Millennial women entrepreneurs in the digital space. The goal of this rhetorical method is to "formulate theoretical constructs" about the characteristics of the genre.[83] In order for this to be a success, I first conducted general observation and researched Black Millennial women with career roots in the digital space that were entrepreneurs and experienced acclaim in mainstream media outlets. This is how Eubanks, Rae, and Robinson each emerged as BMWs who met all of the criteria. Eubanks was featured on the cover of *Black Enterprise* magazine, Rae has been offered television deals with cable networks and Robinson has performed at international televised events. Next, artifacts and background information about their careers were collected. All women had bodies of work available for free on the Internet, the majority of which are written or audiovisual interviews. Third, artifacts were analyzed to determine whether the three women shared similarities with their trails to success. Finally, organizing principles were determined for the genre of Black Millennial Women Digital Entrepreneurs (reported hereafter as BMW DoErs). The *o, r, and s* in *DoErs* was added to create a word representing the actions selected Black Millennial women have taken to make their entrepreneurial digital endeavors successful.

## CONNECTIONS BETWEEN EUBANKS, ROBINSON, AND RAE

### Creating Business Lanes on the Information Superhighway

All three women—Natasha Eubanks, Janelle Monae Robinson, and Issa Rae—were determined to not let others define their paths to success or dictate the heights they would soar to reach their destinies. By calling the shots with their passion projects, they created online communities. Their success and popularity came from loyal followings and visitors of their social media sites. In Robinson's case a mix of social media and underground performances led her following to purchase her albums and attend her concerts. Once these women independently found their own success, it served as confirmation they held the keys to their own futures. They would not need to depend on anyone else to build their brands or have their resumes precede them to obtain sponsorship, endorsements, or investments. Today news clips, Artists & Repertoire (A&R), or Human Resources (HR) are not the only gateways to reaching goals or financial gain.

### My Race and Gender are Real

All three women are aware of the roles race and gender play in society. Most importantly, they are astute to the injustices with portrayals and lack of diversity among representations of women of color in mainstream media. Eubanks began TheYBF to fill a void that left Black celebrities invisible from publications that provided photographs of stars. Robinson did not see many Black women representing her values and morals in popular culture and wanted to ensure she would be a role model for young women to follow. She demonstrates her commitment to inspiring young women to be themselves. Robinson uses herself as an example to show one does not have to take their clothes off to be confident or a star. Additionally, she represents the antithesis of the idea that one has to be a particular *mold* to hold membership in Black culture. Rae experienced being a Black girl with Jewish friends while growing up in Maryland and being the Black girl that "talked white" while attending school in California.[84] She recognized there were not images of corky, awkward Black girls and was determined to bring voice to her experience by starring in her own show.

## Knowledge is Power

Another thread each of the BMW DoErs shared was their enrollment in higher education. Upon graduation from high school, Robinson earned a scholarship and attended the American Academy of Dramatic Arts in New York City.[85] She dropped out when she realized her idea of success did not include standing in lines to compete for a slim number of roles for women of color on Broadway.[86] Instead, she was inspired to move to Atlanta, a place where she saw acts like Outkast were groomed to take the world by storm. Additionally, Eubanks and Rae both graduated from college.

During her undergraduate career, Rae created a show about being a Black student at Stanford University.[87] While it did not become an Internet hit, she continued following her passion and ultimately created *ABG* for her family and friends' enjoyment. It happened to be the project that received the most attention and led to her fame. Prior to *ABG* becoming a hit, Rae was contemplating attending business or law school.[88] Eubanks, on the other hand, graduated from college and attended law school with hopes to be a lobbyist.[89] While living in Washington, DC she now lobbies for advertisers to invest in her readership.

Higher education helped serve as institutions to help BMW DoErs learn more about their passions. For some, it became clear their institution would not play a role in the growth and development they desired to reach their dreams. Yet, for others, it exposed them to friendships and lessons that would aid in their journeys after finishing school. Whether directly or indirectly, higher education propelled BMW DoErs forward.

## Mother Knows Best

All three BMW DoErs have parents that influenced their careers. Robinson wears a black and white uniform whenever she is in the public eye as a way to pay homage to her parents—her mother a former custodian and father, a postal worker. Rae often speaks of her mother's support for her career. This could be attributed to the fact she was an aspiring director that now "lives her dream through Rae."[90] Eubanks knew she had no other choice than to be a successful risk-taker upon telling her mother she did not want to return to law school. Her family had professional backgrounds and was not familiar with the idea of starting a blog as a lucrative career move.[91] Eubanks also knew staying at home was not an option as her parents used tough love to help push her towards success.[92]

## *All* Black Girls Are Not the Same

Through their own art forms, each BMW used the digital space to show that Black women are not a monolithic group. Through Eubanks' use of humor and creative language to express a critical perspective towards the actions, attire, and work of Black celebrities, she provides a counter-discourse that is often invisible in commentaries of popular culture. In contemporary television, Black women are portrayed most commonly on reality shows. Television shows portraying women of color are often surrounding themes of women in relationships (family or romantic) with entertainers or athletes and wealth is often involved.[93] *ABG* reflects none of these characteristics. Through Rae's protagonist, J, she provides an avenue for audience members to connect to the sensibilities of a young Black corky, or *nerdy,* woman. The character, J works a dead end job and enjoys listening to and creating "ratchet" rap music in her spare time as a mode of escapism and therapy.[94]

Robinson's nonverbal communication, alone, speaks volumes and reflects her unique perspective of the world. In their text, *Gender Talk*, Beverly Guy-Sheftall and Johnetta Cole have a chapter entitled, "Personal is Political," which refers to the personal choices one makes in their daily lives that communicate loud messages, or *political* statements for society.[95] When Robinson wears her signature style of natural hair and classic black and white uniform, she is making a statement about the politics of women's bodies in popular culture.[96] In her speeches and interviews, she often emphasizes the importance of women not being objectified, and notes her efforts to have talent as the focal point of her presence and not attire.[97] Robinson also created a dance style mix of James Brown and her own moves, further differentiating herself from others. Her attire and demeanor is a sharp contrast from scantily clad video vixens and women performers that *entertain* audiences with their hypersexual activity.[98]

## Unbought and Unbossed

Like the slogan of the first Black female U.S. presidential hopeful, Shirley Chisholm, these BMWs cannot be bought, bribed, or bossed around! Eubanks, Robinson, and Rae value independence and creative control. The three women do not compromise their perspectives or work for others. They are not afraid to say *no* to offers that do not coincide with their beliefs or the brand they want to present to their audiences. Additionally, they value the integrity of their work and are not willing to compromise solely for financial gain. Robinson upholds her standards with actions such as requiring her potential business partners to learn her core values and read text like *The Big Moo* by Seth Godin.[99] Her commitment to maintaining her voice and created image keeps her protected from others who may try to recreate her based on ideas of who they think she should be. Similarly, Rae is just as adamant about maintaining her creative control of her work and potential partnerships.[100] The importance of defining oneself and maintaining creative control of their works is also reflective of Audre Lorde's famous quote, "If I didn't define myself for myself, I would be crunched into other people's fantasies for me and eaten alive."[101]

## Teamwork Makes the Dream Work

Despite not being willing to relinquish their power to the highest bidders, BMW DoErs are open to helping others' dreams come true. In true Millennial form, these women are collaborators. Eubanks highlights the accomplishments of other Black Millennial women in an array of industries on her blog, and sheds light on those underrepresented or ignored by media. In addition, Robinson's Wondaland Arts Society record label is a collective of "inventors" and creative artists.[102] Rae has signed on to executive produce other web series, such as *RoomieLoverFriends*. Like *ABG* it shares the stories of young Black adults of color.

## BMW DOERS CONTRIBUTION TO RHETORICAL STUDIES

Two pioneering scholars in Black rhetoric, Cummings and Daniel, suggest "there is a need to study the impact of factors such as age, education, caste, social class, and religion on specific aspects of Black Communication."[103] They also argue that many studies in Black communication have come from the perspectives of Black males who hang out on street corners and pool halls, as opposed to an array of diverse Black voices.[104] This research answers Cummings and Daniel's call for research by seeking to discover ways Black women in the Millennial generation use new media in multiple ways. Not only has social media served as a way for Eubanks, Robinson, and Rae to share their passions with the world, they have connected with followers that connect with their work. Hopefully more scholars will investigate the content and dynamics of other communities of color in the digital realm. The hope for this study was to not only identify Black Millennial Women Digital Entrepreneurs, but also to interpret, investigate, and shed light on innovative elements of Black communication dynamics. However, this body of work can also serve as an entrepreneurial business model.

## Dawn of a New Day of Equality

It is interesting to note in both Rae and Robinson's career journeys, they were sought after by Black male contemporary veterans in the music industry—Big Boi, Sean Combs, and Pharrell Williams. Each of the men embraced the BMW DoErs' individuality and allowed the ladies to stay true to their artistic vision and identities. In Robinson's case, both Big Boi and Combs were mentioned often when she discussed her road to success during interviews. For Rae, musician extraordinaire Pharrell Williams funded her second season of *Awkward Black Girl* and distributed her show on his YouTube channel, all while often praising her work.[105] This is a refreshing and new addition to rhetorical studies. Often in research about Black popular culture, there is an idea that if males are a part of a woman's career journey, it is a formula for her being controlled by the male gaze, or his desires for her image.

Additionally, these business partnerships show a new dawn may be on the horizon for healthy gender relations in business and art arenas. Hopefully more young women aspiring to enter the entertainment industry will know their self worth, value their truths, and not conform to the molds and ideas others have for their success. It appears that both Rae and Robinson are unapologetically themselves and exhibit a number of characteristics present in Black Feminism. Because of standing firm on their beliefs, new business models have been created by BMW DoErs that intersect race, age, class, gender, business, and the digital space in a way that has not been investigated before.

Gender roles and stereotypes are also challenged by the success of BMW DoErs, such as Eubanks' celebrity gossip blog. By gracing the cover of *Black Enterprise* magazine, a popular business magazine, Eubanks introduced to many a new viable and lucrative way to experience financial gain in the digital space. Previously, the perception of women *gossiping* was often viewed as a negative pastime. Furthermore, it would commonly be considered an oxymoron as a mode of a lucrative business model. A career in social media, let alone blogging about your favorite celebrity was foreign to many twenty years ago.

## FABULOUS, ELECTRIFYING BLACK GIRLS: DIGITAL ARCHITECTS OF THEIR DREAMS

Eubanks, Robinson, and Rae are representatives of a fleet of BMWs in the digital space, creating their own businesses, and making their own rules. They are also aware of perceptions others may have of their race and gender; however, they do not allow that to compromise their morals, values, or work. Staying true to their artistic goals and visions, while also staying loyal to their fan bases, they set a business model for entrepreneurs of tomorrow. Robinson would consider such bold, courageous, and talented women to be "Electric Ladies"[106] However, for the purposes of this rhetorical genre study, they are called Black Millennial Women Digital Entrepreneurs, or BMW DoErs. They are a small sample of many other BMWs with entrepreneurial spirits and creative business savvy. Smart, culturally astute, collaborative, and family oriented, they reflect the quintessential traits of their generation. Additionally, these women take pride in calling the shots for their careers and are not afraid to work hard for their dreams to come true.

*Going independent* is a popular slang term that refers to someone's plan to take a risk and serve as CEO of his or her own company. It also serves as a synonym for entrepreneurship, which is a growing trend in popular culture. In music, R&B singer Ashanti released her latest album, *Braveheart*, with music inspired by her journey of *going independent*.[107] After spending over ten years in the record industry, she decided to break the typical mold and turn down seven mainstream label offers by starting her own.[108] By distributing her album through pre-sales on iTunes, she experienced 28,000 sales in the first week.[109] In 2014, it is quite a remarkable accomplishment without the support of a major label. Additionally, her album debuted as number one on the U.S. Independent Charts and number two on Billboard's R&B charts.[110]

Other Black Millennial Women, like singer Solange Knowles, recently debuted her new record label, Saint Records. Singer Dondria adapted the tools of a business owner to market her singing abilities through social media. Instead of cutting a demo record and shopping it to interested distributors, she used a free digital platform to launch her music career. By uploading clips to YouTube showcasing her talents, she earned a record deal with So So Def Records.[111]

In the publishing world, public relations guru Arian Simone distributes her own magazine, *Fearless*, along with a series of e-books. She has selected the term "Lifestyle Entrepreneur" to describe her brand, and works to inspire others to live their dreams.[112] Also in the creative content and distribution arena, artists like Haj House have created web series, such as *Funnelcake Flowers and the Urban Chameleons*. The popular web show has turned into a one-woman play with performances at SxSW and across America on its roster so far.[113]

Other BMW DoErs, like Jasmin Goodman, have provided an online distribution platform, Project Blaq, to share the works of women like Rae and Haj. However, she did not leave their work in the digital space or limit it to Black web content. In the fall of 2013, Goodman created the first web-show festival in the southeast region of the United States. The ATL Webfest at Georgia Tech included screenings and workshops to educate content creators of ways to evolve and lucratively profit from their projects. With submissions from as far as Italy, Goodman conducted the majority of the publicity through social media and had over 100 in attendance for its inaugural year.[114]

Finally, this chapter cannot end without revisiting the industry that made the first self-made Black millionairess—hair care. If one were to google *Black hair blog* they would find an array of website options and video tutorial links. From viewing ways to create a wig, shampoo a new sew-in weave hairstyle, or care for *transitioning* hair to reading advice for those beginning a *loc* or natural hair journey, a new cyber friend, ready to offer advice is only a few keystrokes away.[115] Some Black women, like Curly Nikki Walton, have created large online brands and followings that have led to not only international exposure in television and magazines, but also a book deal. Walton and others are sought after as hair experts due to their cult followings in the digital space.

Additionally, BMW DoErs to watch in the hair arena are the founders of Techturized, Inc., "a hair care technology company that incorporates science and technology to revolutionize the way women interact with their hair, information and each other."[116] From pitch competitions for start-up businesses, social media campaigns, and donations, three recent Georgia Tech University graduates have earned over $200,000 for their company. A mobile app and the Miss Naturally Crowned Carolina Natural Hair Beauty Pageant are just a few of their ventures to celebrate hair locs.[117] With a passion to connect Black women, hair products, professional stylists, and personal hair stories through the digital space, they are embodying Madame C. J. Walker's legacy in the twenty-first century.

The new wave of BMW DoErs is blazing a path for younger Millennials and members of the next "generation Z" (born between 1994 and 2010) who yearn to carve their own careers.[118] Some business experts, like Dan Schawbel, believe Generation Z will be even more entrepreneurial than Millennials. It is most important to note BMW DoErs are communicating a message to future entrepreneurs that their goals are attainable, no matter their race, class, gender, age, or geographic location. Eubanks blogged, Robinson sang, and Rae directed, despite what the status quo may have been in their respective industries. They carried the pioneering spirits of Black Women Entrepreneurs of the past and remixed their business models with innovative tools of the future. By letting their fingers do the walking on the information superhighway, their bank accounts can now do great talking. Best of all, it is an exciting day to know gatekeepers are a thing of the past for anyone who yearns to have a dream fulfilled.

## NOTES

1. "griot," *Merriam-Webster*, accessed March 15, 2014, http://www.merriam-webster.com/dictionary/griot.
2. Daryl Dance, *Honey Hush! An Anthology Of African American Women's Humor* (New York: Norton, 1998).
3. Alexa A. Harris, "Diary of a Black Female Millennial Blogger: A Discourse Analysis of theybf.com" (PhD diss., Howard University, 2011).
4. Paul Taylor and Scott Keeter, *Millennials. Confident. Connected. Open to Change* (Washington: The Pew Center, 2010), 4.
5. Ibid.
6. Ibid., 1.
7. Ibid., 10.
8. Lisa Orrell, *Millennials Incorporated: The Big Business Of Recruiting, Managing and Retaining The World's New Generation of Young Professionals* (Deadwood: Wyatt-Mackenzie, 2007), 27.
9. Ibid., 48.
10. "Young Invincible Policy Brief: New Poll Finds More Than Half of Millennials Want to Start Businesses," *Ewing Marion Kauffman Foundation*, 2011, accessed February 12, 2014, http://www.kauffman.org/~/media/kauffman_org/research%20reports%20and%20covers/2011/11/millennials_study.pdf.
11. Jack Nadel, "Experienced Entrepreneurs and Business Leaders: Millennials Need Our Help." *Huffington Post*, February 6, 2014, accessed February 8, 2014, http://www.huffingtonpost.com/jack-nadel/experienced-entrepreneurs_b_4740751.html.
12. Taylor and Keeter, *Millennials. Confident. Connected. Open to Change.*
13. T. J. Becker, "Enter, The Millennials," *Chicago Tribune*, January 31, 1999, accessed August 8, 2010.
14. Scott Beale, *Millennial Manifesto* (Collierville: InstantPublisher, 2003).
15. "The World's Billionaires: #22 Mark Zuckerberg," *Forbes*, accessed February 10, 2014, http://www.forbes.com/profile/mark-zuckerberg/.
16. Elana Joelle Hendler, "Millennial Entrepreneurs-Brand Ethics Intrinsic to Brand Identity," *The Huffington Post*, December 10, 2013, accessed January 28, 2014, http://www.huffingtonpost.com/elana-joelle-hendler/millennial-entrepreneurs_b_4420303.html.
17. Orrell, *Millennials Incorporated.*
18. Ibid.,19.
19. Ibid.
20. Taylor and Keeter, *Millennials. Confident. Connected. Open to Change.*
21. Ibid.
22. Ibid., 29.
23. Ibid.
24. Orrell, *Millennials Incorporated.*
25. Beverly Daniel Tatum, *Why are All the Black Kids Sitting Together in the Cafeteria?* (New York: Basic Books, 2003).
26. Pew Research Center, Millennials a Portrait of Generation Next: Confident Connected Open to Change. February 2010. http://www.pewsocialtrends.org/files/2010/10/millennials-confident-connected-open-to-change.pdf.
27. Dominique Apollon, "Don't Call Them Post-Racial: Millennials' Attitudes on Race, Racism and Key Systems in Our Society," *Applied Research Center*, June 2011, accessed January 28, 2014, http://www.racialequitytools.org/resourcefiles/ARC_Millennials_

Report_June_2011.pdf.

28. Pepper Miller, *Black Still Matters in Marketing: Why Increasing Your Cultural IQ About Black America is Critical to Your Company and Your Brand* (Ithaca: Paramount Publishing Group, 2012), 10; she also notes *The 2009 IMAGES USA Study* about Black Millennials.

29. See other companies focused on Black Millennials, *GlobalHue, IMAGES USA, Lattimer Communications*

30. "Nick History," *Everything Nick: The Home for News About Nick*, accessed March 4, 2014, http://web.archive.org/web/20050127084900/http://www.nick.com/all_nick/everything_nick/history_home.jhtml.

31. A two-hour time slot catered to families on the ABC network from 1989–2000.

32. Popular shows in the 1980s and 1990s showing diverse family dynamics. Broadcast networks aired shows such as *227* (NBC), *Amen* (NBC), *The Cosby Show* (NBC), *Family Matters* (ABC), *The Fresh Prince of Bel Air* (NBC), *Full House* (ABC), *Ghostwriter* (PBS), *Gilmore Girls* (WB/CW), *Hangin' With Mr. Cooper* (ABC), *Married With Children* (FOX), *Moesha* (UPN), *My Two Dads* (NBC), *Roseanne* (ABC), *The Simpsons* (FOX), *Sister Sister* (ABC/WB), *South Central* (FOX), *Thea* (ABC), *The Wayans Brothers* (WB), and *Will and Grace* (NBC), showing an array of family and community dynamics.

33. Alexa A. Harris, "Diary of a Black Female Millennial Blogger: A Discourse Analysis of *theybf.com.*"

34. Ananda Mitra, "Using Blogs to Create Cybernetic Space: Examples from People of Indian Origin," *Convergence* 14, no. 1 (2008): 457–72; Kaye D. Sweester, Guy J. Golan, and Wayne Wanta, "Intermedia Agenda Setting in Television, Advertising, and Blogs during the 2004 Election," *Mass Communication & Society* 11, no. 2 (2008): 197–216.

35. Juliet E. K. Walker, "Black Entrepreneurship: An Historical Inquiry," *Essays in Economic and Business History* 1 (1983), 37–55, accessed January 12, 2014, http://www.thebhc.org/publications/BEHprint/v012/p0037-p0055.pdf.

36. Henry Louis Gates. "Who Was The First Black Millionairess?" *The Root*, June 24, 2013, accessed March 14, 2014, http://www.theroot.com/articles/history/2013/06/who_was_the_first_Black_millionairess.4.html.

37. See film adaptations from books by Black women authors such as *Waiting to Exhale* (1995) by Terry McMillan, *Their Eyes Are Watching God* (2005) by Zora Neale Hurston, and *Beloved* (1998) by Toni Morrison.

38. T. Robinson, "Young Entrepreneurs Position Themselves to Dominate the Business Landscape," *Black Enterprise*, January 2010, 94.

39. Kim Elle, *Interview with Blogger Natasha of Young, Black and Fabulous*, 2006, accessed February 2011, http://www.associatedContent.com/article/84126/interview_with_blogger_natasha_of_young.html?cat=49.

40. Ibid.

41. Vanessa E. Jones, "Believe The Hype: What's Up with Beyonce, Cee-Lo, or Tracee Ellis Ross? Gossip Blogs Devoted to Black Celebrities Tell All," *The Boston Globe*, June 12, 2007, accessed November 4, 2010, http://www.boston.com/yourlife/articles/2007/06/12/believe_the_hype_1181615955/.

42. Robinson, "Young Entrepreneurs Position Themselves to Dominate the Business Landscape."

43. Ibid., 94.

44. Ibid.

45. Caroline Clark, "Interview with Natasha Eubanks for Black Enterprise," 2012, accessed March 4, 2014, http://www.youtube.com/watch?v=DmCkw1IiLrQ.

46. Ibid.

47. Geneva Smitherman-Donaldson, *Black Talk: Words and Phrases from the Hood to the Amen Corner* (Boston: Houghton Mifflin, 1994), 100.

48. Harris, "Diary of a Black Female Millennial Blogger: A Discourse Analysis of *theybf.com.*"

49. Natasha Eubanks, "Live Blog: Ybf, Trey Songz, Jada Pinkett Smith & Carol's Daughter[s] Toast Women At Essence Fest Pop Up Store!," *theybf.com,* July 3, 2010, accessed

November 4, 2010, http://theybf.com/2010/07/03/live-blog-ybf-trey-songz-jada-pinkett-smith-carols-daughter-toast-women-at-essence-fest-p.

50. Natasha Eubanks, "YBF Giveaway: Rachel Roy Clothes!," October 12, 2009, accessed September 12, 2010, http://theybf.com/2009/10/12/ybf-giveaway-rachel-roy-clothes.

51. Robinson, "Young Entrepreneurs Position Themselves to Dominate the Business Landscape."

52. Caroline Clark, "Interview with Natasha Eubanks for Black Enterprise."

53. Robinson, "Young Entrepreneurs Position Themselves to Dominate the Business Landscape."

54. Molly Hagan, "Janelle Monae," *Current Biography* (Amenia, New York: H.W. Wilson/Grey House Publishing, 2013), accessed March 10, 2014, http://www.hwwilsoninprint.com/pdf/CB_May_pgs.pdf; Lyrics from Janelle Monae Robinson's "Q.U.E.E.N." featuring Erykah Badu, Wondaland/Bad Boy records, distributed by Atlantic Records, 2013.

55. Rodney Carmichael, "How Janelle Monae Charmed Diddy," *Creative Loafing Atlanta*, August 13, 2008, accessed March 10, 2014, http://clatl.com/atlanta/how-janelle-monandaacutee-charmed-diddy/Content?oid=1274781.

56. Ibid.

57. Dorian Lynskey, "Janelle Monae: Sister from Another Planet," *The Guardian*, August 26, 2010, accessed March 9, 2014, http://www.theguardian.com/music/2010/aug/26/janelle-monae-sister-another-planet.

58. Hagan, "Janelle Monae."

59. Carmichael, "How Janelle Monae Charmed Diddy."

60. Ibid.

61. Ibid.

62. Nicole Frehsee, "Hot Sci-Fi Beyonce: Q & A With Janelle Monae," *Rolling Stone*, August 28, 2012, accessed March 4, 2014, http://www.rollingstone.com/music/news/hot-sci-fi-beyonce-a-q-a-with-janelle-monae-19691231; Ryan Dombal, "Janelle Monae Talks Robots, Diddy, and Her Genre-Bursting New Album," *Pitchfork*, May 17, 2010, accessed March 4, 2014, http://pitchfork.com/news/38754-janelle-monae-talks-robots-diddy-and-her-genre-bursting-new-album/.

63. Hagan, "Janelle Monae."

64. Ibid.

65. Emily Zemler, "Janelle Monae's Autobiographical Past," *MTV*, June 21, 2011, accessed March 3, 2014, http://www.mtvhive.com/2011/06/21/rock-lit-janelle-monae/.

66. "Q & A: Janelle Monae-Road Trip," *Soul Train*, September 18, 2012, accessed March 10, 2014, http://soultrain.com/2012/09/18/qa-janelle-monae-road-trip/.

67. "Q & A Janelle Monae on new album, Prince, Therapy," *Miami Herald*, November 18, 2013, accessed March 10, 2014, http://www.miamiherald.com/2013/11/18/3755746/qa-janelle-monae-on-new-album.html.

68. Sofia M. Fernandez, "P.Diddy: I Wasn't Such A Control Freak With Janelle Monae, *The Hollywood Reporter*," February 9, 2011, accessed March 9, 2014, http://www.hollywoodreporter.com/news/p-diddy-janelle-monae-grammys-97805.

69. David Greenwald, "Janelle Monae's 'Q.u.e.e.n.' Rules the Funk with Erykah Badu: Listen," April 22, 2013 accessed March 3, 2014, http://www.billboard.com/articles/columns/the-juice/1559107/janelle-monaes-queen-rules-the-funk-with-erykah-badu-listen.

70. Tami Reed, "Singer Janelle Monae New Face of Sonos," *Rolling Out*. October 5, 2012, accessed March 3, 2014, http://rollingout.com/music/singer-janelle-monae-new-face-of-sonos/#_.

71. Chris Hernandez, "KSHB Kansas City. From Quindaro to the White House, Janelle Monae Shares Her Success Story," November 25, 2011, accessed March 22, 2014, http://www.kshb.com/news/local-news/singer-janelle-monae-returns-home-with-a-message.

72. Janelle Monae's Myspace page, https://myspace.com/janellemonae/music/songs.

73. Awkward Black Girls homepage with web-episodes, http://awkwardBlackgirl.com.

74. Vanessa Hua, "Awkward Stage: A Web Sitcom's Quirky Black Heroine is Poised for Takeoff," *Stanford Magazine*, May/June 2012, accessed February 13, 2014, http://alumni.stanford.edu/get/page/magazine/article/?article_id=53330.

75. Ibid.
76. Ibid.
77. Emma Gray, "Issa Rae, Creator of 'Awkward Black Girl,' Felt Like Her Voice was Missing from Pop Culture-So Here's What She Did," *Huffington Post*, November 5, 2011, accessed March 9, 2014, http://www.huffingtonpost.com/2013/11/05/issa-rae-awkward-Black-girl_n_4209313.html.
78. "Exclusive Interview With Issa Rae: The Awkward Black Girl," Necolebitchie.com, June 21, 2012, accessed March 13, 2014, http://necolebitchie.com/2012/06/exclusive-interview-with-issa-rae-the-awkard-Black-girl/.
79. Ibid.
80. Myeisha Essex, "ABC Passes on Issa Rae and Shonda Rhimes' Comedy Series 'I Hate L.A. Dudes' [Exclusive]," *Hello Beautiful*, August 9, 2013, accessed March 3, 2014, http://hellobeautiful.com/2013/08/09/abc-passes-on-issa-rae-shonda-rhimes-comedy-series-i-hate-l-a-dudes-exclusive/.
81. Ibid.
82. Nellie Andreeva, "HBO Developing Comedy Series from Larry Wilmore & Issa Rae to Star Rae," *Deadline*, August 6, 2013, accessed January 28, 2014, http://www.deadline.com/2013/08/hbo-developing-comedy-series-from-larry-wilmore-issa-rae-to-star-rae/.
83. Sonja Foss, *Rhetorical Criticism Exploration and Practice* (Long Grove: Waveland Press, 2008).
84. Issa Rae, "Black Folk Don't Like to be Told They're Not Black," *The Huffington Post*, August 4, 2011, accessed February 9, 2014, http://www.huffingtonpost.com/issa-rae/Black-folk-dont-movie_b_912660.html.
85. "The Griot's 100: Janelle Monae, of-the-Moment Artist with Timeless Appeal," *The Griot*, February 22, 2011, accessed November 4, 2013, http://thegrio.com/2011/02/22/2011-janelle-monae/.
86. "Q & A: Janelle Monae-Road Trip," *Soul Train*, September 18, 2012, accessed March 10, 2014, http://soultrain.com/2012/09/18/qa-janelle-monae-road-trip/.
87. "'Awkward Black Girl' Creator Issa Rae Talks About Her Web series and Television Ambitions," *Blackbook*, March 7, 2013, accessed January 25, 2014, http://www.bbook.com/awkward-Black-girl-creator-issa-rae-talks-about-her-webseries-and-television-ambitions/.
88. Gray, "Issa Rae, Creator of 'Awkward Black Girl,' Felt Like Her Voice Was Missing From Pop Culutre-So Here's What She Did."
89. Clark, "Interview with Natasha Eubanks for Black Enterprise."
90. "Exclusive Interview With Issa Rae," Necolebitchie.com.
91. Clark, "Interview with Natasha Eubanks for Black Enterprise."
92. Ibid.
93. See *Basketball Wives* (VH1), *Love and Hip Hop: Atlanta* (VH1) and *Love & Hip Hop: New York* (VH1), *The Real Housewives of Atlanta* (Bravo).
94. See episodes and more information about *Awkward Black Girl* on Issa Rae's Homepage, http://www.issarae.com.
95. Beverly Guy-Sheftall and Johnetta B. Cole, *Gender Talk* (New York: One World/Ballantine, 2003).
96. Hagan, "Janelle Monae."
97. Ibid.
98. Lola Ogunnaike, Janelle Monae Cover Story, *Essence Magazine*, May 2013, accessed February 4, 2014, http://www.essence.com/2013/04/02/janelle-monae-essence-may-cover/.
99. Zelmer, "Janelle Monae's Autobiographical Past."
100. "'Awkward Black Girl' Creator Issa Rae Talks About Her Web series and Television Ambitions," *Blackbook*.
101. Denise McFall, "Women's Research and Resource Center: Marking 25 Years of Changing the World Through Feminist Intellectual Thought," *Spelman Messenger*, Winter/Spring 2006, 12.
102. Issa Rae homepage, http://www.issarae.com.

103. Melbourne Cummings and Jack Daniel, "The Study of African American Rhetoric in Golden," in James L. Golden et al. (Eds.), *The Rhetoric of Western Thought: From the Mediterranean World to the Global Setting* (Dubuque: Kendall/Hunt, 2007), 457.

104. Ibid.

105. "'Awkward Black Girl' Creator Issa Rae Talks About Her Web series and Television Ambitions," *Blackbook.*

106. See *Electric Lady* album by Janelle Monae, Wondaland Arts Society/Bad Boy records, distributed by Atlantic Records, September 6, 2013.

107. Brad Wete and Ericka Ramirez, "Ashanti Gives Five Craziest Murder Inc Moments, Bosses Up With 'Braveheart' Album: Watch Here," *Billboard*, March 14, 2014, accessed March 20, 2014,

108. http://www.billboard.com/articles/columns/the-juice/5937510/ashanti-gives-five-craziest-murder-inc-moments-bosses-up-with.

109. Keith Caulfield, "Rick Ross Rules with Fifth No. 1 Album On Billboard 200," *Billboard*, March 12, 2014, accessed March 20, 2014, http://www.billboard.com/biz/articles/news/chart-alert/5930455/rick-ross-rules-with-fifth-no-1-album-on-billboard-200.

110. Ibid.

111. Jayson Rodriquez, "Jermaine Dupri Relaunches So So Def with Dondria: Producer Goes Independent with Dallas Singer He Discovered On Youtube," *MTV*, February 19, 2010, accessed February 20, 2014, http://www.mtv.com/news/articles/1632277/jermaine-dupri-relaunches-so-so-def-with-dondria.jhtml.

112. See Arian Simone's website, http://ariansimone.com.

113. See Haj House's web channel, http://tickles.tv/.

114. See website for ATL Webfest, *atlwebfest.com.*

115. Transitioning is a term used in the natural hair community that refers to the process of growing out a hair relaxer to embrace natural hair locs. Two hair textures, natural and relaxed, are present, thus the hair is "transitioning" from one texture to another.

116. See Techturized, Inc websites, techturized.tumblr.com, madameyou.com, and http://www.myavana.com.

117. Ibid.

118. Dan Schawbel, "Why 'Gen Z' May Be More Entrepreneurial Than 'Gen Y'" *Entrepreneur*, February 3, 2014, accessed February 10, 2014, http://www.entrepreneur.com/article/231048.

# BIBLIOGRAPHY

Beale, Scott. *Millennial Manifesto*. Collierville: InstantPublisher, 2003.

Cole, Johnnetta B., and Beverly Guy-Sheftall. *Gender Talk: The Struggle for Women's Equality in African American Communities.* New York: One World/Ballantine, 2003.

Cummings, Melbourne, and Jack Daniels. "The Study of African American Rhetoric in Golden." In *The Rhetoric Of Western Thought: From The Mediterranean World To The Global Setting,* edited by James L. Golden, Goodwin F. Berquist, William E. Coleman, and J. Michael Sproule, 443–61. Dubuque: Kendall/Hunt, 2007.

Dance, Daryl. *Honey Hush! An Anthology Of African American Women's Humor.* New York: Norton, 1998.

Foss, Sonja. *Rhetorical Criticism Exploration and Practice*. Long Grove: Waveland Press, 2008.

Miller, Pepper. *Black Still Matters in Marketing: Why Increasing Your Cultural IQ About Black America is Critical to Your Company and Your Brand*. Ithaca: Paramount Publishing Group, 2012.

Orrell, Lisa. *Millennials Incorporated: The Big Business of Recruiting, Managing And Retaining The World's New Generation Of Young Professionals.* Deadwood: Wyatt-Mackenzie, 2007.

Tatum, Beverly D. *Why are All the Black Kids Sitting Together in the Cafeteria?* New York: Basic Books, 2003.

*Chapter Thirteen*

# The Classification of Black Celebrity Women in Cyberspace

## Andre Nicholson

Cyberspace may be one of the only forms of media that allows people to determine, define, and redefine the way they want to be portrayed and/or identified. Through this medium, unlike with others, an individual has more control over what he or she wants to say, write, or display. Although cyberspace is also a breeding ground for an exaggeration of the truth or untruth about people, the medium allows for people to combat those untruths in a manner that is swift and appropriate for them. Cyberspace, better known as the Internet, also allows people to be generators of content versus mere consumers. When people have control over the text and images that define them, it is possible that a certain level of satisfaction is achieved through the use of this technology, therefore drawing them back for continued use.

In the past, the images that have been portrayed in media through platforms such as television and print have not always been the most flattering, or even the most accurate portrayals of certain races and genders. Scholars such as Patricia Hill Collins and bell hooks have paved a road for acknowledging and understanding how Black women, in particular, have been historically stereotyped and represented in the media. The purpose of this chapter is to explore and understand the way Black women are classified in cyberspace, particularly on social networks. Also, this research aims to identify whether these portrayals are similar to the way Black women have been historically classified in other media or whether the participatory nature of social networks has elevated Black women into another, more flattering, classification. For the purpose of the current research, classification is defined as systematically placing Black women into categories.

It is important to recognize the representations of Black women have expanded from past to present; however, the content of these images or characters has not. The reality is that images have simply been rebranded to fit modern day culture. For example, "The remnants of the foundational Jezebel, Mammy, Matriarch, and Welfare Mother images of Black womanhood remain today, as exemplified by similar, yet more sexually explicit scripts that include the Freak, Gold Digger, Diva, and Dyke."[1] Dionne Stephens and Layli Phillips suggest these representations are more than simple visual images of people and should be discussed in terms of sexual scripts.[2] The sexual scripts that represent Black women stem from negative stereotypes that have been in existence for decades. More current representations of Black women in the media include eight scripts that are reflections and adoptions of youth culture: The Diva, Gold Digger, Freak, Dyke, Gangster Bitch, Sister Savior, Earth Mother, and Baby Mama.[3] These scripts are problematic in that: (1) they reinforce how Black women have learned to view themselves; and (2) it reinforces how others, both inside and outside their race and gender, have come to view Black women.[4] People have come to recognize these messages and images through the traditional mass media, such as print, radio, and television. These channels of media use a one-way mode of communication. The messages and images transmitted to the mass audience are done so by one individual or entity to many different audiences. New media such as the Internet, on the other hand, uses a two-way line of communication in that it allows for both senders and receivers of messages to interact with each other through virtual responses. This two-way engagement could provide an opportunity for groups that feel misrepresented, based on their race or gender, to define or redefine how they would like to be classified and identified to the world. This research seeks to explore voices that are often ignored in scholarship about the practices of underrepresented groups and their use of social media. Jane Rhodes reports, "Women of color often fall through the cracks, unless a deliberate effort is made to study them as subjects, audiences, and producers of mass communication."[5] This is especially true of "mass communication research that has done little more than document the absence of African American women in the media."[6]

## THE MASS MEDIA'S INFLUENCE

The mass media serves many purposes. One of its primary functions is to offer consumers information on topics that may be unknown.[7] In this sense, the media acts as a knowledge provider. The power yielded by media can influence and have an immediate or long-term effect on its audience. Viewers can develop an understanding of certain issues from various media perspectives, instead of having limited exposure to these issues based on minimal outlets sources.[8] This is problematic because one presentation may or may not be the most accurate. Robert Entman suggests that when people do not have interaction with certain groups, they use media messages and images to draw conclusions about those people.[9] When the presentations of certain races or genders are one-dimensional and demeaning, it can be detrimental to how others perceive them.

Media images are constantly recycled, which leads to limited portrayals and perpetuated stereotypes within the majority of content shown to viewers. Jennifer Pozner argues on a larger scale, these images can be used to justify racist treatment toward individuals and institutions as a whole.[10] Rhodes states that mainstream press has portrayed Black women, in particular, in a stereotypical fashion that is detrimental.[11] With mass media being so multifaceted, the stereotypical images of Black women are not restricted to one medium. The same images you find in television can be found in social media. When studying images of Black women in cyberspace—as one of the newer media forms—it is helpful to consider how this group has historically been presented in other popular media. This helps to understand any evolution, or lack thereof. Furthermore, it can reveal which images have managed to cross mediums. Before turning our attention to cyberspace, it would be beneficial to first review stereotypical images of Black women and their presence in other media. This will provide a context for our discussion of Black women and social media.

## Stereotypes and Sexual Scripts

In studying the stereotypes that have been put forth about Black women in the media, one has to contemplate how and where these presentations develop. Robin Means Coleman suggests the images of Black women in traditional media have often been misrepresented in order to paint a particular picture.[12] Social Darwinism, a theory by Charles Darwin, suggests that the African race is lowest on the hierarchy of humans in terms of intelligence, health, and civility.[13] White males are considered to be at the highest end of human beings and those of African heritage are considered to be closer to the animal kingdom.[14] George Cuvier, a scientist with an expertise in zoology, examined the dead body of a young African woman named Saarah Baartman, from the Khoikhoi tribe in Africa. Baartman later became known as The Hottentot Venus.[15] The conclusions that Cuvier drew were in comparison of Baartman's body to orangutans and their mating habits. His findings were used as the foundation for sexual scripts in which Black women have been labeled, as wild, sexually uninhibited, and exotic.[16] In this sense, "Sarah became the bedrock of African female sexuality, reinforcing the exotic, animal image that separated people of African descent from Whites."[17] Understanding the pathology White males have used to define and present Black women to the world through mass media could assist consumers to separate the perception from the reality. Such knowledge can also help us understand some of the long-standing sexual scripts about Black women.

According to Collins, the Jezebel is the hypersexual woman who uses her sex appeal to gain attention and material possessions. This long-standing sexual stereotype was used to justify the dehumanization and objectification of slave women by slave masters for their sexual gratification. On the opposite end of the spectrum is the image of the asexual being known as Mammy. The Mammy is a caregiver and domestic servant to the White family. She is conditioned to put her White family's needs before her own or those of her family. On the other hand, the image of the Welfare Mother suggests that African-American women bear children without any concern for the financial or emotional burden it places on them or society. The Welfare Mother is content with birthing children and collecting government assistance.[18] There is also the image of the controlling, angry female who does not need a man beyond using him to have a child. The image of the Matriarch portrays African-American women as dominating, independent, and emasculating toward their male counterparts.[19]

## Limited Portrayals of Blacks on Television

Oftentimes, media executives' standards of Black people are that they should fit into one framework. They are not allowed to be multidimensional outside of those established frameworks. Janette Dates and Carolyn Stroman suggest that Black people are usually portrayed in two ways: financially comfortable in the middle class, educated, and employed; or as a criminal, uneducated, and poor.[20] Unfortunately, there are often limited images outside of such stereotypes. One has to wonder the effect these images have on the race and gender of those portrayed. This is especially true since these images have managed to travel throughout television, even within new types of programming that have emerged—such as reality television.

Reality television (RTV) has become a growing genre of television programming. Through the use of non-actors, RTV is programming that attempts to capture participants in their natural lives without scripted material, as the name implies. The portrayal of people in these programs continues to perpetuate stereotypes originally presented in fictional programming. Scholars who have studied RTV suggest the programming reinforces stereotypes rather than challenges them.[21] Black women on RTV are often assumed to represent an entire race and gender. Due to their actions in these programs, presentations can be harmful to the perception others have of them.[22]

Programs such as the Oxygen's *Bad Girls Club*, Bravo's *The Real Housewives of Atlanta*, and VH1's *Basketball Wives* offer viewers a full episode of neck rolling, finger snapping, and, oftentimes, physical altercations. The

RTV formula has proven to be successful, as each of the shows has aired for numerous seasons. But success and ratings do not automatically equate to quality and fair images. For example, Siobhan Smith's research on BET's program *College Hill* suggests Black women were portrayed more negatively than Black men on the RTV program.[23] However, these negative presentations continue to add to the reinforcement and stigma of common stereotypes such as the *Angry Black woman*.

In addition to scripted and unscripted television, music videos (most often aired on television) also present one-dimensional presentations of Black women. Hip hop is a genre of music that developed out of youth culture.[24] The genre addresses adolescents' concerns and beliefs and has therefore become quite popular among that population. Rap music, a form of hip hop, often includes videos that objectify women and present them as mere body parts for the consumption of male desires.[25] These women have come to be known as the Video Vixen and they fulfill the new sexual scripts of the Diva, Gold Digger, Freak, Dyke, Gangster Bitch, Sister Savior, Earth Mother, and Baby Mama.[26] Stephens and Phillips describe these new sexual scripts as such:

> Divas are viewed as "having an attitude," where they see themselves as someone to be worshiped and adored. It is the attention they receive that is important. Sexually they are sultry or tempting, but never explicit. Divas select men based on how their achievements can enhance what she already has. A Gold Digger is a woman who explicitly seeks material and economic rewards above all else, and is willing to trade sex for it. Where trading social status for sex describes the Diva, it is the Gold Digger who trades sex for a harder currency. A Freak is sexually aggressive and wild, a woman who simply loves to have sex without any emotional attachment. Where Freaks have sex with other women and allow men to watch or join in, Dykes do not let men have any role in their sexual interactions. However, unlike the Dyke, Gangster Bitches do not challenge the pervasive patriarchy or sexism. In fact, they indicate this through the valuing of men as partners in their struggle for daily survival in urban American culture.[27]

Unlike the other scripts described above, the Sister Savior and Earth Mother did not evolve from male involvement. For these women, the source of their decision and self-worth came from a higher existence such as church or some spiritual framework, not the hip hop culture. Although the Earth Mother does have a presence in the popular culture, she is not defined by it. The last script, the Baby Mama encompasses all four of the foundational images discussed earlier—Jezebel, Mammy, Welfare Mother, and Matriarch. This script glorifies single motherhood and is not viewed as a negative.[28] Each of these images are communicated and reinforced in media, which can impact Black women's experiences.

## Engagement with Social Networks

A benefit of online social networks is that it allows users to create their own reality, unlike traditional media. Rather than being restricted to the images created by others, social networks allow people to control their own representations. Social media represents one of the world's largest vehicles for interaction that permits people to share stories and experiences with one another through its application.[29] It delivers information via the web by people who intend to engage in communication. Damian Ryan and Calvin Jones offer the following definition for social media:

> The umbrella term for web-based software and services that allow users to come together online and exchange, discuss, communicate and participate in any form of social interaction. That interaction can encompass text, audio, video and other media, individually or in any combination. It can involve the generation of new content; the recommendation of and sharing of existing content; reviewing and rating products, services and brands; discussing the hot topics of the day; pursuing hobbies, interests and passions; sharing experience and expertise—in fact, almost anything that can be distributed and shared through digital channels is fair game.[30]

As the definition points out, any digital format can be incorporated into social media communication, allowing participants' unlimited engagement. Solis and Breakenridge suggest social media is anything that uses the Internet to facilitate conversations.[31] This engagement offers those who may not otherwise have a voice in traditional media a carved out space online to define who they want to be and how they want to be perceived.

A 2012 report on social media by Nielsen states, "social media and social networking are no longer in their infancy. Today, social networking is truly a global phenomenon."[32] Although Facebook and Twitter continue to be among the most popular social networks, Pinterest emerged as one of the most used social media sites in 2012. The site allows users to post images, videos, and other objects for others to see. It boasted the largest year-over-year increase in both unique audience and time spent of any social network across all platforms such as PC, mobile web, and apps.[33] The report states women use Pinterest more than males across all platforms. Similar to Pinterest is Instagram, which also allows users to post images and videos in order to connect with others. More than half of Instagram users visit the site once a day and 35 percent visit on multiple occasions throughout the day.[34] One of the features of several social networking sites is the ability to follow celebrities. However, personally knowing a person is still a significant factor when users decide to connect with someone through social media.[35]

In the Pew Research Center's recent report on African Americans and Technology, they found that 98 percent of Black women, eighteen to twenty-nine years old, use the Internet followed by 92 percent of thirty to thirty-nine year olds. Also, nearly three out of four Black women use at least one social networking site.[36] This report suggests Black women are using the Internet, and more specifically social networks, as much, if not more, than men and other races. Their use extends the two-way line of communication they can have online and lack through traditional media. This engagement opens a path for Black women, as well as others, to write their own scripts and use the platform to change the sexual scripts that have been historically presented in the media. Research can reveal whether Black women have used the social media landscape as a platform to do just that. Is it possible that a balance of images and messages presented through social networks can have a counter effect to the negative stereotypes that have been the standard in other media forms for so long? Sue Jewell suggests that without a more holistic and accurate reflection of Black women in the media, they will continue to be maligned.[37]

## METHODOLOGY

This research seeks to answer the question: How are Black women classified on image based social media websites? In order to do so, I examine two social media websites—Instagram and Pinterest. The purpose of the study is to examine whether Black women are classified in a particular way in cyberspace and does that classification offer new scripts through cyberspace communities. Gerald Schoening and James Anderson refer to this community-based approach as Social Action Media Studies.[38] This theoretical approach outlines six premises that will frame the analysis: (1) the meaning that people receive is not from reading or viewing a message itself, but from their own interpretive processes; (2) meaning from media messages is produced actively by audiences; (3) meanings shift often as individuals use different media; (4) meanings may vary depending on the person, however, it is a community activity; (5) the actions we take toward media and the meaning that arises from those actions are based on social interaction; and (6) researchers temporarily become part of the community they study.

Cyberspace obviously covers all aspects of the Internet; therefore, for the purpose of this study only two social media sites were examined. The sites were selected based on recent social media research by Nielsen and the Pew Internet & American Life Project. According to those reports, although Facebook still remains the top used social media site, both Pinterest and Instagram are among the most used social media sites by Internet users as well.[39] These two sites, in particular, are based on images that people post. For this reason, each was selected for this analysis, as the aim was to understand how users view and relate to images of Black women online.

Pinterest is defined as "a tool for discovering things you love, and doing those things in real life . . . we've helped millions of people pick up new hobbies, find their style and plan life's important projects. Pinterest is a tool for collecting and organizing the things that inspire you."[40] The social media site allows users to *Pin* specific images they like so they can reference them at a later time Users can also comment on images posted by others. The site also states the importance of expressing who you really are versus accumulating lots of followers. Another popular, social networking site is Instagram, ". . . a fun and quirky way to share your life with friends through a series of pictures. Snap a photo with your mobile phone, then select a filter to transform the image into a memory to keep around forever."[41] The image sharing website began as a mobile based application that allowed users to upload pictures through the use of their cell phone or digital device such as a tablet. Today, users can also access the site using a computer. The site is also compatible with other popular sites such as Facebook, Twitter, and Flickr (another photo-sharing site).[42] According to the Pew study more than half (57 percent) of the people who use Instagram, visit the site at least once a day and 35 percent visit it several times a day.[43] For Black female celebrities in the current study who have profiles on Instagram, it is a great way for their fans/followers to see images of them and make comments. For this study, I analyzed comments made in reference to images posted on the Pintrest and Instagram pages of four famous Black women.

In order to identify four popular, Black women in the public spotlight, I began with a Google search with the terms *Most Searched Black Female.* The search results provided several pages of links to articles. However, many did not provide information about the most searched Black female. I then randomly looked at ten of the articles and compared the names of the women who appeared the most on those lists. There were four celebrities who consistently appeared among the most searched Black females: singer, Beyoncé [Knowles/Carter][44]; rap artist, Nicki Minaj; former talk show host and now media mogul, Oprah Winfrey; and singer Rihanna (Fenty). All four women are well-known entertainers who generate massive interest online. Of course their popularity and success is due largely in part to their careers. Yet, their online personas, through images, could also have an impact on the public's opinion. For this reason, examining their use of popular social media sites is research worthy. The Google search results also revealed Kim Kardashian as being a name that showed up on each list. However, since this research focuses on Black women, as she is not classified as such, she was excluded from the analysis.

User comments on Instagram and Pinterest served as the data corpus for the analysis. It was important to examine an equal number of posts from each celebrity's profile page for the validity of the study. This helped with obtaining a complete picture of how followers viewed these Black women, which was a goal of the study. In order to analyze comments, the images from each celebrity's page had to be selected. This was a challenging selection process as each celebrity had a variety of images and some had more than others.

Celebrity Instagram and Pinterest posts on Instagram, images that portrayed the celebrity (alone or with others) were selected. The only exception was Oprah; on each of her web pages, the majority of her images were of inspirational quotes she created. Therefore, some of these posts were also included in the analysis. Because of the large amount of comments posted under the Instagram photos, twenty-five images were selected from each of the celebrities' Instagram webpages. This helped to make the amount of comments more manageable, while also allowing for an analysis of the women's more recent posts. This accounted for one hundred images among the four women.

Once the Instagram images were selected, comments made by users about the specific images were viewed more closely. As anticipated (and discussed earlier), the number of comments was astronomical. For example, due to her 8.9 million Instagram followers, one of Beyoncé's images could garner thousands of comments. Rihanna, who has 11 million followers, received nearly half a million *likes* on a single photo. Again, to help with manageability, only the first ten comments were selected for each of the twenty-five images, resulting in 1,000 comments. However, several comments were either in another language or only included a symbol such as a smiling animated character or punctuation; they were excluded from the final analysis, which lowered the amount to 726 comments on Instagram.

Next in the selection process, posts were chosen from the celebrities' personal pages on Pinterest. Duplicate images and those that did not fit into the guidelines of the study, were eliminated. This generated 1,990 total images between the four celebrities. On Pinterest, the total number of comments was much less than those found on Instagram, with some of the images only generating *likes* by users, and no comments. The total of comments in the final analysis for Pinterest was 991. After combining the information accessed from both sites, the final total 1,717 comments were used for a thematic analysis.

## RESULTS AND FINDINGS

Before analyzing the comments attached to the celebrities' images, it is important to acknowledge that each individual user is participating in an online conversation. Because of the interactivity of social media, users are collectively discussing how they view each Black female celebrity's presentation of self. Themes that emerge throughout such conversations can help reveal how the Black female celebrities are presented through cyberspace, as discussed by the viewing public.

The analysis revealed several repeated patterns between both sites. The patterns were categorized into three themes, each with notable key findings. As explained by Virginia Braun and Victoria Clarke, "A theme captures something important about the data in relation to the research question and represents some level of patterned responses or meaning within the data."[45] In a thematic analysis, it is important to establish prevalence in order to identify patterned data. For the sake of this analysis, patterned was defined as three or more users making similar comments, but also understanding that the responses captured the meaning across the entire data set. The three themes identified in the current analysis are titled as "Cyberspace Classification Scripts for Black Female Celebrities." See table 13.1 for a summary and description of themes.

The difference between scripts found in traditional media and those found in this analysis is that these cyberspace scripts are based specifically on how users feel about an image posted by a celebrity. This is unlike the sexual scripts found in traditional media, which are placed on Black women by those controlling a particular medium. The celebrity has control over her image on each respective site, even if a member of her publicity team posts that image. She can deem what images are appropriate or inappropriate unlike with those displayed in traditional media. Each of the three themes found during the analysis—the inspirer, the cyber sexy, and the unattainable beauty—help answer the question: How are Black women classified on image based social media websites? To help show the way in which themes were communicated, I provide examples of users' comments. None of the wording was changed, in order to maintain the authenticity of their original comments.

## The Inspirer

One theme found across all four celebrities' pages was the inspirer. This captures the breadth of posts that users made in reference to how they felt

Table 13.1. Summary of Themes

| Theme | Summary |
| --- | --- |
| The Inspirer | *Captures the breadth of posts that users made in reference to how they felt about the celebrity.* |
| The Cyber Sexy | *Captures the breadth of users' posts that discuss the celebrities' look and sex appeal.* |
| The Unattainable Beauty | *Captures users' posts that discuss their inability to achieve the look of the celebrity.* |

about the celebrity. Several (803) users comments were written with strong adulation and love for these particular Black women. The theme title *Inspirer* appears to capture their passion for these celebrities. The majority of posts centered on love, praise, and even eager requests to meet the celebrity due to the fan's adoration. A notable finding is Oprah's Instagram and Pinterest sites had the greatest number of comments made about inspiration. Her Pinterest site is comprised of images with motivational quotes she has written or posted from other sources. This potentially frames comments from users. Some users posted comments that said:

> Oprah Pinterest User post: *yes Oprah is the most inspirational person on this earth. Would give my right arm and left arm to meet her—so inspiring.*

> Oprah Pinterest User post: *Dream to meet her.*

> Oprah Instagram User post: *Ma'am you inspire me to reach heights that before I believed to be impossible! Thank you for your existence and good character. One day I'll be able to give tremendously to those around me and other parts of the world.*

> Oprah Instagram User post: *You inspire us!*

Oprah is known for being an inspirational figure, as can be seen on her program, *Oprah's Lifeclass* that airs on her OWN television network. Several images on both sites are taken from *Lifeclass* programs or interviews that she has held with both famous and unknown people. These images all seem to frame the comments and conversations on respective social media sites and capture the sentiments expressed by users.

These sentiments were also found in the comments users posted to the sites of Rihanna, Beyoncé, and Nicki Minaj. Although followers posted comments about being inspired by these three Black female entertainers, the majority of their comments were geared toward the love followers had for them. Followers praised the images that portrayed the celebrity at different events such as walking the red carpet, attending a social gathering, or posing in a high fashion styled picture. Therefore, it is the image itself that inspires or garners adulation for these Black women versus the words that they have written or spoken. The following is a comment made on the Instagram site of Nicki Minaj:

> Nicki Minaj Instagram User post: *Nicki I know you probably won't notice me but I want to say that I love you so much and you are my inspiration in life. You taught me to be me and to be no one else. You taught me to not f _ _ _ over anybody and everybody who gets in my way of getting to my*

dream. My dream is to be a famous singer. I love you so much. I have your perfume and 12 of your shirts. I don't know if I would be here without you right now.

This follower is not only expressing their love for the entertainer, but also how he or she feels inspired by her and what she has taught him or her. The follower goes so far as to state how he or she would not be living if it were not for Nicki Minaj. Below are examples of users on Beyoncé's Pinterest and Instagram pages who made similar comments.

> Beyoncé Pinterest User post: *I love Beyonce, she such a beautiful person inside and out.*
>
> Beyoncé Pinterest User post: *Amazing, something rare and spectacular? Love you Beyoncé.*
>
> Beyoncé Instagram User post: *Beyonce, you're such an inspiration to us all. I love your new album.*
>
> Beyoncé Instagram User post: *Really love you and your husband. You're the best!*

## The Cyber Sexy

The next theme, or rather classification script, captures the breadth (691) of users' posts who commented on the celebrities' appearance and sex appeal. As stated earlier in the previous theme, images posted to the sites of selected Black female celebrities are what framed the comments and conversations, which led to this theme's development. The theme also highlights one notable finding. The sentiments expressed on both sites of each celebrity revealed that followers of Nicki Minaj were more likely to use profanity in their comments to express how they felt about her looks and/or sex appeal. Followers' comments on surface level may appear negative by the use of certain profane terms, but for all intended purposes followers were attempting to be positive toward the celebrity. For example:

> Nicki Minaj Instagram User post: *Aww you're f'n cute.*
>
> Nicki Minaj Instagram User post: *You still look f_ _ _ _ _ _ flawless with short hair.*
>
> Nicki Minaj Instagram User post: *Nicki you're gorgeous and you're a bad ass b _ _ _ _.*

Another notable finding in this theme was its prevalence within images posted to Rihanna's social media sites. There were a greater variety of images of the entertainer on her sites than there were of the other three Black women. For example, Rihanna's pages have images of her even when she is not wearing glamorous clothes and makeup, unlike what was mostly found on Beyoncé's and Nicki Minaj's sites. This was also the case for Oprah's pages in the few images of her that are posted. Instead, followers can see images of Rihanna in everyday wear or on vacation in a bikini. Rihanna's sites offer her followers images one could consider to be more relatable to their own lives. An image of Rihanna in a bikini generated the following comments:

> Rihanna Instagram User post: *Sex appeal off the chain. Could be eating a cracker and do it sexier than anyone ever done it before.*

> Rihanna Instagram User post: *You have such a tiny waist, you look fabulous.*

> Rihanna Instagram User post: *You are amazing . . . perfect*

> Rihanna Instagram User post: *You're a sexy woman. Would you marry me?*

> Rihanna Instagram User post: *I absolutely love this woman and her style.*

These four Black women have different styles, but one can only assume their audience or fans are similar in demographic and the celebrities share many of the same followers. Thus, the conclusion cannot be drawn that users look similar to their favorite celebrities, causing them to like the photos. However, findings do illustrate how users enjoyed the photos of the women and considered them physically attractive.

## The Unattainable Beauty

The last theme captures the breadth of users' comments that expressed a desire to look like the celebrity. Interestingly, these comments also insinuated users would not be able to achieve that celebrity look. In the prior theme, followers simply expressed that they liked or even loved a celebrity's appearance, but this theme goes a step further. There were not as many comments (138) within this theme in comparison to the others; however, it was still necessary to point out these findings in that it demonstrates how followers of these celebrities compare their own personal style, appearance, and/or talent to these Black celebrity women. This theme highlights the power and influence of the media, in this case social media, through the images users see.

Beyoncé Instagram User post: *How can you be so perfect? Like everything, your voice, your face, your body. I want to be like you.*

Beyoncé Pinterest User post: *It's amazing you can be that beautiful. I want to look like you.*

Oprah Pinterest User post: *You're such a strong business women. I wish I could be like you.*

Rihanna Instagram User post: *Rihanna I love your style and beauty. I want to be like you but I know I never could.*

Rihanna Pinterest User post: *I wish I could sing like her!*

Nicki Instagram User post: *Nicki your body is amazing. Did you have plastic surgery? I want to look like you.*

The comments followers made in this theme touch on a few broader topics such as self-esteem and body alteration. Findings show that followers admire these Black women so much that some would consider plastic surgery to achieve their look. But, also the success these women have accumulated serves as motivation for their followers to strive for although some may perceive the celebrities' beauty and success unattainable.

## DISCUSSION AND CONCLUSION

Overall, this research illustrates that followers of Rihanna, Oprah, Beyoncé, and Nicki Minaj commented on the women's posted images in similar ways. These comments, when examined using a thematic analysis, can be placed into three main themes—The Inspirer, The Cyber Sexy, and The Unattainable Beauty. It is critical to understand that these "Cyberspace Classification Scripts of Black Female Celebrities" are not ones bestowed upon them by themselves, but they capture the essence of how their followers view and feel about their images. This is a departure from how traditional labels or scripts are placed on Black women. Historically, Black women as a whole have been stereotyped in traditional media to fit into both past and present sexual scripts as identified by scholars discussed earlier, such as Collins, bell hooks, and Stephens and Phillips.

So, how can a Black woman be seen beyond the stereotypes that are placed on her by traditional media? This research offers that new media such as social media websites could be a portion of the solution. Through social media people can engage with one another more freely, quickly, and openly than they can through traditional means. This engagement lends itself to

Black women, not only celebrities, by helping them take back the power that has been stripped away by those in powerful media positions who make decisions on representations of Black women. These media moguls have the ability to portray Black women, or any group for that matter, in ways they deem appropriate for financial gain. Social media sites, such as Instagram and Pinterest, allow people to define and redefine how they want to be perceived through the images they post. These images can then be received and viewed by users to draw their own perception of these women.

Although the majority of comments on these sites were positive about the four Black women, there were instances that the comments were not so pleasant. Again, this strengthens the argument for the power and influence these sites offer. Users who follow these Black women came to their defense when negative comments were posted by someone. When a negative comment was made about a celebrity's image, users were quick to respond with a rebuttal or vehemently urge the negative poster to get off the site. This protective nature was noted during the analysis but was not reported in the results because of its low occurrence. However, the ability to answer back illustrates the participatory nature of social media and how that can contribute to discussions of Black women in popular culture. The Instagram and Pinterest users were able to have a voice in the discourse surrounding the Black female celebrities. They are able to be participants in the conversation about representations and portrayals, of at least these four women, rather than being outliers on the margins of the greater media landscape where Black women and others are often silenced.

Lastly, it is important to address images posted to the sites used in this analysis framed the comments users made about the Black women selected for the study. Also, many of the images were taken from events that were also featured in traditional media, like television or magazines. The celebrities were able to highlight the media coverage of themselves that they wanted to share with their fans. Although social media should be highly considered as a means by which Black women can take back their rightful identity in the eyes of the world, we must also understand the integral role traditional media still plays in the representations, and resulting perceptions, of Black female celebrities. Social media can provide an opportunity to create your own public image, but traditional media can still continue with its own representations—whether flattering or not. What is promising is that Instagram and Pinterest, as well as other social media sites, contribute to celebrities' ability to reach a broader audience and present their own self-image. It also allows the audience to feel a sense of engagement with the celebrity that otherwise would not be attained through traditional mass media. More research in this area is needed to examine and understand how Black women who are not famous but use media sites are classified, and if they fit into any of these cyberspace classification scripts.

## NOTES

1. Dionne Stephens and Layli Phillips, "Freaks, Gold Diggers, Divas, and Dykes: The Sociohistorical Development of Adolescent African American Women's Sexual Scripts," *Sexuality & Culture* (2003): 3.
2. Ibid., 5.
3. Ibid., 11.
4. Ibid., 15.
5. Jane Rhodes, "Falling Through the Cracks: Studying Women of Color in Mass Communication," in *Women in Mass Communication*, ed. P. J. Creedon (Newbury Park: Sage, 1993), 24–31.
6. Ibid., 25–26.
7. George Gerbner et al., "Growing up with Television: Cultivation Processes," in *Media Effects: Advances in Theory and Research*, 2nd ed. Jennings Bryant and Dolf Zillman (Mahwah: Erlbaum, 2002), 43–67.
8. Dolf Zillman and Hans-Bernd Brosius, *Exemplification in Communication: The Influence of Case Reports on the Perception of Issues* (Mahwah: Erlbaum, 2000), 21.
9. Robert Entman, "Policy Issues for Telecommunication Reform: Reports of the 2005 Aspen Institute Conferences on Telecommunication and Spectrum Policy," accessed December 18, 2013, Aspeninstitute.org/policy.
10. Jennifer L. Pozner, *Reality Bites Back: The Troubling Truth About Guilty Pleasure TV* (Berkeley: Seal Press, 2010).
11. Rhodes, "Falling Through the Cracks," 29.
12. Robin Means Coleman, *African American Viewers and the Black Situation Comedy: Situating Racial Humor* (New York: Garland Publishing Co, 2000).
13. Nancy Krieger and Elizabeth Fee, "Man-Made Medicine and Women's Health: The Biopolitics of Sex/Gender and Race/Ethnicity," in *Man-Made Medicine: Women's Health, Public Policy and Reform*, ed. Kary L. Moss (Durham: Duke University Press, 1996), 15–36.
14. Jared Diamond, "A Tale of Two Reputations: Why We Revere Darwin and Give Freud a Hard Time," *Natural History* 110 (2001): 20-25.
15. Anne Fausto-Sterling, "Gender, Race, and Nation: The Comparative Anatomy of Hottentot Women in Europe, 1815–1817," in *Deviant Bodies: Critical Perspectives on Differences in Science and Popular Culture*, ed. Jennifer Terry and Jacqueline Urla (Bloomington: Indiana University Press, 1995), 19–46.
16. Ibid., 31.
17. Stephens and Phillips, "Freaks, Gold Diggers, Divas, and Dykes," 7.
18. Patricia Hill Collins, *Black Feminist Thought: Knowledge, Consciousness, and the Politics of Empowerment*. 2nd ed. (New York: Routledge, 2000).
19. Jean Carey Bond, "Is the Black Male Castrated?" in *The Black Woman: An Anthology*, ed. Toni Cade (New York: Mentor Books, 1970).
20. Janette Dates and Carol Stroman, "Portrayals of Families of Color on Television," in *Television and the American Family*, ed. Jennings Bryant and J. Alison Bryant (Mahwah: Erlbaum, 2001), 207–25.
21. Mark P. Orbe, "Constructions of Reality on MTV's The Real World: An Analysis of the Restrictive Coding of Black Masculinity," *Southern Communication Journal* (1998): 32–47, accessed December 27, 2013. doi: 10.1080/10417949809373116; Pozner, "Reality Bites Back."
22. Camille O. Cosby, *Television's Imageable Influences: The Self-Perceptions of Young African Americans*, (New York: University Press of America, 1994); Dwight E. Brooks and Lisa P. Herbert, "Gender, Race, and Media Representation," in *The Sage Handbook of Gender and Communication*, ed. Bonnie J. Dow and Julie T. Wood (Thousand Oaks: Sage, 2006), 297–317; Collins, *Black Feminist Thought*; bell hooks, *Black Looks: Race and Representations* (Cambridge: South End Press, 1992).
23. Siobahn Smith, "And Still More Drama!: A Comparison of the Portrayals of African American Women and African American Men on BET's College Hill," *The Western Journal of Black Studies* 37 (2013): 39–49.

24. Stephens and Phillips, "Freaks, Gold Diggers, Divas, and Dykes," 11.
25. Beverly Guy-Sheftall, *Words of Fire: An Anthology of African American Feminist Thought* (New York: New Press, 1995).
26. Stephens and Phillips, "Freaks, Gold Diggers, Divas, and Dykes," 11.
27. Ibid., 15–33.
28. Collins, *Black Feminist Thought*, 58.
29. Donald Wright and Michelle Hinson, "An Analysis of New Communications Media Use in Public Relations: Results of a Five-Year Trend Study," *Public Relations Journal*, 4 (2010), accessed November 18, 2011, http://www.prsa.org/Intelligence/PRJournal/Spring_10/.
30. Damian Ryan and Calvin Jones, *Understanding Digital Marketing* (Philadelphia: Kogan Page Limited, 2009), 152.
31. Brian Solis and Deirdre Breakenridge, *Putting the Public Back in Public Relations: How Social Media is Reinventing the Aging Business of PR* (Upper Saddle River: Pearson Education, Inc, 2009).
32. "State of the Media: The Social Media Report 2012," Nielsen, accessed December 15, 2013, http://www.nielsen.com/us/en/newswire/2012/social-media-report-2012-social-media-comes-of-age.html.
33. "The Social Media Report 2012," 10
34. "Social Media Update 2013," Pew Internet & American Life Project, accessed December 30, 2013, http://pewinternet.org/Reports/2013/Social-Media-Update/Main-Findings.aspx?view=all.
35. "The Social Media Report 2012."
36. "African American and Technology Use," Pew Internet & American Life Project, accessed December 30, 2013, http://pewinternet.org/Reports/2014/African-American-Tech-Use/Main-Findings.aspx.
37. Sue Jewell, *From Mammy to Miss America and Beyond: Cultural Images and the Shaping of US Social Policy* (London: Routledge, 1993).
38. Gerard T. Schoening and James A. Anderson, "Social Action Media Studies: Foundational Arguments and Common Premises," *Communication Theory* 5 (1995): 93–116.
39. "The Social Media Report 2012"; "Social Media Update 2013."
40. "For Members of the Press," Pinterest, accessed December 15, 2013, http://about.pinterest.com/press/.
41. "FAQ," Instagram, accessed December 17, 2013, http://instagram.com/about/faq/.
42. Instagram's website provides a slideshow presentation that discusses its growth as a social networking site. The timeline/slideshow appears at the bottom of the site's press page, http://instagram.com/press/ , after clicking on the button that reads, "Our Story."
43. "Social Media Update 2013."
44. When Beyoncé's full name is referenced, she is sometimes referred to using her maiden name "Knowles." However, people also refer to her as Mrs. Carter, as she is married to Shawn "Jay-Z" Carter. For example: Mrs. Carter's World Tour.
45. Virginia Braun and Victoria Clarke, "Using Thematic Analysis in Psychology," *Qualitative Research in Psychology* 3 (2006): 77–101.

# BIBLIOGRAPHY

Bond, Jean Carey. "Is the Black Male Castrated?" In *The Black Woman: An Anthology*, edited by Toni Cade. New York: Mentor Books, 1970.
Boylorn, Robin. "As Seen on TV: An Authoethnographic Reflection on Race and Reality Television." *Critical Studies in Media Communication* 25 (2008): 413–33. Accessed December 27, 2013 doi: 10.1080/15295030802327758.
Braun, Virginia, and Victoria Clarke. "Using thematic analysis in psychology." *Qualitative Research in Psychology* 3 (2006): 77–101.
Brooks, Dwight, and Lisa Herbert. "Gender, Race, and Media Representation." In *The Sage Handbook of Gender and Communication*, edited by Bonnie J. Dow and Julie T. Wood, 297–317. Thousand Oaks: Sage, 2006.

Cosby, Camille. *Television's Imageable Influences: The Self-Perceptions of Young African-Americans*. New York, NY: University Press of America, 1994.

Dates, Janette, and Carol Stroman. "Portrayals of Families of Color on Television." In *Television and the American Family*, edited by Jennifer Bryant and J. Alison Bryant, 207–25. Mahwah: Erlbaum, 2001.

Diamond, Jared. "A Tale of Two Reputations." *Natural History* 110 (2001): 20–25.

Entman, Robert. 2006. *Policy issues for telecommunications reform: Reports of the 2005 Aspen Institute Conferences on Telecommunication and Spectrum Policy*. Aspen Institute. Accessed December 18, 2013 Aspeninstitute.org/policy.

Fausto-Sterling, Anne. "Gender, Race, and Nation: The Comparative Anatomy of "Hottentot" Women in Europe, 1815-1817." In *Deviant Bodies: Critical Perspectives on Difference in Science and Popular Culture*, edited by Jennifer Terry and Jacqueline Urla, 19–46. Bloomington: Indiana University Press, 1995.

Gerbner, George, Lance Gross, Michelle Morgan, Nartty Signorielli, and James Shanahan. "Growing up with Television: Cultivation Processes." In *Media Effects: Advances in Theory and Research*, 2nd ed., edited by Jennings Bryant and Dolf Zillman, 43–67. Mahwah: Erlbaum, 2002.

Guy-Sheftall, Beverly. *Words of Fire: An Anthology of African-American Feminist Thought*. New York, NY: New Press, 1995.

Hill Collins, Patricia. *Black Feminist Thought: Knowledge, Consciousness, and the Politics of Empowerment*. 2nd ed. New York: Routledge, 2000.

hooks, bell. *Black Looks: Race and Representations*. Cambridge: South End Press, 1992.

Jewell, K. Sue. *From Mammy to Miss America and Beyond: Cultural Images and the Shaping of US Social Policy*. London: Routledge, 1993.

Krieger, Nancy, and Elizabeth Fee. "Man-Made Medicine and Women's Health: The Biopolitics of Sex/Gender and Race/Ethnicity." In *Man-Made Medicine: Women's Health, Public Policy and Reform*, edited by Kary L. Moss, 15–36. Durham: Duke University Press, 1996.

Means Coleman, Robin. *African American Viewers and the Black Situation Comedy: Situating Racial Humor*. New York, NY: Garland Publishing Co, 2000.

Nielsen. "State of the Media: The Social Media Report 2012." Accessed December 15, 2013 http://www.nielsen.com/us/en/newswire/2012/social-media-report-2012-social-media-comes-of-age.html.

Orbe, Mark P. "Constructions of Reality on MTV's 'The Real World': An Analysis of the Restrictive Coding of Black Masculinity." *Southern Communication Journal* (1998): 32–47. Accessed December 27, 2013 doi: 10.1080/10417949809373116.

Pew Internet & American Life Project. "Social Media Update 2013." Accessed December 30, 2013, http://pewinternet.org/Reports/2013/Social-Media-Update/Main-Findings.aspx?view=all.

Pew Internet & American Life Project. "African Americans and Technology Use." Accessed December 30, 2013 http://pewinternet.org/Reports/2014/African-American-Tech-Use/Main-Findings.aspx.

Pozner, Jennifer L. *Reality Bites Back: The Troubling Truth About Guilty Pleasure TV*. Berkeley: Seal Press, 2010.

Rhodes, Jane. "Falling Through the Cracks: Studying Women of Color in Mass Communication." In *Women in Mass Communication*, edited by Pamela J. Creedon, 24–32. Newbury Park: Sage, 1993.

Ryan, Damian, and Calvin Jones. *Understanding Digital Marketing*. Philadelphia: Kogan Page Limited, 2009.

Smith, Siobahn. "And Still More Drama!: A Comparison of the Portrayals of African American Women and African American Men on BET's College Hill." *The Western Journal of Black Studies* 37 (2013): 39–49.

Solis, Brian, and Deirdre Breakenridge. *Putting the Public Back in Public Relations: How Social Media is Reinventing the Aging Business of PR*. Upper Saddle River: Pearson Education, Inc, 2009.

Stephens, Dionne, and Layli Phillips. "Freaks, Gold Diggers, Divas, and Dykes: The Sociohistorical Development of Adolescent African American Women's Sexual Scripts. *Sexuality & Culture* (2003): 3–49.

Wright, Donald, and Michelle Hinson. "An Analysis of New Communications Media Use in Public Relations: Results of a Five-Year Trend Study." *Public Relations Journal* 4 (2010). Accessed November 18, 2011 http://www.prsa.org/Intelligence/PRJournal/Spring_10/.

Zillman, Dolf, and Hans-Bernd Brosius. *Exemplification in Communication: The Influence of Case Reports on the Perception of Issues*. Mahwah: Erlbaum, 2000.

*Chapter Fourteen*

# Identity as a Rite of Passage

*The Case of Chirlane McCray*

Sheena C. Howard

Currently, there is no notable research that offers a critical examination of the first lady of New York, Chirlane McCray, through the lens of identity politics. This chapter will deconstruct the ways in which McCray's transitional identity queers the prescribed categorizations of sexual orientation, reinforces heteronormative values, as well as male mythology, whilst simultaneously sending ambivalent messages around progressive politics and public opinion. As a result of this ambivalence and ambiguity around McCray's sexual identity, Bill de Blasio was able to gain access to the votes of various minority groups—including the LGBT (lesbian, gay, bisexual, and transgender) community.

Within the current political landscape of the twenty-first century, or what I call *new politics*, "spouses are a big money shot in the high-stakes show business that constitutes presidential politics."[1] Therefore, McCray, wife of Bill de Blasio, had no choice but to play her best supporting spouse role on the national stage as Blasio ran for public office as the Democratic mayoral nominee in 2013.

## POLITICS AND POPULAR CULTURE

Today, politics and popular culture are interconnected. A political candidate running for public office will find that utilizing social media such as Twitter and Facebook, referencing celebrities, and using YouTube to gain voter support, if done correctly, can drastically improve one's campaign success. Eric Louw has argued that there has been a narrowing in the gap between politics and entertainment.[2] In his definition of "pseudo-politics" Louw suggests there has been a PR-isation of issues "in which celebrities are now enlisted to whip up mass public opinion."[3] For example, President Barack Obama utilized several avenues within popular culture to generate support during his race for presidency in 2008. Obama utilized the U.S. entertainment–politics nexus to seek Everyday Maker support when he appeared as a senator on popular talk shows such as *The Oprah Winfrey Show* (1986–2011) and as a "rock'n'roll" candidate he effortlessly mixed with celebrity endorsers including Oprah Winfrey herself.[4] At the time, Winfrey was one of the United States most internationally recognizable figures and in 2008 she held the top spot in *Forbes Magazine*'s hundred most powerful American celebrities. Her endorsement of Obama prior to the 2008 Democratic Presidential Primary generated a statistically and qualitatively significant increase in the number of votes received as well as in the total number of votes cast.[5] Consequently, Democrats have successfully utilized popular culture during political campaigns to increase political support.

This juxtaposition of politics and popular culture has been no different for the campaign that Bill de Blasio ran as Democratic mayoral nominee in 2013. The children of Blasio and his wife—first lady of New York—have also spent time in the spotlight. Their son, Dante, generated fame of his own during Blasio's campaign appearing on a television campaign advertisement, which can be readily viewed on YouTube. In addition, on December 24, 2013, Chiara de Blasio, the daughter of the New York City Mayor-elect Blasio, revealed in a video put out by Blasio's transition team that she struggled with alcohol, drugs, and depression. Chiara discussed removing substances from her life, and encouraged viewers to seek help and get sober. Her revelation did open up the discussion around alcoholism as a disease and the need for support for those who suffer from drug and alcohol addiction. According to a December 24, 2013, article in *Politico*, the video also caught the attention of the Obama Administration and the White House Drug Policy Director Gil Kerlikowske who commended Chiara for encouraging an open discussion of mental health and substance abuse.[6] Popular culture tools such as social media and online streaming aid in visibility and virility of content, especially during political campaigns as evidenced here. In addition, McCray has been, and continues to be an avid Twitter user.

McCray's Twitter topics include education reform, the ways in which her husband and she raise their children, and pictures of her attending social events, amongst other things. Furthermore, she is no stranger to the political landscape and human rights activism. This chapter seeks to focus on the narrative of McCray's identity politics as a journey, which queers the prescribed categorizations of sexual orientation and reinforces heteronormative values, as well as male mythology—all of which is accomplished through various popular culture tools. The aforementioned cannot be examined without first providing a brief overview of McCray. The following overview of McCray is inherent to the central argument of this chapter as the transitional identity politics surrounding McCray's life reveal the ways in which the observable silencing around her sexual identity is deafening as it acts as a vehicle to reinforce heteronormativity, through a ritualized narrative.

## CHIRLANE MCCRAY: LIFE IN POLITICS AND ACTIVISM

In a 1979 *Essence* article titled, *I Am A Lesbian,* McCray provides insight into a number of Black lesbian and feminist organizations of the 1970s and 1980s that she actively participated in, including the Combahee River Collective, SistaSoul, and Jemima. During the publication of the 1979 *Essence* article McCray was in her mid-twenties and discussed *coming out* as a lesbian. This essay and membership into the above-mentioned groups provides insight into McCray's participation and interest in the political scene, particularly the women's movement, as a young adult. As previously mentioned, McCray was a member of the Combahee River Collective (CRC), which is said to have coined the term *identity politics*.

The Combahee River Collective (CRC) ran from 1974-1980 and was a mutual-support organization for African-American feminist writers, especially Black lesbian feminists. The CRC was considered a political movement seeking to combat all forces of oppression that women of color face. CRC member activities included abortion-rights work, lesbian activism, and activities related to Third World Women's International Women's Day. Other activities sponsored by CRC members included workplace and labor organizing, rape-crisis work, and child-care concerns. Members of the Combahee River Collective would meet on several occasions to discuss participant publications; the last meeting was held in Washington, DC, in February of 1980. This meeting was a few months after McCray shared with the group the publication of her September 1979 *Essence* article *I am a Lesbian*, which was groundbreaking.

McCray remained active in the political arena and on the activism front, through membership with the Salsa Soul Sisters. Salsa Soul Sisters galvanized around issues pertinent to women of color, especially lesbian women of color. In 1974 the Black Lesbian Caucus reformulated itself as the Salsa Soul Sisters, Third World Wimmin Inc., an autonomous group of Black and Latina lesbians offering its members a social and political alternative to the lesbian and gay bars, which had "historically exploited and discriminated against lesbians of color."[7] Eventually, The Jemima Writers Collective was formed by members of the Salsa Soul Sisters to "meet the need for creative/ artistic expression and to create a supportive atmosphere in which Black women could share their work and begin to eradicate negative self images."[8] McCray was also a member of the Jemima Writers Collective.

McCray eventually expanded her focus from Black lesbian and feminist activism to a broad range of political endeavors in the 1990s, further continuing her involvement on the political front. After moving to New York, she spent nearly a decade in magazine publishing, working as a writer, editor, and marketing research analyst. In addition, she did freelance writing for *Essence* magazine and performed spoken word poetry. In 1983, her work was published in *Homegirls*, a black feminist anthology still used in college classes today.[9]

McCray's own resume includes stints as a speechwriter; she worked in this capacity for Mayor David N. Dinkins, State Comptroller Carl McCall, and City Comptroller Bill Thompson. She also served as a political appointee during the Clinton Administration at the New York Foreign Press Center.[10] In addition, McCray worked in public relations for Citigroup. From 2005 to 2010, she held a six-figure job in marketing at Maimonides Medical Center, which some criticized as a political quid pro quo between de Blasio and the Brooklyn hospital.[11]

## RATIONALE

McCray, as a narrative around Blasio's campaign trail and her own transitional sexual identity, functions as a liminal journey of discovery in which a self-identified Black feminist lesbian marries a heterosexual White man; this offers spectators a series of contradictory messages which reinforce heteronormative values and the male mythology that: "lesbians just need a good fuck, that is, a phallic intrusion to break up the threatening duo."[12] The aforementioned is accomplished through various modes of popular culture tools. The ambiguity and silencing around McCray's journey from being a self-proclaimed lesbian (which was very public) to a woman in a twenty-year heterosexual marriage poses observable threats to the gay and lesbian liberation movement, which makes McCray's narrative worthy of analysis.

While part of the gay and lesbian rights movement is the freedom and liberation for one to define and redefine oneself without restriction, another very real and important part of the movement is deconstructing the notion that a gay or lesbian identity is stable—not a phase and certainly not a choice. McCray's narrative contradicts the latter. In short, anti-gay supporters will use and have already began to use her narrative as an example that being gay or lesbian is a choice and an identity which is unstable and fleeting. Whether intentional or unintentional, McCray's silence on the issue and ambiguity as it relates to her journey from being a self-proclaimed lesbian to a woman in a long-term heterosexual relationship is harmful to the gay and lesbian rights movement and to gay and lesbian individuals.

The implied messages displayed throughout the narrative of McCray are multi-faceted, complex, and contradictory on three levels: (1) her narrative symbolically sends a message to spectators that lesbianism is fleeting, unstable, and incomplete without the ultimate sexual desire for the male penis; (2) her narrative reinforces heteronormative ideologies around male mythology; and (3) her narrative queers the categorizations of rigid labels. These messages are implicit in McCray's narrative and accomplished through a ritual formula that follows the traditional sequence characteristic of rites of passage.[13] The rites of passage treatment serves as a heteronormative formula consisting of 1) separation, 2) liminality, and 3) re-assimilation, which is expounded upon in the following sections.

## SEPARATION

As previously stated, rites of passage begin with separation of ritual initiates and end with (re)integration. Arnold Gennep, author of *The Rites of Passage*, states, "These are constants of social life . . . for groups as well as individuals; life itself means to separate and to be reunited, to change form and condition, to die and to be reborn."[14] In the case of McCray, her 1979 article published in *Essence* magazine, titled *I Am A Lesbian*, distinctly signifies her departure from what was considered the social norm in the late 1970s, as the American Psychiatric Association did not yet consider lesbianism a viable or acceptable way of life. In this groundbreaking article, McCray identifies herself as a lesbian, discusses coming to terms with her identity, and displays a clear social separation from conforming to the status quo as far as her sexual orientation is concerned. McCray notes, "I wanted my voice to reassure those who feel as isolated and alone as I once did, those who desperately seek answers to all the 'whys' when none exist, those who are embroiled in a struggle to be themselves in a society that frowns on differences."[15] The aforementioned quote illuminates a clear struggle and coming to terms with the social isolation and separation that one faces when a gay or lesbian identity poses serious risks, especially in the 1970s and 1980s. The 1970s were a time of community organizing as well as fierce discrimination for members of the LGBT community.

In the late 1970s and early 1980s there was a lot of community organizing within and across the gay and lesbian community. However racial minorities found the gay liberation movement to be racist and classist. In Eric Marcus' *Making Gay History*, Deborah Johnson, Black female lesbian, recalls:

> You can be sure that being black had an impact on how people dealt with me. I had the advantage of at least being educated on an undergraduate level. This

was an advantage because I found there was a lot of academic bias within the gay and lesbian movement. The activist tended to be fairly well educated.[16]

For the gay and lesbian liberation movement at large, the fight for equal rights had evolved through three distinct periods by the early 1970s: the development of organizations and discussion groups beginning in 1950; the tiny, although persistent, homophile movement of the 1960s; and the explosive gay liberation movement, which paralleled the rise of the leftist and anti-Vietnam activism in the late 1960s through the early 1970s.[17] Despite these achievements, gay and lesbian people of color continued to struggle with a unique set of issues and concerns. Johnson continues her recollection:

> There are a lot of good grass roots activists who are very bright people but who don't have college experience. I have watched time and time again for their opinions to be devalued or not to be taken seriously, particularly if they're people of color. I encountered this attitude constantly. And there was just a lot of racism.[18]

These unique challenges make McCray's 1979 *Essence* article trailblazing as one can only postulate the amount of courage, fear, and strength she experienced when writing such an open and intimate piece around her identity, in a culture that considered lesbianism an abomination and often devalued Black female voices. This article enacted symbolic codes around identity, visibility, and liberation. A symbol, most simply, is an object, idea, or action that is loaded with cultural meaning. Following Clifford Geertz, it is "any object, act, event, quality, or relation that serves as a vehicle for conception—the conception is the symbol's meaning."[19] The article, *I Am A Lesbian* makes a very public and political statement that Black lesbians exist. Furthermore, the publication of the article is a symbolic action that challenged the social structures of the 1970s and 1980s. Thus, the action of McCray *coming out* during that time signified a social separation from the dominant social structure.

## LIMINAL LICENSE

Liminaltiy is central to rites of passage sequentially and in terms of ritual focus.[20] Aden describes liminality as both a transitory state and a transitory process.[21] Those liminally positioned are, according to Turner, "betwixt and between."[22] Thus, they are paradoxically a part of, yet a part from, a group. In the case of McCray, spectators find her transient identity *betwixt and between* when her 1979 *Essence* article resurfaces as Blasio runs for Democratic Mayor of New York in 2013.

McCray is, at least, emblematically a part of the LGBT community, yet apart from it as her marriage signifies heterosexuality. This, whether intentional or unintentional, transient identity worked to provide the Blasio campaign with a political platform that allowed the candidate to connect with the Black, female, and LGBT voters—through his wife. McCray has never stated that she views her identity as transient or liminal. Yet spectators are provided with contradictory messages as McCray, who was once very vocal around her sexual orientation and identity, is ambiguous about her transition from lesbianism to a twenty-year marriage to a man. In a November 2013 interview on *HuffPost Live*, when asked what she now identifies as, McCray responds, "Why should I explain my sexuality? I don't know what I will be like ten years from now." In a May 2013 *Essence* article titled, "Chirlane McCray: From Gay Trailblazer to Politician's Wife" by Linda Villarosa, McCray is asked directly if she considers herself a bisexual. She responds:

> I am more than just a label. Why are people so driven to labeling where we fall on the sexual spectrum? Labels put people in boxes, and those boxes are shaped like coffins. Finding the right person can be so hard that often, when a person finally finds someone she or he is comfortable with, she or he just makes it work. As my friend Vanessa says, "It's not whom you love; it's that you love."[23]

While the gay and lesbian liberation movement galvanizes around the ability for one to define and redefine oneself without restriction, McCray's 1979 *Essence* article begs the question as to why be silent now? The silence is louder than anything, as the obscurity around her sexual orientation leaves the door wide open for staunch criticism from anti-gay supporters that lesbianism is a phase and perpetuates male mythology that lesbians ultimately will desire penis.

The average male can identify with Blasio as a regular guy and, by extension McCray's narrative validates the notion that lesbians just need a good fuck. The heteronormative formula symbolized through her narrative is often the central image in mainstream media used to control representation in order to draw back the female from entering the realm of lesbian desire. In short, it symbolically sends the message that regardless if one claims to be a lesbian, there will be desire for male penis.[24] However, McCray has and continues to have the opportunity to be as open today as she was in 1979; or at most address, in some fashion, her struggle and journey from being a self-identified lesbian who wrote one of the defining articles in the late 1970s shedding light on Black female sexuality. Furthermore, her narrative effectively works to queer categorizations around sexual orientation. Many scholars have written about the limitation of labels and necessity to move away from such categorizations. In *Black Queer Identity Matrix: Towards An Integrated Queer of Color Framework*, Sheena Howard notes:

> Categories such as lesbian, gay, bisexual, and others are essentially approximations of reality. Not everyone perfectly or neatly fits into those categories—which is why they keep adding letters to the acronym LGBTQ. Categories never quite get it right. For example, someone will call themselves "lesbian" if their experiences have involved only same-sex attraction and behavior because that's who they're principally attracted to, but that doesn't necessarily mean that they'll never be involved with a member of the opposite sex or at least find a member of the opposite sex attractive or sexually attractive. Ultimately, I believe if social expectations and enforcements were removed, people would grow however they felt best fit them. In other words, people wouldn't feel the need to conform to "Blackness" or a "lesbian" identity, and so on—they would simply be. Labels tend to limit possibilities of what one can or does become.[25]

This notion is significant as society moves towards a more sexually fluid, accepting environment. However this should not undermine the validity of lesbianism as a fleeting or unstable identity. Oftentimes narratives, such as McCray's, do agitate the understanding that a gay/lesbian identity is stable. This is dangerous for those everyday individuals who are gay and lesbian. In addition, McCray's narrative is largely used as a tool to hinder LGBT rights, as anti-gay supporters insist a lesbian or gay identity is a choice. This is primarily the danger in McCray's narrative; she remains a part of, yet apart from, an identity which conveniently and simultaneously allows her to queer categorizations, perpetuate the notion of lesbianism as a phase whilst representing as an ally of the LGBT community. This formula of liminality allowed the Blasio campaign to court the Black, LGBT, female, and heterosexual vote—through his wife, McCray. She remains safe for Black, female, and heterosexual voters and a part of the in-group of various identities. Blasio, as a result, is framed as an LGBT ally, sensitive to the plight of Black Americans, and a heterosexual male in support of the politics of feminism. In addition, he has made it public that McCray is an active participant in the political decisions he makes. Thus, McCray shapes his politics. The end of the liminal stage and the opening of the integration stage begins when Blasio is sworn in as the 109th mayor of New York (McCray as the first lady of New York) on January 1, 2014.

## REINCORPORATION

If McCray's sexual identity was ever in question or unclear for spectators, the ultimate swearing in ceremony of Blasio as the mayor of New York symbolically validated heteronormative ideals and values around the idyllic family structure and image needed for a prominent political family—which always includes a man married to a woman. Spectators are not threatened or forced to remember McCray's identification as a lesbian, which ultimately works to minimize the social *threat* of lesbianism. Simultaneously, members of the LGBT community feel a sense of representation as those individuals recall the queer sexual identity of McCray, which ultimately provides a connection between the Blasio family and the LGBT community.

Whatever the specific details, the function of rites of passage and of specific rites within the ritual scheme remains the same. That consequence is the revitalization of society by facilitating transitions in social relations in ritualized settings where the values and relationships of the society are expressed and reaffirmed.[26] Thus, the swearing in of Blasio acts as a symbolic enactment of cultural beliefs or values.

In the third phase, reincorporation (or re-assimilation), the passage is consummated. Having completed the rite and assumed a *new* identity, one re-enters society with a new status. Re-incorporation is characterized by elaborate rituals and ceremonies (such as the swearing in ceremony previously discussed) and by outward symbols of new ties. Thus "in rites of incorporation there is widespread use of the 'sacred bond', the 'sacred cord', the knot, and of analogous forms such as the belt, the ring, the bracelet and the crown."[27] Ritual works by sending messages to those who perform and those who receive or observe it. Therefore the election of Blasio embodies heteronormative values by rewarding the Blasio family as one that is acceptable and safe. In addition, it bi-directionally sends a message to observers that they are a stable heteronormative family. Consequently, McCray's use of silence and ambiguity around her sexual orientation allows her to re-assimilate effortlessly as the first lady of New York as she remains a part of a traditional heterosexual family structure where her past as a sexual *deviant* is essentially erased from cultural memory.

## THE CEREMONY

The swearing in ceremony conducted at City Hall was well attended by thousands of New Yorkers, politicians, and celebrities. Former President Bill Clinton, who officiated the ceremony, was joined by his wife, Hillary Clinton. Governor Andrew Cuomo and former Mayor of New York Michael Bloomberg were also in attendance. At the ceremony, Democrat Letitia James was sworn in as public advocate and Democrat Scott Stringer was sworn in as comptroller. The celebrities in attendance were singer Harry Belafonte, who opened the event, as well as actresses Cynthia Nixon and Patina Miller.

During Blasio's remarks, he pledged to pursue a liberal agenda and reshape New York City. He lso promised to improve economic opportunities in minority and working-class neighborhoods and decried allegations of abuse under the police department's stop-and-frisk policy, which disproportionately affects Blacks and Hispanics.[28] Blasio was administered the oath by Bill

Clinton on the historic bible given to Franklin Delano Roosevelt at his first presidential inauguration in 1933.

The imagery around the swearing in ceremony of Blasio, as the family looks on, is a poignant message. It solidifies the ways in which McCray makes a bold statement about her transitional identity from a self-proclaimed lesbian to a woman in a non-offensive, safe heterosexual relationship. McCray, who once challenged the social structure of sexual orientation through social separation, is re-incorporated or re-assimilated into mainstream values and ideals through this ritualized ceremony; where actions speak louder than words. The ceremonial act ameliorated any social threat of lesbianism or disturbance around traditional social relations within a political family.

The formal rite of incorporation, prescribed by the city of New York, ceremonially incorporated the Blasio family through a ritual that bestowed a new and elevated social status equal to that of first lady of New York City and mayor of New York City. The ritual, as previously stated but worth placing emphasis on, was augmented by the inauguration event on January 1, 2014, in New York City, where former President of the United States Bill Clinton officiated the ceremony.

## CONCLUSION

Chirlane McCray's narrative represents a transitional identity from a self-proclaimed lesbian to a woman in a twenty-year heterosexual marriage. Her narrative queers the prescribed categorizations of sexual orientation, reinforces heteronormative values and male mythology, all while simultaneously sending ambivalent messages around progressive politics and public opinion. This is accomplished through a ritual formula that follows the traditional sequence characteristic of rites of passage, which ultimately represents identity as a rite of passage. In short, McCray's heterosexual marriage to Bill de Blasio, allows entry into a new and elevated social status as first lady of New York—or acts as a rite of passage to said position. The aforementioned dynamics of transition discussed in this essay are accomplished through various modes of popular culture, such as magazine articles and social media.

McCray's social separation or dissociation from heterosexuality was made very public in the publication of the 1979 *Essence* article, titled "I Am A Lesbian." In 1991, McCray met Blasio while she was working for David Dinkins as a speechwriter. In 1993, the two were married and ultimately had two children, Dante and Chiara. In 2013, Blasio is on the campaign trail running as New York City's next Democratic mayor. During the campaign trail, knowledge of the 1979 *Essence* article "I Am A Lesbian" resurfaces on several news outlets and print publications. Once the article resurfaces,

McCray remains silent and ambiguous on the subject of her transition from a self-proclaimed lesbian to a woman married to a man. She is very public about resisting labels and categorizations, which is in stark contrast to her philosophy in the late 1970s, where she proclaimed to be a lesbian. McCray's silence and ambiguity around her sexual orientation allowed her to remain apart of, yet apart from, the LGBT community. As such, she ultimately was able to court the LGBT, Black, and female vote and portray her husband as an ally for the LGBT, Black, and female community. On January 1, 2014, Blasio was sworn in as the 109th mayor of New York City.

During the swearing in ceremony at City Hall, membership into the new social status of New York City mayor destroys the symbol of McCray's alternative sexual orientation as she, along with Blasio and their children, represent a family that parallels the heteronormative ideals of a typical first family.

For spectators, the swearing in ceremony of Blasio acts as a mechanism of erasing cultural memory around McCray's sexual orientation by symbolically reinforcing heteronormative values through representation and imagery of a traditional family structure. In addition, McCray's symbolic identity as a heterosexual is safe for heterosexual and Black voters who are not accepting of members of the LGBT community. It also allows her a superficial connection to members of the LGBT community by aligning her as an ally due to past initiation into the LGBT community.

As this chapter concludes, one can reason from the narrative of events outlined here that public opinion around sexual orientation is becoming more progressive. However, the swearing in of the Blasio family symbolically reinforces the normative family structure of a man and woman within the political arena. McCray's silence and ambiguity around her transitional identity and rejection of labels allowed the campaign to erase the cultural memory of her sexually *deviant* past and validate traditional cultural beliefs and values.

The McCrays' narrative perpetuates the male mythology that lesbians will ultimately desire penis, which is a pervasive image within popular culture.[29] Her narrative acts as a danger to the lesbian and gay rights movement as it destabilizes lesbianism as a viable and stable identity; which is a harmful narrative for everyday individuals living as lesbians and gay men. More specifically, her narrative provides anti-gay supporters ammunition in hindering the gay and lesbian rights movement by portraying lesbianism as a choice. Rites of passage as a ritualized narrative within popular culture and politics needs to be a continuous area of study as the lesbian and gay rights movement gains support and breaks down barriers. Symbolic messages play a large role in shaping public opinion and changing public policy.

# NOTES

1. Jaime Stiehm, "For Better or Worse, Politics Is Show Business," *New York Times*, September 5, 2012.
2. Eric Louw, *The Media and Political Process* (London: Sage, 2005).
3. Ibid., 191.
4. Mark Wheeler, "The Democratic Worth of Celebrity Politics in an Era of Late Modernity," *British Journal of Politics & International Relations* 14, no. 2 (2012): 407–22.
5. Wheeler, "The Democratic Worth"; Craig Garthwaite and Tim Moore, "The Role of Celebrity Endorsements in Politics: Oprah, Obama, and the 2008 Democratic Primary." http://econ-server.umd.edu/~garthwaite/celebrityendorsements_garthwaitemoore.pdf (2008).
6. Jose Delreal, "Bill de Blasio Daughter Reveals Drug, Alcohol Abuse," *Politico*, December 14, 2013. Retrieved from http://www.politico.com/story/2013/12/bill-de-blasio-daughter-reveals-drug-alcohol-abuse-101511.html.
7. Molly Mcgarry and Fred Wasserman, *Becoming Visible: An Illustrated History of Lesbian and Gay Life in Twentieth-Century America* (New York: Penguin Studio: 1998), 187.
8. Gloria Joseph and Jill Lewis, *Common Differences: Conflicts in Black and White Feminist Perspectives* (New York: South End Press, 1986), 36.
9. *Meet Chirlane*. http://www.billdeblasio.com/meet-the-de-blasios/about-chirlane.
10. "Bill de Blasio For Mayor," last accessed April 12, 2014, http://www.billdeblasio.com/meet-the-de-blasios/about-chirlane.
11. Heidi Evans, "Bill de Blasio's Wife Chirlane McCray No Stranger to Politics, Will Be 'Activist' First Lady if He's Elected," *New York Daily News*, October 27, 2013.
12. Barbara Creed, "Lesbian Bodies: Tribades, Tomboys and Tarts" in *Sexy Bodies: The Strange Carnalities of Feminism,* ed. Elizabeth Grosz and Elspeth Probyn (London: Routledge), 115.
13. Arnold Gennep, *The Rites of Passage* (Chicago: The University of Chicago Press, 1960); Celeste Lacroix and Robert Westerfelhaus, "From the Closet to the Loft: Liminal License and Socio-Sexual Separation in 'Queer Eye for the Straight Guy,'" *Qualitative Research Reports in Communication* 6, no. 1 (2005): 11–19.
14. Gennep, *The Rites of Passage,* 189.
15. Chirlane McCray, "I Am A Lesbian," *Essence,* September 1979, 91.
16. Eric Marcus, *Making Gay History: The Half-Century Fight for Lesbian and Gay Rights* (New York: Perennial, 2002), 191.
17. Ibid.
18. Ibid., 191.
19. Clifford Geertz, *Religion as a Cultural System* (Waukegan: Fontana Press, 1993), 93.
20. Lacroix and Westerfelhaus, "From the Closet to the Loft."
21. Roger Aden, *Popular Stories and Promised Lands: Fan Cultures and Symbolic Pilgrimages* (Tuscaloosa: University of Alabama Press, 1999).
22. Victor Turner, Sacred Reals Essays in Religion, Belief and Society—Oxford "Betwixt and Between the Liminal Period in 'Rites de Passage,'" *Myth, Ritual, Symbolism and Taboo* 6, no. 1 (2005): 47–53.
23. Linda Villarosa, "Chirlane McCray: From Gay Trailblazer to Politician's Wife," *Essence,* May 9, 2013.
24. Sheena Howard, "The Kids Are All Right: A Mediated Ritual Narrative," *Women and Language* (2014): 81–89.
25. Sheena Howard, *Black Queer Identity Matrix: Towards An Integrated Queer of Color Framework* (New York: Peter Lang, 2014), 99.
26. Thomas Lemon, *The Rites of Passage in a Student Culture* (New York: Teachers College Press), 1972.
27. Caroline Keating, et al., "Going to College and Unpacking Hazing: A Functional Approach to Decrypting Initiation Practices Among Undergraduates," *Group Dynamics: Theory, Research, and Practice* 9, no. 2 (2005): 104–26.

28. "De Blasio Takes Formal Oath in Ceremony Officiated by Bill Clinton." Last accessed April 12, 2014, http://www.nbcnewyork.com/news/local/Bill-de-Blasio-Inauguration-Swearing-In-New-York-City-Mayor-January-2014-238324341.html.

29. For additional information see: Sheena Howard, "The Kids Are All Right: A Mediated Ritual Narrative," *Women and Language* (2014): 81–89.

# BIBLIOGRAPHY

Aden, Roger. *Popular Stories and Promised Lands: Fan Cultures and Symbolic Pilgrimages.* Tuscaloosa: The University of Alabama Press, 1999.

Combahee River Collective (CRC). In *Encyclopedia of African-American writing*. 2009. http://library.rider.edu:4048/login?qurl=http%3A%2F%2Fathena.rider.edu%3A2334%2Fcontent%2Fentry%2Fghaaw%2Fcombahee_river_collective_crc%2F0.

Creed, Barbara. "Lesbian Bodies: Tribades, Tomboys and Tarts." In *Sexy Bodies: The Strange Carnalities of Feminism,* edited by Elizabeth Grosz and Elspeth Probyn, 86–104. London: Routledge, 1995.

Davis-Floyd, Robbie. *Birth as an American Rite of Passage*. Los Angeles: University of California Press, 1992.

De Blasio Takes Formal Oath in Ceremony Officiated by Bill Clinton. NBC Universal Media. 2014 http://www.nbcnewyork.com/news/local/Bill-de-Blasio-Inauguration-Swearing-In-New-York-City-Mayor-January-2014-238324341.html.

Delreal, Jose. "Bill de Blasio daughter reveals drug, alcohol abuse." *Politico*. December, 24, 2013. http://www.politico.com/story/2013/12/bill-de-blasio-daughter-reveals-drug-alcohol-abuse-101511.html

Evans, Heidi. "Bill de Blasio's Wife Chirlane McCray No Stranger to Politics, Will be 'Activist' First Lady if He's Elected." *New York Daily News*. October 2013.

Garthwaite, Craig, and Tim Moore. "'The role of celebrity endorsements in politics: Oprah, Obama, and the 2008 democratic primary.'" 2008. http://www.stat.columbia.edu/~gelman/stuff_for_blog/celebrityendorsements_garthwaitemoore.pdf.

Geertz, Clifford. "Religion as a Cultural System." In *The Interpretation of Cultures: Selected Essays*, edited by Clifford Geertz, 87–125. Fontana Press, 1993.

Gennep, Arnold. *The Rites of Passage*. Chicago: The University of Chicago Press, 1960.

Howard, Sheena. "The Kids Are All Right: A Mediated Ritual Narrative." *Women and Language* (2014): 81–89.

Howard, Sheena. *Black Queer Identity Matrix: Towards An Integrated Queer of Color Framework*. New York: Peter Lang Publishers, 2014.

Joseph, Gloria, and Jill Lewis. *Common Differences: Conflicts in Black and White Feminist Perspectives*. New York: South End Press, 1986.

Keating, Caroline and Others, "Going to College and Unpacking Hazing: A Functional Approach to Decrypting Initiation Practices Among Undergraduates." *Group Dynamics: Theory, Research, and Practice* 9, no. 2 (2005): 104–26.

Lacroix, Celeste and Westerfelhaus, Robert. "From the Closet to the Loft: Liminal License and Socio-sexual Separation in 'Queer Eye for the Straight Guy.'" *Qualitative Research Reports in Communication* 6, no. 1 (2005): 11–19.

Lemon, Thomas. *The Rites of Passage in a Student Culture*. New York: Teachers College Press, 1972.

Louw, Eric. *The Media and Political Process*, London: Sage, 2005.

Marcus, Eric. *Making Gay History: The Half-Century Fight for Lesbian and Gay Rights*. New York: Perennial, 2002.

McCray, Chirlane. "I Am A Lesbian." *Essence*, September 1979.

Mcgarry, Molly, and Fred Wasserman. *Becoming Visible: An Illustrated History of Lesbian and Gay Life in Twentieth-Century America*. New York: Penguin Studio, 1998.

*Meet Chirlane, 2013* New Yorkers for de Blasio. http://www.billdeblasio.com/meet-the-deblasios/about-chirlane.

Salsa Soul Sisters (N.D.), *Where it Can All Come Together*, brochure, LHA Organization. Files/Salsa Soul Sisters.

Shockley, Anne (1979, Nov 30). The Salsa Soul Sisters. *Off Our Backs. ProQuest.* Web. 12 Jan. 2014.

Smith, Barbara. *Homegirls: A Black Feminist Anthology.* New York: Kitchen Table, 1983.

Stiehm, Jaime. "For Better or Worse, Politics Is Show Business." *New York Times.* September, 2012.

Turner, Victor. "Betwixt and Between the Liminal Period in *Rites de Passage*." *Myth, Ritual, Symbolism and Taboo* 6, no. 1 (2005): 47–53.

Wheeler, Mark. "The Democratic Worth of Celebrity Politics in an Era of Late Modernity." *British Journal of Politics & International Relations* 14, no. 3 (2012): 407–22.

# Index

AAAA. *See* American Association for Advertising Agencies
*ABG. See The Misadventures of Awkward Black Girl*
Abrams, Molly (fictional character), 58
*According to Our Hearts: Rhinelander v. Rhinelander and the Law of Multiracial Family* (Onwuachi-Willig), 21
Adichie, Chimamanda Ngozi, 156, 163
advertising: Aunt Jemima and, 209–211, 211; BFT and, 206; for Campbell's soup, 209; celebrities in, 214; Civil Rights Movement and, 211; complexities and contradictions in, 204–206; conglomerate monopolies in, 205; convergence and, 205; Creative Revolution in, 202, 210; in *Ebony*, 225–240; electronification and, 200, 204–205; employment discrimination in, 212; empowerment with, 219; in *Essence*, 225–240; for fade creams, 233; future of, 215–220; Gender Pluralism and, 211; Generation X and, 202–203; hip hop for, 203; hypersexuality in, 213–214; in Industrial Revolution, 207–208; Internet and, 203, 217, 218–219; Jezebel in, 213–214; Mammy in, 208, 209, 213; market segmentation in, 219; mass media and, 201; Matriarch in, 213; meaning of, 200–202; in 1960s, 202, 211–212; in 1970s, 212; in 1980s, 202–203, 212; objectification and, 207; paradigm shift in, 199–220; popular culture and, 201; privacy and, 219; racial slurs in, 208; skin color in, 225–240; slavery and, 207; stereotypes and, 199–220; Strong Black Woman in, 214–215; Welfare Queen in, 214; wenches in, 207; on YBF, 256
advertising stamps, 208–209
Africa Channel, 255
Akil, Mara Brock, 17, 18
Ak'Sent: "All I Need" by, 142; "Zingy" by, 138
*All about Love* (hooks), 168
Allen, Brenda, 2
Allen, Debbie, 3
"All I Need" (Ak'Sent), 142
*All My Baby Mommas* (TV program), 5
*All That, Gullah Gullah Island* (TV program), 252
"All That I Got is You" (Ghostface Killah), 115–116
Ambi, 233–234, 234–235
American Association for Advertising Agencies (AAAA), 212
*An American Family* (TV program), 39
*American Idol* (TV program), 6
American Life Project on Millennials, by Pew Research Center, 251, 279
*America's Top Model*, 254

Amin, Takiyah Nur, 30
*Amos 'n' Andy* (radio and TV program), 16, 25; Sapphire on, 36
Anderson, James, 279
Angelou, Maya, 92, 253; on skin lightening products, 233; West and, 114
Angry Black Woman, 39, 58; *I'm Gonna Get You Sucka* and, 83; *Madea* and, 59
Angus, Ian, 56–57
Applied Research Center, 252
"Area Codes" (Ludacris), 179
The Artist Empowerment Firm, 254
arts, BMW DoErs in, 253–255
*At the Dark End of the Street* (McGuire), 27
Aubrey, Jennifer, 126
Aunt Esther (fictional character), 25
Auntie, 208, 209
Aunt Jemima, 209–210; advertising and, 209–211, 211; Mammy and, 24, 210
*Awkward Black Girl* (webseries), 4

Baartmann, Saartjie (Sarah), 2, 275
Baby Mama, 37, 274; in rap music, 119
bad Black father, 100
bad Black mother, 100
*Bad Girls Club* (TV program), 39, 276
Badu, Erykah, 258
Bankable Productions, 254
Banks, Azealia, 141
Banks, Tyra, 254
Baraka, Amiri, 233
Barnette, Neema, 3
Barras, Jonetta R., 97
*Basketball Wives* (TV program), 3, 39, 276
Beale, Scott, 249–250
beauty: of celebrities, 285–286; skin color and, 227–228
Beavers, Louis, 16
Becker, T. J., 249
*being mary jane* (TV program), 18
Berkely, Elizabeth, 58
BET. *See* Black Entertainment Television
*The Beulah Show* (TV program), 16
Bey Feminism, 155–169
Beyoncé, 4, 5, 28, 280; body image and, 160; as bottom bitch, 161–163; in Destiny's Child, 155, 158; feminism and, 155–169, 156; as inspirer, 283–284; Pinterest and, 281; sexuality and, 160; social media and, 156
*Beyoncé: The Visual Album*, 155–169
"Beyoncé Serenaded Teenage Boys and Black Feminists" (blog), 167–168
BFT. *See* Black Feminist Thought
Big Boi, 257, 264
*Big Momma* (films), 58, 83
*The Big Moo* (Godin), 258, 263
*The Birth of a Nation* (Griffith), 99
Bitch: bottom bitch, Beyoncé as, 161–163; Gangster Bitch, 274, 277. *See also* Black Bitch
"Black," meaning of, 226–228
Black Bitch, 39, 178; anger of, 44; *I'm Gonna Get You Sucka* and, 78, 83
Black Codes, 207
*Black Enterprise* (magazine), 255–256, 264
Black Entertainment Television (BET), 3, 18, 34, 38, 255, 277; Millennials and, 252
blackface, 24; Aunt Jemima and, 210
Black Feminist Thought (BFT), 130–131, 143, 157–158; advertising and, 206; HHT, 180–181; hip hop and, 175–176; "How to Love" and, 180–181; principles of, 206
Black is Beautiful movement, 227, 229; skin lightening advertisements and, 231
Black Lady, 37, 43; in *For Colored Girls*, 94; Mammy and, 37
Black Lesbian Caucus, 295
Black liberation movement, 157
*Black Looks: Race and Representation* (hooks), 96
Black Millennial Women Digital Entrepreneurs (BMW DoErs), 247–266; in arts, 253–255; in fashion, 256; gender and, 264; generic criticism and, 259–260; going independent by, 265; men and, 264; in publishing, 253–254; in rap music, 254; rhetorical studies and, 263; sports franchises and, 255; television and, 254–255
Black Power Movement, 25
Black Queen, 37
*Black Queer Identity Matrix: Towards An Integrated Queer of Color Framework*

(Howard), 299–300
*Black Still Matters in Marketing* (Miller), 252
*Black Women's Blueprint* (reports), 27
Blake, Mike, 130
Blaxploitation films, 17, 58; funk music in, 75; history of, 84n1; sheroes of, 75; soul music in, 75
bleaching cream, 231, 232
Blige, Mary J.: Eve and, 137; with Ghostface Killah, 115–116; "Runaway Love" by, 179
blogs, 2, 4, 39; "Beyoncé Serenaded Teenage Boys and Black Feminists," 167–168; "Feminists Everywhere React to Beyoncé's Latest," 165–166; "Five Reasons I'm Here for Beyoncé," 166–167; hair care, 266; *For Harriet*, 229; Luvs and, 216–217; "On Defending Beyoncé: Black Feminists, White Feminists and the Line in the Sand," 164–165; "The Problem with Beyhive Bottom Bitch Feminism," 160–163; *Statigram*, 235; YBF, 255–256
"Blow" (Beyoncé), 160
blues, 127–128
*The Bluest Eye* (Morrison), 92, 225, 240
BMW DoErs. *See* Black Millennial Women Digital Entrepreneurs
Bobo, Jacqueline, 5
body image: Beyoncé and, 160; skin color and, 225–240
Bogle, Donald, 72, 99
Boomers, 203
bottom bitch, Beyoncé as, 161–163
Boulet, Jennie (fictional character), 17
"Bow Down/I Been On" (Beyoncé), 5
Bowers, Vivian (fictional character), 18
Bowser, Yvette Lee, 255
branded entertainment, for advertising, 201
Braun, Virginia, 282
bravado, in rap music videos, 139–141, 146
BRAVO, 38
Braxton, Tamar, 1, 4, 41, 45–46
Braxton, Toni, 41, 45
Braxton, Towanda, 41
Braxton, Traci, 41

Braxton, Trina, 41
*Braxton Family Values* (TV program), 4, 40–41, 42; audience identification with, 48; drama in, 47–48; potential of, 48–49; sexuality in, 46–47; sisters in, 44–46; working mothers in, 43–44
*Breaking Bad* (TV program), 29
breeder stereotype. *See* Welfare Mother
Breedlove, Claudia (fictional character), 240
"Brenda's Got a Baby" (Tupac), 119
Brown, James, 262
Brown, Jamie Foster, 253
Brown, Monica, 34
brutal Black buck, 99
Burruss, Kandi, 1, 254
Bush, George H. W., 18
*The Butler* (film), 22

Cake Soap, 230
Calloway, Cab, 127
Campbell, Erica, 41, 42
Campbell, Tina, 41, 42
Campbell's soup, 209
*Candid Camera* (TV program), 39
Carmichael, Stokely, 25
Carol's Daughters, 253; YBF and, 256
Carroll, Diahann, 17, 22
Carter, Monifah, 34
Carter, Shawn. *See* Jay-Z
Castleman, Michael, 28
"Cater 2 U" (Beyoncé), 160
CBS. *See* Columbia Broadcasting System
celebrities: in advertising, 212, 214; beauty of, 285–286; hypersexuality and, 214; as inspirers, 282–284; on Internet, 273–288; in RTV, 42–48; sexuality of, 284–285. *See also specific celebrities*
*Celebrity Apprentice* (TV program), 4
celebrity docusoaps, 34
*Charlie's Angels* (film), 158
Chenzira, Ayoka, 3
Cherry (fictional character), 76–81
Cheryl (fictional character), 76–81
Chicken Head, 39
Chisholm, Shirley, 263
Civil Rights Movement, 36; advertising and, 211; Millennials and, 252
Civil War, 207

Clark, Caroline, 255–256
Clarke, Victoria, 282
*Cleopatra Jones* (film), 17
Clinique, 237–238
Clinton, Bill, 18
Clinton, Catherine, 24, 26
Clyburn, Mignon, 216
*Coffy* (film), 17
Cole, Johnetta B., 5, 177, 262
Cole, Keyshia, 5, 143
Coleman, Robin Means, 92, 206, 275
*College Hill* (TV program), 277
Collins, Patricia Hill, 5, 37, 57–58, 146, 157, 181, 273; on "othering" of Black female body, 227
colorism. *See* skin color
*The Color Purple* (Walker), 92
Columbia Broadcasting System (CBS), 204
Columbia Records, 176
Combahee River Collective (CRC), 157–158, 215, 295
Combs, Sean "Puffy," 257, 258, 264
Common, 111
Communist Party, 16
"Conceited" (Remy Ma), 139
Confederacy, 24
conglomerate monopolies, in advertising, 205
Congressional Black Caucus, 212
convergence, advertising and, 205
the coon, 99
Cooper, Anna Julia, 24
Cooper, Britney, 21
Cosby, Bill, in advertising, 212
*The Cosby Show* (TV program), 17, 22–23, 36
Cottle-Harris, Tomeka, 34
Cover Girl, 258
CRC. *See* Combahee River Collective
Creative Revolution, in advertising, 202, 210
*Crunk Feminist Collective*, 166–167
Crystal (fictional character), 95
Cult of True Womanhood, 23
*Cultural Politics In Contemporary America* (Angus and Jhally), 56–57
Cuvier, George, 275

"Dance" (Nas), 116–117
Dance, Daryl Cumber, 90, 247–248
dancing, in rap music videos, 147–148
*Dangerously in Love* (Beyoncé), 155
*Dark Girls* (film), 229, 230
dark spot removers, 231, 232, 237
Darwin, Charles, 275
Dash, Julie, 3
data mining, 219
Dates, Janette, 276
Davis, Angela, 129, 131
Davis, Viola, 55
Dawes, Dominique, 138
Dead Prez, 111
"Dear Mama" (Tupac), 115, 179
de Blasio, Bill, 293–303, 294
*Deception* (TV program), 17–18
Dencia, 230
Dennis, David, 23
Denzin, Norman, 130
Derrida, Jacques, 226–227
Destiny's Child, 155, 158
diapers, 216–217
"Did It On 'Em" (Minaj), 139–140
*A Different World* (TV program), 17
Dionne, Evette, 40
Diva, 274, 277
*Django Unchained* (film), 18
Dobson, Tamara, 17
docusoaps, 34, 42
"Does Tyler Perry have a Problem With Black Men" (Smith, M.), 98–99
Dondria, 265
Downey, Sharon, 113
Dr. Fred Summit, 242n49–243n50
Draper, Betty (fictional character), 27
Dreamtone Skin Tone Correcting Serum, 236
"Drunk In Love" (Beyoncé), 28, 161–162
Dubois, W. E. B., 252
Dubrofsky, Rachel E., 8
DuMont Network, 16
DuVaernay, Ava, 3–4
Dyke, 274, 277
Dyson, Michael Eric, 22–23, 111, 112, 178

Earth Mother, 274, 277
*Ebony* (magazine), 22; advertising in, 225–240; *Dark Girls* and, 230; skin

color in, 225–240
*The Electric Lady* (Robinson, J.), 258
electronification, advertising and, 200, 204–205
Elle, Kim, 255
Elliott, Missy, 254
Emancipation Proclamation, 207
emasculation, of men, 81
employment discrimination, in advertising, 212
empowerment: with advertising, 219; in rap music videos, 133, 136–138
Entitled Diva, 39
Epps, Edwin (fictional character), 26
*ER* (TV program), 17
*Essence* (magazine): advertising in, 225–240; McCray in, 295, 297; skin color in, 225–240
Estée Lauder, 236
*The Ethel Waters Show* (TV program), 15
Eubanks, Natasha, 4, 255–256; connections with Rae and Robinson, J., 260–263
Evans, Florida (fictional character), 25
Eve, 137–138, 139
Even Better Clinical Dark Spot Corrector, 237–238
Even Skintone Illuminator, 236

Facebook, 250, 278, 293
fade creams, 231, 232, 233, 234–235, 239
*Fame* (TV program), 17
*The Family Hustle* (TV program), 34
fashion, 256
Fashion Fair Cosmetics, 231
father deprivation, 97
fat suits, 83
FDA. *See* Food and Drug Administration
*Fearless* (magazine), 265
*The Feminine Mystique* (Freidan), 27
femininity: "How to Love" and, 176; mass media and, 130, 130–131; in popular culture, 127; skin color and, 228
feminism: Beyoncé and, 155–169; *For Colored Girls* and, 89–103; definitions for, 158–159; HHF, 180–181; radical, 158; rap music videos and, 130–131. *See also* Black Feminist Thought

"Feminists Everywhere React to Beyoncé's Latest" (blog), 165–166
femiphobia, 112
*Fifty Shades of Grey* (Roiphe), 28
film. *See* Blaxploitation films; *specific films*
Fisher, Luchina, 20
"Five Reasons I'm Here for Beyoncé" (blog), 166–167
Flavor Unit, 254
"***Flawless" (Beyoncé), 156, 162, 166, 167
Flyguy (fictional character), 75
Food and Drug Administration (FDA), 231
*For Colored Girls* (film), 89–103; images of women in, 91–93; lessons on black men in, 97–101; lessons on black women in, 95–97; putting words in Black women's mouths, 101–102; reclaiming ourselves and, 102–103; sexuality in, 96; stereotypes in, 93–95
*For Colored Girls Who Have Considered Suicide When The Rainbow Is Enuf* (Shange), 91
*For Harriet* (blog), 229
Foss, Sonja, 113, 117
Fox-Genovese, Elizabeth, 26
*Foxy Brown* (film), 17, 75
Frazier, Franklin E., 227
Freak, 181, 274; rap music and, 277
freak show, 2
Freidan, Betty, 27
Frisby, Cynthia, 126
*Fruitvale Station* (film), 22
"Fuck Friends" (Tupac), 119
funk music, in Blaxploitation films, 75
*Funnelcake Flowers and the Urban Chameleons* (web series), 265

*The Game* (TV program), 17, 26
game doc, 39, 51n33
Gangster Bitch, 274, 277
Gates, Henry Louis, Jr., 22–23
gay, 293–303
Geertz, Clifford, 298
gender: BMW DoErs and, 264; Millennials and, 248–251. *See also* men
Gender Pluralism, advertising and, 211
*Gender Talk* (Sheftall and Cole), 262

gender violence, 175–188; in hip hop, 175–188; Jezebel and, 183–184; reimagining realities and, 185–187. *See also* sexual abuse
Generation X, 202–203
Generation Z, 266
generic criticism: BMW DoErs and, 259–260; MAR and, 113–114
Gennep, Arnold, 297
*Get Christie Love!* (TV program), 17
"Getting Some" (Shawnna), 140
Ghetto Girl, 39
Ghostface Killah, 112, 115–116
Gibson, Laurieann, 42
Gilbert, Whitley (fictional character), 17
Giovanni, Nicky, 114
*Girlfriends* (TV program), 17
*Girls* (TV program), 28
Godin, Seth, 258, 263
going independent, by BMW DoErs, 265
Goldberg, Whoopi, 101
Gold Digger, 38, 181, 274
Golden, Marita, 229
The Goldmind, Inc., 254
*Gone with the Wind* (film), 24
Goode, Meagan, 18
Goodman, Jasmin, 266
*Good Times* (TV program), 25
*The Good Wife* (TV program), 21
Graham, Lawrence, 227
Grant, Lydia (fictional character), 17
Green, Nancy, 24, 210
*Grey's Anatomy* (TV program), 18, 255
Grier, Pam, 17, 58
Griffith, D. W., 99
griots, 247
Guerrero, Ed, 73, 75
Gutman, Herbert, 25
Guy-Sheftall, Beverly, 5, 177, 262

hair care: blogs, 266; natural-hair movement and, 229, 266
Haj House, 265
Harpo studios, 254
Harrell, Jackson, 113
Harris, Clifford, 34
Harris, LaKeisha, 29
Harris, Tina, 58
Harris, Trudier, 93

Harris-Perry, Melissa, 112, 214
The Harvard Report, 176
*Hawthorne* (TV program), 17
*The Hazel Scott Show* (TV program), 16
HBCU. *See* Historically Black University
*The Help* (film), 24
Hemings, Sally (fictional character), 20–21, 26
Hendler, Elana J., 250
"Here We Go" (Trina), 135–136, 136, 142
Heron, Gil Scott, 22, 127
"Hey Mama" (West, K.), 114–115
HHF. *See* hip hop feminism
Hight, Christopher, 75
Hill, Lauryn, 111
hip hop, 1, 111–112, 277; for advertising, 203; BFT and, 175–176; commercialization of, 176–177; gender violence in, 175–188; history of, 127–129; "How to Love" and, 175–188; hypermasculinity in, 178; hypersexuality in, 177, 178; objectification in, 178; as paradoxical, 187–188; sexism in, 178–180; stereotypes in, 126. *See also* rap music
hip hop feminism (HHF), 180–181
Historically Black University (HBCU), 229
HIV, 64, 65, 185–186
Holyfield, Evander, 28
*Homegirls!* (McCray), 296
homophobia, 175
*Honey Hush* (Dance), 247–248
Hoochie, 181
hooks, bell, 5, 66, 81, 96, 175, 212; *All about Love* by, 168
Hootchie Mama, 39
Horne, Lena, 22
Hottentot Venus, 2
Howard, Sheena, 299–300
"How to Love" (Lil' Wayne), 175–188; BFT and, 180–181; Jezebel and, 181, 183–184; as paradoxical, 187–188; reimagining realities and, 185–187
HQ. *See* hydroquinone
*Huffington Post's Black Voices*, 216
Hughes, Cathy, 254
Hull, Akasha, 90, 92
Hunter, Karen, 253

Hunter, Margaret, 226, 228, 233
Hunter, Wendy Williams, 254
Huxtable, Claire (fictional character), 17, 22, 36–37, 37
Huxtable, Cliff (fictional character), 22
hydroquinone (HQ), 232, 237
hypermasculinity, 75, 81, 179; in hip hop, 175, 178
hyperpigmentation, 238
hypersexuality, 17, 58, 276; in advertising, 213–214; celebrities and, 214; of Gold Digger, 38; HHF and, 181; in hip hop, 177, 178; in *Temptation: Confessions of a Marriage Counselor*, 57, 65. *See also* Jezebel

*I Am A Lesbian* (McCray), 295, 297
*I Am Other* (YouTube channel), 259
identity politics, 293–303
Žižek, Slavoj, 82
"If I were a Boy" (Beyoncé), 160
"I Get Around" (Tupac), 119
"I Got a Thing for You" (Trina), 136, 143
*I Hate LA Dudes* (TV program), 259
*I Know Why The Caged Bird Sings* (Angelou), 92
*I Love New York* (TV program), 39
"I Made It" (Jay-Z), 116
IMC. *See* Integrated Marketing Communications
*I'm Gonna Get You Sucka* (film), 71–84; Black women's bodies and, 81–84; men in, 73–76
*The Impact of Fatherlessness on Black Women* (Barras), 97
"Inauguration Day" (Spillers), 82
*Incidents in the Life of a Slave Girl* (Jacobs), 26
"Independent Woman" (Beyoncé), 158
Industrial Revolution, advertising in, 207–208
*In Living Color* (TV program), 84n4
inspirers, celebrities as, 282–284
Instagram, 278, 279, 280–281
Integrated Marketing Communications (IMC), 201, 218, 219
Internet, 7–8; advertising and, 203, 217, 218–219; celebrities on, 273–288. *See also* blogs; social media

interracial kiss, on *Star Trek*, 16–17
Izrael, Jimi, 93

Jackson, Janet, 28
Jackson, Michael, 212
Jacobs, Harriet, 26
Jay-Z, 28, 112; Beyoncé and, 159, 160, 161–162; "I Made It" by, 116
Jefferson, Louise (fictional character), 17
Jefferson, Thomas, 21
*The Jeffersons* (TV program), 17, 20, 30n11
Jemima Writers Collective, 295
Jemison, Mae, 16
Jewell, Su, 279
Jezebel, 23, 24, 36, 276; in advertising, 213–214; in *For Colored Girls*, 94, 98; gender violence and, 183–184; "How to Love" and, 181, 183–184; *I'm Gonna Get You Sucka* and, 83; *Madea* and, 59; Pope as, 26; slavery and, 181, 213–214
Jhally, Sut, 56–57
Jim and Jane Crow, 25, 207
"John (If I Die Today)" (Lil' Wayne), 187–188, 188
Johnson, Deborah, 297–298
Johnson, Fern, 233
Johnson, Shelia, 255
Jones, Calvin, 278
Jones, Hettie, 233
Jones, Lisa, 233
Jones, Quincy, 1
Jordan, Michael, 212
Joseph, Peniel, 25
*Journal of Sex Research*, 28
Judith (fictional character), 55–66
*Julia* (TV program), 16, 17, 22

Karenga, Maulana, 25
Kartel, Vybz, 230
Kauffmann Foundation, 249
"Keep Ya Head Up" (Tupac), 119, 179
Keeter, Scott, 248, 250–251
Kendall, Mikki, 164–165
Kennedy, John F., 210
Kerlikowske, Gil, 294
Kerner Report, 211–212
Kickstarter, 259
King, B. B., 22

King, Deborah K., 130
King, Martin Luther, Jr., 16, 211
King, Rodney, 73
*Kingdom Come* (Jay-Z), 116
Kinnon, Joy Bennett, 228
Knowles, Solange, 265
Knowles-Carter, Beyoncé. *See* Beyoncé

Lampkin, Chrissy, 1
Lancôme, 236
*The Last King of Scotland* (film), 18
The Last Poets, 127
*Late Registration* (West), 114
Lawrence, Martin, 58, 83
Leakes, Nene, 4, 34
Lee, Spike, 92, 99, 229
Lena, Jennifer C., 128
lesbian, gay, bisexual, and transgender (LGBT), 293–303
"Lettin' Go" (Robinson, J.), 257
Lewinsky, Monica, 18
Lewis, John, 21
LGBT. *See* lesbian, gay, bisexual, and transgender
"L.I.F.E." (Lil' Mama), 135
Lifestyle Entrepreneur, 265
"Lighters Up" (Lil' Kim), 137
Lil' Kim, 136, 137
Lil' Mama, 135, 140
Lil' Wayne: "How to Love" by, 175–188; "John (If I Die Today)" by, 187–188, 188; "Mrs. Officer" by, 179; as paradoxical, 187–188
liminality, 298–300
Lincoln, Abraham, 24
Linkugel, Will, 113
"Lip Gloss" (Lil' Mama), 140
Littlefield, Marci, 130
*Living Single* (TV program), 17, 255
Locasto, Joanna (fictional character), 18
Lorde, Audre, 263
L'Oreal, 216
Lost Cause myth, 24
L'Ouverture, Toussaint, 100–101
Louw, Eric, 293–294
*Love and War* (Braxton), 4
*Love & Hip-Hop* (TV program), 3, 39
love/relationships/intimacy, in rap music videos, 141–143, 145–146

*Loving v. Virginia in a Post-Racial World* (Maillard), 21
Lozada, Evelyn, 1
Lucas, Ted, 144
Ludacris, 179
Lupe Fiasco, 111
Luvs, 216–217

Ma Bell (fictional character), 76–81
*Madea* (films), 58–59, 83
Madison, Paula, 255
*Mad Men* (TV program), 27, 29
Maillard, Kevin Noble, 21
*Making Gay History* (Marcus), 297–298
male heroism, 73
Malone, Naomi (fictional character), 58
Mammy, 3, 23, 24, 36, 276; in advertising, 208, 209, 213; Aunt Jemima and, 24, 210; Black Lady and, 37; in *For Colored Girls*, 94; in *Gone with the Wind*, 24; *I'm Gonna Get You Sucka* and, 83; *Madea* and, 59; male version of, 99; monument for, 24–25; qualities of, 58
MAR. *See* Mother Appreciation Rap
Marcus, Eric, 297–298
Margolis, Harriet, 74
Marguilies, Julianna, 21
market segmentation, in advertising, 219
*Martin* (TV program), 25
Martin, Kim, 40, 41
*Mary Mary* (TV program), 4, 41, 42; audience identification with, 48; drama in, 47–48; potential of, 48–49; sexuality in, 46–47; sisters in, 44–46; working mothers in, 43–44
masculinity: *For Colored Girls* and, 89–103. *See also* hypermasculinity
"Massive Attack" (Minaj), 139–140
mass media: advertising and, 201; convergence of, 8; exclusion by, 3, 36; femininity and, 130, 130–131; racism in, 57–59; sexism in, 57–59; socialization by, 2; stereotypes and, 274–275. *See also* Blaxploitation films; Internet; music; publishing; television; *specific films*
Matriarch, 276; in advertising, 213; in *For Colored Girls*, 94

Maxwell, Brandon, 23, 23–24, 25, 26
McCarthy, Joseph, 16
McCarty, CeCee, 253
McCray, Chirlane, 293–303; liminality and, 298–300; reincorporation and, 300–301
McDaniel, Hattie, 16, 24
McGuire, Danielle, 27
McKenzie, Mia, 164–165
"Me, Myself and I" (Beyoncé), 160
Mellie (fictional character), 27
men: BMW DoErs and, 264; as brutal Black buck, 99; as the coon, 99; defense of in rap music videos, 132–133; emasculation of, 81; gender violence and, 175–188; male heroism of, 73; rap music and, 111–120; as Uncle Tom, 99; virility of, 81
men in drag, 58–59, 84
*Metropolis* (Robinson), 257–258
*Middle of Nowhere* (documentary), 3
Miles, Tiya, 21
*The Millennial Manifesto* (Beale), 249–250
Millennials, 203, 248–253; BET and, 252; Civil Rights Movement and, 252; gender and, 248–251; racism and, 252; social media and, 250, 250–251; technology and, 249; television and, 252–253. See also Black Millennial Women Digital Entrepreneurs
Miller, Pepper, 252
Million Man March, 73
Minaj, Nicki, 4, 132, 280; advertising by, 214; "Did It On 'Em" by, 139–140; as inspirer, 283–284; "Massive Attack" by, 139–140; "Right Thru Me" by, 141–142; "Super Bass" by, 142
"Minnie the Moocher" (Calloway), 127
*The Misadventures of Awkward Black Girl* (*ABG*), 259
misogyny: hip hop and, 175; rap music and, 119–120
Miss America, 229
Missy, 138
*Moesha* (TV program), 17
monopolies, in advertising, 205
Moore, Sylenna Johnson, 34
Morgan, Joan, 180
Morrison, Toni, 92, 225, 240, 253

Mos Def, 111
Mother Appreciation Rap (MAR), 111–120; "All That I Got is You" and, 115–116; analysis of genre, 117–120; "Dance" and, 116–117; "Dear Mama" and, 115; generic criticism and, 113–114; "Hey Mama" and, 114–115; "I Made It" and, 116
motherhood, rap music and, 111–120
Moynihan Report, 94, 95
*Mr. and Mrs. Smith* (film), 18
Mr. Big (fictional character), 71
Mrs. Carter Show, 160
"Mrs. Officer" (Lil' Wayne), 179
MTV, 38
Multicultural Millennials, 252
Murphy, Eddie, 58, 83
music: blues, 127–128; Robinson, J., and, 257–258. See also hip hop; rap music; specific artists and songs
"My Black is Beautiful," by Proctor & Gamble, 229
*My Brother and Me* (TV program), 252
*My Mic Sounds Nice* (documentary), 3

NAACP. See National Association for the Advancement of Colored People
Nadel, Jack, 249
Nadinola, 232–233
Nas, 112, 116–117
National Association for the Advancement of Colored People (NAACP): *Amos 'n' Andy* and, 16; *Scandal* and, 29
natural-hair movement, 229, 266
"Naughty Girl" (Beyoncé), 160
Neal, Mark Anthony, 119
*The New Normal* (TV program), 4
Nichols, Nichelle, 16–17
*Norbit* (film), 83
Norman, Christian, 216
Northrup, Solomon, 26
Norwood, Sonja, 254
Nussbaum, Emily, 21
Nyong'o, Lupita, 31n39, 230

Obama, Barack, 18, 20; criticism of, 22; Winfrey and, 294
Obama, Michelle, 20; skin color of, 229

objectification, 2, 3; advertising and, 207; in hip hop, 178; in rap music videos, 277. *See also* stereotypes
O'Grady, Lorraine, 226
Okazawa-Rey, Margo, 227
OkCupid, 21
Oliver, Tracey, 259
"Olivia Pope and the Scandal of Representation" (Maxwell), 23
"On Defending Beyoncé: Black Feminists, White Feminists and the Line in the Sand" (blog), 164–165
O'Neal, Shaunie, 3
Onwuachi-Willig, Angela, 21
*Oprah's Next Chapter* (TV program), 23, 55
*The Oprah Winfrey Show* (TV program), 294
Orrell, Lisa, 249, 250, 251
"othering" of Black female body, 226–227
Outkast, 257
OWN television network, 254

Palcy, Euzhan, 3
Paley, William, 204
Palmer's, 235–236, 242n49–243n50
paradigm shift, in advertising, 199–220
"Partition" (Beyoncé), 160
patriarchy, 59; in *Temptation: Confessions of a Marriage Counselor*, 65
Patterson, Robert, 59
Patton, Jonetta, 254
Pearl Milling Company, 210
Peirce, Charles, 200–201
Perry, Tyler, 4; *For Colored Girls* by, 89–103; stereotypes and, 55–66; *Temptation: Confessions of a Marriage Counselor* by, 55–66
Perry-Harris, Melissa, 23
Pew Research Center, 251, 278–279, 279
Phillips, Layli, 38, 129, 132–133, 133, 138, 274, 277
Pickaninny, 208, 209
pigmentocracy, 227
Pimp Theory, 161
Pinterest, 278, 279, 280, 280–281
*The Plantation Mistress* (Clinton, C.), 26
Pleas, Arnetra, 29
Poitier, Sidney, 29

politics, popular culture and, 293–295
*Pondy Woods* (Warren), 90
Pope, Olivia (fictional character), 15–30; as Jezebel, 26; as post-racial heroine, 20–23
popular culture: advertising and, 201; femininity in, 127; politics and, 293–295. *See also* mass media
poster stamps, 208–209
post racial society, 252
Powell, Adam Clayton, Jr., 16
Pozner, Jennifer, 39
Price, Janeen, 27
Price, Lisa, 253
Prince, 258
privacy, advertising and, 219
*Private Practice* (TV program), 255
"The Problem with Beyhive Bottom Bitch Feminism," 160; blog, 160–163
Proctor & Gamble, 216–217, 229
product placement, 201
Project Blaq, 266
pseudo-politics, 293–294
Publicis Omnicom Group, 219
publishing, 7; BMW DoErs in, 253–254. *See also specific magazines and books*
punk rock, 127

Queen Latifah, 17, 129, 254
Qureshi, Bilal, 165–166

race products, 232
racial ambiguity, 8
racial capital, 226, 238
racial discrimination, 227
racial slurs, 208
racism: in media, 57–59; Millennials and, 252; rap music and, 127; skin color and, 227
radical feminism, 158
Radio One, 254
Rae, Issa, 4, 259, 260–263
Randolph, Amanda, 16
rape: in *Scandal*, 27–28; in slavery, 65, 94
rap music: blues and, 127–128; BMW DoErs in, 254; commercialization of, 128, 144; men and, 111–120; motherhood and, 111–120; sexism and, 175–176; stereotypes in, 119; thematic

content of, 129; voyeurism in, 128. *See also* Mother Appreciation Rap
rap music videos: "All I Need," 142; bravado in, 139–141, 146; "Conceited," 139; dancing in, 147–148; defense of men in, 132–133; "Did It On 'Em," 139–140; empowerment in, 133, 136–138; feminism and, 130–131; "Getting Some," 140; "Here We Go," 135–136, 136, 142; "I Got a Thing for You," 136, 143; "L.I.F.E.," 135; "Lighters Up," 137; "Lip Gloss," 140; list of, 147; love/relationships/intimacy in, 141–143, 145–146; "Massive Attack," 139–140; new themes in, 138–143; objectification in, 277; respect in, 132–133, 134–136; "Right Thru Me," 141–142; self-help in, 133, 136–138; "Single Again," 138, 142; solidarity in, 133, 136–138; stereotypes in, 129–130; "Super Bass," 142; "Tambourine," 137–138, 139; themes in, 134; "We Run This," 138; "Whoa," 136; by women, 125–148; "Zingy," 138. *See also* "How to Love" (Lil' Wayne)
Rashad, Phylicia, 22, 23, 101
Rasputia (fictional character), 83
Ravera, Gina, 58
*Ray* (film), 18
*R&B Divas-Atlanta* (TV program), 34
*Real Colored Girls* (website), 160–163
*The Real Housewives of Atlanta* (TV program), 4, 34, 39, 276
reality television (RTV), 1, 2, 5, 38–40, 276–277; celebrities in, 42–48; as constructed reality, 33; potential of, 48–49; stereotypes in, 34; on VH1, 3. *See also specific programs*
*The Real World* (TV program), 39
Reconstruction, 207, 208
Recording Industry Association of America (RIAA), 131–132
Reddick-Morgan, Kerri, 129, 132–133, 133, 138
Red Scare, 16
Reid-Brinkley, Shanara R., 37
reincorporation, McCray and, 300–301
Remy Ma, 139

respect: in rap music videos, 132–133, 134–136; sexuality and, 185
"The Revolution Will Not Be Televised" (Heron), 22
Rewind and Reframe, 217
Rhimes, Shonda, 6, 18, 255, 259
Rhone, Sylvia, 254
RIAA. *See* Recording Industry Association of America
"Right Thru Me" (Minaj), 141–142
Rihanna, 28, 280; advertising by, 214; as inspirer, 283; Pinterest and, 281
*The Rites of Passage* (Gennep), 297
*Road Rules* (TV program), 39
The Roaring Twenties, 201
Roberts, Robin, 129
Robinson, Chris, 182–183
Robinson, Janelle Monae: connections with Eubanks and Rae, 260–263; *The Electric Lady* by, 258; *Metropolis* by, 257–258
Robinson, Tracy, 227
Roddenberry, Gene, 16
Rodgers, Raymond, 113
Roiphe, Katie, 28
role models, 1
"Rope Burn" (Jackson, J.), 28
Rose, Tricia, 144, 179
Rowland, Kelly, 136
Roy, Rachel, 256
RTV. *See* reality television
"Runaway Love" (Blige), 179
"Run the World (Girls)" (Beyoncé), 160
Rutt, Chris L., 210
Ryan, Damian, 278
Rye Rye, 141

Salsa Soul Sisters, 295
Salt-N-Pepa, 129
*Sanford and Son* (TV program), 25
Sapphire, 3, 25, 36; anger of, 44; in *For Colored Girls*, 94; *I'm Gonna Get You Sucka* and, 83
*Saturday Night Live* (TV program), 18
*Scandal* (TV program), 6, 15–30, 255; NAACP and, 29; rape in, 27–28; stereotypes and, 23, 23–29, 25
Schoening, Gerald, 279
*School Daze* (film), 229

Scott, Hazel, 16
self-determination, 158, 184
self-directed stereotypes, 74
self-help, in rap music videos, 133, 136–138
*Set It Off* (film), 58
*Sex and the City* (TV program), 29
sexism: in Black Power Movement, 25; in hip hop, 178–180; in media, 57–59; rap music and, 119–120, 127, 175–176; skin color and, 227
sexual abuse: in slavery, 26. *See also* rape
sexuality: Beyoncé and, 160; in *Braxton Family Values*, 46–47; of celebrities, 284–285; in *For Colored Girls*, 96; in *Mary Mary*, 46–47; respect and, 185; stereotypes and, 275–276. *See also* hypersexuality
sexual orientation, 293–303
Sexual Siren. *See* Jezebel
*Shaft* (film), 75
Shakur, Tupac. *See* Tupac Shakur
Shange, Ntozake, 91, 92
Shatner, William, 16–17
Shawnna, 140
Shawty Lo, 5
Shayon, Robert Lewis, 22
sheroes, of Blaxploitation films, 75
*Showgirls* (film), 58
Simmons, Mabel "Madea" (fictional character), 4
Simone, Arian, 265
"Single Again" (Trina), 138, 142
"Single Ladies (Put A Ring on It)" (Beyoncé), 160
SistaSoul, 295
*Sister Citizen* (Harris-Perry), 23
Sisterlee Productions, 255
Sister Savior, 274, 277
*Sister to Sister* (magazine), 253
*60 Minutes* (TV program), 56
skin bleaching creams, 230, 237
skin brightener, 233
skin color: in advertising, 225–240; body image and, 225–240; in *Ebony* and *Essence*, 231–238; effects in other countries, 241n10; meaning of "Black" and, 226–228; public discourse on, 228–230; racial discrimination and, 227; racism and, 227; sexism and, 227; skin lightening advertisements, 231–238; slavery and, 227; as standard for beauty, 227–228; Twitter and, 230
skin discoloration, 238
Skin Success Eventone, 235–236
skin tone correctors, 232
slavery, 25; advertising and, 207; Jezebel and, 181, 213–214; rape in, 65, 94; sexual abuse in, 26; skin color and, 227
"S&M" (Rihanna), 28
Smalls, Joan, 236
Smith, Barbara, 131
Smith, Jada Pinkett, 17
Smith, Judy (fictional character), 18
Smith, Mychel Denzel, 98–99
Smith, Siobhan, 277
Smollett-Bell, Jurnee, 57
Social Construction of Reality theory, 130, 143
Social Darwinism, 275
social justice movements, 210
social media, 2, 4–5, 278–279; Beyoncé and, 156; Millennials and, 250, 250–251; Robinson, J., and, 257–258; stereotypes and, 279. *See also specific websites*
solidarity, in rap music videos, 133, 136–138
*The Sopranos* (TV program), 29
soul music, 75
*Soul Talk* (Hull), 90, 92
Spade, Jack (fictional character), 71–84
Spillers, Hortense, 82
sponsorships, 201
sports franchises, 255
*Star Trek* (TV program), 16–17
*Statigram*, blog, 235
Steele, Tanya, 165–166, 167, 167–168
Stein, Lacey, 114
Stephens, Dionne, 38, 129, 132–133, 133, 138, 274, 277
stereotypes, 3, 36, 72; advertising and, 199–220; in *For Colored Girls*, 93–95, 100; in hip hop, 126; mass media and, 274–275; of men, 99; Perry and, 55–66; in rap music, 119; in rap music videos, 129–130; rebranding of, 274; in RTV, 34; *Scandal* and, 23, 23–29, 25;

sexuality and, 275–276; social media and, 279; Strong Black Woman as, 214–215; troublesome images of, 57–59. *See also specific stereotypes*
"Stick It" (film), 138
*Still Standing* (TV program), 34
Stone, Angie, 34
storytelling: by griots, 247; rap music and, 127, 131
Stowe, Harriet Beecher, 99
Stroman, Carolyn, 276
Strong Black Woman, 214–215
Summer's Eve, 217, 222n65
"Super Bass" (Minaj), by Minaj, 142
super stars, 212
*Sweet Sweetback's Baadasssss* (film), 75, 84n1
"Tambourine" (Eve), 137–138, 139

Tatum, Beverly Daniel, 251
Taylor, Paul, 248, 250–251
technology: Millennials and, 249. *See also* Internet
Techturized, Inc., 266
*Teen Summit* (TV program), 252
television: BMW DoErs and, 254–255; limited portrayals of Blacks on, 276–277; Millennials and, 252–253. *See also* reality television; *specific programs*
*Temptation: Confessions of a Marriage Counselor* (film), 55–66; devaluation of Black women in, 59–60; storyline of, 60–64
TheGrio.com, 39
*theYBF.com*, 4
Third World Wimmin Inc., 295
Thirteenth Amendment, 207
Thomas, Clarence, 73
*The Tom Joyner Morning Show* (TV program), 42
"Tramp" (Salt-N-Pepa), 129
transactional sex, 178
Trina: "Here We Go" by, 135–136, 136, 142; "I Got a Thing for You" by, 136, 143; "Single Again" by, 138, 142
Trump, Donald, 4
Truth, Sojourner, 129
Tubman, Harriet, 129

Tupac Shakur, 112, 179; "Brenda's Got a Baby" by, 119; "Dear Mama" by, 115; "Fuck Friends" by, 119; "I Get Around" by, 119; "Keep Ya Head Up" by, 119, 179
Turner, Ike, 28, 162
Turner, Tina, 28
Turner, Victor, 298
TV One, 254
*12 Years a Slave* (film), 22, 26, 31n39, 230
Twitter, 4, 5, 6, 278; skin color and, 230
"212" (Banks, A.), 141
Tyree, Tia, 39, 119
Tyson, Cicely, 18
Tyson, Mike, 28, 162

Uhura (fictional character), 16–17
Uncle Tom, 99
*Uncle Tom's Cabin* (Stowe), 99
Union, Gabrielle, 18
"U.N.I.T.Y." (Queen Latifah), 129
US Organization, 25

Van Peeble, Melvin, 84n1
Vested In Culture, 254
VH1, 34; RTV on, 3
*Vibe* (magazine), 1
Vick, Michael, 18
victimization, 64
Video Vixen, 277
"Violet Stars Happy Hunting!" (Robinson, J.), 257
virility, of men, 81
*Vogue* (magazine), 17
voyeurism, in rap music, 128

Wade, Earnestine, 16
*Waiting to Exhale* (film), 58
Walker, Alice, 92
Walker, C. J., 253, 266
Walton, Curly Nikki, 266
Ward, Janie Victoria, 227
Ware, Cellestine, 158
Warren, Robert Penn, 90
Washington, Kerry, 18–19
Waters, Ethel, 15
Watkins, Craig, 178
Wayans, Damon, 84n4

Wayans, Keenan Ivory, 84n4; *I'm Gonna Get You Sucka* by, 71–84
Welfare Mother (Queen), 37, 214, 276
wenches, in advertising, 207
"We Run This" (Missy), 138
West, Cornel, 225
West, Kanye, 112; "Hey Mama" by, 114–115
WE tv, 4, 40–42
White, Constance C. R., 229
"Whoa" (Lil' Kim), 136
*Why are All the Black Kids Sitting Together in the Cafeteria* (Tatum), 251
Williams, Jo-na A., 254
Williams, Pharrell, 259, 264
Williams, Vanessa, 229
Williams, Wendy, 5
Willis, Helen (fictional character), 20, 30n11
Willis, Tom (fictional character), 20, 30n11
*The Will to Change: Men, Masculinity, and Love* (hooks), 175
Wilmore, Larry, 259

Winfrey, Oprah, 5, 21–22, 254, 280; as inspirer, 283; Obama, B., and, 294
*The Wire* (TV program), 29
*Within the Plantation Household* (Fox-Genovese), 26
womanism, *For Colored Girls* and, 89–103
Wondaland Arts Society, 257, 263
Woods, Tryon, P., 176
working mothers, 43–44

YBF. *See* Young, Black, and Fabulous
Yochim, Emily Chivers, 206
Young, Black, and Fabulous (YBF): advertising on, 256; blog, 255–256; Carol's Daughters and, 256
Young, Mona Scott, 3
YouTube: Dondria and, 265; *The Misadventures of Awkward Girl* on, 259; politics and, 293

Zimmerman, George, 22
"Zingy" (Ak'Sent), 138
Zuckerberg, Mark, 250

# About the Contributors

**Robin M. Boylorn**, PhD, earned her doctorate in 2009 from the University of South Florida. She is currently a faculty member at the University of Alabama where she teaches and writes about issues of social identity and diversity, focusing primarily on the lived experiences of Black women. She is author of the award-winning book *Sweetwater: Black Women and Narratives of Resilience* (Peter Lang Publishing, 2013) and co-editor, with Mark Orbe, of *Critical Autoethnography: Intersecting Cultural Identities in Everyday Life* (Left Coast Press, 2014). She has written within the academy and without (as a member of the Crunk Feminist Collective) about issues related to the representation and construction of Black women in media and popular culture.

**Rachel Alicia Griffin**, PhD, is assistant professor in the Department of Communication Studies at Southern Illinois University (SIU), cross-appointed in Africana studies and women, gender, and sexuality studies. As a critical intercultural scholar, her research interests span Black feminist Thought, critical race theory, popular culture, gender violence, sport, and education. In 2012 Dr. Griffin was awarded the Judge William Holmes Cook Professorship by the Office of the Associate Chancellor for Institutional Diversity at SIU and in 2013 she was awarded the College of Liberal Arts Early Career Faculty Excellence Award. Most recently, Dr. Griffin has published in *Critical Studies in Media Communication*, *International Journal of Qualitative Studies in Education*, and *The Howard Journal of Communications*. She is also fortunate to be a frequent guest speaker on campuses all over the country.

**Mark C. Hopson** (PhD, Ohio University) is associate professor at George Mason University. His research interests include critical intercultural communication and studies in Black masculinity. Additionally he has presented seminars on violence prevention strategies for more than 7,000 teens and adults. Currently Dr. Hopson facilitates "Changing Lives Through Literature," a nationally recognized alternative sentencing program for young men. Dr. Hopson's publications include *Notes from the talking drum: Exploring Black communication and critical memory in intercultural communication contexts* (Hampton Press); and *Masculinity in the Black imagination: Politics of communicating race and manhood* (Peter Lang).

**Sheena C. Howard** (PhD, Howard University, Intercultural/ Rhetorical Communication) is assistant professor in the Department of Communication and Journalism at Rider University in Lawrenceville, NJ. Dr. Howard is the first editor (along with Ron L. Jackson) of the edited book, *Black Comics: Politics of Race and Representation* (2013). She is also the author of *Black Queer Identity Matrix: Towards An Integrated Queer of Color Framework*.

**Christopher K. Jackson**, PhD, is assistant professor of speech, communications, and theatre at Borough of Manhattan Community College in New York City, NY. His most recent publication includes "Exploring Sustainable Development in Kibera: A Case Study" in *Journalism and Mass Communication*. His primary research interests are how Black women are portrayed in the news and in popular culture.

**Joanna L. Jenkins**, PhD, is a strategic communicator, advertising creative professional, media specialist, and professor. Within the industry, Joanna has led numerous creative initiatives and worked with notable clients and advertising agencies including Calvin Klein, Topps Inc, Verizon, The U.S. Census, Globalhue, Draft, McCann, etc. She has produced IMC creative works in diverse media ranging from television and print to radio, interactive and digital. Joanna received a doctorate in mass communications and media studies from Howard University with a central focus in cognitive processes and personality engagement. Prior to that she graduated with honors from Pratt Institute with an MS in visual communications.

**Mackenzie Jordan**, PhD, is an experienced professional of communications strategy with an emphasis on training/development and social media. With a doctorate from Howard University in communication and culture, she has now gone on to be the proud owner of Greenbriar Associates, a company through which she conducts trainings, workshops, and consultations related to her expertise. Prior to owning her own business, Mackenzie has gained tactical experience in her field through her employment at colleges and universities in multiple capacities including: student services, admissions, curriculum development, classroom instruction, and retention programs. She continues to write publications relevant to her specific interest of aging in addition to pursuing many personal hobbies.

**LeRhonda S. Manigault-Bryant**, PhD, is associate professor of Africana studies at Williams College. She is the author of *Talking to the Dead: Religion, Music, and Lived Memory among Gullah/Geechee Women*

(Duke University Press, 2014), and co-author of *Womanist and Black Feminist Responses to Tyler Perry's Productions* (Palgrave Macmillan, 2014) with Tamura A. Lomax and Carol B. Duncan. A proud native of Moncks Corner, South Carolina, she navigates the academy as a scholar-artist, and teaches courses that merge her life as a vocalist with her interdisciplinary specializations in religion, gender, race, and popular culture.

**Andre Nicholson**, PhD, received his doctorate in mass communication and media studies from Howard University in Washington, DC. His research interests are social media, public relations/advertising, political communications, and media effects. His most recent research deals with young adults' use of social media and how they identified with President Obama during the 2008 presidential campaign.

**Joshua Daniel Phillips**, MA, is a PhD candidate in the Department of Communication Studies at Southern Illinois University (SIU). His academic focus includes rhetoric and intercultural communication with particular interest in the areas of sport, sexual violence, popular culture, and poverty. His latest publication with co-author Dr. Rachel Alicia Griffin is "LeBron James as Cybercolonized Spectacle: A Critical Race Reading of Whiteness in Sport" in *Sports and Identity: New Agendas in Communication*.

**Simone Puff**, PhD, is currently assistant professor of American studies at the University of Graz in Austria. Previously, she was a post-doctoral researcher of North American literary and cultural studies at Saarland University in Saarbrücken, Germany, and assistant professor (pre-doc, non-tenure-track) at Alpen-Adria-Universität Klagenfurt in Austria. She received her PhD in English and American studies with emphases on African American studies and gender studies from Alpen-Adria-Universität Klagenfurt in 2012. Among her publications are articles on Zora Neale Hurston, discourses on skin color in the United States, and representations of the Black Feminist movement in the media. She is the co-editor of *Almighty Dollar* (LIT Verlag 2010).

**Elizabeth Y. Whittington**, PhD, is a graduate of Howard University. She is currently a visiting assistant professor at Portland State University, where she teaches classes on race, gender, and sexuality in the media, advanced intercultural and interpersonal communication courses, as well as a graduate course on critical cultural methodologies. Her areas of research include race and gender dynamics in the perceptions of negotiations of sexual consent, the discourse surrounding sexual assault and sex within minority communities, and the awareness of prevention programs available for students at colleges and universities. She is currently examining how Black students at a Historically Black University (HBCU) negotiate sexual consent in casual sex relationships and the influence of parent and peer messages about sex.

**Joshua K. Wright**, PhD, is assistant professor of history and coordinator for the Social Studies Teacher's Education program at the University of

Maryland Eastern Shore. He holds a PhD in history from Howard University. He is the founder of the Hip-Hop & Higher Education at Howard University. His research interests focus on issues of race, gender, popular culture, and politics in nineteenth- and twentieth-century America. Dr. Wright is currently completing the manuscript for his first book, "Bad Men: The Curious Case of Black Male Empowerment in America."

# About the Editors

**Adria Y. Goldman**, PhD, is assistant professor of communication at Gordon State College in Barnesville, GA. Dr. Goldman's research examines media representations of Black womanhood as well as groups that are underrepresented in media. She enjoys examining the way in which such representations impact viewers' construction of reality. Most recently, her attention has turned to messages within reality television and social media. She received her PhD in mass communication and media studies (along with a graduate certificate in women's studies) from Howard University in Washington, DC.

**VaNatta S. Ford**, PhD, is assistant professor of communication studies at Columbia College in Columbia, SC. Before joining Columbia, she spent two years as an ACM-Andrew W. Mellon Postdoctoral Fellow of African American Rhetorical Studies, at Ripon College. Dr. Ford's teaching and research interests include: hip hop culture, color and identity politics, gender, and African American rhetorical traditions. She earned her PhD in rhetoric and intercultural communication from Howard University in Washington, DC. In addition to Dr. Ford's scholarly endeavors, she serves as the second vice chair of the Black Caucus of the National Communication Association.

**Alexa A. Harris**, PhD, is a communications consultant in Washington, DC. Her background is filled with a myriad of experiences in the media, ranging from television, film, and print journalism to marketing, event planning, and public relations. Dr. Harris earned a doctorate from Howard University, holds a masters degree in documentary film and history from Syracuse University, and a bachelors of arts from Spelman College. In her spare time, she enjoys working with organizations to encourage and empower young women to follow their dreams.

**Natasha R. Howard**, PhD, is a graduate of Howard University. In addition to being a freelance writer, she has taught communications courses at Montgomery College (Rockville, MD), Howard Community College, and the Community College of Baltimore County. She is currently assistant professor of communication at Bronx Community College. Her research interests include media effects, hip hop culture, images portrayed in music videos and reality television, and the portrayals of race, gender, and sexuality in the media and their effects on communication as a whole. She holds a PhD in mass communications and media studies with a women's studies graduate certificate.